THE
PUERTO RICAN
EXPERIENCE

This is a volume in the
ARNO PRESS collection

THE PUERTO RICAN EXPERIENCE

See last pages of this volume
for a complete list of titles

EQUAL EDUCATIONAL OPPORTUNITY

HEARINGS

BEFORE THE

SELECT COMMITTEE ON
EQUAL EDUCATIONAL OPPORTUNITY

OF THE

UNITED STATES SENATE

NINETY-FIRST CONGRESS

SECOND SESSION

ON

EQUAL EDUCATIONAL OPPORTUNITY

PART 8—EQUAL EDUCATIONAL OPPORTUNITY FOR PUERTO RICAN CHILDREN

WASHINGTON, D.C., NOVEMBER 23, 24, AND 25, 1970

ARNO PRESS
A New York Times Company
New York – 1975

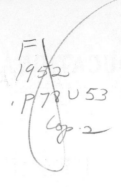
Reprint Edition 1975 by Arno Press Inc.

The Puerto Rican Experience
ISBN for complete set: 0-405-06210-9
See last pages of this volume for titles.

Publisher's Note: This title was originally
part of a series. The pagination is correct.

Manufactured in the United States of America

———◆———

Library of Congress Cataloging in Publication Data

United States. Congress. Senate. Select Committee on
    Equal Educational Opportunity.
    Equal educational opportunity for Puerto Rican
children.

    (The Puerto Rican experience)
    Reprint of the 1970 ed. published by the U. S. Govt.
Print. Off., Washington, which was issued as pt. 8 of
Equal educational opportunity.
    1. Puerto Ricans in the United States--Education.
2. Segregation in education--United States. I. Title.
II. Series. III. Series: United States. Congress.
Senate. Select Committee on Equal Educational Oppor-
tunity. Equal educational opportunity ; pt. 8.
[KF26.5.E6 1970a]   370.19'344   74-14255
ISBN 0-405-06240-0

EQUAL EDUCATIONAL OPPORTUNITY

HEARINGS

BEFORE THE

SELECT COMMITTEE ON
EQUAL EDUCATIONAL OPPORTUNITY

OF THE

UNITED STATES SENATE

NINETY-FIRST CONGRESS

SECOND SESSION

ON

EQUAL EDUCATIONAL OPPORTUNITY

PART 8—EQUAL EDUCATIONAL OPPORTUNITY FOR PUERTO RICAN CHILDREN

WASHINGTON, D.C., NOVEMBER 23, 24, AND 25, 1970

Printed for the use of the Select Committee on Equal Educational Opportunity

U.S. GOVERNMENT PRINTING OFFICE

46–125

WASHINGTON : 1970

SELECT COMMITTEE ON EQUAL EDUCATIONAL OPPORTUNITY

WALTER F. MONDALE, Minnesota, *Chairman*

JOHN L. McCLELLAN, Arkansas
WARREN G. MAGNUSON, Washington
JENNINGS RANDOLPH, West Virginia
THOMAS J. DODD, Connecticut
DANIEL K. INOUYE, Hawaii
BIRCH BAYH, Indiana
WILLIAM B. SPONG, Jr., Virginia
HAROLD E. HUGHES, Iowa

ROMAN L. HRUSKA, Nebraska
JACOB K. JAVITS, New York
PETER H. DOMINICK, Colorado
EDWARD W. BROOKE, Massachusetts
MARK O. HATFIELD, Oregon
MARLOW W. COOK, Kentucky

WILLIAM C. SMITH, *Staff Director and General Counsel*
A. SIDNEY JOHNSON, *Deputy Staff Director*

(II)

CONTENTS

CHRONOLOGICAL LIST OF WITNESSES

Page

EQUAL EDUCATIONAL OPPORTUNITY FOR PUERTO RICAN CHILDREN

MONDAY, NOVEMBER 23, 1970

U.S. SENATE,
SELECT COMMITTEE ON
EQUAL EDUCATIONAL OPPORTUNITY,
Washington, D.C.

The committee met at 10 a.m., pursuant to call, in room 1318, New Senate Office Building, Hon. Walter F. Mondale (chairman of the committee) presiding.

Present: Senators Mondale, Javits, and Brooke.

Present also: William C. Smith, staff director and general counsel; A. Sidney Johnson, deputy staff director; and Leonard P. Strickman, minority counsel.

Senator MONDALE. The committee will come to order.

This morning, we are commencing hearings on the problems of educational opportunity which affect the Puerto Rican children of this Nation.

I will ask Senator Javits, at whose request these hearings were called, to introduce our panel this morning.

Senator Javits?

STATEMENT OF HON. JACOB K. JAVITS, A U.S. SENATOR FROM THE STATE OF NEW YORK

Senator JAVITS. Mr. Chairman, thank you very much.

We have a very interesting situation in New York which involves the community of Puerto Rican ethnic extraction. In fixing our attention on the problems of school desegregation and school integration, I thought it was critically important that we should hear from the Puerto Rican community. So, our first witness this morning is Miss Antonia Pantoja, founder of Aspira, a Puerto Rican community organization. Miss Pantoja is a very distinguished woman, and very, very active in her work for her people.

She will be followed as a witness by a panel which I will call as soon as Miss Pantoja has concluded.

The panel consists of Mrs. Silvia Fox from Chicago Aspira; Armando Martinez of Boston, the director of Puente, a community organization; Hector Vasquez of the Puerto Rican Forum; and Nathan Quinones, Puerto Rican Educators Association, and chairman of the Department of Foreign Languages of the Benjamin N. Cardozo High School in New York.

Is Miss Pantoja here?

All right.
Will you come forward, please?
This is the first witness.
Senator MONDALE. Yes. We have met.

STATEMENT OF MISS ANTONIA PANTOJA, WASHINGTON, D.C., FOUNDER, ASPIRA, INC.

Miss PANTOJA. Good morning.
Senator MONDALE. You have a prepared statement. You may proceed as you wish.
Senator JAVITS. Miss Pantoja, the statement, from what I can see, will probably take about 20 minutes to read. If there are any abbreviations you wish to make, we will leave that up to you.

Now, may I explain for the record that I am a member of the Foreign Relations Committee which this morning is going to consider the genocide treaty after 20 years. It is a matter for which I have had the laboring oar. So; I hope the witnesses will understand if I am called away it is not anything other than a high call of duty, but our chairman will be here and I will return the minute I get through with the other meeting.

Senator MONDALE. Thank you.
If you will, proceed.
Miss PANTOJA. You have my full statement which will be in the record. I will limit myself to commenting on several portions of my statement.

Senator MONDALE. The full statement will appear as though read. You may comment on it any way you wish.

Miss PANTOJA. First of all, I would like to let you know that I am speaking here as a professional person as well as a Puerto Rican who has experienced the types of problems that I will be speaking about.

I am a social worker, the founder of an agency called Aspira; the organizer of another agency called the Puerto Rican Forum, and subsequently I have been a professor at Columbia School of Social Work at the new School for Social Research and at the University of Puerto Rico.

I have also been a member of the Bundy panel on decentralization of the school system in New York City.

At present, I am in Washington trying to organize a national Puerto Rican research and resource center.

I am living in Washington but I have lived for the past 25 years in New York City where I had migrated from Puerto Rico in 1944.

Now. why do I want this committee of leaders in this Nation to know the educational problems of Puerto Ricans? I will explain this to you with various arguments.

LOCATION OF PUERTO RICAN POPULATION

First of all, I think that it should be made clear that Puerto Ricans are not solely residents of New York City or New York State. Puerto Ricans live throughout the northeast and the middle west.

Senator MONDALE. Could you go over for me the size of Puerto Rican populations and where they are located? That would be helpful to me.

Miss PANTOJA. Yes. Unfortunately, you don't have exact statistics about the Puerto Rican population in the United States, because the 1970 census did not list us as a separate category in the general count. So, from the 1960 figures and from estimates—educated estimates—that have been done, of the growth of population, specifically taking two examples, one can reach the conclusion that there must be about 2 million Puerto Ricans in the entire Nation.

For example, the 1960 census lists for the area of New York 55,351 Puerto Ricans in the 1960 census. But we know from the figures obtained from the Board of Education, the Department of Education of the State of New Jersey, that they have an estimated 200,000 Puerto Ricans in that State. For example, in New York City, when the census in 1960 listed 642,622 Puerto Ricans living in the State of New York, by 1964 we know that there were 701,500 Puerto Ricans living in the city alone.

So that you see that there has been a very meaningful increase in the population of Puerto Ricans as witnessed the number of Puerto Ricans living in these two States. You can accordingly figure an increase in the whole area where we are concentrated. We are concentrated in precisely those areas experiencing the urban crisis, so that we share in the problems of that crisis.

Since here we are concerned with education and the problems of education, I will then give you some figures, the kinds of figures that are available.

I repeat again the kind of data which is taken for granted for all the minority people in this country, does not exist about Puerto Ricans. This is a handicap that we are constantly working under.

DROPOUT RATE

For example, in Chicago. In Chicago, you find that of 18,000 Puerto Ricans enrolled in the public school system, by the time they get to the high schools you find a figure of 4,000. From figures we have obtained from the Aspira of Illinois, we find out that Puerto Ricans dropout—or as we more appropriately say we are pushed out—at a rate of 60 percent before we finish high school.

In the area of Newark, you have 7,800 Puerto Rican students in the public school system last year and only 96 survived to the 12th grade. So that is even a more dramatic situation.

In Philadelphia, of 7,989 Spanish-speaking students—and here I want to call to your attention one of our problems—you don't know how many of those Spanish-speaking are Puerto Rican. So, in Philadelphia, by the time you reach the junior high school, you find 1,547 Spanish-speaking students and 903 in the senior high school.

From figures obtained from the State department in that State we find that approximately 70 percent is the rate of dropout for Spanish-speaking students.

I want to call your attention to the fact that in New York City we do have a study that was done in 1964 which is a more comprehensive study and it provides a profile of our community in that area. Actually, the profile that you have in New York City could be extended to the rest of the cities where we live in large numbers. We have proceeded on that assumption.

In New York City, you find that our children suffer a good deal of academic retardation. The study called the 1964 study of poverty conditions in the New York-Puerto Rican community shows that less than 10 percent of the Puerto Rican children in the third grade were reading at their grade level or above. By the eighth grade, the degree of retardation of Puerto Ricans was even more severe. While 30 percent of the Puerto Ricans were reading at a grade level, almost two-thirds were retarded almost 3 years.

So the story goes, the more you go to school the more retarded you get.

The same study also showed that in 1963—and now we go into the possibility of entering college—of 21,000 academic diplomas granted, only 331 were to Puerto Ricans, 1.6 percent. We are 7.2 percent of the academic high school population in that year. That is the high school that prepares you with the diploma which to enter college.

I am going to move further down in my presentation, again reinforcing the need for accurate data.

So far as I know, this year in preparation there is only one study that will give us a better picture of the Puerto Rican population of Newark. The study is coming out in December by Prof. Hilda Hidalgo of Rutgers University. I know of no other study that will paint the picture with the type of data we need.

We need accurate and comprehensive data of the problems, needs, and general description of the Puerto Rican population for program design and for evaluation purposes, to be able to do things in an intelligent way.

We would like the committee to know also that we have been named the poorest people in the northeast. We are the poorest people, the poorest group, even when you consider the terrible situation in which our brothers, the blacks, find themselves. We are in a worse situation than the blacks.

ECONOMIC AND RACIAL BARRIERS

Some people will ask, aren't you going to make it the way the European migrants did who came to this country under the same conditions?

There are two reasons why we are not making it in the same manner in which the previous migrants who came in the 1800's made it. The first reason is the fact that we come in a different historical time and under different economic conditions. The country is already made. There is no more frontier. You cannot say any more, if you have the willingness to work and you have muscle to offer you will obtain a job; if you will grab a piece of land out in the west and set up a farm that you will do as the previous people who came here did.

There is no more frontier. You do not need unskilled hands, no matter how willing they are. This country needs developed minds and skilled arms. So that we are obsolete as a people. Unskilled people no matter how willing to work have no place in this kind of society.

Employment is related to education and training.

The second reason for Puerto Ricans "not making it" is a racial reason. We are a mixed people and in this country, you know that race—other than the white race—is a liability. So that we suffer from the same prejudices and discrimination as other people of color; as the blacks do; as the Chicanos do, as the Indians.

We do not have the type of experience and tradition to fight this. Unfortunately, there has not been enough cooperation and understanding with our brothers, the blacks, to be able to develop common lines of approach even though we are partners in poverty.

Senator MONDALE. What do you mean by that comment that they have very little experience?

LACK OF POWER

Miss PANTOJA. We haven't had the years of tradition in organizing to fight discrimination. In Puerto Rico, you don't find that type of organization. So that when you arrive here you don't know how to do it.

In the 50-some years that we have been here, we have been separated from the organizations that have done this. We have the beginnings of such organizations of our own but we have not been able to establish coalition with the people who have done this type of fighting effectively.

The problem of our people is basically a problem of lack of power. The problem of being trapped in a cycle of poverty. The cycle of poverty is very well delineated in the study I quoted before, the 1964 study of poverty conditions of Puerto Ricans in New York City. There the cycle of poverty goes this way. The people who arrive are people who have low educational attainment; they are unskilled. They have the worst, the lowest types of jobs, the lowest pay, the lowest prestige. They have the highest percentage of unemployment.

Because of this, of course, they inherit the slums and the attendant problems of the slums. Their children go to the school system in this country. Instead of the prophecy coming true that once the children of the migrant go through the school system their problems are over, what happens is that they drop out before they finish.

So, the cycle of poverty is established because they then drop out without a high school diploma in a country where the lowest paid job needs at least a high school diploma. Then they continue to be in the lower rung of the ladder and continue to add Puerto Ricans to the poverty group. Any details on the situation of poverty of our group could be found in that study.

I would like to then proceed with my next reason for wanting to speak to this committee.

We are not only the poorest people in the areas where we live, but we are invisible and silent because we are poorly organized and we are powerless.

IMPORTANCE OF LANGUAGE AND CULTURE

I would like very much to leave with you the understanding that language and culture are two very important factors to our being able to survive the crisis of migration. They are not only the treasures that we as poor people possess, but they are the lifesavers in a situation of crisis while we try to overcome the problems of migrating and of adjusting to a new home, we are culturally different than the majority community not only because of our racial attitudes but also because of the fact that we speak a different language, Spanish, by the fact we have different values, customs, family patterns, and different patterns of interpersonal relationships.

We are the bearers of another culture, the Puerto Rican culture, not the Spanish culture, which is the culture of Spain, but the Puerto Rican culture. Now, as Mr. Luis Nunez says in a presentation he made before the Morton Wollman distinguished lectures:

Simply put, a Puerto Rican New Yorker [A Puerto Rican in the United States] might conduct all of his business, professional and most of his social life in English, but with his parents, with his friends from the Island, and when he journeys to Puerto Rico, he speaks Spanish. The differences between the situation of the Puerto Rican and the situation of the previous . . . newcomers is that the ties [with their culture] seem to strengthen with time rather than lessen. The emerging Puerto Rican professional and businessman travels to Puerto Rico two or three times a year. He has a genuine desire to retain his cultural identity and not to disappear into the mainstream as some would urge us. The liberal concept of cultural pluralism is a fact now with many Puerto Ricans [in the United States].

So that, retaining the Spanish language is not only an emotional necessity but a material necessity. The matter of acquiring the English language is crucial to functioning in the vital day-to-day world, not only for survival but for securing the basic needs that man needs to be healthy.

But in the immediate present, retaining and developing the Spanish language, is for the Puerto Rican a means of having one tool of communication while developing mastery over another.

This brings me to the fact that the schools have mounted an attack on the child who speaks Spanish and who is different; an attack to force him to give this up. What happens as a result is that the child is ashamed of himself and his parents, and ashamed of his speaking Spanish. This hurts these children's motivation and ability to learn. Because, you know that if you don't think well of yourself you are not going to be able to achieve in the learning of a new language, or in the learning of new skills.

NONREPRESENTATION

In the same manner, the adult Puerto Rican is timid and finds it difficult to attend community activities where he could go and represent himself. So, you will find that we are always represented by somebody else. We are always represented and we are always spoken about and hidden away in the phrase "Negroes and Puerto Ricans," or "Spanish-speaking," or the "browns." What you find is that in the end, at the service end, we are left out.

I would like to give an example of the type of thing I mean when I say we are left out by these coverall phrases. I would like the committee to be aware of the fact that there is a Cabinet Committee for the Spanish-speaking, and there is also in the Office of Education, an office for the Spanish-speaking American affairs. In both these agencies there is no Puerto Rican staff and there is no concern or programs relating to, or for Puerto Ricans. This is what I mean by—you use the coverall phrase, but then we are left out when it comes to service and when it comes to funds and when it comes to staff.

Senator MONDALE. Are you saying in this Cabinet committee that there is not a single Puerto Rican?

Miss PANTOJA. As a matter of fact, I would like to ask a question of this committee, and I would like this committee to find out the answer to the question. I would hope that the answer is other than the one I suspect. The question is, how many Puerto Ricans are there employed at policy levels in the Office of Education, for example?

I suspect the answer to that is none, here in Washington in the Office of Education.

Senator MONDALE. We will write the Office of Education asking that question.

Miss PANTOJA. It is also true of the Cabinet committee.

Senator MONDALE. We will also write to the Cabinet committee and ask how many Puerto Ricans are represented on the committee.

Miss PANTOJA. The name of "Cabinet Committee" was recently changed to "For Spanish Speaking", instead of for Mexican American.

I would like to read a series of recommendations directly from my written presentation since they are very few:

FUNDS FOR PRIVATE NONPROFIT EDUCATIONAL AGENCIES

No. 1: Through new legislation or amendments to existing legislation the Committee must provide grants to Puerto Rican—and other minorities—nonprofit private educational agencies, to establish complementary programs to the public systems of education, which we claim they have failed in providing. We have arrived at the conclusion that they have failed and they will never be able to provide certain functions. I refer to such functions as motivation, guidance and programs to develop a positive identity in the children. Those functions, we in the Puerto Rican community can do best for our own children. But there are very few Federal laws under which a private nonprofit agency, such as the ones we have established—we have very few, but we have some—can receive funds.

So far as I know, there is only one source of Federal funds which can be granted to a private educational agency, and that is from the Talent Search, in the division of Special Services to Students, Office of Education. This particular program has a very little amount of money to cover the entire United States. Somewhere in one of these education laws, an amendment could be added to make private agencies eligible to receive Federal monies. Private minority agencies could receive funds from such a program as the Bilingual Program, such programs as title I, to be able to do the kinds of things that the school systems cannot do or have failed to do.

You cannot continue to put massive amounts of monies into the same systems that failed and that constantly continues to fail. There were 3.1 billion dollars assigned in financial assistance to pre-school, elementary and secondary education in the year 1970. None of that money could go to private agencies, but public school systems who received it did not show any substantial improvement in their ability to teach as a result of the extra funds.

Senator. Mondale. What are you proposing here is funding of non-profit private agencies and the circumventing of the local education agencies?

Miss Pantoja. Yes.

Senator Mondale. We are exploring the possibility of setting aside 10 percent of the title I money for this purpose. How would such an educational agency work? Would you establish competing elementary schools, would you set up part-time after-school hour programs or what?

EVALUATION

Miss Pantoja. I wouldn't say that we set up competing systems. Besides, the responsibility of educating the children is the responsibility of the State. We would set up programs which the school system cannot possibly do. We can set up programs that will be watchdog programs. We can do evaluation of programs that the school system does. Sometimes what happens is that the legislator thinks that the only place where you find the kind of capability to keep the school system honest is the university. There is capability and there is know-how and knowledge in the Puerto Rican community, and I am sure in other minority communities, to keep the school system honest.

For example, how many of these evaluations of title I are done by separate private institutions and separate private institutions of the minority people who are the affected people? I have done evaluation for title I, and usually what happens is that the final evaluation says that the school is trying very hard to come forth with what is expected, but it never says right out that they have failed because of this and this and this and that.

Now, I don't know if I answered your question or not.

Senator Mondale. My understanding is that the implementation of your first recommendation would result in the funding of primarily work community groups, in this case including, I gather, Puerto Rican professionally trained leaders, to make the system respond to motivational, language and cultural sensitivities.

PRIVATE, BILINGUAL EDUCATION

Miss Pantoja. I am talking about that and to perform certain tasks that we think the school cannot perform. For example, we know that our children can be motivated to learn. We know that it is necessary for them to have a positive self image. We know that, in the case of teaching the Puerto Rican culture, in fact in the case of the bilingual programs, we could conduct such programs with better effectiveness.

Senator Mondale. In other words, in that case you might conduct bilingual education classes outside the school system?

Miss Pantoja. Yes. As a matter of fact, Senator Mondale, there is already a precedent. Children go out to receive religious education and it is done in released time. I don't want to go too much in detail in this area, because I think one of the coming speakers is going to present to you in more detail this type of program. But there are many things that could be done and there is talent and the creativity, and, we have ideas. The school system has been failing for years; so, if we fail, the money should be withdrawn from us, in the same manner as the money should not be given to the school systems. They continue to fail year after year after year, and continue to be given more and more funds in spite of their demonstrated failure.

This is the second recommendation:

RESISTANCE TO CHANGE

This committee can be instrumental in the creation of the type of climate which will open the doors for the introduction of new concepts into the present educational scheme in the schools of the large cities of this country. The schools cannot continue to do business as usual. What I mean is, that you find study after study of the situation of education. When you deal with a school system at the administrative level and at the teachers level, you find a recalcitrant system that will continue to tell you they are doing things in the way educators believe best and you are not an educator, and should not meddle into what they are doing.

There are already existing in this country programs which should be instituted as regular programs of the school system, but they will not be accepted voluntarily by that school system. For example, a program which I am familiar with, the Job Corps. I don't know why, for the love of me, the Job Corps, which has been unimaginative program, has been emasculated and put away somewhere in the depth of the Department of Labor.

Children could choose, when they are finishing their junior high school, to go into an academic high school, into a commercial, into a vocational, or they could choose to go into a Job Corps center, a residential center. I don't mean just the hard core dropout. People consider the Job Corps as a place to send children who have criminal records or who have completely been forgotten and discarded by the educational system. I mean any child could voluntarily choose to go to a Job Corps center. A child who would like to leave home because there is a terrible atmosphere and condition at home; a child who would like to go away and live with his peers and find himself out, have an opportunity to try a number of skills, should have this alternative in the regular school system.

This is the kind of things that we would like to see happening in the school system, ideas such as the Job Corps. Instead of considering Job Corps one of the many training programs geared to employment for political reasons, destroying its creativity as a new educational approach.

Another recommendation I would want to leave with the committee.

BILINGUAL EDUCATION

One other innovative program which should be given full opportunity to succeed is bilingual education. To have a fair chance to demonstrate its validity bilingual education as it is today needs a number of changes and expansions. First, the few existing projects are all under the control of the same school system which failed at monolingual education.

This committee should request the necessary funds for the expansion of the program at the same time that it changes the eligibility criteria so that other educational agencies—particularly those of Puerto Rican, Chicanos, Chinese, et cetera—can establish programs with the aid of universities or known experts in bilingualism.

Second, the bilingual programs must be required to be bicultural as well as bilingual as the law stipulates.

Third, the bilingual education law should provide funds for separate evaluative and teacher training efforts. What happens is that the monies are granted without insisting on an evaluation design along with the project proposal so there is no evaluation. No evaluations designs exist at present for evaluating this type of program. There are not enough bilingual teachers, so you find that the projects hire unprepared professionals. There should be monies for training and monies for creating an evaluation design that would give us the proper evaluation of this program.

Fourth, bilingual education has to be established throughout the elementary, junior and senior high schools. It should be a complete program.

NEED FOR PUERTO RICAN INVOLVEMENT AT FEDERAL LEVEL

My fourth recommendation: The committee must be instrumental through new legislation, amendments to existing legislation or some other means to create structures at the Federal level that will develop concern, promote the development of programs and the employment of professionals, secure the assignment of funds and gather complete and accurate data on and about Puerto Ricans in the Office of Education and other agencies related to education.

I finish my presentation with the question. How many staffs are there in policy levels in the Office of Education?

I have spent hours trying to find out where are there funds in the Office of Education? How does one get these funds to be able to mount programs, to be able to save our children from this horrible cycle of poverty, from this horrible trap? I know that there are funds. But, I have not been able to go through the whole complicated structure of the Office of Education. Besides, when one is inside, when one is a staff member inside, one learns ways that are not on the law or on the guidelines. If you know the administrative procedures, one learns of new programs that are being instituted, and one learns in time to present a proposal and to request money. We usually learn about these things when it is too late.

Senator MONDALE. Do you know how much bilingual education money is going to assist Puerto Rican children?

Miss PANTOJA. That, I don't know. But that information could be secured.

Senator MONDALE. What percentage is it?

Miss PANTOJA. That, I do not know. But that might be a good question to find out. I know of a bilingual project which is under the control of a board of education, has a director, an English-speaking director, who does not speak Spanish.

Senator MONDALE. Where is this?

Miss PANTOJA. In the area of Camden. I was present at a conference for bilingual programs and a committee of community people
approached me to find out if there was a way in which they could
find out how to stop this. I asked them, "Don't you have an advisory
committee to this program?"

They said, "Yes, we have an advisory committee, but nevertheless
the superintendent of schools was the one who approved the director
of the program." This is what I mean by having the bilingual programs under the control of the very system that has failed on monolingual education.

I thank the committee for the opportunity to come here to speak
to you. If you have any other questions, I will answer them.

(The prepared statement of Miss Antonia Pantoja follows:)

PREPARED STATEMENT OF MISS ANTONIA PANTOJA

I am Antonia Pantoja, a social worker, founder of ASPIRA (an agency dedi-
cated to leadership development through education), organizer of the Puerto
Rican Forum, Inc., also subsequently, a professor of social work at Columbia
University, the University of Puerto Rico and the New School of Social Re-
search, one of the members of the Bundy Panel (The Advisory Panel on the
Decentralization of New York City Schools). At present I am working on the
establishment of a national Puerto Rican Research and Resource Center in
Washington, D.C.

Although I have been living in Washington for the last three months, my
home for twenty-five years was New York City where I migrated from Puerto
Rico in 1944. I speak before this hearing as a professional person reinforced
by the "expertness" provided by having lived through the problems I will describe. When I arrived in New York I lived in its slums, I worked in its sweat-
shops, I completed my undergraduate education in the evening and my graduate
work with part time employment and scholarship help. My accent kept me out
of the New York City School System, even though I had been a teacher in
Puerto Rico, but maybe helped me keep my identity.

Now, why do we Puerto Ricans in the United States want to make you, some
of the leaders of the nations, aware of our desperate educational problems?

We want to make you aware of the fact that although Puerto Ricans live in
the 50 states of this country, they are concentrated in about eight states and
in precisely the cities and metropolitan regions which share the urban crisis.
According to the 1960 U.S. Census, the highest areas of Puerto Rican concentration in that year were: Connecticut, 15,247; Florida, 19,535; Ohio, 19,940;
Pennsylvania, 21,206; California, 28,108; Illinois, 36,081; New Jersey, 55,351;
New York, 642,622.

There has been considerable Puerto Rican population growth since the 1960
Census. If it were not for the fact that the 1970 Census did not include Puerto
Ricans as a category in its general count we would know exactly the nature of
that growth. But two examples of the Puerto Rican population growth will
suffice to indicate that the educated estimate of approximately 2 million Puerto
Ricans in the country by 1970 is valid. According to statistical data obtained
by ASPIRA of New Jersey in 1969 from the State Department of Education,
the Puerto Rican population of New Jersey was approximately 200,000 which
is a substantial increase from the 55,351 figure obtained from the 1960 Census.
New York City alone indicated a very significant increase in its Puerto Rican
population. By 1964, the City had 701,500 Puerto Ricans while the 1960 Census
listed 642,622 for the state as a whole. So when we speak of Puerto Ricans in
the United States we are talking about two million people. They reside in massive concentrations in the large cities and towns from New York City fanning
inland through New Jersey and Pennsylvania, North along the Eastern seaboard to Massachusetts and inland through Ohio to reach Illinois. Common to
all these Puerto Ricans is a vehement concern for education—the education of
their children and their youth. It is very important that you know that the
commonly held impression that Puerto Ricans are primarily located in New
York is wrong.

We want you to be aware that Puerto Ricans have arrived at the same conclusions which many highly respected educators and social scientists have ar-

rived at, after investigation of the urban school systems of this nation. No studies are available which have placed the spotlight on the full dimension of the educational problems of Puerto Rican children. Although the following details do not tell the entire story we can begin to sketch some of the known facts. We ourselves do not know the entire story although we suspect it.

In the City of Chicago there are 18,000 Puerto Ricans enrolled in the public elementary schools, but only 4,000 are enrolled in the public high schools. Some children "drop out" (or as is better known among Puerto Ricans are pushed out) in the transition between the junior and senior high school. The approximate rate of dropout is 60%. The ASPIRA of Illinois reports that of the thousands of Puerto Ricans in the high schools of Chicago only 107 were admitted to colleges and universities this year.

Out of 7,810 Puerto Rican students in the public school system of Newark last year, only 96 survived to the 12th grade. There are approximately 150 Puerto Rican college students in that state, some of whom are out of state residents.

In 1970 there were 7,989 Spanish speaking students in the public schools of Philadelphia: 1,547 of them in the junior high school and 903 in the senior high school. The school system in that city reports that Puerto Rican children drop out before they reach high school at a rate of approximately 70%.

New York City offers somewhat more specific information because the *1964 Study of Poverty Conditions in the New York Puerto Rican Community* gathered a profile of the Puerto Rican educational situation in more depth than had been done in other cities. The situation which emerged in 1964 showed that Puerto Rican youth were severely handicapped in achieving, more so than any other group of youths in the public school system of that city. It showed that less than 10% of Puerto Rican children in the third grade were reading at their grade level or above. By the eighth grade the degree of retardation of Puerto Ricans was even more severe. While 13% of Puerto Rican youth were reading at grade level, almost two thirds ($\frac{2}{3}$) were retarded more than three years.

The same study also showed that in 1963 of 21,000 academic diplomas granted only 331 were to Puerto Ricans (1.6% of the total number of academic diplomas granted), although that year Puerto Ricans constituted 7.2% of the total enrollment of the high schools which prepare students for college entrance. In New York City Puerto Ricans drop out of school before finishing high school at an approximate rate of 50%. This is not surprising considering that by the eighth grade $\frac{2}{3}$ of them are retarded more than three years in reading. The longer Puerto Ricans attend the schools the more retarded they become. The existence of the kind of information and reliable data, which is taken for granted for most minority groups, does not exist about Puerto Ricans. Not too much more than what has been summarized here can be found. In December of this year a study by Prof. Hilda Hidalgo of Rutgers University will be published which will offer a profile of the Newark Puerto Rican population. There is an obvious need for gathering the kind of basic data on the educational needs of the Puerto Ricans that can serve as the basis for program designs and evaluatory purposes.

We want to make this committee aware of what is meant when we have been described as "the poorest group in the Northeast". Why are Puerto Ricans "not making it" as the emigrants from Europe who came during the eighteen hundreds did? There are two main reasons among others of lesser importance.

1. The Puerto Rican migration has come (and is coming) to this country during different historical and economic conditions. The country has already been made; the frontier does not exist anymore; the labor unions have been organized, etc. . . . The country has no need for unskilled poor people even if they are industrious and ready to work. Employment has a direct relationship to the development of skills or to the acquisition of training for a profession. Many menial jobs require at least a high school diploma. Unskilled, willing hard workers are obsolete. The country needs developed educated minds and skilled hands.

2. Puerto Ricans are a racially mixed people. Color (other than white) is a liability in the United States. The group shares with the Blacks and other minorities the prejudice and discrimination with its attending suffering and deprivation. Because of a lack of tradition and experience as to how to mount a fight against these evils and because of a refusal of Puerto Ricans to divide

themselves as Black Puerto Rican and White Puerto Rican, very few bridges of cooperation and understanding exist with their Black American brothers although we are partners in poverty.

The findings of the *1964 Study of Poverty Conditions in the New York Puerto Rican Community*, quoted before in this presentation, showed that by merely collecting existing. data, that Puerto Ricans in New York were caught in a trap, a cycle of poverty, which would not only relegate them to an indigent status but would produce cultural disintegration. The study is the only attempt to date which breaks the veil of silence and ignorance which hides the situation of Puerto Ricans in the United States. Its findings can be extended, if multiplied, to the situation of Puerto Ricans in other major cities where they have migrated. In essence the profile of Puerto Rican poverty can be drawn as follows:

Puerto Ricans fall on the poverty line at the rate of one out of every two, in other words 51.4% of the total Puerto Rican population of New York lived in poverty circumstances in 1960. Puerto Rican poverty is characteristic of family life and large families including children. Also more than 47% of the males and 45% of the females were under 20 years of age in 1960. So poverty casts a shadow over a present and future generation of youth.

As a result of the large number of children in the Puerto Rican group a relatively small number of them are at their best working ages. Puerto Rican adults have the lowest level of formal education of any identifiable ethnic or color group in New York City. Eighty-seven percent of them had dropped out without graduating from high school and more than half, 52.9% of Puerto Ricans in New York City of 25 years and older, had less than an eighth grade education in 1960.

In 1961 a study of a Manhattan neighborhood showed that fewer than 10% of the Puerto Ricans in the third grade were reading at their grade level or above. Three in ten were retarded one and a half years or more in the middle of their third year of school. By the eighth grade the degree of reading retardation was more severe; while 13% of the Puerto Rican youth were reading at grade level or above, almost ⅔ were retarded more than 3 years.

Of the few who remain in high school an infinitesimal number graduate with a diploma which prepares them for a college education and of those only a handful go to college and can survive there to emerge with a profession.

In 1963 Puerto Ricans were 7.2% of the academic high schools (those preparing for college), 22.5% of vocational high schools (those preparing for a trade), and 29.1% of special schools. (Special schools include mostly those where youth with serious behavior problems are sent.)

Since the· educational attainment of first generation migrant Puerto Ricans and second generation is so extremely low it is not surprising to find a negative situation when it comes to employment, unemployment, and housing. The findings of the *1964 Study of Poverty Conditions in the New York Puerto Rican Community* in these three areas are summarized as follows:

Employed Puerto Ricans, more than any other group in the city, are concentrated in the occupations with the lowest pay and status.

In 1960 one in 10 Puerto Rican men were unemployed and looking for work. In other words Puerto Rican unemployment was at a rate of 9.9% compared to 6.9% for Blacks and 4.3% for Whites.

Among both the first and second generation a trend is evident for the occupational status of employed women to improve relative to that of the employed men. If the trend continues, it may have unfavorable implications for the stability of traditional Puerto Rican cultural patterns of family life.

The housing situation of Puerto Ricans in New York City emerges logically out of the previous negative picture. Puerto Ricans live in housing units that are the most deteriorated or dilapidated and the most crowded in New York City.

So the Puerto Ricans are poor migrants, racially mixed, do not speak English. They have a low educational attainment, no skills, hold the lowest prestige and lowest paying jobs; have the highest degree of unemployment; live in the worst houses; and inherit the worst conditions of living which surround the slums. Their children are racially mixed, do not speak English or Spanish well, cannot read well, drop out of school without a high school diploma, etc., etc. . . . The cycle goes on and on. We Puerto Ricans *are* the poorest people in the Northeastern United States and we are also silent and invisible.

We want very much to leave with you the understanding of how important our language and our culture are to us. They are not only the treasures we as a poor people possess, which enrich our lives, but they are also the life savers which will succor us in this our hour of crisis. We are culturally different than the majority community in this country not only in our racial attitudes, but also in the fact that we speak a different language—we speak Spanish. . . We are also different in our values, mores, customs, and patterns of family life and other interpersonal relationships. We are the bearers of a culture—The Puerto Rican culture. Quoting Mr. Louis Nunez, the president of ASPIRA of America, Inc., in his lecture as part of the Morton Wollman Distinguished Lectures for 1969-70, "Simply put, a Puerto Rican New Yorker [a Puerto Rican in the U.S.] might conduct all of his business, professional and most of his social life in English, but with his parents, with his friends from the Island, and when he journeys to Puerto Rico, he speaks Spanish. The differences between the situation of the Puerto Rican and the situation of the previous . . . newcomers is that the ties [with their culture] seem to strengthen with time rather than lessen. The emerging Puerto Rican professional and businessman travels to Puerto Rico two or three times a year. He has a genuine desire to retain his cultural identity and not to disappear into the mainstream as some would urge us. The liberal concept of cultural pluralism is a fact now with many Puerto Ricans [in the U.S.]." For Puerto Ricans in the U.S. the matter of retaining the Spanish language is an emotional as well as a material necessity. The matter of acquiring the English language is crucial to functioning in the vital day to day world, not only for survival, but to succeed in securing the basic needs that make men healthy. In the immediate present, retaining and developing the Spanish language is for the Puerto Rican a means of having one tool of communication while developing mastery over another.

The school systems which Puerto Rican children attend in their new home have mounted a formidable attack upon the child's language and culture. The child is made to feel ashamed of both and by so doing, he is made to feel ashamed of himself and his family. As a result most Puerto Rican children are silent, withdrawn and non-receptive. They acquire a very poor self-image. Children who do not believe in themselves have difficulty in learning and have poor motivation and low aspirations.

This quality of silence and withdrawal is also true of the adult Puerto Ricans. The language difficulty which creates timidity in participating, coupled by the rejection and exclusion of the overall community, make the group absent from parent associations and other school boards and committees. As a result others usually speak or represent Puerto Ricans. This happens to such an extent, that usually Puerto Ricans' needs and problems become hidden in such phrases as "Negroes and Puerto Ricans" or in a generalization such as "Spanish speaking". The result of such mergers is always that Puerto Ricans are left out when services, benefits or rights are secured under these joint banners. A very good example for this Committee of this type of problem is the establishment of two structures at the level of the Federal government. First there is the Cabinet Committee for the Spanish Speaking, and second, there is in the Office of Education the Office for Spanish Speaking American Affairs. In both agencies there is no Puerto Rican staff and there is no concern or programs relating to or for Puerto Ricans!

Recommendations:

I want to leave the following recommendations for this Committee to consider in their preparation of legislation or their influencing the development of new programs under existing federal agencies:

1. Through new legislation or amendments to existing legislation the Committee must provide grants to Puerto Rican (and other minorities) non-profit-private-educational agencies to establish complementary programs to the public school system. There are functions which are at present the responsibility of the public schools, at which they have failed, and which they will always be incapable of fulfilling successfully. For example, the motivational and guidance programs and programs to develop a positive identity in the children is something we Puerto Ricans know we can do best for our children. There is another function, keeping the school systems honest, which usually is contracted with universities or industry because it is thought that only there is found the ex-

pertise to evaluate and audit the special federally funded programs. Puerto Rican professionals and Puerto Rican professional agencies can also perform these functions. The Federal government cannot continue to pour massive monies for assistance to the very systems which have failed (for example 3.3 billion dollars in financial assistance for pre-school, elementary and secondary education was given in the year 1970). It is preposterous if responsible, professional, private minority group agencies who know the children best who are the victims of the schools are not permitted to offer their solutions to the crisis of education.

2. This Committee can be instrumental in the creation of the type of climate which will open the doors for the introduction of new concepts into the present educational scheme in the schools of the large cities of this country. The schools cannot continue to do business as usual. They exist in a new world which requires changed institutions. There are a few new approaches which are considered valid by many respected educators and which are producing results where the old methods failed. To mention one of them, I want to voice my amazement at the efforts to hide away and emasculate the Job Corps, burying it in the Department of Labor as just one more program to teach skills or a trade for employment aimed at hard core dropouts. It seems to many of us that Job Corp is one innovative concept of education which should be offered as one more alternative for youths to pursue in the same manner that academic, vocational, commercial or general courses are alternatives. Any youth should have the opportunity to enter in residence a Job Corps Center in search of personal development, in search of a vocational choice, in search of clarifications to personal and emotional confusions, as well as to continue his or her basic education. Such centers as part of the regular school systems can offer a normal young person and those with a troubled life, an opportunity to work out his or her problems through the every day living experiences with peers who are doing the same. These centers are succeeding with youths who were discarded by the regular school systems because the Job Corps starts by viewing the learning needs of each youth and his learning capabilities as unique, and because they start with the concept that all children and youth can learn. That is most certainly innovative when compared to the typical urban school.

3. One other innovative educational program which merits being given the full opportunity to succeed is bilingual education. To have a fair chance to demonstrate its validity, bi-lingual education as it is today needs a number of changes and expansions. First, the few existing projects are all under the control of the same school systems which failed at mono-lingual education. This Committee should request the necessary funds for the expansion of the program, at the same time that it changes the eligibility criteria so that other educational agencies (particularly those of Puerto Ricans, Chicanos, Chinese and other bi-lingual groups) can establish programs with the aide of universities or known experts in bi-lingualism. Second, the bi-lingual programs must be required to be bi-cultural as well as bi-lingual as the law stipulates. Third, the bilingual education law should provide funds for separate evaluative and teacher training efforts. Fourth, bi-lingual education has to be established throughout the elementary, junior and senior high schools.

4. The Committee must be instrumental through new legislation, amendments to existing legislation or some other means, to create structures at the federal level that will develop concern, promote the development of programs and the employment of professionals, secure the assignment of funds and gather complete and accurate data on and about, and for Puerto Ricans in the Office of Education and other agencies related to education and the Puerto Rican. I would want to know how many Puerto Ricans are employed in policy making positions in the Office of Education? I suspect the answer to my question is none or almost none. Thank you.

INTEGRATION AND PUERTO RICAN NEEDS

Senator MONDALE. Senator Brooke?

Senator BROOKE. Mr. Chairman, I have been very much interested in what Miss Pantoja has said. I certainly understand her great feeling of the need for Puerto Rican children to understand their own identity and have a sense of pride in themselves and their heritage and culture.

As I understand it, you believe the basic obstacle to educating Puerto Ricans is language; is that correct?

Miss PANTOJA. Language and a negative self image. Also another obstacle is a school system that continues to function business as usual, and does not institute effective programs to bring these children up to par, a school system that is insensitive to the needs of this particular group of people who, in many instances—I was going to say minority, but they are not; numerically, in many instances they are the majority in some areas.

Senator BROOKE. Now you are not advocating by any means a nonintegrated system. You believe in an integrated system?

Miss PANTOJA. Yes. I believe that in order to integrate effectively, when you are a group that lacks the tools of language and when you are a group that has been under the impact of an attack upon your very image, upon who you are, you need to have alongside with efforts at integration, you need to have the special programs to bring you up to par.

I don't mean remedial experiments and little pilot projects, because of those we have thousands. If you contact the one board of education that I know best, which is New York City, they will give you a list of hundreds and hundreds of programs they have for Puerto Ricans. But you will find out that these are programs for 200 kids, for 300 kids; and I am speaking of thousands of children. So I am talking about programs within the regular school day, everyday. Integration alongside a school system aware and sensitive to the fact that this country has always had language groups coming in. And let us hope that it will always have language groups coming in, and that it develops this kind of special attention to children who do not speak the language.

PARALLEL INSTRUCTION

Senator BROOKE. Now are you talking only of language courses, or are you talking of history, Puerto Rican history, Puerto Rican culture, other types of courses that could be integrated into the school curriculum?

Miss PANTOJA. I am talking about those, and I am also saying that the system is so incapable of looking at people who are different in a positive way that we concluded that we would like to have monies ourselves, to teach ourselves these in parallel, complementary systems.

Senator BROOKE. Outside of the school system?

Miss PANTOJA. Yes, in cooperation with the system, having the system release our children to come over to acquire such knowledge. We know of courses on the history of Puerto Rico are being taught by people who do not know anything about our history. Let me give you an example, a book which a school system put out, in which the heroes used for Puerto Rican children are some people from the community who the children themselves know are questionable people in their practices and the way they live in the community. They refuse to go into our history and into the experiences of the Puerto Rican, into our past. Let me tell you it is ignorance, it is ignorance of what has gone on, who we are, where we come from.

There are people who say, "Well, we would like very much to institute some courses on Puerto Rican culture, but is there a Puerto Rican culture?" Then they will institute a course on the culture of Spain. Well, Spain, to us, is another colonial power. You see, studying Spain is fine. Our culture is based basically on the Spanish root, but there are Indian and black roots in that culture.

RELATIONSHIP WITH OTHER MINORITIES

Senator BROOKE. Let me ask a further question, Mr. Chairman.

I think in your paper you stated you do not have the cooperation of blacks. Is there much cooperation between diverse Spanish-speaking groups?

Miss PANTOJA. No, I am sorry to say. Some of the very militant kids say that the establishment keeps us divided. I must say that that is so. We are divided. You know, we poor people and we people who need to be together are divided. In many instances you will find that the blacks and the Puerto Ricans have either no communication or negative communication. In areas where politically we stand much to gain when we work together, we compete with one another.

The Chicanos are on the other side of the country. There is all the reason in the world why we should get together and set up some cooperative effort because really we don't have that many reasons to compete. We could extend lines of communication. But we don't have them. If a structure existed for Chicanos and Puerto Ricans, to establish good lines of cooperation, the only place where they could compete, because they share the crumbs of the slum, is in Chicago. But in the rest of the nation we are so far apart geographically that we should be able to cooperate with one another.

With the blacks what happens is that at the bottom we compete for the horrors of the slums.

Senator BROOKE. Thank you.

Senator MONDALE. On that last point, having served for some time on the Indian Education Subcommittee and having served some time with the Mexican American Subcommittee, I have found that the complaints heard are almost identical—lack of sensitivity to language, lack of sensitivity to culture and history evinced by a system which seems to be unresponsive to the needs of the child who in turn must fend for his own self—while the details differ somewhat the complaint is almost the same.

FAILURE OF THE EDUCATIONAL SYSTEM

Then coupled with these objections is this tremendous frustration which develops from having tried to make the systems respond and then finding that it won't, it can't understand; In any event the tragedy continues.

You cite figures in New York and elsewhere which show that most children are not making it, not even through high school, let alone through or even into college.

In Chicago, of 18,000 Puerto Rican children enrolled in the public elementary school, only 4,000 made it in high school and a scant 107 went on to college or universities. Of 7,800 Puerto Rican students in

Newark, 968 survived through the 12th grade. 1st grade is characterized by a majority of Puerto Ricans, a majority of Mexicans, majority of Indians. But by the time these minority children get to the high school, particularly the 12th grade, you need an FBI investigator to find one. Yet this continues.

Senator BROOKE. Mr. Chairman, I was wondering, after hearing the witness—and she is absolutely correct—the Puerto Ricans have made contributions to this nation, the blacks have made it, the Mexican Americans have made it. All of us have come from all over the world—Italians, French, Spanish speaking people—and I was just wondering, because, as you have said, Mr. Chairman, as we have listened to other groups their problems have been practically the same. They have advocated in essence the same type of programs.

SEPARATE MINORITY PROGRAMS

I am just wondering, are we headed toward a society and educational system in which we have a public school system here and then separate programs for each minority group? Because they do vary a bit, even though their goals are the same, the languages might be the same, their cultures are the same. Are we going to ever really get together, to have this one single school system in the nation in which, of course, you might have Spanish, Puerto Rican culture, Mexican culture, African culture, Portuguese culture—right down the line. I am wondering are we going to be able to have a system with all these variables on the outside of the main school system?

Miss PANTOJA. You see, it is not really a peculiar thing. It has been done in this country in other areas. The public money coupled with private money in private institutions has created new ideas. These have been the type of activities that has kept the public institutions honest; have served as watchdogs, have set standards, have had the opportunity to experiment in other fields.

It is not strange that in the educational system you develop that type of pattern and still keep a single educational system. I don't say that we should pull our children out of the general educational system and set up our own schools. That would be foolish. We are a very poor people and we can't support a system like that.

Senator BROOKE. Even if you could support it, would you want to do it?

Miss PANTOJA. No, I would not want it.

Senator BROOKE. Among the blacks there is a great movement for separatism, as you well know. A number of blacks want a separate school system. They want all black faculty, subjects as chosen by them, a black principal—the whole system. They want a separate system.

Is there a movement among Puerto Ricans in this direction, for separatism?

Miss PANTOJA. I would judge—and the other witnesses can answer that for you also. I would judge there is no movement for that type of separatism as a nation. We already have a little island in the Caribbean.

Senator BROOKE. You have it there, you don't have it here in the United States. You have a large number of Puerto Ricans living in the United States, say, in New York or my own city of Boston. Now is there any movement there for separatism?

Miss PANTOJA. No, because we already are separated in our ghettos. We consider that in the case of people who come from another culture and have another language, the ghetto is going to serve as a cushion to be able to jump into the general world. I would say you have to have experiences in the general community and the school system is one area where you have such experiences.

But you must provide people with the manner and the ways in which they learn a new culture, a new language, new ways; and it does not have to be by depriving them and taking away from them their culture and their language. You see, people are not like a pot where, if you have water in it and you are going to put milk, you have to throw the water out. Fortunately, human beings are fantastic creatures. They can hold more than one language, more than one culture, more than one piece of knowledge in their head. So it is not necessary to clean out one to put in another one.

What I am advocating is that there are aspects of this that the people themselves, Puerto Ricans themselves, can do very effectively, much more effectively than the school system and that, with public monies, we can help these children overcome the crisis which is robbing them of their future. We are talking about the lives of people.

Without saying that you are destroying the central system—which I am not advocating—sometimes people get all shaken up if you say you are going to set up a parallel system on the side. We are not advocating a parallel school system, but we are advocating complementary services to the school system.

PRESCHOOL PROGRAMS

Senator BROOKE. Would you advocate preschool classes for Puerto Rican children, prekindergarten classes?

Miss PANTOJA. Yes. For example, bilingual classes. We tried in New York, we experimented with a bilingual nursery, only we lost the money when the OEO funds were cut. That is what happens.

Senator BROOKE. Thank you.

Senator MONDALE. You mean there has been no preschool Head Start type of experimental bilingual educational effort for the Puerto Rican people?

Miss PANTOJA. I don't know if there is a bilingual program that goes down into the preschool. But Headstart does not have bilingual programs.

Senator MONDALE. So at this point they have not even tried one?

Miss PANTOJA. We tried one.

Senator MONDALE. But OE or OEO has not tried one?

Miss PANTOJA. I don't think so.

Senator MONDALE. It is unbelievable. There is one point I want to make. I think I am correct. On the Navaho Reservation when they finally set up their own schools, set up a bilingual education program taught by Navaho teachers, after the second year the children were more proficient in both languages than they would have been if English language instruction had been conducted solely in English as before. The point is that they learned English faster through bilingual education than they would have learned if you had tried to stuff English down the throat of a child who can't understand what you are talking about.

Miss PANTOJA. I know there is a school in New York City, in Brooklyn, a junior high school, that had an experiment where they put together a group of Puerto Rican children. They were kept year after year together. They received all their subjects in Spanish and they participated also in classes in English. They even received their counseling in Spanish, together.

These kids had an Aspira Club also. This is the agency we have in New York and in various cities. We know that the majority of those children are right now in college. Looking at them, you knew these were the kind of children who were going to drop out and get into trouble. They were on the Brooklyn waterfront, that type of environment. These children demonstrated a fantastic advancement in their learning and in their holding power in the school. But they were having the whole component. They were having guidance, they were having an identity program. They were having classes in English and in Spanish.

So there are evidences that this is possible and this kind of thing is effective.

Senator MONDALE. What percentage of the Puerto Rican children attending school this year, first graders, would you estimate are proficient in English?

Miss PANTOJA. First graders?

Senator MONDALE. The children entering the first grade.

Miss PANTOJA. I am not able to tell you the percentage. As I told you, there is very little data about us. It is like we do not exist. I know, for example, that talking to a man in the Office of Education who is an expert in bilingualism, Dr. Bruce Gaarder, he told us when we were planning the bilingual nursery that children coming to the first grade have acquired a certain number of words in their own language at home. The teacher mounts on top of these words that they have learned at home, the teaching of English.

SPANISH—BASIC HOUSEHOLD LANGUAGE

You take for granted that at home they have acquired a certain number of words and phrases. This is a basic necessity to start the teaching of English. The Puerto Rican children who at home speak Spanish—and that happens in all our households—they get that basic language in Spanish. The teacher starts mounting on top of a base which is in Spanish, English. This is why to begin with, the Puerto Rican child, starts with handicaps.

Senator BROOKE. This is quite different from the Italians. I have made a study of that. The second generation of Italians, the child did not speak Italian, does not know how to speak Italian. He spoke English. They would understand a bit of Italian from the parents, but they never spoke it in the home. In the Puerto Rican home Spanish is spoken all the time, so the child grows up speaking Spanish?

Miss PANTOJA. Yes. Before you came in, I had pointed to the fact that we have the kind of migration that returns to Puerto Rico. You see, you return to the island and you keep using the language. Many children even go home for vacation.

PUERTO RICAN STATEHOOD

Senator BROOKE. I go with them back and forth. I take the flight on Eastern Airlines. I know what you mean. Tell me this, is the status of Puerto Rico a factor in this problem at all? I refer to commonwealth, independence or statehood. I spend a lot of time in Puerto Rico, Mr. Chairman. I am very much familiar with the debate raging in Puerto Rico at the present time as to whether they should have their independence or whether they should be a state or whether they should remain a commonwealth as they are at the present time.

I know the president down there. I know the battles that have been going on. I am just wondering whether this is a factor in the problem of young people, Puerto Rican children who are in the United States at the present time. Is that a factor?

Miss PANTOJA. Yes, it is. You will find that the young militant Puerto Rican in the university or in the high school will be concerned with these issues. The central theme, the central cord for their militancy will be the independence of Puerto Rico. So that you will find they have communication with the established independence party in Puerto Rico, a recognized party in Puerto Rico. They have contact with university students in Puerto Rico who are for the independence of Puerto Rico. This is an important issue for them.

Senator BROOKE. You say it is an issue?

Miss PANTOJA. Yes.

Senator BROOKE. How does it manifest itself so far as the young people are concerned?

Miss PANTOJA. Well, it manifests itself in going back to the life of the writers who are the leaders for independence in Puerto Rico, Betances, Campos, De'Diego, and the study of the struggle for independence, not only in the days of Spain, but of the days of certain massacres and activities that went on in Puerto Rico.

SEPARATISM

Senator BROOKE. I did not phrase my question properly. I understand that. Your answer was responsive. Has this brought about a general feeling for separatism here in the United States? For example, are Puerto Rican children now more apt to want their own schools, their own school system—want to be separate?

Miss PANTOJA. As far as I know, not separate schools, but it has brought about the demand for Puerto Rican studies in universities. Of course, not only the kids who believe in the independence of Puerto Rico want that. The other young Puerto Ricans who might believe in statehood or who might believe in the commonwealth have gone after and have fought for Puerto Rican studies also.

I don't think that you have the same thing, it is not parallel with the same thing that has happened with the black militant. We don't have a struggle for the development of a separate nation in the United States, because we already have it in our island. There is a struggle for projecting forth the fact that the island has a political status which is questionable.

You know that kind of statement is a statement that you will hear your statehood person say also, that the island has a sort of neo-colonialism in which the citizens are not full citizens. Some people say the answer to that is independence, and other people say the answer to that is statehood.

Senator BROOKE. But this has given rise to more militancy in the Puerto Rican communities, has it not?

Miss PANTOJA. It has been the theme of the militants, and we do have a militant group, or a couple of militant groups. Maybe I shouldn't say any number, because there are several militant groups that exist in the Puerto Rican community of the United States whose central preoccupation along with problems that exist here—problems of poverty, problems of garbage collection, problems of low educational attainment—is also independence for the island of Puerto Rico.

Senator BROOKE. It has made them more militant concerning conditions as they exist in the United States?

Miss PANTOJA. And they equate the situation of the deprivation here and the situation of silence and the situation of being left out as a result of the island being a colonial island.

Senator BROOKE. They question whether or not they are truly citizens of the United States in that respect?

Miss PANTOJA. They question that, yes.

Senator MONDALE. I would like to continue, but we have a panel we have to hear before noon. Thank you very much for your testimony.

ENGLISH PROFICIENCY

I would conclude with one final question, if I might. Did I understand your answer to my question of how many first graders, Puerto Rican first-graders, were proficient in English from the standpoint of the average public school to be that for all practical purposes none of them are?

Miss PANTOJA. None or very few.

Senator MONDALE. Almost all of them come with a basic Spanish language and culture?

Miss PANTOJA. That is correct.

Senator MONDALE. Thank you very much.

Let me ask you one final question. How many public schools build upon that Spanish language as a cultural base and then works into English, rather than the other way around?

Miss PANTOJA. Very few. You know, there is a study, it is not really a study, it is not a statistical study but it is a sort of review of the situation of Puerto Ricans throughout the nation that was put out by Aspira. Aspira commissioned it. It is called the Lucers. I hope that some of the coming speakers will give "The Losers" as appendix for the record. These give incidents when the types of conditions where a child would urinate in his seat because he had been trying to tell the teacher in Spanish he wants to go to the bathroom.

The teacher does not understand and is oblivious to what he is trying to say. It is as basic a thing as that.

You find a system trying to say that the children will not learn; but not saying: it is our responsibility to teach them.

Senator MONDALE. Do you know how many Puerto Rican children are in the District school system here in Washington, D.C.

Miss PANTOJA. No.

Senator MONDALE. Are there some?

Miss PANTOJA. There are some, because I know that when the city established a new program in the Human Resources Administration, they established a new program for the Spanish speaking. I know that the man who headed the effort for that is a Puerto Rican, and that there are a number of Puerto Ricans living in the Columbia Road-16th street area. But I don't know how many because the figures we have are the figures from the largest areas of concentration.

There is a need for data, Senator. You can't function if you don't know the dimensions of your problem.

Senator MONDALE. Thank you very much.

Our next panel is composed of Mrs. Sylvia Fox, Mr. Armando Martinez, Mr. Hector Vasquez; and Mr. Nathan Quinones. We will start with Mr. Martinez, of Boston.

Perhaps you would like to introduce him.

Senator BROOKE. Mr. Chairman, I regret I will be unable to stay to hear Mr. Martinez' testimony, and other members of the panel. I would like very much to do so. I do have another commitment, as I told you, Mr. Chairman. I have read Mr. Martinez' statement, and the statements of other members of the committee.

Mr. Martinez is a founder of Puente Fund, Inc., which I understand is a sister organization to a group called BRIDGE, which is a black organization in the City of Boston. I think it is probably the first time that the Puerto Rican organization and blacks have cooperated and organized and worked together. It has been to help Puerto Ricans go to college.

I think we have some shocking statistics to come from Mr. Martinez. I think we have only had four or five Puerto Rican graduates from high school in our city in the last four or five years, and the population is steadily increasing.

I understand further, I am ashamed to say, there are reports that less than half of the Puerto Rican children are even enrolled in the schools. Mr. Martinez, of course, can give us more statistics on this, but this is a very shocking statistic, if this is a fact. We are hopeful that we will certainly be able to correct this condition which does exist in the city.

I don't know whether you have statistics about other parts of the State, Mr. Martinez, but I understand that the statistics for the other parts of the State are not much better than those in the City of Boston.

Why don't you proceed, Mr. Martinez? I certainly shall review very carefully the statements of all the members of this panel.

Thank you for appearing.

STATEMENT OF ARMANDO MARTINEZ, BOSTON, MASS., DIRECTOR, "PUENTE"

Mr. MARTINEZ. Before I explain what I know about the problem of education among my people, I would like to make it clear that what I say or speak about are not mere educational theories or conclusions arrived at from books. I am not just a spectator of my people's history and condition in this country. My ideas have risen from experience and total involvement with my people's problems.

First as a student and then as a teacher and educator, I have felt and seen the educational injustices that this country has committed against our linguistic and cultural minority.

Our children are faced with an alien language and new concepts which result in classroom difficulties. Our children not only must adjust to a new culture, with new standards, but also a new tongue, as well.

There are a number of factors that contribute to the possibility of scholastic retardation and illiteracy among Puerto Rican children in America. Children between five and seven use language at an accelerated rate for purpose of problem solving. To switch a child to a second language without first developing cognitive skills in the mother tongue can lead to what is called a nonlingual, a premature bilingual, whose function in both languages develops only in limited ways.

"ENGLISH-ONLY" POLICY

The UNESCO commission asked the governments of the world not to reject linguistic minorities when setting up national educational programs. In America, the "English-only" policy contributes to a student's alienation from home and culture. Every effort should be made to provide education in the mother tongue, because they understand it best. Not to do this is a great mistake. Literacy in the mother tongue rather is the means to the culture and language of the nation.

The command of the national tongue must be insured. There are ways, however, to secure this goal and at the same time secure the education of the individual.

Research studies indicate that one of the best predictors of success in the national language is mastery of the mother tongue first. Children who are instructed in the beginning school years in their first language and then advance to the second language quickly learn the second language and at the same time become balanced bilinguals capable of functioning in two languages.

In our modern and accelerated world, flexibility is essential, and if we are able to do all that will be required of us to develop the hemisphere and the world, it is essential that we begin to think in linguistic terms.

ADVANTAGE OF LINGUISTIC POTENTIAL

What better way for America to develop a heterogeneous linguistic population to meet the present and future than to take advantage of the linguistic minorities and develop their already clear potential?

At the same time, we would be treating linguistic minority children in such a way that their disadvantage under our present educational policy would become an advantage under the new one.

To think that a non-English-speaking child can learn to read and write in a language that he cannot speak is totally unrealistic and irrational. To continue forcing on our children the triple disadvantage of having to learn to speak English—a period of 2 to 3 years—before learning to read or write, forcing on them the frustrations of not understanding the language spoken around them, and leaving them only with nonverbal clues for communication, is unjust. The result of this practice kills whatever motivation the child brings to the classroom, and breeds in him a strong feeling of inadequacy.

Not being able to solve the problem of adjusting to the new environment, new language, new life, and new culture, the child tries to seek support from parents, who suffer from identical problems—aggravated by their struggle for existence. Therefore, if the child fails, he suffers further indignity. He may reason that it is better not to try. Doing this, he reasons a justification for failure. He may remain indifferent, uninvolved, apathetic.

The linguistic and cultural shock are responsible **for our failure.** We need your help to overcome this. Please help us.

STATISTICS OF FAILURE—BOSTON

I am sorry for having read this to you in this way, but I think it is very important to point out the following statistics I bring to you from Boston.

In Boston, we have a 90-percent-dropout rate among the Puerto Rican children, a dropout rate not from high school, but junior high school, seventh and eighth grades. This dropout rate, let me just say, I personally documented.

We have 3,000 children out of school, according to the Children Out of School Task Force in Boston. They estimate 3,000 to 5,000—I am giving you the low figure—Puerto Rican children.

Senator MONDALE. These children never went to school?

Mr. MARTINEZ. These are children who were never in school.

Senator MONDALE. What about the truancy laws?

Mr. MARTINEZ. We don't have one truancy officer in the entire Boston school system that can speak English.

Senator MONDALE. You have 3,000 to 5,000 Puerto Rican children who never attended any school?

Mr. MARTINEZ. Right. Of this number, I personally documented, in the summer migrant program in Boston, in 1969, a program designed for 4,000 Puerto Rican children, 62 children who had lived in Boston for more than 1 year, and who had never registered in a Boston school or attended a Boston school.

Furthermore, of this number, the Spanish Education Council, a council made up of teachers and of community-conscious people in the Boston area, in a door-to-door search documented 1,000 cases, in a door-to-door survey of children who were not attending school this past year.

Senator MONDALE. This migrant education, is that federally funded?

Mr. MARTINEZ. Yes.

Senator MONDALE. Do some of the Puerto Rican migrate with the crops?

Mr. MARTINEZ. Almost 90 percent of the Puerto Ricans who come into Massachusetts come from a migrant agricultural background.

I would like to bring this point up later, because it is part of something I would like to discuss.

Senator MONDALE. All right.

Mr. MARTINEZ. Now, in the Puerto Rican community in Boston, these are some more statistics. We have one policeman. We don't have one engineer. We don't have one executive. We have two teachers who are Puerto Rican, out of 5,800 teachers in the Boston schools, and I know of no other Puerto Rican teachers that exist in the State of Massachusetts.

We have two Puerto Ricans in the State of Massachusetts who hold a master's degree, and I am the only one in the doctoral program, presently at Harvard. This is out of a possible Puerto Rican population in the State of Massachusetts, we don't have the correct statistics, probably, but we estimate that there are somewhere between 100,000 and 150,000.

These figures come from the Commonwealth of Puerto Rico migrant statistics, and in the State.

Senator MONDALE. You estimate between 100,000 and 150,000 Puerto Ricans in Massachusetts?

Mr. MARTINEZ. Yes.

Senator MONDALE. You know of only two Puerto Rican teachers in the State?

Mr. MARTINEZ. That is right.

Senator MONDALE. You estimate from 3,000 to 5,000 children of school age are not going to school at all?

Mr. MARTINEZ That is right.

We in the city of Boston have only 62 children in preschool programs, out of an estimated number of preschool children of 3,200.

Senator MONDALE. Sixty-two?

Mr. MARTINEZ. Sixty-two.

We have one bilingual school, for 300 children, which the Spanish Education Council and APCROSS helped set up in February.

Senator MONDALE. Who is funding that school?

Mr. MARTINEZ. OEO is funding part of it. The other part was funded through something called the Educational Development Center in Newton. They gave only $80,000. We were able to get the rest of the money through the Boston school system. This year OEO took it over.

Up to this year, we have not had one high school program in the entire city of Boston that has met our children's needs through bilingual education. It is this year that Puente has worked with the system and helped set up three classes in bilingual education for our children.

ENGLISH COMPREHENSION

Senator MONDALE. Would you agree with the previous witness that most, if not all, Puerto Rican children start school with no adequate comprehension of the English language from the standpoint of what is being taught?

Mr. MARTINEZ. That is correct.

In a study conducted by Deliah Vorhauer in APCROSS, we found there was, in a cross-sectional study of Puerto Rican families in the city of Boston, 99 percent of the families spoke Spanish only at home.

Senator MONDALE. What percentage of those Puerto Rican children, when they start in the first grade, will receive training in their mother tongue?

Mr. MARTINEZ. In Boston?

Senator MONDALE. Yes.

Mr. MARTINEZ. Very few.

Senator MONDALE. How many will receive training in what is called bilingual education?

Mr. MARTINEZ. The 300 children that we have in the bilingual school now.

Senator MONDALE. That is not a public school?

Mr. MARTINEZ. It is a public school.

Senator MONDALE. It is?

Mr. MARTINEZ. Yes, it is.

Senator MONDALE. 300 of them would receive bilingual education?

Mr. MARTINEZ. Right. That covers elementary school and junior high school.

Senator MONDALE. All first graders?

Mr. MARTINEZ. No, that covers elementary and junior high school, the 300 children.

Senator MONDALE. So that some of these children will have gone through sixth and seventh grades in school, and at this late date in their career, the schools are going to try to teach them English?

Mr. MARTINEZ. That is correct.

Between 1965 and 1969, we documented only four Puerto Ricans as having graduated from Boston schools. This is out of an estimated Puerto Rican student population of about 7,000 in the city of Boston.

Senator MONDALE. Out of 7,000, they graduated four?

Mr. MARTINEZ. Right, in 4 years. This year we did a little bit better. We were able to graduate seven, three from public schools, four from parochial schools.

Senator MONDALE. Would you say that parochial schools are doing a better job, on the basis of those figures, than the public schools?

Mr. MARTINEZ. That is really not a significant—I can't answer that.

As you can see today, statistics are witness to a hopeless future for my people, considering that education is a key to success in this country, and literacy the means of survival, for it is only in learning to read a help advertising, and in knowing how to fill out the application required for the job, that one can get a job.

My people are today among the worst off in this nation. As economic slaves, I see no future for them to overcome their problem until American education is democratized.

ECONOMIC PRESSURES

The effect of the educational policy in Puerto Rico has been the brutal manipulation of an entire population that has shifted by economic pressures to the mainland so that they might fill the job vacuum left by the black man.

This I feel very, very strongly about. I feel our people have been forced out of their lands into the urban areas, and something has got to be done for their children. I have very little hope right now for our adult population. There is very little I can do for them, but I am not going to stand by and see our children slaughtered the way they are slaughtered today. It is unjust.

This is the price Puerto Ricans must pay for development. It could have been done through education.

There are two ways of developing any underdeveloped area. One is through education, the other one is through mass migration. Unfortunately, we were unable to do it through education, because of the linguistic suppression policy that was conducted in our island for 38 years, beginning with the Clark policy in 1898, which forbade education on the island in Spanish. It was an on-and-off fashion that went on for 38 years, not allowing a definite all-Spanish education policy in the island.

There were intervals when we were allowed to educate our children for, maybe, one, two, three, maybe elementary school only, in our language. Most of the education, meaningful education, had to be done in English. This is linguistic suppression. That is why today in Boston we have a 62 percent illiteracy rate, not only in English but in Spanish, among our adults. This is why today we don't have enough professionals to meet the need of our people.

Senator MONDALE. You made a point in your testimony which strikes me as central to the educational problems of Puerto Rican children.

LOSS OF SELF ESTEEM

You take a Puerto Rican child who comes from a family which speaks Spanish, learns his values and his self-worth from his parents. When he enters the first grade in a public school where they speak only English, and teach a different culture, he is going to be totally frustrated.

The second step is that he goes home seeking help from his parents. They cannot help him. So I assume that what happens is that he not only loses respect for himself, but he quickly loses respect for his parents and the value system and the language that they taught him.

In other words, they have proved inadequate through his eyes, and he is left with nothing. Is that accurate?

Mr. MARTINEZ. Very accurate.

Now, failure on the part of Anglo-Saxon America to permit the democratization of culture has resulted in what are the deepest roots in American education today. It will not be enough to permit our people to just read and write their language, or the language that they speak. It will be necessary for them to know themselves also as historical beings.

These ideas I put forth are the expression of my people's political emergence, and practical reflection about it.

Education for identity, education for a better America, a democratic America, literacy, has no significance for us, unless it deals with the history lived by my people.

PUERTO RICAN EDUCATIONAL PROBLEMS—NEW ENGLAND

Now the problem in education among Puerto Ricans in the New England area:

On October 16, 17, 18, the Puerto Rican community in New England held a conference in Hartford, Conn. The conference was funded by the New England Regional Council of the Department of Community Affairs. The objective of the conference was to identify problems of our community, and to discuss ways of combating these problems.

The participants in the conference came from all of the New England States, and the following cities and towns were the most concerned with the educational problems of our community.

I was really surprised to see our people scattered up in Maine, New Hampshire, Vermont, in significant numbers. I knew they were in Connecticut, Rhode Island, and Massachusetts.

Senator MONDALE. I am told that this report entitled "The Way We Go to School" is an excellent one. I am going to ask that it be made a part of the record of this hearing and be included in the material of our final report.

Mr. MARTINEZ. Now, some of the cities that expressed chronic educational problems were: Boston, Chelsey, Lawrence, Lowell, Springfield, New Bedford, Holyoke, Framingham, Cambridge, Lenester-Fitchburg, Mass.; Norwalk, New Brittain, Waterbury, Conn.; Providence, Pawtucket, Central Falls, R.I.; and numerous other towns throughout the New England area.

COMMON PROBLEMS

At this conference, the following problems in education confronting our people were identified as being common:

1. Many towns and cities documented a 90 percent and more dropout rate from junior high school. In Boston, for example, we can document four Puerto Rican students as having graduated from high school between 1965 and 1969. This year we graduated seven, four from parochial schools and three from public schools. This is out of a student populated estimated in the 7,000.

2. Many towns and cities spoke about the alarming rate of school age children who were not attending school. In Boston, the Children Out of School Task Force has estimated that there are between 3,000 and 5,000 Puerto Rican children who do not attend school. I personally documented 62 out of 4,000 children in the summer migrant education program of 1969. The 62 children had lived in Boston over one year, yet had never enrolled or attended a Boston school. The Spanish Education Council in a door-to-door survey documented 1,000 names of children who were not attending school.

Senator MONDALE. I notice this point 3, about members of the mentally retarded classes. Similar complaints have been widely made in Texas. When a child has a language problem, the school responds by putting him in mentally retarded classes and labeling him dumb. In that way, the school cannot be considered to have failed. It was the kid's fault.

Do you find a good deal of this going on elsewhere?

Mr. MARTINEZ. I was in a mentally retarded class until I was 13 years old. I have a master's from Harvard, and I am in a doctoral program in Harvard today.

Senator MONDALE. Our witness, Dr. Palmarez, who is regarded as one of the great American educators, also spent two or three years in a mentally retarded class, I think in California, was it not?

Mr. MARTINEZ. Mine was in Pawtucket, R.I.

Let me continue.

3. Many towns and cities complained about Puerto Rican children being placed in classes for mentally retarded. In many cases these were children who were put in these classes merely because they could not communicate in English.

Springfield, Mass., is one of the cities I would like to identify as practicing it. Boston did so until about 4 years ago.

4. There exists at present no testing mechanism to fairly evaluate our children.

We are constantly fighting the battle to get our children in colleges. They evaluate our children by SAT scores that are not culturally oriented to us, or linguistically oriented to us.

5. Bilingual education programs are needed at all levels. They are needed at preschool, elementary school, junior high school, high school, technical school, vocational school, adult education, literacy, university and college.

I say universities and colleges because I feel that we have every right to intellectualize ourselves in our own language as much as possible.

We want bilingual education, and that means exactly that. It does not mean to learn and write our language. It means to learn and think in it, as well.

6. There is a great need to reeducate our people to their concrete social, economic, and racial situation. There is a need to develop a group concept and identity, so that those that develop skills can return to our communities to help us develop them. I am a firm believer in control over our own destiny.

Senator MONDALE. One of your strong recommendations is community control of the schools. Is that what you are saying?

Mr. MARTINEZ. If not involvement.

Senator MONDALE. There is a lot of difference between the two.

Mr. MARTINEZ. I am still debating that. One month I am on one side. The next month I am on the other. Nothing is constant except change, I am afraid.

7. Very few communities are in the process of planning to deal with the educational problems of the Puerto Rican community.

Boston, which is supposed to be the furtherest ahead, leaves much to be desired at this point. Their negligence is incredible. Their lack of responsiveness is alarming.

8. There is a great need and demand for bilingual teachers who are native Spanish speaking. This means that teacher training programs and curriculum development programs are needed.

In Boston, there is not one guidance counselor in the entire Boston school system that can even speak Spanish. Not one.

9. There is a need to disseminate information about programs, laws, and means that will improve our social situation. This dissemination of this should be done in Spanish.

This is a question that I would post Government agencies.

REASONS FOR FAILURE

Now, the reasons why our children failed, I have identified as primarily three, two categories in one of them, linguistic and cultural problem.

There is a need for a bilingual education program. By bilingual education, I don't just mean the linguistic aspect of it. I also mean the bicultural aspect of it. This is the best way that I know that our children can develop their cognitive skills. By this I mean reading, writing, arithmetic, and consciousness of themselves.

However, solving this problem by all means is not going to solve our problem, and I see it very clearly.

There are two other problems that face our children. A second is economic. The Vorhauer study again showed that more than 80 percent of our family, averaging six members per family, were living on an income of less than $85 a week.

This tells me a lot of why these 13-, 14-, 15-, 16-, 17-year-old boys leave school, to go to work.

Third, the racial problem. We are forced into a society that distinctly makes the line separating white from black. We are a people of many peoples. It is unjust to force us to decide what side of the fence we should lie on.

In Boston, for instance, one of the reasons why children are not in school, and I can tell you this from experience, because I worked for six years at the Martin Luther King School, an all-black school in the Roxbury area of Boston, our people have filled a vacuum of housing that exists between the black and white community.

In a city like Boston, all you have are black or white schools. When our children go to all-black schools, they are not black enough. When our children go to all-white schools, they are not white enough. It has created a racial situation that is affecting the education of our children. Whether we want it or not, I see no alternative except separatism. I hate to see it, but it is a matter of educating our children or not.

RECOMMENDATIONS

Now, some recommendations, ways to help Puerto Ricans reach educational equality.

We need laws to help implement programs. It is not enough to say, "This is a good program." We need legislation to force some of these school systems to implement some of these programs. Not just national, but State as well.

We need additional moneys to increase bilingual education in this country; $24.5 million is not enough for the entire Nation. Only a fraction of that is going to the Puerto Rican community. Most of it is going to the Mexican American community.

Senator MONDALE. And they are not getting enough.

Mr. MARTINEZ. They are not today, no.

I would like to repeat what Miss Pantoja has suggested, that more staff be hired by Government programs. The Bureau of Spanish Affairs, up to last year, and I think he has left his position, had only one Puerto Rican on the staff. That is disgraceful. Where is our representation in this Government? They are needed in different parts, especially the poverty area section. We are not getting our share.

The model cities program in Boston, 33.3 percent of our people live in their area. Last year, the higher education program, 288 students, 15 whites, two orientals, all the rest black, not one Puerto Rican in their higher education program. This is only one segment of the model cities program last year. Where is equality here?

I believe that a special fund should be set aside to combat the problems of the Puerto Ricans. I believe that we need a program to develop our own curriculum. We cannot use Puerto Rico's curriculum here. This is our new area. Massachusetts is my people's area now. We need a curriculum relevant to Massachusetts.

We need a teacher training program that will turn out a significant number of bilingual teachers, teachers who are trained in bilingual methodology, and there are several of them, teachers who are trained in methodologies to combat poverty, to combat racism. There are such things.

We need a vehicle to collect more information about our people. We are here. We know we are here. But somehow, someone has tried to erase us or camouflage us. I want to know more about my people. You can only act on a situation when you identify it and know it well. This is what I seek now.

MIGRANT EDUCATION

Now, migrant education funds. You might be able to help us here. I think the allocation is $50-plus million in the country, of which I think the State of Texas this year returned $1 million because they were unable to use it. I wish we had it.

You see, the migrant education fund enables us to set up supplementary programs, for instance, summer programs that could help our children.

However, even though 99 percent of the Puerto Ricans reaching Massachusetts come from an agricultural migrant background, they worked in agriculture on the island, and as you know, the shift from agriculture to industry——

Senator MONDALE. How many still are in the migrant stream in the United States?

Mr. MARTINEZ. I was going to get to that.

The problem is that they come from a migrant agricultural background. There is no doubt. However, migrant education guidelines, or migrant fund guidelines force the migrant to go from one State to another. Our people don't do this, especially in places like New England, where you have an agricultural span of only several months.

So, instead, what they do, rather than going from a cold area to another cold area, they stay in a local town and local city and try to get a factory job or busboy job or cleaning some bank or something. Eventually, they do stay in the city.

Somehow, I think the migrant education fund has a responsibility to our people, just as well. You know, for generations their people worked in agriculture on the island. The shift from agriculture to industry has forced them out of the island. They come into Massachusetts to work in the tobacco fields, in the cranberry fields, in the apple orchards, the tomato fields in the western part of the State. However, they do not migrate to other States.

It is this that is preventing our people from getting migrant funds to supplement them with educational programs in the summer. I think this past year all we had in the State was $200,000, which is very little money to meet our needs.

So I would suggest that the definition of migrant agricultural worker be worked on a little closer so that our people can be included in this.

Secondly, I am now directing a program in Boston called Puente. Puente is very similar to Aspira. We try to work with our youth. We try to open up avenues of opportunity for them somehow. This program comes out of a budget of $5 million allocated to talent search for the entire nation.

I would like to see more money there, because I think programs like Aspira and like Puente make a big, significant difference. For the first time in the State of Massachusetts this year we have 46 students in colleges in Massachusetts, this year. Thirty were dropouts, not even a high school diploma, but we were able to get them into a junior college program, a higher education program of model cities, which enables them, with supplementary services, to work through 2 years of college, and get credit for it. The other 16, most of them had degrees from Puerto Rico.

What I am saying is that programs like this are very meaningful, because they give us control over our own destiny. Somehow, they make a significant difference.

Five million dollars certainly is not enough to cover even our problem alone, let alone the problem of the poor white, the black, the Indian, the Mexican American, and the Puerto Rican. It is areas such as this one that more money should be spent on, not the war.

That is my presentation. Thank you.

Senator MONDALE. Thank you very much for your most useful contribution.

(The statement of Mr. Martinez follows:)

LITERACY THROUGH THE DEMOCRATIZATION OF EDUCATION

(By Armando Martinez)

(This paper presented on January 7, 1970 at the symposium held by the Harvard Educational Review, at the Harvard School of Education, on the problem of illiteracy in America. The paper will be one of a series of articles that will appear in the spring issue of the Harvard Educational Review.)

Before I explain what I have worked out as a possible solution to the problems of education among my people I would like to make it clear that what I say, or speak about are not mere educational theories. I am not just a spectator of my people's history and condition in this country. My ideas have risen from experience. I am one of the close to ten million Hispanic Americans in the United States. My father was a Puerto Rican; my mother, a Cuban. I was raised as an urban migrant and encountered all the problems that our people have had as a result of suppression inflicted upon them. You do not have to kill a people to eradicate them, or put chains on them to make them slaves. Both these aims can be accomplished by silencing them. In 1845, all Spanish educational institutions were stifled in the Southwest. In 1898, the same thing was done in Puerto Rico. Not until 1934, did all schools in Puerto Rico once again use Spanish as the medium of instruction, and then it was only through grade eight.[1] Only recently have the Mexican Americans regained that right.

We are now reaping the harvest of educational injustice. Our cities are flooded by migrations of Hispanic Americans, —in the West by Mexican Americans and in the East by Puerto Ricans and Cubans. My people flood the urban areas along with all the others who have been cheated by a system that professes democracy and equal rights for all. They contribute to the disparity and hopelessness of today's society. Moving into tenements where the black man once lived, the Hispano clings to his illiterate spoken Spanish, and feeds on rice and beans. He does this almost in defiance against a system that has treated him unjustly, hoping, always hoping, that the future will be different for his children. The Mexican American has seen up to five generations of this and the Puerto Ricans have seen three.

Today's statistic are witness to a hopeless future for my people, considering that education is the key to success in this country and literacy the means of survival. For it is only in learning to read a help wanted advertisement and in knowing how to fill out the application required for the job that one can get a job. My people are today among the worst off in the nation. As economic slaves I see no future for them to overcome their problems until American education is democratized.

To understand the literacy problem of my people, it is essential to talk of the circumstances that have led to the insulting educational practices that have made almost unbelievable statistics.

In the Southwest State of Texas, in section 288 of the Penal Code, made it illegal for education in that state to be administered in any language other than English. Other states in the area set up similar laws. Result: 52% of Mexican Americans in the state over 25 have finished only 4 years of school. A mere 11% go to high school. (This doesn't mean that they graduate.) The City Manager of San Antonio says that 44.3% of all Mexican Americans under his jurisdiction are functional illiterates. The 1960 census shows that 20% of all adult Mexican Americans in Baster County Texas have not completed any school at all.[2]

The effect of the educational policy in Puerto Rico has been the brutal manipulation of an entire population that is shifted by economic pressure to the mainland so that they might fill the "job vacuum" left by the black man. Puerto Rico, the "Poor House of the Caribbean", is becoming a developed land area only through means of migration.[3] (In 20 years one-third of the population of the island has been shifted to American cities.[4]) This has been the price Puerto Ricans must pay for development. It could have been through education; but unfortunately because of the American government's policy in education for the island, it was impossible. Thirty-seven years of an entire population being without literacy in our language left the island without professionals who could have met the demand when development began to take place.[5] The result, sad as it was meant a majority of Puerto Ricans had to find a home elsewhere on the mainland. The economic policy forced on the island tripled the standard of living in a short period of time and failed to create jobs for the general population of unskilled labor. Big capital investments lured to the island by the new tax policy failed to provide sufficient jobs and operated on a minimum of personnel. Many of the new jobs created could not be filled by Puerto Ricans and recruitment on the mainland took place. Nine television stations imposed middle class values as desirable, creating great psychological pressure on the population. The channels bombard the population with American middle class programs translated into Spanish.

In 1960 there were 995 Puerto Ricans in Boston.[6] Today, we estimate around 30,000.[7] Five families averaging six members per family arrive daily.[8]

In the 1969 Migrant Education Program that I directed in Boston this past summer, we interviewed the families of 400 students who took part in the program. We found that 93% of the adults were illiterate and could only sign their name by making a cross. The average grade finished by them was fourth grade. Among the children we found that 62 of the children who were above the third grade could neither read nor write in English or Spanish.

Fifty-two children who had lived in Boston over one year had never attended a Boston school. Many of the children who had gone to Boston schools for two years or more continued to speak only Spanish and knew little if any English. Today, it is estimated that 5,000 Hispanic children, who should be in Boston schools do not attend any school at all.[9]

Not surprisingly the statistics of the Hispano on the Southwest are similar to those of the Hispano in the East.

The feeling of "peoplehood" among the Hispano grows more and more as they become aware of the injustices against them as a minority. Our language, religion, customs, beliefs, myths, and mores, food and even folk medicine, give us a group consciousness that has existed for over a thousand years.

We are heirs of a people who are among those contributing most to world culture and civilization. (The Hispano is a mixture of Carthegenian, Celtic, Goth, Roman, Greek, Phonecian, Moore, Indian, and Negro.)

Our forefathers came from a country that produced some of the world's greatest religious and political leaders, philosophers, writers and painters.

Rome-Hadrian, Trajan and Marcus Aurelius, emperors of Rome, were Spaniards. Our peoples ancestors created the greatest colonial empire the world has ever known; and were discoverers, explorers, civilizers, and colonizers of much of the New World. Our ancestors founded over 200 major towns and cities in America; established the first Christian churches; brought the first printing presses, published books; wrote the first dictionaries, histories, and geographies; and founded the first newspaper in the New World.

There have been Spanish schools for over 400 years and three Spanish universities had been graduating students for nearly one hundred years before Harvard was founded.

Our people introduced the cow, horse, sheep, and many other animals to this country. Agriculture, stock raising and mining in Americas were established by our ancestors.[10]

These facts are omitted or distorted in the schools. For example, American history books portray the Hispanos as a cruel people, only seeking gold, stripping the local population of self-government, and not interested in civilizing or colonizing the New World. In fact, however, between 1500 and 1800 over three million men, women, and children were sent from Spain to colonize America. The Hispano also set up his own town councils and elected legislative assemblies, much like the English did in Virginia and Massachusetts.

Our children have been cheated out of this information. These facts are impot.ant because their use, along with literacy in our own language first, will enable us to overcome the educational and cultural injustices which my people have fallen victims to.

Our children are faced with an alien language and new concepts which result in classroom difficulties. Our children not only must adjust to a new culture, with new standards but also to a new tongue as well.

There are a number of factors that contribute to the possibility of scholastic retardation and illiteracy among the Hispano children in America. Children between 5–7 use language at an accelerated rate for purpose of problem solving.[11] To switch a child to a second language without first developing cognitive skills in the mother tongue can lead to what Zintz calls a "non-lingual," a premature bilingual whose function in both languages develops only in limited ways.

Knowlton[12] points to the Southwestern schools that graduate students who are functionally illiterate. The same can be said of many major cities in the country.

With the backing of research done with Sweden, Mexico, Miami, San Antonio and some of the Asiatic and African Nations, the UNESCO commission asked the governments of the world not to reject linguistic minorities when setting up national educational programs.[13] In America the "English-only" policy contributes to a student's alienation from home and culture. Every effort should be made to provide education in the mother tongue. Children should begin their education through the medium of the mother tongue because they understand it best. I do not say that education in the mother tongue should be an end in itself. To do this would be a great mistake. Literacy in the mother tongue rather is the means to the culture and language of the nation. The command of the national tongue must be insured. There are ways however, to secure this goal and at the same time secure the education of the individual. Research studies have indicated that one of the best predicators of success in the national language is mastery of the mother tongue first.[14] Children who are instructed in the beginning school years in their first language and then advance to the second language quickly learn the second language and at the same time become balanced bi-linguals capable of functioning in two languages.

In our modern and accelerated world flexibility is essential; and if we are to do all that will be required of us to develop the Hemisphere and the world, it is essential that we begin to think in linguistic terms. What better way for America to develop a hetrogeneous linguistic population to meet the present and future than to take advantage of the linguistic minorities and develop their already clear potential. At the same time we would be treating linguistic-minority children in such a way that their disadvantage under our present educational policy would become an advantage under the new one.

To think that a non-English-speaking child can learn to read and write in a language that he can not speak is totally unrealistic and irrational. To continue forcing on our children the triple disadvantage of having to learn to speak English (a period of two to three years) before learning to read or write forcing on them the frustration of not understanding the language spoken around them and leaving them only with nonverbal clues for communication is unjust. The result of this practice kills whatever motivation the child brings to the classroom, and breeds in him a strong feeling of inadequacy. Not being able to solve the problem of adjustment or the new environment, new language, new life, and new culture, the child tries to seek support from his parents who suffer from identical problems—aggravated by their struggle for existence. Therefore, if the child fails, he suffers further indignity. He may reason that it is better not to try. Doing this, he reasons a justification for failure. He may remain indifferent, uninvolved, apathetic.

The "linguistic and cultural shock" are responsible for our bondage. It is a miracle that we do not have a 100% illiteracy and school drop-out rate among my people. How much better it would be to allow the child to learn to read in the language he already understands, introducing him later to the second language, a language in which he could easily apply the previously learned skills of reading and writing.

Failure on the part of Anglo-Saxon America to permit the democratization of culture has resulted in what are the deepest roots of American educational problems today. It will not be enough to permit our people to read and write the language that they now speak; it will be necessary for them to know themselves as historical beings. These ideas I put forth are the expression of my people's political emergence and practical reflection about it; education for freedom, education for identity, education for a better America, a democratic America. Literacy has no significance unless it deals with the history lived by my people.

FOOTNOTES

1. Juan J. Osuna, "*A History of Education in Puerto Rico*," *San Juan Review*, June 1965, p. 30.
2. Robert Coles and Harry Huge, "Thorns on the Yellow Rose of Texas," *New Republic*, April 19, 1969, pp. 13–17.
3. Stanley Friedlander, *Labor Migration and Economic Growth*, Cambridge, Massachusetts, MIT Press, 1965, p. 6.
4. William C. Baggs, "Puerto Rico: Showcase of Development." 1962 *Brittanica Book of the Year*.
5. Juan J. Osuna, op. cit., p. 30.
6. "*A Summary in Facts and Figures, Progress in Puerto Rico*," 1964–65 edition, p. 18, quoted from "1960 Census Population," Bureau of the Census.
7. Rosemary Whiting, "*An Overview of the Spanish-Speaking Population in Boston*," August 1969, p. 1. Unpublished mimeographed report prepared for the Mayor's Office of Public Service.
8. Source: Denison House, 25 Howard Avenue, Dorchester, Massachusetts.
9. "*The Education Needs of Spanish-Speaking Children*." Report of Task Force on Children Out of School, Roxbury, (Mass.) Multi-Service Center.
10. Daniel T. Baldes, "The U.S. Hispano," *Social Education*, April 1969, pp. 441–442.
11. S. H. White, "Evidence for Hierarchical Arrangement of Learning Processes," in *Advances in Child Development and Behavior*, Ed. Vol. II. Lipsitt, L. P. and Spiker, C. C. (Eds.), New York: Academic Press, 1965.
12. Knowlton, C. S. "Bilingualism—A Problem or an Asset," ERIC Documentation Reproduction Service No. ED 010 744, December, 1965.

13. UNESCO, "Foreign Languages in Primary Education: The Teaching of Foreign or Second Languages to Younger Children." Hamburg: UNESCO Institute for Education, 1963.

14. H. Singer, "Bilingualism and Elementary Education," *Modern Language Journal*, 40: pp. 44–58; 1956.

Senator MONDALE. We have eight minutes to noon. I am willing to stay beyond that time.

I will ask each of you to summarize as quickly as you can. If you have statements, they will be inserted in the record as though read. Mrs. Fox?

STATEMENT OF MRS. SYLVIA FOX, ESQ., EXECUTIVE DIRECTOR, ASPIRA OF ILLINOIS, INC.

Mrs. Fox. I must apologize for laryngitis.

The first two pages of my presentation are devoted to placing the Puerto Rican population within the context of the city of Chicago. We constitute approximately 4.5 percent of the population. Together with other Spanish speaking, we make up 9.8 percent of the population of the city, itself. We calculate the total Puerto Rican population as approximately 130,000 in the city of Chicago.

The figures from Health, Education, and Welfare place the population officially, updated figures, at 80,000. Estimates for the cities of Aurora, Waukegan, and Elgin are equally erroneous, by approximately 40 to 50 percent underestimated.

This question of being undercounted is part of the same problem that the gentleman from Boston was referring to. We have a people who has been almost erased from the national landscape.

Many of our problems I will not repeat. They have been stated already by the prior witnesses.

Out of our population, there are only 30 Puerto Ricans attending college. After 1 year of operation, we have increased that number to 170 freshmen who have been placed this year.

However, our program finds itself frustrated by the absence of other services, and other institutions of bilingualism are missing. It is frustrating to the education program aimed at bilingualism.

In high school, where the effort is geared at adapting the student to the administrative convenience of keeping him passively in attendance for 10 or 12 years, this is not a very meaningful pastime from the point of view of having solved some basic social educational problems.

I will skip the enumeration of specific problems, because they have already been discussed.

COMMUNITY INVOLVEMENT IN DECISIONMAKING

The need for redefining the criterion for admission to the creative talent program, where we measure way below average. I myself was given an official IQ of 20 on the Wechsler-Bellevue scale.

Senator MONDALE. That would make you a dropout from a subnormal institution.

Mrs. Fox. That would make one walk out of windows.

Our problem basically is one of alienation, of the problem of decisionmaking. All of us have special problems that we are discussing, which must first be tackled by guaranteeing that our community make a significant input into the problem of making decisions about schooling, particularly our education in general.

Unfortunately, we are faced in Chicago with a highly bureaucratized situation. Only 4.2 percent of the faculty is at present Puerto Rican, and we have no people in decisionmaking positions. The students who have firsthand information of where the educational problems lie are energetically and systematically excluded from voicing their comments.

The whole area of bilingual education is critical, and is misconceived as such by the community. We have only 500-some-odd students participating in the bilingual programs in Chicago. in total, of which the number of Puerto Ricans participating. and this figure needs to be inserted in my presentation. because they were not available at the time I made it, the exact figure of Puerto Ricans participating in the programs are not available. They are not counted that way. The only reason we are counted now at all. as of 2 years ago the Federal Government required these figures.

The answer we have always received when we requested information has been that since the system does not discriminate. it does not need to count the Puerto Ricans.

The fact remains that the Puerto Rican is dropping out and underachieving at a rate of 10 times higher than that of the national norm. Our children are approximately 4 years behind in reading skills. That is, the children in school. We have no way of estimating the retardation of the other school population.

ADVISORY COUNCIL

So that in general I would say that the recent proposal to reduce the participation of parents in the educational process through advisory councils is a tragic indicator of where we are in terms of insight into the problems of the education of minorities.

As I have recommended in recommendation 6, I urge you to intervene with this additional attempt of disfiguration of the original intention of the educational ESEA.

The role of the community in this advisory council has been limited by the regulation of withholding information and making available only at the last moment the agendas of related things. But rather than destroying the opportunity for this rare encounter of people with different class backgrounds and different races and different language backgrounds, what this body should insure is that the nature of participation be improved by earmarking funds for the development of the capability for participation among the community.

Problem 7, which is referring to the role of student participation, to me is a variant of the parental participation.

In general, I think the solution lies in developing a system of complementary education which is fully community controlled, and in which students have appropriate roles for participation appropriate to their age, and appropriate to their developing knowledge.

Discussing the difference between community control and community participation, it seems to me that community participation with the aim of eventual community control is the meaningful desire. The community should have the education of its own children.

This would be one way to bring meaning to education, to make it relevant to the problems of living, and this will be the only way that the capability for participation will be developed among the community, start debating at the level which they are now capable.

The failure of the schools has been dramatic enough, publicized enough. The experimental programs have been dramatic enough. The only way to bring this new knowledge to bear upon the development of new curricula and correction of all problems will be to somehow change the power structure and develop some kind of countervailing institution which will help eliminate the terrible differential of power between an ignorant and disorganized community and a well organized army of professionals whose main aim, as demonstrated in the results of their programs, has been to maintain itself entrenched.

Thank you.

Senator MONDALE. Your full statement will be included in the record as though read.

(Prepared statement of Sylvia Herrera Fox, Esq., follows:)

PREPARED STATEMENT OF SYLVIA HERRERA FOX, ESQ.

Ladies and Gentlemen of the Senate, by any conceivable index, the public school system has failed to meet the learning needs of the Chicago Puerto Rican, and of the Chicago community at large. For our particular minority the crisis is great and requires immediate intervention from all responsible quarters. A fundamental revision of the objectives and methods of schooling is needed, as well as restructuring of the lines of responsibility for decision-making and program evaluation.

Certain specific and glaring inequities require your attention: Problem 1. Irrational underutilization of human resources. There are 26,176 Puerto Ricans enrolled in the Chicago Public Schools. Puerto Ricans thus comprise 4.5% of the total student population, and the largest Spanish Speaking minority. Together with 24,066 Mexican Americans (4.2%); 2,673 Cubans (.4%) and 3,459 others (.6%) the Spanish Speaking comprise 9.7% of the total public school population of 577,679. The balance of this total is comprised by .1% American Indians; .2% Orientals; 199,669 Caucasians (34.6%) and 316,711 Blacks, (by far the largest single component, and an absolute majority of 54.8%).[1]

By contrast to the 4.5% Puerto Rican representation in the student body, there are in Chicago zero Puerto Rican principals, assistant principals or administrators of any kind, and only 47 teachers out of a total of 24,546, amounting to a mere .2% of the total faculty. The equivalent percentages for Mexican Americans, Blacks and Caucasians are .3%; 34.5%; and 64.2% respectively.[2]

These incredible disparities are only one of the many reflections of the failure of the public schools to prepare the Chicago Puerto Rican to undertake occupational training commensurate with his equal intellective potential. Our own motivational and guidance work indicate that teaching and social services continue to be the most favored career choice, the expressed aspirational values of our Chicago population conforming to those of the island culture.

Clearly, the explanation lies not in lack of interest in these occupations. Margolis[3] found in 1968 only thirty Chicago Puerto Ricans attending college in the Metropolitan area. Aspira's own current search for Puerto Rican professionals to aid us in our identity program with adolescents has led us to identify only 2 physicians, 5 clergymen, 3 lawyers, and one dentist, all except one of whom were educated at their own families expense while the latter resided in Puerto Rico.

---

[1] Chicago Board of Education, *Student Racial Survey*, October 7, 1970.
[2] Chicago Board of Education, *Teacher Racial Survey*, October 7, 1970.
[3] Margolis, Richard J., *The Losers: A Report on Puerto Ricans and the Public Schools*, May, 1968.

There have been placed this Fall, as a result of Aspira's first year of operation of its motivational and counseling program, 107 students in college, 78% of whom did not qualify for regular admissions, and only one of whom was not below the poverty line. A midwestern "first", exemplary but minuscule program for training bilingual teachers for teaching in bicultural settings was developed with the School of Education of the University of Illinois at the Chicago Circle Campus.

The small successes achieved only point out the necessity to marshal great resources for a massive attack on the problem of underachievement. He should be able in the mainland, to repeat the Operation Bootstrap which was the self-help marvel, legislatively initiated and governmentally executed, of the decades of the 40's and 50's.

As a first priority, an effective cadre of professionally trained Puerto Ricans must be developed by a concentrated commitment to special educational programs aimed at salvaging the dropout, and overcoming the language and cultural barriers, coupled with meaningful in-service training opportunities for the young adult.

Certification and other requirements which systematically exclude persons whose native language is not English must be abolished from federally funded programs. Too many of the few Puerto Rican psychologists, teachers and social workers do not get hired by the Board of Education because of failure to pass certification requirements which rely heavily on language, even when the crucial skill for the position is the ability to speak in Spanish. In the meantime, thousands of non-English speaking children are being tested, taught, diagnosed and treated in a language which they do not fully understand. And while this is going on, armies of truant officers and community relations personnel, who cannot carry on a simple conversation with the parents, are being paid to retain the youth in school. Given the rigidity of curriculum in the public schools, these problems are not only applicable to arrivals within the last two years, but to all those students who were automatically put back a year or two, "because of the lack of English," as if grade retardation had some magical connection with acquiring a second language, and to all those students who fall behind because of the language trauma and forever stay behind because the system is not one in which the ones behind can ever catch up.

It would seem greatly more feasible and more economical to develop the bicultural person's technical skills than to attempt to impart to full grown monolinguals a second language and an appreciation for the nuances of a second culture, as is being done.

Problem 2. Disproportionate neglect of the physically handicapped Puerto Rican. At present federal aid for the education of the handicapped is reactive rather than proactive, and permits unwise criteria such as the superior capability of the more affluent regions to generate programs and proposals, to determine allocation patterns.

Recommendation 2. Legislation must establish guidelines which mandate proportionate share by Puerto Rican and other minorities according to need and population proportions.

Problem 3. Exclusion from Programs for the Gifted. At present the Puerto Rican is systematically being excluded from these programs. This constitutes a perfect example of institutional discrimination, as distinct from any personal racist pathology. Puerto Rican students measure very low in every kind of so called achievement and intelligence tests. Because these tests were standardized for children from other cultural and language backgrounds, their administration to Puerto Rican children is unscientific, abusive and discriminatory, and that it should be permitted, reflects the callous indifference of the companies that produce them, and the hopeless bureaucratization of the professionals who administer knowing full well their total invalidity. Our college placements have measured as low as the fifth percentile on some tests, and average around the 30th. Most are doing well, in spite of their limited academic preparation. Unless you are ready to assume genetic inferiority of some ethnic groups, you must recognize the necessity to mandate that the criteria for participation in such benefits must be made culture free.

Recommendation 3. That Congress mandate the equal representation of all ethnic groups, Puerto Rican and others in programs for the gifted.

Problem 4. Exclusion from migrant benefits. Present legal definitions of the migrant are not up to date in recognizing the urban character of the vast sector of the Puerto Rican and Mexican-American migrations. The Puerto Rican at present is penalized for being a U.S. citizen. Federal legislation, for example, contemplates the special educational needs of the Cuban immigrant, but, as poignantly portrayed in the film, "Papi", ignores the plight of the Puerto Rican migrant.

Problem 5. Miniature bilingual programs, which do not incorporate the scientific rationale for bilingual education, and which are unrelated to the rest of the system. The present bilingual programs in Chicago are 5 miniature programs only servicing 541 students of which an unascertained number are Puerto Ricans, and ranging in quality from fair to pathetic. Disproportionately few Puerto Ricans participate because the typical Puerto Rican child arrives knowing a very limited English, but enough to disqualify him from the Bilingual Programs, which are misconceived as temporary concessions to programs aimed at teaching English as a second language. Mastery of English as a Second Language is an independent and most critical priority, but it should not confuse the goals of bilingual programs, nor limit eligibility to them. The true bilingual-bicultural program addresses itself to the possibilities of "riding", pedagogically speaking, the intellective energies that are released by an integration of two or more distinct, and equally rich, cultural and linguistic experiences. Research on the subject has amply demonstrated the positive effect of the full bilingual experience (as distinct from stunted development in two simultaneous and confused languages and cultural settings, as is common) in the achievement of higher intellectual performance levels and a healthier emotional configuration as compared with the monolinguals, or with the situation where limited linguistic development occurs in several languages simultaneously.

Recommendation 5. Truly bilingual and bicultural programs must be made available whenever a significant (10%) of the student body speaks some language other than English as its mother tongue. Rather than an additional expense, this approach to the cultural pluralism of the city turns a false liability (foreign language) into an educational asset. Foreign language requirements could be eliminated and language skills would abound without the painful expensive necessity of training adult executives in the rudiments of foreign languages.

Problem 6. Minimal parent participation and resulting alienation between school and community. The causes underlying most of the deeply negative attitudes toward school and learning which characterize the Chicago student could begin to be identified and resolved if a meaningful dialogue were maintained between the school and community. To talk about alienation between school and community amounts to saying that learning is estranged from living, so only "schooling" transpires. The atmosphere of too many of our schools is one of prisons where children have been sentenced to for the crime of being under age 16, and where special penalties are enforced for the additional crime of speaking with something other than the pronunciation approved by the State and having the wrong physical type, and poor, bewildered and easily cowed parents. A vast portion of the school's resources is aimed at resocializing these imperfect Americans by a well meaning, tired and frustrated team of experts whose lack of effectiveness relates to the fact that skills and mores offered have no survival value, and at best a neutral meaning, for affecting their indifferent charges life chances.

Parent participation until recently required by administrative guidelines for Title I programs, has often been ineffectual in the case of the Puerto Rican and other minority communities because adequate provisions were not made to establish definite programs to help develop participant's capability. Consequently in many instances the role of the community advisory councils has been to rubber stamp the actions of the school administration. Within this context, the comment by Terrel H. Bell, Acting Commissioner, U.S. Office of Education of last October 9, to the effect that [4] ". . . you people want the Commissioner to use his office to provide parents what they don't have the gumption to ask for themselves . . ." reveals a surprising ignorance of group process and the dynamics of citizen participation. It is strongly reminiscent of the laissez faire railings against interference with the starving worker's freedom to contract his life away. To my best understanding the new administrative guidelines will not require parent councils but will only "encourage" them.

Recommendation 6. I urge this body to intervene with this threatened additional disfiguration of the original purpose of the ESEA. With all its limita-

---

[4] Quoted from *News*, NCSPS, October, 1970 Washington D.C.

tions, the community Advisory Council have facilitated class and race encounters which are preciously rare in our tragically polarized society. Rather
than destroying this incipient development, parent participation should be mandated legislatively. The Administration should be held responsible for its effective implementation with a view towards assisting the development of councils
which will be able to assume effective and responsible community control.

Problem 7. Student Participation is Viewed as a Threat to Law and Order.
The views on student participation in the decisionmaking process concerning
his educational experiences have reflected the degree of youth-centered anxiety
of the view-holders more than realistic assessments of educational objectives and
methodological alternatives as presented by specific kinds of situations. Many
of our thoughtless assumptions about the role of the school, such as the ana-
chronistic notion that an impersonal bureaucracy could conceivably act in *loco
parentis* to a child, date back to the days when the few who attended schools
were sufficiently protected by the traditions of class as to be impervious to
abuse negligence of indifference at the hands of their mentors. Orphanages and
correctional institutions actually provided the model of much of what today
passes unquestioned as standard administrative procedure, such as, for example, unilateral evaluation of the child by the teacher and not vice-versa. Why
are the defenders of the freedom to contract so still when it comes to voicing
the inequities in bargaining power of the tender in years and the poor?

Whatever the historical reasons, the fact remains that the human mind can
only be opened from the inside. In its zest to standardize its product and mer-
chandize it, our society has permitted the minds of the vast majority of our
children to become locked as a defensive maneuver against a system of schooling which seeks to leave out the human factor in learning for efficiency of
Administration's sake. Our schools are so efficient at canning knowledge that
the minds of the children have flown the classrooms and are not available for
further conditioning.

Recommendation 7. Student participation is not a dimension of learning that
can be legislated in or away, rather subject participation is the sine qua now
of the learning process itself. It would therefore seem imperative to legislate
that in federally funded programs appropriate roles be defined for student participation and autonomy compatible with elementary principles of learning.

Problem 8. Lack of self-corrective input from adequate evaluation research.
Present evaluations frequently do not fulfill the intent of the law's evaluation
requirements. They frequently consist of questionnaires administered to the
staff responsible for carrying out the program, and as such are self serving
and inadequate. This limitation is not overcome even if a sophisticated statistical analysis is superimposed on the essentially inadequate data, a flaw which
is aggravated by the fact that the evaluating firms are often educational research establishments whose very existence is predicated on a good relationship with their main client, the local Board of Education.

Recommendation 8. In the area of accountability present practices are pseudo-
scientific and predicated on the sovereign immunity of boards of education.
The federal government can assume the leadership in resocializing schools to
our commonly held values as to the American principle of accountability in
public service. Requirements must be built into all federal funding contracts
which a) condition initial finding on prior definition of performance objectives,
b) condition subsequent funding on presentation of evidence that objectives are
being reasonably met, and c) condition salaries raises, dismissals, retention
and general personnel policies upon successful completion of adequate and
measurable criteria developed for that task. Students and parents, as well as
participating staff, must participate in evaluation if it is to accomplish its
didactic function and be something other than a complex ritual of revalidation
of the authority hierarchy.

Problem 9. School Failure. Within the present structure of the public schools,
there are certain inherent destructive forces generated which only the excep-
tionally gifted, dedicated and well trained teacher can overcome. Banking on
such unlikely virtuosity is not a wise policy for institution building.

The full meaning of centralized bureaucracy reaches the new idealistic
teacher as well as the student, except that the student can't leave until he is
16. As long as decisionmaking is not a natural outgrowth of the interaction
between the professing adult (teacher) the community, and the student, schooling will continue to be a sterile ritual as far as meeting the learning needs of
each new generation. As far as its social and political control functions are
concerned, it is already a dangerous escalating exercise in totalitarianism.

The fear of social change by an entrenched bureaucracy of vested interests makes the school system almost totally impervious to any corrective external input, and defensive in the face of the best intentioned criticism, even from sources whose objectives are identical to theirs, namely that more students should learn more about more important matters.

A book such as *Down These Mean Streets* by the Black, New York Puerto Rican author. Piri Thomas, was banned from Tuley High School, one of Chicago's high schools by its principal. This autobiographical novel offers great sociological insight into life conditions parallel to those of the thousands of Puerto Rican youths attending that particular school. It is written in the language of their lives. It was therefore dangerous, because the students would have understood the full resonance of its protest, the full pain, since it was also their own.

Daily hundreds of these anti learning decisions are being made in our schools. They drive the students and many of the best teachers away. Public Schools are not fit to educate because mammoth bureaucracies cannot keep the soul of each individual child in luminuous perspective as their central value, and constantly make the myriad delicate adjustments necessary to maintain this clear focus. Instead, the Public School system is adept, like any other structure of its kind, at preserving its boundaries impermeable to external interference. Almost the total effort is geared to obtaining the compiance of the *object* of the schooling. When meeting with success the system fails because it has destroyed the subject. which alone is capable of learning, and at most a highly depreciable product emerges which has very limited usefulness. When the system fails in destroying the subject, we have the pushouts who. in a society where schooling has acquired the monopoly of legitimacy, all too frequently soon become destroyed.

Recommendation 9. a) Greater administrative decentralization coupled with increased conscious use of the regulatory powers of a centralized fiscal policy, as opposed to quasi criminal sanctions and program surveillance. b) The recognition must be made that all education is public, in that it is vested with crucial public interest, and private in that it is an intimate process not amenable to handling as another market commodity without suffering fundamental deformation. c) Funding policies must kindle those innovative sparks evinced in small private programs everywhere. d) The dynamics of the countervailing power need to be reestablished in education by strengthening the so called private school, in a more effective pursuit of the public good, and insuring that those efforts do not compromise the traditional virtues of the public school: freedom from religious, racial or political bigotry. e) A complementary, rather than a competing relationship between the public and private educational systems must be encouraged. The community school is, by its very structure, more likely to succeed in those areas of learning relating to attitude formation which the public schools have either neglected or heroically, and disastrously undertaken. This includes counseling, community relations, cultural identity, ethics. civics. or just about any aspects of the humanities or applied social sciences. For that matter, contrast the U.S. 20% of problems among students learning to read as opposed to Finland's 1%. Could it simply be due to the fact that in Finland knowing how to read is a prerequisite for admission to school? Maybe Johnny can't read, in many cases because nobody cared that *he* learn. If such is the case, then, why don't we think of programs where Libraries on wheels are prepared with materials and methods assistance to help mothers teach? Our vision of the objectives of education is blurred in that we have forgotten that the most effective learning group is the self regulated community, as it evolves its own problem solving capability. To the extent that community life has been destroyed, opportunities for real learning have begun to disappear. An unmentioned ecological hazard. We have attempted to pick up the pieces by putting children in boxes for scheduled time periods, and feeding them pellets of facts at regular intervals. We have been as successful in this attempt as in trying to solve atmospheric pollution by locking ourselves up in air conditioned boxes and consuming vast amounts and antihistamines. It is time that we take an honest look around the space ship, check the trajectory and cross check with the resources still available. Some fast course corrections are in order.

Senator MONDALE. Mr. Hector Vazquez, of New York City.

STATEMENT OF HECTOR VAZQUEZ, NEW YORK CITY, PUERTO RICAN FORUM, INC.

Mr. VAZQUEZ. Thank you, Mr. Chairman.

I was drafted about Wednesday night to appear before this committee.

Senator JAVITS. Mr. Vazquez, will you speak a little louder?

Mr. Vazquez is one of our most distinguished New Yorkers in this field.

Mr. VAZQUEZ. I think I have to relate my qualifications to appear before the committee.

I arrived in New York at age of 15 from Puerto Rico, and I am a high school dropout in the New York school system. You can say I am a runaway from the system. I also went to the Army and came out, got a master's degree, and later on was the first Puerto Rican on the New York City Board of Education. My tenure was very short, a whole year. The board was abolished by a new regulation. You might say I am a casualty of a skirmish in the urban crisis.

We have noticed that Puerto Ricans have been arriving in this country for the last 25 years with one hope: to improve their life. They have soon found out that the jobs they could fill are not there.

They have also noticed that the school system, which has been the traditional way to assimilate, participate in society, was very successful with early migrants. For the domestic minorities, the blacks, the Indians, the Spanish speaking, Mexican Americans, Puerto Ricans, the system has failed.

Now, you have heard before the statistics that point out that we have dropout rates of 80, 85, 90 percent throughout different cities in the United States. New York City is just about that, too.

Our graduates are coming out of high school with an eighth-grade reading level, and sometimes very deficient in their oral English. We have a large number of high school graduates getting a general diploma, which in itself is not a passport to college. It is actually a certificate of attendance.

INADEQUATE SKILLS

We have also students coming out with skills that are not useful in today's technological society. There has been a tendency to lump the educational needs of the Puerto Ricans with those of the total poverty community, including the black community.

As former Secretary of Health, Education, and Welfare Robert Finch points out, if the student cannot understand the language the teachers are using, it is hopeless to expect him to learn.

In New York City, you have 118,000 non-English-speaking Puerto Rican students, out of 250,000 Puerto Rican students in New York City's school system. That is approximately 23 percent of the total school enrollment.

Senator MONDALE. That would be a much higher percentage of non-English speaking than——

Mr. VAZQUEZ. Yes. You have second- and third-generation Puerto Ricans in New York. The fact is that you have less than 500 Puerto Rican teachers. You would need I would say 10,000, really, to deal with this problem, if you are trying to develop a bilingual educational system.

The New York City Board of Education has tried to develop means to deal with this problem. They are trying to provide English as a second language education for these non-English speaking students, which also include Chinese, Haitians, Dominicans, students from other countries.

ENGLISH INSTRUCTION

Now, their plan includes classroom ESL for one period a day for those who are in mixed classes—mixed classes means students who are English speaking students—or small group ESL instruction outside the classroom given by teachers of English as a second language.

Now, our research that we have been carrying out this last year points out that very little instruction in ESL is actually taking place in the classroom. Most teachers don't have the basic qualifications for ESL training.

Secondly, they have very little time to dedicate to the non-English-speaking student, when he has a mixed classroom, and the demands of the English-speaking students is there continuously.

You have also throughout the whole system many non-English-speaking students who are just sitting there not knowing what is going on. An example of this is the fact that for a long time in the Bronx a young girl was classified as non-English speaking, and actually she was deaf. So there was no way of screening to find out what was the problem.

VOLUNTEERS

Now we see that the system is trying to develop alternative ways to deal with the problem. One of them is a volunteer system of bringing in persons who are interested in helping out to give some of their time freely to handle the problem. I have an article here from the Puerto Rican press of yesterday in which they are trying to get recruits, persons to do this. The basic qualifications are that you have to have a high school diploma, age 28 or older, and ability to travel short distances to a school. It says that you don't have to have a knowledge of another language. It also points out that a lot of volunteers live in Queens, where non-English children are moving.

I don't know the situation in New York in which we are trying to get changes in the matter of qualifications of teachers. We believe that State qualifications are sufficient to teach. They receive tremendous opposition. The board of examiners that screen and actually certify teachers claim that their qualifications are very high for America in terms of capability and background.

Well, if we can get volunteers with no educational experience to teach, we could certainly believe that persons who go through a 4-year educational background in college and get a State certification could possibly be prepared to do this kind of work.

We have a lot of Puerto Ricans who meet this qualification, but they can't go through the screening process of the board of examiners.

Now, one other thing I found out is that the board of education has no standard measure for screening the NE's students in order to put them in the right classes.

The board of education carried out a study in 1967, at a cost of $1 million. One of the recommendations of the study was that appropriate screening procedures be developed. Now, this year, 1970, our investigation discovers that none of the four tests that were recommended has been either developed, or any kind of similar testing is provided.

The only thing that is used is subjective open-book tests, which are considered somehow better than nothing by specialists in non-English students, but it is not an adequate solution.

The report also points out the need for materials, the yearly testing to demonstrate any improvement, reception classes for students who are right from Puerto Rico, other countries, to be able to prepare them to get into mixed classes. None of this has been put into effect.

TEACHER TRAINING

There were very strong recommendations of teacher training. Here we believe that a great opportunity was lost, because this study was done 10 years ago. In New York City you have a 50 percent turnover of teachers every 5 years.

One of the recommendations was that teachers should be required to learn to teach English as a second language, and that this course should be taken in college. Well, that recommendation has never been applied, and the teachers that are coming out now are not prepared to deal with an increasing problem, believe there is definite need for massive efforts in bilingual education, taking into consideration that we have students that come in at the preschool level, persons who come into our intermediate high school, and also high school level, from Puerto Rico, so the problem cannot be isolated at one particular entry point.

We believe that bilingual education might be the way, and that separate facilities might have to be set up just to deal with this type of students.

We have now two schools in the South Bronx, bilingual schools, and several smaller programs throughout the city. They can only handle 4,000 students in 1970. We need similar and possibly more ample facilities throughout East Harlem, the Lower Side of New York City, Manhattan, Williamsburg, New York, and Brooklyn, and other parts of the Bronx and Queens. Of course, as you have heard this morning, similar facilities in Connecticut, Massachusetts, New Jersey, and even in the Midwest, where a lot of Spanish-speaking people are settling down.

One of the points that a previous spokesman mentioned was this fact of the migrant workers. I hear from OEO the philosophy to try to get migrants to settle down, who want to get out of the migrant stream. However, when we notice that they settle down as Puerto Ricans, we find there is no money or facilities to deal with them. Here we are asking them, or trying to get them to settle down, and then we don't provide the means to make that possible.

CIVIL RIGHTS VIOLATION

Now, in May 1970, the Secretary of Health, Education, and Welfare warned school districts throughout the country that failure to provide equal educational opportunity for non-English-speaking pupils is a violation of the 1964 Civil Rights Act, and that such violation prohibits use of Federal funds for programs that discriminate as to race, color, or national origin.

Now, we believe that the public school systems in New York State, and the whole northeastern region, are in violation of this directive, so we call for a Federal investigation of the educational practices in those States in relation to the NE's. New York State alone stands to lose $100 million in Federal funds, under title I, if this thing can be enforced, if corrective action is not taken immediately.

We also demand that the educational authorities begin to develop a well coordinated State, regional, Federal effort geared to meet the special needs of the non-English-speaking pupils in the region, and such effort should begin by implementing the recommendations.

SCHOOLS FOR NON-ENGLISH SPEAKING STUDENTS

One, immediate consideration should be given to the establishment of schools made up of only NE's. Pupils of similar language background should be placed in the same schools, whenever possible. The personnel of such schools should be bilingual.

I know what I am saying here tends to sometimes sound like separatism. Gentlemen, we are not advocating separatism by color, or any other category of nonracial separation of people. What we are saying here is that we have students who have a problem, and special attention and special facilities should be provided to meet their needs.

We do have facilities like this for handicapped children, for mentally retarded children. We are asking in this particular time students should receive special attention, and be able to receive it where it is most suitable.

NE's should not be placed in regular classes until they have acquired a knowledge of English. Such knowledge must be provided by standardized tests. There must be speedy development of such tests, and proper screening procedures. All classroom teachers are to learn the principles of teaching English as a second language. But teaching teachers must be started soon.

ADMINISTRATION RESPONSIBLE RE NON-ENGLISH-SPEAKING STUDENTS

We also advocate establishment within the New York City Central Board of Education of a deputy superintendent in charge of education of non-English-speaking pupils, to be directly responsible to the board at central headquarters. I believe a staff should be provided for this office.

We also believe such a similar position is needed in New York State in the Department of Education, and the education departments of other States with sizable concentrations of Spanish speaking residents.

The establishment of an independent citizens' commission, to be financed by public educational funds and provided by State and Federal Government, is needed to oversee progress of bilingual education throughout the northeast region.

Appointment within the U.S. Office of Education of an Assistant Commissioner to deal specifically with the educational needs of Puerto Ricans is long overdue.

Ladies and gentlemen, the need of the non-English speaking child has been neglected for too long. Many potential careers have already been ruined by such neglect. Continued inaction on the part of educational authorities and the Government can only result in increased waste of human resources and dependency. We certainly cannot afford another generation of functional illiterates. I think it is better for the nation if such an event does not happen.

Thank you very much.

Senator MONDALE. Thank you very much for a most useful statement.

(Mr. Vazquez's prepared statement and an analysis, entitled "Analysis of Puerto Rican and Black Employment in New York City Schools," follow:)

PREPARED STATEMENT OF HECTOR I. VAZQUEZ

For over twenty five years we, the Puerto Ricans have been arriving in New York in search of a better life for ourselves and our children. We came here believing the axiom that "all men are created equal", and that anyone if they make the effort can "make it" in this society.

However, we arrived at a time of high technological advancement; we found that America offered a free educational system which everyone could attend. This system of education was presented as the avenue through which migrants, as they arrived, became socialized and acculturated into the American way, and were thus prepared to partake of the wealth brought forth by this new technology in this country. However, not everyone that attended this school system became educated.

In looking at this myth, because that is exactly what it is, one has to realize the educational limitations that are self evident when a closer look is taken at the public educational system of the United States, and specifically that of New York City.

Traditionally, the school has been the socializing agent used by this country to integrate newly arrived groups into the life mainstream of the United States. In order to do this efficiently, the system attempted to eliminate the different social and cultural aspects that make people distinguishable from each other and give them a national identity. To a great extent during the early year of this century this succeeded the results being that we have become intolerant of groups that refuse to conform to our vision of what an American is.

The damage done by this educational system can be seen today in the Blacks, Chicanos, and Puerto Ricans. By and large, these three groups have become the main educational problem in this country. But, are we the problem or does the problem reside within the unchanging educational structure?

Education has failed, failed miserably and in the process it has managed to destroy generations of Puerto Rican children. How can we ever reach the fabled "American Dream" if the results of education among us is:

1. Retardation of more than 2 years in Reading and Mathematics.
2. Inadequacy in oral English at graduation level.
3. Large number of Puerto Rican youngsters in General Courses in high schools.
4. Exceedingly high rate of drop-outs.
5. A general negative self concept.
6. Non-marketable skills amongst most Puerto Rican youngsters when they leave schools.

Let me make it clear to you, gentlemen, that these are not vacuous statements, each of these can be backed up by a series of facts provided by the Board of Education of New York City itself. As the noted educator Dr. Kenneth Clark has pointed out. Achievement in Reading is fundamental to all other learning. All normal children can and should be achieving at or above grade level in reading. A tabulation of 1969, Fifth Grade reading scores for pupils in 87 schools with Puerto Rican majorities, found 85 out of 100 pupils are below grade level in reading. One third of these pupils are over 2 years below grade level.

An analysis of 8th Grade reading scores in 1969, in the 23 junior high schools in the City with Puerto Rican majorities disclosed 79% of the pupils are below grade level. 1 out of 4, was over 4 years below grade level in Reading. More than 6 out of 10 are anywhere from 2 to over 5 years below.

Based on these figures, it can be projected that of the 250,000 Puerto Ricans in the schools in October 1969, 155,000 will end up more than two years below grade level in reading, and thus emerge from the schools educationally crippled unless drastic changes take place in the education of the Puerto Rican children in general, and particularly in terms of the chief extra barrier they have—which makes their educational problem even more serious than that of the Blacks—the language barrier.

New York City offers its students a variety of high school diplomas, vocational, commercial, general and academic; of these, the academic diplomas is granted to those students in the college preparatory program. In 1966, 10,142 Puerto Rican students entered the 10th Grade in New York City. Two years later, there were only 4,393 in the 12th Grade—a drop-out rate of 56.7%. During the same period, the drop-out rate for Blacks was 46%, and for others, mostly Whites, it was 28.9%. To make matters even more critical, many of the 4,393 Puerto Ricans never graduated, even though they reached the senior year.

Of the 4,393 Puerto Ricans who did reach the 12th Grade in May 1969, only 1,628 were eligible to receive academic diplomas, which might possibly have provided them with the requirements for entering college. The largest number 1,922, were eligible to receive general diplomas, termed "inferior" by the Public Education Association, and 843 were eligible to receive commercial diplomas.

The low number of Puerto Rican seniors in the academic track (1,628) resulted in a small number of such diplomas in predominantly Puerto Rican high schools. In June, 1969, three of the four academic high schools with the highest percentage of Puerto Ricans had the lowest percentages of pupils receiving academic diplomas: Benjamin Franklin, 6%; Morris, 7.8%; Haaren, 9.6%. Eastern District, with the second largest percentage of Puerto Ricans, was sixth from the bottom, with 16.3% academic diplomas.

By comparison, the average city percentage was 48.4%; 70.3% receiving academic diplomas in John Bowne; 64.9% in Abraham Lincoln; 67.6% in Bayside; 61.3% in Flushing.

The number of Puerto Rican students in those schools receiving academic diplomas was pitifully small: 22 of 365 candidates for graduation in Benjamin Franklin; 28 of 359 in Morris; 24 out of 250 in Haaren; 54 of 324 in Eastern District.

Of the total 4,393 Puerto Ricans in the 12th Grade in May, 1969, an unknown number received no diplomas in June, 1969. More than one of every five graduation candidates was refused a diploma in Benjamin Franklin and Haaren.

These figures, dismal as they are, do not present the complete picture, since we have not included those pupils that drop out between the 7th and 9th grade. If these were added the percentage figure might rise to 80% or possibly as high as 85%.

Wholesale firings of executive and other types of staff would have occurred in any corporation that failed so dismally to produce the product for which it was geared. Structural change and new way of doing things would have been tried. However, the Board of Education is not run like a corporation and like "Old Man River, it just keeps rolling along". What the educational system in New York is producing are educational cripples condemned to the most menial and degrading type of work in our society.

The particularly high drop-out rate among Puerto Rican students in the City's high schools, even as compared to Blacks; combined with the extremely low reading scores discussed above, point to the fact that the educational system in New York City has yet to cope adequately with the special needs of Puerto Rican pupils.

There has been a tendency to lump the educational needs of the Puerto Rican child in the poverty-area schools with those of the Blacks. And while there are many similarities, the Puerto Rican student has some special needs. One of them, as former Secretary of Health, Education and Welfare, Robert H. Finch, put it: "if students cannot understand the language their teachers are using . . . it's hopeless to expect them to learn." (*New York Daily News,* May 25, 1970).

In New York where there are over 89,000 Puerto Rican students that are officially classified as Non-English speaking and a total of less than 500 licensed

Puerto Rican teachers, the statement by Mr. Finch is dramatized most vividly. When you add to the language barrier the social and cultural differences between teacher and pupil we can then begin to perceive the obstacles that the Puerto Rican child is expected to overcome because it is he that is expected to make all the modifications within his person and adapt to the system—the system stays rigid and impenetrable.

In the teaching-learning situation it is required that motivation take place all along. If the teacher does not have clear insights into the social and cultural background of her, or his students, he or she will not be able to create a classroom atmosphere that will be conducive to learning, this is magnified when teacher and pupil cannot communicate.

In New York City where today Non-English speaking students comprise over 10.6% of the total school population needed changes have to be made in order to insure an education for these students.

The critical problem faced by the Non-English is learning to read and write English competently enough to keep up with the work of the regular mixed classes, including English-speaking children where most Non-English students are placed.

To provide its pupils with ESL instruction, the Board of Education has had two major approaches: 1) Classroom ESL instruction for one period a day for those NE's in mixed class, 2) Small-group ESL instruction outside the classroom given by TESLS—Teachers of English as a Second Language.

Research done this year by the Puerto Rican Forum on these two approaches disclosed that:

Classroom Instruction: Little ESL instruction actually takes place in the classroom. This is the opinion of 35 Board of Education specialists who work with NE's in over 100 city public schools. These specialists report that few classroom teachers have training in teaching ESL, and that teachers generally find it difficult, if not impossible, to ignore other pupils in the classrooms while they concentrate on the NE's. Consequently, they report, many NE's are found in classrooms throughout the city who sit in class day after day not knowing what is going on or what is said or read. (Few teachers speak Spanish—the language of 88% of NE's.) Consequently, these specialists report, the NE's feel more and more educationally inadequate and disillusioned with school.

Small-group ESL Instruction Outside the Classroom: The number of TESLS assigned in the entire city is approximately 200, and can hardly provide even one period a day of ESL instruction for 10,000 NE's—less than one-tenth of the total of 118,000 in the schools.

Significantly, the Board of Education has done no research on: 1) How many children receive how much instruction in ESL in the classroom or in small groups outside the classroom; or 2) How effective the ESL instruction given has been.

The gross inadequacy of these two major activities of the Board of Education to assist the vast number of NE's pupils with their special language problems has turned many classrooms into veritable chambers of horrors for the neglected N.E. students.

Furthermore, a substantial sampling made for the Puerto Rican Forum Study on Conditions of the N.E. Students, brought forth that 341 public schools in New York City containing 102,000 NE's, seventy five percent (75%) receive no help at all with their special language problem. Pupils in bilingual programs, NE classes, or those receiving any amount of small group ESL instruction—even two periods a week—are not included in the above total.

Other areas where the NE students suffered because of Board of Education procedures were the following:

Poor Screening Procedures: There are no standard screening procedures mandated for NE's so that a proper evaluation of their educational and language ability can be ascertained. *The Puerto Rican Study of 1953-1957,* that the Board of Education carried out at a $1 million, recommended that four standard tests be given the NE's as part of the screening procedure:

1. understanding spoken English
2. ability to speak English
3. ability to read English
4. ability to read Spanish

Specific tests by name in each category were recommended. In 1970, this investigation discovered that *none of the four screening tests are in use,* nor has one *ever been made officially available or recommended.* Some NE's receive subjective open-book tests, considered better than none by NE specialists, but not considered adequate.

Poor Placement Procedures: There is no Board of Education policy on class placement of NE children. In practice, NE specialists report, NE's end up in the classes with children with the most serious discipline problems and the least experienced teachers. Little consideration is given of their individual abilities or individual problems. One brutal example of what the latter can lead to is the placement of a young NE girl into a regular class where she remained for seven weeks before it was discovered she was completely deaf!

Other recommendations made by the "1953-1957 Puerto Rican Study" that have been ignored are:

Materials: Although the Puerto Rican Study recommended production of materials for NE's on subject matter, only one book including such materials has come out during the past twelve years. Teachers in 1970 complained of a shortage of such material.

Periodic Testing: Although the Puerto Rican Study recommended special NE tests be used for their periodic testing, no such special tests are used. Instead the NE's at the lowest level of English proficiency (C, D, and F categories) which compose two thirds of all NE's are given the standard English reading test in which they are bound to score low. Too often these low scores become the basis for improper placement of NE's.

Reception Classes: The Puerto Rican Study recommended such classes for pupils newly arrived in the country, where they could be oriented to their new environment and taught some English, before being placed in mixed classes. In 1970, there were few such reception classes found in the entire school system, nor was there a policy that they be organized.

Teacher Training: The Puerto Rican Study particularly stressed the need for teachers to take courses in college to learn how to teach English as a Second Language. A simple requirement that all teachers must take such courses would have effected this vital need. This was never done. Thus, thousands of teachers enter schools yearly (there is 50% teacher turnover every five years) without the minimum education needed to help the NE **child.**

A similar requirement that all teachers take courses in Spanish would facilitate communication between teachers and most parents who don't speak English.

These recommendations made over thirteen years ago go unheeded until this day. What happens to the students that pass through this process? Three sociologists from San Diego State University who followed 2,617 youngsters through their high school years found that students experiences in school, instead of helping steer them clear of trouble, are the cause of most delinquency. The frustration of youths at their inability to succeed in school to any degree forces them to turn to other pursuits—like delinquency—to find achievement and self-esteem. Why wait until our young rebel and engage in violent confrontations to initiate the changes necessary to insure everyone of an equal opportunity in this country? Puerto Ricans are no longer willing to wait for the system to go through its very slow process of change. We cannot tolerate another generation of functional illiterates.

Certain things can be done to right the many wrongs inflicted on our children. One of them is to establish a bilingual system of education in areas with a high NE student body. In New York there are two bilingual schools in the South Bronx, plus a few smaller bilingual programs in other areas of the city. All told they totalled less than 4,000 pupils receiving bilingual instruction in the school year 1969–70.

The basic aims of the bilingual programs is to use the child's first language as a bridge to understanding the second language—English, and to use his first language to teach him subject matter while he learns English. This saves valuable time.

An extended aim being implemented in the two bilingual schools—is to make the pupils competent not only in English, but in Spanish as well. Many Spanish-speaking pupils do not know how to read or write the language of their fathers. Many educators consider essential the acquisition of this knowledge for developing adequate self-image and motivations. This concept has not been accepted officially by the Board of Education, and has yet to be made policy by the newly elected school boards. Current Board of Education guidelines suggest that junior high school pupils should be near grade level in English, before they can take Spanish, or other foreign language.

Pupils in the bilingual schools receive ESL instruction in English classes or in classes where subject matter is taught in English. Meanwhile, the pupils learn subject matter in Spanish, and save valuable educational time.

They also learn more English and more subject matter in English than pupils in mixed classes in other schools.

There are enormous advantages of grouping the NE's in such separate schools. The educational advantage is that pupils learn all day in a language and at a level they understand; they also have teachers who can communicate with them in their own (the pupils) first language.

For the English-speaking pupils this is also a great advantage; when no NE's are in their classes—they can receive uninterrupted instruction in English. At present throughout the more than half the schools in the city which have sizeable numbers of NE's—anywhere from 50 to over 1,000—teachers are forced to attempt to teach the two enormously different groups of pupils—the NE's and the English speaking pupils, in one classroom. As a result, neither group obtains the full benefit of the teachers efforts; neither group obtains uninterrupted instruction.

There is also a financial advantage. At present the city is wasting millions of dollars in providing classroom space and teachers for NE's pupils who do not know what is going on.

Tens of thousands of pupils and even a greater number of parents are unable to communicate with school personnel because the latter do not speak their language.

This problem of communication not only includes the NE's, but pupils who, although they themselves may speak English, have parents who can't. More than one of every four pupils in the last school census was listed as coming from either Spanish-speaking or Oriental home.

The Puerto Rican Forum has published a study showing that less than 1% of professionals in the schools are Puerto Rican. Schools are found where small children are used as interpreters.

A specific area involving Puerto Ricans are the Spanish-speaking Bilingual Teachers in School and Community Relations, a group of professionals employed by the schools to facilitate communication between the school, the pupils and the parents.

Employment of such professionals in all schools with over 100 Spanish-speaking pupils, was urged by the Puerto Rican Study twelve years ago. In 1970, this investigation found not a single one in any Academic or Vocational High Schools, and only two in the Junior High Schools. There were 188 in the elementary schools which needed at least one, and some, with as many as 1,000 Spanish-speaking pupils needed two or three. In addition, a disturbing number of these BT's were found assigned to other tasks not involving Spanish-speaking pupils.

Increased hiring of Spanish-speaking para-professionals has helped matters. However, not only are more of them needed, but additional professionals as well.

In May, 1970, the Secretary of Health, Education, and Welfare (H.E.W.) warned school districts throughout the country that failure to provide "equal educational opportunity for Non-English speaking pupils is a violation of the 1964 Civil Rights Act, and that such violation prohibits use of Federal Funds for programs that discriminate as to race, color, or national origin." Since the public school system in New York State and in fact the whole Northeast Region are not granting "equal educational opportunity" we call for a Federal investigation of the educational practices in these States. New York State alone stands to lose over $100,000,000 in Federal funds under the Title I of the Elementary and Secondary Education Act, if corrective action is not taken immediately.

We also demand of the states in the Northeast that they begin immediately:

To develop a well coordinated State, regional, federal effort geared to meet the special needs of the non-English speaking pupils in the region. Such an effort should begin by starting to implement the following recommendations:

NE's should not be placed into regular classes until they have acquired an adequate knowledge of English. Such knowledge must be proven by standardized tests.

All children should have the right to acquire a knowledge of a foreign language.

Immediate consideration should be given to the establishment of schools made up only of NE's. Pupils of a similar language background should be placed in the same schools, wherever possible. The personnel of such schools should be bilingual.

Speedy consideration should be given to establishment of NE schools in areas which contain high concentrations of NE's such as in the South

Bronx, Williamsburg, East New York, East Harlem, the Lower East Side in New York City, and in cities across the nation with the same situation.

Speedy development of tests needed for proper screening.

Establishment of proper placement procedures.

Development of special tests to measure annual progress of NE's as part of an accountability process.

All classroom teachers to learn principles of teaching English as a Second Language.

Vast increase in programs for training bilingual teachers.

Increase the number of Bilingual Teachers in School and Community Relations, not only Spanish-speaking, but those who speak other languages.

The establishment within the New York City Central Board of Education of a Deputy Superintendent, in charge of the Education of non-English-speaking pupils, to be directly responsible to the Board at Central headquarters. Adequate staff and budget should be provided for this office.

The establishment of a similar high position in the New York State Department of Education, and in Education Departments of other states with a sizable concentration of Spanish-speaking residents.

Each school district with over 1,000 NE's should have a special top assistant to the District Superintendent responsible for the education of the non-English-speaking pupils.

The establishment of an independent citizens commission to be financed by public education funds, provided by State and Federal governments, which would be a watchdog on progress of bilingual education throughout the Northeast Region.

Appointment within the United States Office of Education of an Assistant Commissioner to deal specifically with the educational needs of Puerto Ricans.

Ladies and Gentlemen: the needs of the Non-English speaking child has been neglected for too long. Many potential careers have already been ruined by such neglect. Continued inaction on the part of educational authorities and state, local and federal governments can only result in increased waste of human resources and dependency.

Only by acting *now* can we control a situation that everyday becomes more acute and more costly to deal with effectively.

I will end my statement by asking you to think and reflect upon this question. What will be the effect upon our already troubled inner cities when they have to deal with an increasing poorly educated population: frustrated by their miserable living conditions: unable to secure and hold jobs that would provide them with the basic increase to lead a decent life? At what cost can we then try to retrieve these human beings? Will they wait for such programs or vent their frustrations violently against a society that they feel has let them down?

ANALYSIS OF PUERTO RICAN AND BLACK EMPLOYMENT IN NEW YORK CITY SCHOOLS

(By Richard Greenspan)

Although sizable numbers of Puerto Rican pupils have been recorded as attending New York City public schools for nearly two decades, employment of Puerto Ricans in the school system, according to recently released data, discloses none employed at the middle-management levels; an infinitesimal number (less than 1%) at professional levels; with a somewhat-higher percentage—but still not in proportion to the percentage of pupils—recorded in the lower-paid non-professional and civil service positions. (See Table I.) Nor are any Puerto Ricans to be found at the top levels in the educational bureaucracy, according to recent inquiries.

The number of Puerto Ricans in public elementary schools alone in 1953 amounted to 53,932—9.2% of the pupils at that level.[1] (No ethnic census was taken for other levels that year.) In September, 1957, the number of Puerto Ricans at all levels amounted to 128,980—13.5% of the total school population.[2]

By the school year 1968-69 Puerto Ricans in the public schools numbered 240,746—21.5% of the total.[3] In the same school year, according to the March, 1969, public school personnel census taken by the Office of Personnel of the New York City Board of Education, no Puerto Rican was employed in the middle-management levels of the central board as either a director or assistant director; and the number and percentage of Puerto Ricans employed in the major professional categories was as follows:

TABLE I.—ETHNIC DISTRIBUTION OF NEW YORK CITY BOARD OF EDUCATION PERSONNEL FOR THE MONTH OF MARCH 1969

	Total Number	Whites		Blacks		Puerto Ricans		Other Spanish speaking		Orientals		Others[1]	
		Number	Percent	Number	Percent	Number	Percent	Number	Percent	Number	Percent	Number	Percent
Directors and assistant directors:													
Directors (licensed and acting)	38	36	94.7	2	5.3					1	0.1	4	0.4
Assistant directors and assistant administrative directors (licensed and acting)	121	106	87.6	15	12.4					1	(2)	6	.3
Pedagogical personnel and supportive staff:													
Principals (appointed and acting)	969	923	95.3	37	3.8	4	0.4						
Assistant principals (appointed and acting)	2,039	1,781	87.3	239	11.7	10	.5	2	0.1				
Teachers in charge	40	32	80.0	8	20.0								
Department chairmen (licensed and acting)	1,192	1,128	94.6	57	4.8	4	.3	1	(2)	1	(2)	1	(2)
Teachers (regular and substitutes)	59,108	52,827	89.4	5,395	9.1	464	.8	181	.3	133	.2	108	.2
Guidance counselors (regular and acting)	1,529	1,335	87.3	179	11.7	10	.7			3	.2	2	.1
Bureau of child guidance (regular, acting, or Subs)	605	491	81.2	104	17.2	3	.5	2	.3	3	.5	2	.3
Paraprofessionals	15,794	6,232	39.5	6,832	43.3	2,483	15.7	112	.7	54	.3	81	.5
Others:													
Administrative employees (civil service)	5,672	4,450	78.5	1,000	17.6	138	2.4	59	1.0	10	.2	15	.3
School lunch employees	9,226	5,496	59.6	3,109	33.7	584	6.3	21	.2	3	(2)	13	.1
Total	96,333	74,837	77.7	16,977	17.6	3,700	3.8	378	.4	209	.2	232	.2

[1]American Indians, east Indians, Arabs, and others not designated. [2] Less than 1/10 of 1 percent.

Source: Computer Sheets, Personnel Census, March 1969, Office of Personnel, New York City Board of Education.

PARTIAL SUMMARY OF TABLE I

	Number	Percent
Directors and assistant directors:		
Directors	(¹)	5. 3
Assistant directors	(²)	12. 4
Other professionals:		
Principals	37	3. 8
Assistant principals	239	11. 7
Department chairmen	57	4. 8
Guidance counselors	179	11. 7
Bureau of child guidance	104	17. 2
Teachers	5, 395	9. 1
Other categories:		
Civil service	1, 000	17. 6
School lunch employees	3, 109	33. 7
Paraprofessionals	6, 832	43. 3

¹ 2 of 38.
² 15 of 121.

TOP POSITIONS

The personnel census* did not include an ethnic analysis of the relatively small number of extremely important top-level positions. A check at the Board of Education in April, 1970, discloses essentially the same situation that existed during the March, 1969, personnel census: of the 50-odd assistant superintendents there are two Blacks—no Puerto Ricans. No Blacks or Puerto Ricans occupy any of the four topmost positions in the Board bureaucracy—positions of enormous power: Superintendent of Schools (now Acting)** and three Deputy Superintendents—for Personnel, Business Administration and Instructional Services.

Where the Blacks and Puerto Ricans do have some positions of influence is on the five-person Board of the Board of Education, which has one Puerto Rican and one Black among its members; both were appointed by a borough president of the same ethnic background.

However, the Board itself is of an interim character, to be replaced in July, 1971, by a seven-person board, five of whom are to be elected and two of whom are to be appointed by the Mayor.

TABLE II.—EXTENT OF UNDERREPRESENTATION OF BLACKS AND PUERTO RICANS IN MAJOR PROFESSIONAL CATEGORIES IN RELATION TO PUPIL ETHNICITY (NEW YORK CITY BOARD OF EDUCATION, SCHOOL YEAR 1968–69)

	Percent blacks	Percent Puerto Ricans	Number of times underrepresented in employment in proportion to pupil population		How many more times Puerto Ricans underrepresented compared to blacks
			Blacks	Puerto Ricans	
Pupil ethnicity	32. 2	21. 5			
Professional personnel:					
Principals	3. 8	. 4	8. 5:1	53. 8:1	6. 3:1
Assistant principals	11. 7	. 4	2. 8:1	53. 8:1	6. 3:1
Department chairmen	4. 8	. 3	6. 7:1	71. 7:1	10. 7:1
Teachers	9. 1	. 8	3. 5:1	26. 9:1	7. 7:1
Guidance counselors	11. 7	. 7	2. 8:1	30. 7:1	11. 0:1
Bureau of child guidance	17. 2	. 5	1. 9:1	43. 0:1	22. 6:1

* The personnel census figures on 96,333 persons obtained by the Puerto Rican Forum, while including most major personnel categories, did not include school secretaries because the information wasn't available. Other groups may have been left out, since the Board of Education, in another publication, reported having "approximately 113,000 employees." (See Board of Education of the City of New York, *Facts and Figures, 1968–1969*, p. 35.)

** The current Acting Superintendent of Schools is to be replaced by a Chancellor to be chosen by the present Board of Education for a three-year period.

RATIO OF PROFESSIONAL POSITIONS TO PUPIL ETHNICITY

In the 1968–69 school year the extent of underrepresentation of blacks and Puerto Ricans according to pupil ethnicity in the 65,482 professional positions—where most of the higher-paid and prestigious positions are to be found—(as shown in Table II), is as follows:

Teachers: Blacks 3.5 times underrepresented; Puerto Ricans, 26.9 times.

Guidance Counselors: Blacks 2.8 times underrepresented; Puerto Ricans, 11 times.

Bureau of Child Guidance: Blacks 1.9 times underrepresented; Puerto Ricans, 22.6 times.

Department Chairmen: Blacks 6.7 times underrepresented; Puerto Ricans, 71.7 times.

Assistant Principals: Blacks 2.8 times underrepresented; Puerto Ricans, 53.8 times.

Principals: Blacks 8.5 times underrepresented; Puerto Ricans, 53.8 times.

RATIO OF PUERTO RICANS TO BLACKS IN PROFESSIONAL POSITIONS

The relative position of Puerto Ricans to Blacks, taking into account the differences in pupil ethnicity figures, in terms of underrepresentation in professional positions held, is as follows:

Teachers: 7.7 to 1.
Guidance Counselors: 11.0 to 1.
Bureau of Child Guidance: 22.6 to 1.
Department Chairmen: 10.7 to 1.
Assistant Principals: 6.3 to 1.
Principals: 6.3 to 1.

Thus, as seen by all the material presented here, while there is a great degree of Black underrepresentation in all professional positions in relation to pupil ethnicity, the extent of Puerto Rican underrepresentation is at least six times greater than that of the Blacks in any one of the positions. It is more than 7½ times greater among the 59,000 teachers where the bulk of the professional positions are to be found, and it is more than 22 times greater in the Bureau of Child Guidance.

SELF IMAGE AND PRINCIPALS

For both the Blacks and Puerto Ricans the position of Principal is held to be key at the school level because of the position's importance to Black and Puerto Rican pupil self-image. While this is generally true, it must be held especially true in those schools where Blacks and Puerto Ricans constitute a majority of the pupils.

According to a Puerto Rican Forum tabulation of 1968–69 New York City public school figures, there were 183 schools where Black pupils made up more than 50% of the student body and 131 schools where Puerto Rican pupils numbered more than 50%. (See Table III)

In contrast there was a total of 37 Black and four Puerto Rican principals.

A three-year Ford Foundation-supported program at Fordham University to grant full-support scholarships to Negroes and Puerto Ricans with Master's degrees to take the scholastic credits needed to apply for principal and assistant principal examinations will be completed this year. Forty-four Blacks and 18 Puerto Ricans will have completed this course of study when the present grant ends.

TABLE III.—NUMBER AND PERCENTAGE OF NEW YORK CITY PUBLIC SCHOOLS ⁴ WITH OVER 50 PERCENT OF PUPILS BLACK OR PUERTO RICAN, DECEMBER 1968

Types of schools	Total number of schools	Schools with over 50 percent blacks		Schools with over 50 percent Puerto Ricans	
		Number	Percent	Number	Percent
Elementary	621	140	22.5	101	16.3
Junior high	149	33	22.0	23	15.4
Academic high	62	7	11.3	3	4.8
Vocational high	28	3	10.7	4	14.3
Total	860	183	21.3	131	15.2

OTHER CATEGORIES

As seen by the personnel census, the extent of Black and Puerto Rican employment generally rises where the salaries paid descend. Significantly, the lowest-paid, the paraprofessionals, have the highest proportion of positions held by Puerto Ricans (15.7%—2,483 out of 15,794), while the percentage of Black paraprofessionals—43.3%—is even higher than the 32.2% Black pupil population. A similar case is seen in the percentage of school lunch employees where Blacks make up 33.7%. Puerto Ricans, on the other hand, make up 6.3%.

Where the Blacks and Puerto Ricans—especially the latter—are underrepresented is in the administrative civil service employees—a category which covers clerks, specialists, custodial employees and the like—where the range of salaries is from low to near-high. In this category—of the 5,672 persons employed, 1.000 Blacks make up 17.6%; 138 Puerto Ricans make up 2.4%.

Sources

1. Board of Education of the City of New York, *The Puerto Rican Study—1953-1957*, p. 169. Published 1958
2. Board of Education of the City of New York, Bureau of Educational Program Research and Statistics, *Special Census of School Population, Summary Tables*, February, 1959, Publication No. 140
3. Board of Education of the City of New York, *Annual Census of School Population, December 17, 1968, Summary Tables*, Table #1. Prepared by Margaret S. Langlois and Florence Adler. Published July, 1969. Publication No. 324
4. Board of Education of the City of New York, Bureau of Educational Program Research and Statistics, *Annual Census of School Population, December 17, 1968.* Computer Sheets: Composition of Register by School Within Level by District

Senator MONDALE. Mr. Quinones.

STATEMENT OF NATHAN QUINONES, VICE PRESIDENT, PUERTO RICAN EDUCATORS' ASSOCIATION

Mr. QUINONES. Gentlemen, I am representing the Puerto Rican Educators' Association of New York City, and my focus is on the status of the Puerto Rican student in New York City as we currently find him.

I will just select some pertinent areas of my study, leaving out those that have been mentioned already, so that we don't have constant repetition of the horrible facts that we have heard this morning.

We need not wait for the genetic manipulation prophesied for us in "A Brave New World" to produce the Epsilons needed by society. We have a system operating now that has assured us of an ample supply of menial laborers for at least the next generation. An integral cog in the production of these miscasts is our schools, and the human raw material is the Puerto Rican.

"The American Dream" has each boy envisioning himself as a potential President. The Puerto Rican reality is that its children will continue to be the dishwashers, boys, girls, busboys, and chamber maids to meet the needs of the Alphas and the Betas.

PUERTO RICAN SIZABLE MINORITY

Currently, as we have heard, there are 250,000 Puerto Rican pupils in the schools of New York City. We are no longer a small minority. The total enrollment, as we have heard also, in the schools of New York City is comprised of over 20 percent of Puerto Rican children. Now, these are relatively up-to-date figures.

They do indicate the increased numbers of our students, but the educational status of the Puerto Rican youngsters cannot be said to have improved to any degree, since the last hearings held in May of 1967 by the Special Subcommittee on Bilingual Education.

SCHOOL DROPOUTS

Let me focus back to that recent year. Of the total number of Puerto Rican students in the 10th grade during the year of those hearings, over 56 percent dropped out by their 12th year. The comparable figure for blacks was 46 percent, 10 percent lower, and for others, primarily whites, 28.9 percent, almost half as many.

This waste is of a staggering proportion for all groups, but please notice the educational demise of so many of those who are already on the very lowest rung of our socioeconomic ladder.

The 56 percent is also very inconclusive. We have to add to that the numbers of children that did not even make it to junior high school. We have to add to that the number of children who did not achieve an academic diploma, the usual passport for further education in New York City.

To pinpoint this a bit more specifically, in 1969, the four academic high schools in New York City with the highest percentage of Puerto Rican pupils reflected the following findings:

Benjamin Franklin High School had 22 Puerto Rican candidates for an academic diploma. Morris High School had 28.

These are not percentages. These are actual numbers of students.

Eastern District High School in Brooklyn had 54. Haaran High School had 24 students, a total of 128 potential candidates for a diploma, a goal, needless to say, some of these children did not attain.

The citywide percentage of diplomas at the same time was 48 percent.

I think we have to be concerned about the quality of education for all children throughout the United States, that we are focusing on only one minority.

We have seen the recent book by Silberman, "Crisis in Our Classrooms," which indicates that our middle class, white, Anglo-Saxon Protestant children are receiving an inferior education. What can we then expect that our blacks, Indians, Puerto Ricans, Mexican children are receiving within the schools of our country?

ACADEMIC RETARDATION

In 1969, seven elementary schools with over 50 percent Puerto Rican population revealed that 85 percent of their children read below grade level in the fifth grade. Sixty-seven out of every 100 pupils were in such a crisis in their reading ability that it was questionable whether they would ever catch up.

In the junior high school it was not appreciably better. In the eighth grade, 89 percent were reading below level, and again below level is rather vague. To be more precise, 62 percent were in the critical range, 2 to 5 years behind.

This is a basic ingredient for social dynamite, with the fuse being ignited in very early life.

Again, I think that it would be disastrous to think that these figures are dwindling. Seventeen years ago, there were 40,000 children classified as non-English in New York City. In 1958, the figure rose to over 48,000. Currently, as we have heard, it is 118,000. Of this group, 75 percent, or close to 90,000, are Puerto Rican children.

Can we, on the basis of these figures, anticipate fewer children in this category next year, or 1975, or 1984?

OFFICIAL INSENSITIVITY

It is this group, however, that reflects the greatest insensitivity by the hierarchy of educators of the Board of Education.

The term "non-English" or "NE" is a misnomer. They are in fact new Epsilons, created with intent.

We have heard mention of the Puerto Rican study to which the New York City Board of Education devoted $1 million 12 years ago; spending money for suggestions to ostensibly improve the education that these youngsters were to receive. Yet, 12 years later, not one of those proposals has really been put into effect.

The recent figures provided by Aspira also indicate a fantastic dropout rate of the few who do make it into college, at least 60 percent for those Puerto Ricans admitted.

Unfortunately, I cannot end this presentation on any optimistic note, but must ask, What is the future of the Puerto Rican in this land of opportunity when his educational lifeline is strangling him?

NDEA INSTITUTES FOR BILINGUAL EDUCATION

I will not repeat many of the suggestions made concerning the improvement of the education of the Puerto Rican child, but will limit myself to asking for the reestablishment of NDEA institutes. We had them, and functioning most effectively, in the area of foreign languages and science, but these recommended NDEA institutes should direct themselves toward the training of bilingual teachers, bilingual guidance counselors, and bilingual psychologists.

From the few testimonies that we have had presented this morning, you can see how critically important it is not to classify so many of our potential youngsters as mentally retarded, or deaf, or even below the moronic stage of IQ.

I think within New York City there must be some concern to see whether any Federal laws have been broken, when we see the infinitesimally small number of educators on levels of decisionmaking affecting pupils with Spanish-speaking backgrounds.

For example, in New York City, as of this moment, there is not one fully qualified principal out of the 1,000 schools that we have who is of Puerto Rican background.

Senator MONDALE. Not one?

Mr. QUINONES. Not one. Mr. Matthews who is now a district superintendent, has left that one position he occupied vacant.

Now, this is within New York City.

The amount of reaction that the current superintendent of schools, Dr. Scribner, has received by both the United Federation of Teachers and the Council of Supervisory Associations also indicates the formidable opposition to any criticism of the status quo, and certainly to any implementation of bringing in people who might be somewhat more sensitive to the situation that has continued in our schools throughout these many years.

Thank you very much.

(Mr. Quinones' prepared statement follows:)

THE STATUS OF THE PUERTO RICAN STUDENT IN NEW YORK CITY

(By Nathan Quinones, Vice President, Puerto Rican Educators' Association)

We need not wait for the genetic manipulation prophesied for us in "*A Brave New World*" to produce the Epsilons needed by society. We have a system operating now that has assured us of an ample supply of menial laborers for at least the next generation. An integral cog in the production of these mis-casts is our schools and the human raw material is the Puerto Rican.

"The American Dream" has each boy envisioning himself as a potential president. The Puerto Rican reality is that its children will continue to be the dish-washers, boys, girls, bus-boys and chamber maids to meet the needs of the Alphas and the Betas.

Currently in New York City there are close to *250,000* Puerto Rican pupils. That massive number of pupils bears repeating—*250,000*. A quarter of a million young Puerto Ricans—destined to what? It is a formidable minority making up 23.9% of all pupils in the Elementary Level; 21.8% of the Junior High School population; 13.3% Academic High Schools; 29.9% in Vocational High Schools and 29.2% in Special Schools. In toto 21.5% of the public school pupils in New York City are Puerto Ricans.

These figures are up-to-date and do indicate the increased numbers of our students, but the educational status of the Puerto Rican youngster can not be said to have improved to any degree since the last hearings held in May 1967 by the Special Sub-Committee on Bilingual Education. Of the total number of Puerto Rican students in the 10th grade during the year of those hearings 56.7% dropped out by their 12th year—1968–1969. The comparable figure for Blacks was 46%—10% lower—and for others, primarily whites, 28.9%—almost half as many. The waste is of a staggering proportion for all groups, but please notice the educational demise of so many of those who are already on the very lowest rung of our socio-economic ladder. To that 56.7% must be added an untold number that had dropped out prior to their 10th year in school, as well as those who received less than an academic education. It should be noted that the academic diploma has traditionally been the passport to further education in New York City. In 1969 the four academic high schools in New York City with the highest percentage of Puerto Rican pupils reflected the following findings:

Benjamin Franklin H. S. had 22 Puerto Rican candidates for an academic diploma.

Morris High School had 28 Puerto Rican candidates for an academic diploma.

Eastern District H. S. had 54 Puerto Rican candidates for an academic diploma.

Haaran High School had 24 Puerto Rican candidates for an academic diploma.

A total of 128 potential *candidates* for a diploma—a goal some of whom, needless to say, did not achieve, reducing even further the paltry figure already cited. The city-wide percentage of academic diplomas at the same time was 48.4.

What leads up to this educational decimation, however, is really a continuum with its roots in the elementary school and its bitter fruit scattered in a steady progression.

The Metropolitan Achievement Test is an examination in English given throughout the city to all pupils a number of times during their school life.

In 1969, 87 elementary schools with over a 50% Puerto Rican population revealed that 85% of their children read below grade level in the 5th grade. Sixty-seven (67) out of every 100 pupils were in such a crisis in their reading ability that it was questionable whether they would ever catch up.

A similar study of 23 Junior High Schools with a majority of Puerto Rican children enrolled, indicated that in the 8th grade, 79% were below level in reading. Below level, however, is rather vague. To be more precise—62% were in the critical range, two to five years behind. This is a basic ingredient for social dynamite—with the fuse being ignited in early life.

What are some causative factors behind these figures? Unless one accepts the reason as inherent intellectual inferiority then we must search out the sources.

We have to acknowledge within society the conditions affecting the schools, the children and the teachers, but this can readily serve to absolve the educators of their own responsibility; a responsibility that has willfully not been met by the top administrators of the Board of Education of New York City. The prime example of this can be seen with the children in our schools classified as—Non-English. They are not a sudden apparition on the educational scene and will not soon disappear—regardless of how they are neglected.

Seventeen (17) years ago there were 40,000 children classified as Non-English in New York City. In 1958 the figure rose to over 48,000. Currently it is 118,000. Of this group 75% or close to 90,000 are Puerto Rican children. Can we, on the basis of those figures anticipate fewer children in this category next year, or 1975 or 1984?

It is this group however, that reflects the greatest insensitivity by the hierarchy of educators of the Board of Education. The term Non-English or NE is a misnomer. They are NEW EPSILONS—created with intent.

One million dollars is a considerable amount of money to spend on educational research. It was worth considerably more in 1958, and amounts to a formidable waste when many of the proposals in the *Puerto Rican Study* have yet to be implemented. Among the recommendations made were: Screening tests for the proper placement of Non-English pupils, recommendations concerning bi-lingual teachers and instruction of the Non-English child. These are recommendations sought and paid for by the Board of Education of New York City and then apparently abandoned as the children have been.

The statistical picture I have presented shows an early start in mis-education from one end, to the outpouring of incomplete youngsters to the streets of our cities. The infinitesimally few who do enter the colleges suffer a similar fate. Recent figures provided by Aspira indicate a drop-out rate of 60% for these Puerto Ricans admitted to college.

Unfortunately I can not end this presentation on any optimistic note but must ask:

What is the future of the Puerto Rican in this land of opportunity when his educational lifeline is strangling him?

Senator JAVITS. How many acting principals are there of Puerto Rican background?

Mr. QUINONES. I would say the two bilingual schools mentioned by Mr. Hector Vazquez, one run by Mr. LaFontaine, P.S. 25, even after 3 years of setting up the school, almost personally, is still not fully qualified as a principal in New York City.

Senator JAVITS. How many acting principals are there? That is one you named.

Mr. QUINONES. I would think possibly no more than four or five. That is out of a total of 1,000 schools in New York City.

Senator JAVITS. Now, the witnesses have certainly pictured the situation very vividly and very dramatically; it is clear, that there is very serious educational deprivation in the Puerto Rican community in New York City, and elsewhere. The deprivation heavily contributes to the lack of motivation and language facility.

Now, we have had a difficult time trying to get the NDEA institutes funded. Your testimony may help us to get them funded.

I am the ranking minority member of the Labor and Public Welfare Committee which handles this matter—this is a Select Committee which Senator Mondale heads. I have also been on the Appropriations Committee. I have fought like a tiger to get money for those institutes, but without success. But we will try again.

On the other question, you raise the issue of the culturally and
minority isolated position of the Puerto Rican. It is normally thought
in New York that the Puerto Rican pattern would not follow the
pattern of New York's black community, but would rather follow the
pattern of the traditional New York immigrant community.

I think it was very interesting when Miss Pantoja made clear the
difference between the situation which faced my parents as immigrants at the turn of the century and the situation which faced the
Puerto Rican community beginning in the 1940's. It will have an
impact on what we do, and on what we recommend.

DESEGREGATION LEGISLATION

We have, as you gentlemen and lady know, a bill pending before
us, not here, but in the Legislative Committee, for almost a billion
and a half dollars. How we direct that money to be administered is
what you have emphasized, and one of the big things which I get
from your testimony is that it is not only a matter of discrimination
at the instructional level, that it is a matter of the built-in basis on
which there is racial isolation, using the word "race" in its very broad
sense. Really, it is ethnic. That is what we are going to have to direct
our attention to.

We are getting that impact from other sources. Your testimony
will give great cumulative weight to the approach which we take
against not only an un-American, unconstitutional deprivation because of segregation and discrimination, but against the real isolation
of a whole community of two million people in our country. In New
York City I estimate the figure is well over a million, with a very
large proportion of the public school attendance. Certainly the figures
you have given are very vivid on that score.

You have helped us enormously. I am pleased, myself, that you
have been able to appear.

We will have more testimony tomorrow. I think the weight of it is
going to help us when we come to decide what the U.S. money is to
be used for, to see that within this community, it is used more effectively than it would otherwise be.

Thank you, Mr. Chairman.

EDUCATIONAL "STARVATION"

Senator MONDALE. What strikes me about this testimony that we
have heard this morning and others that we have heard, is that in
many ways educational problems of minorities are analogous to this
Nation's hunger problem. Not just a few but millions are starving
educationally in ways which might be a little more difficult to describe, but just as completely and just as fully as a child starving of
malnutrition. In the city of Chicago, only two doctors and perhaps
six or seven professional men can be identified as Puerto Rican, and
all but one of them were trained in Puerto Rico. Only one of them
is a product of our institutions.

In New York City you can identify a student body of 250,000. In
the main Puerto Rican high school, fewer than 150 graduates are

apparently headed for college, and you can predict 60 percent of them are going to drop out.

You have at least a national scandal—human suffering and denial that is tortuous. Yet I must say in all candor the professional educational response has amounted to little more than studies, conferences and hollow promises.

We have Dr. Marland, a very fine man, a commissioner of education. If he were asked what he thought of the funding strategy, he would say, "We really don't know what to do until we have some more studies. There is no point in putting more money into the system."

In terms of integration, he feels that should be a fairly long-term solution. In terms of what kind of compensatory strategy will work, he says there are some studies coming in pretty soon.

I don't mean to be critical of him, because I think that is the standard response that we have been hearing. Meanwhile, according to these studies backed up by your own personal experience, there must have been 20,000 bright-eyed little Puerto Rican kids that went to school full of hope this fall, who by now are glassy eyed, have lost confidence in themselves and are beginning to doubt their parents. It is impossible to measure the disaster of these repercussions upon their lives, the enormous loss to this country among so many other things in terms of their talent, their affections and their hopes.

I think the more we open up this issue, the more we see the indescribably tragic proportions of the failure that we are visiting upon these children, and upon these people.

You have said it a lot better than I can. Something had better happen around here pretty fast.

Thank you very much for your most useful testimony.

The subcommittee will recess until tomorrow morning.

(Whereupon, at 12:35 p.m., the subcommittee recessed, to reconvene at 10 a.m., Tuesday, November 24, 1970.)

EQUAL EDUCATIONAL OPPORTUNITY FOR PUERTO RICAN CHILDREN

TUESDAY, NOVEMBER 24, 1970

U.S. SENATE,
SELECT COMMITTEE ON
EQUAL EDUCATIONAL OPPORTUNITY,
Washington, D.C.

The committee met at 10 a.m., pursuant to recess, in room 1318, New Senate Office Building, Hon. Walter F. Mondale (chairman of the committee) presiding.

Present: Senators Mondale and Javits.

Present also: William C. Smith, staff director and general counsel; A. Sidney Johnson, deputy staff director; Emon Mahony, professional staff counsel; Cornell Lewis, legislative counsel; Mike Baroody, professional staff member; and Leonard P. Strickman, minority counsel.

Senator MONDALE. The committee will come to order.

This morning our first witnesses consist of a panel of Mrs. Antonetty and Prof. Federico Aquino.

I will ask Mrs. Antonetty to come to the witness table along with Professor Aquino.

I understand Professor Aquino has a plane to catch. So, if there are no objections, perhaps you could begin with your testimony and you can make the plane.

STATEMENT OF PROF. FEDERICO AQUINO-BERMUDEZ, NEW YORK CITY, CITY UNIVERSITY OF NEW YORK

Professor AQUINO-BERMUDEZ. Before I proceed, I would like to state that there is further material that I would like to include in my statement. Today I will just talk briefly.

Senator MONDALE. We will put your full statement in the record as though read. You may make such points as you wish.

Professor AQUINO-BERMUDEZ. Mr. Chairman and distinguished members of the Select Committee on Equal Educational Opportunity of the U.S. Senate.

I am Federico Aquino-Bermudez. I am here on behalf of the Puerto Rican Forum, Inc., and as a private citizen interested in the education of the Puerto Rican children.

RACISM AND PUERTO RICAN EDUCATION

Today, I will talk to you about the impact of racism upon the education of Puerto Rican children.

My first task is to clarify and define the term "racism." Thus, enabled to determine the effects, if any, it has upon the education of Puerto Rican children and its projected effects on their economic and social opportunities and for their achievement.

To me, this is necessary because of the nature of racial perception in two dissimilar environments. Two key points need be made here: One is the different model of racial relations in Puerto Rico and the United States; the other is culturism as a mode of racism in America.

Professor Eduardo Seda-Bonilla, in a paper entitled "Two Models of Racial Relations," states that the discrepancies in the Puerto Rican and the American racial models make for instability among the Puerto Ricans with intermediate skin-color-texture in the United States: he indicates that whereas there is a twofold perception—black-white—in the United States, the Puerto Rican has three—"blanco, triqueno y negro"—white, intermediate, and black. (Eduardo Seda Bonilla, "Two Models of Racial Relations," paper presented to the XXII annual meeting of the Society for Applied Anthropology, Mar. 22, 26, 1964.)

He indicates that the intermediate type then loses his assigned socioracial place in the new environment, thus creating a frustrating situation for him. If this is true, as it seems to be, then racial identification for many Puerto Ricans in the United States becomes a stigma of inferiority and social disadjustment.

In short, what I am suggesting is that even before the public schools receive the Puerto Rican children, racism has already created a difficult, if not a devastating and deviating position for a miscegenated group such as the Puerto Rican. This is so because the new environment requires people to identify as black or white.

Therefore, the intermediate in taking an "inferior role," identified as black, feels alienated racially; in addition, the other two racial roles, black and white, also suffer because they are assigned a tribal or national identification—Puerto Rican—which indeed is characterized as non-white; therefore, perceived by the North Americans as inferior.

CULTURISM

Secondly, culturism, as defined by Dr. Elena Padilla, as a basis for racism in America. Her point is made eloquently when she states (Elena Padilla, "Up From Puerto Rico," New York: Columbia University Press, 1958, p. 70):

Culturism involves the assumption that each individual is representative of his whole national or minority group culture, and that regardless of the uniqueness of his personality of change in circumstances of his life and of the learning situation available to him he will continue to be immutably attached to the standards of behavior of his ancestors and to the cultural traditions of his group.

She further states:

Both racism and culturism are forms of prejudice each using a point of reference for its justification regardless of whether the members of a group are all considered to be "good" or "all bad."

If these two points are true, as they seem to be, then Puerto Ricans are indeed looked upon as inferior by the majority of Américans. If one adds to this, the stigmata of different language and of foreign-ness, one can begin to see the Puerto Rican children's predicament in the social order as well as in the schools.

Studies on the Mexican Americans indicate similar experiences between the two groups. These facts are substantiated by Leo Greb-ler, et al., in The Mexican American People, the Nation's Second Largest Minority. (Leo Greber, et al., The Mexican American People, The Nation's Second Largest Minority, New York: The Free Press, 1970. Special attention should be given to chapters 6 through 12, also in "Education of the Culturally Different, a Multi-Cultural Ap-proach, a Handbook for Educators," by Jack D. Forbes, U.S. Gov-ernment Printing Office, Washington, D.C., first edition, January 1969.)

Having set forth what I consider a viable and workable definition of racism or culturism permits me to present what I consider de-ficiencies in the education of the Puerto Rican children, many of which emanate from the impact of racism and culturism upon the group.

In this presentation I will point up some of the effects of these im-pacts in the development of the Puerto Rican personality and upon his educational achievement.

Generally speaking, the Puerto Rican children enter the educa-tional world with a perception based on the fact that there are people of different colors, even within their families. They, by and large, find that these people do not hold an inferior or superior place in this structure.

SCHOOLS ESTABLISH PATTERN OF INFERIORITY

Upon entering school, parents are not fully aware of the educa-tional inequities and inferiorities based on color discrimination their children face because their experiences in Puerto Rico have proven that in public education everyone is supposed to be equal—and I underline "equal." They, nevertheless, see segregation beginning in kindergarten and through the elementary school, unless the school is situated in a solid Puerto Rican neighborhood where homogeneity of the Puerto Rican is present.

The parents slowly come upon the realization which indicates to them that there are two groups of children to be taught: One group which is perceived as inferior, and one that is perceived as superior. Indeed, they see that the superior group is composed of white Amer-ican children; the other group, the inferior, is composed of Puerto Rican and black children.

Parents, furthermore, see white children placed in advanced or IGC classes. Later, parents discover, if they are somewhat sophisti-cated, that the selection is based on tests in which their children can-not succeed, and that sometimes placement is based on selective methods based on biases of school personnel. They also learn that their children are categorized as non-English speaking, culturally deprived, low achievers, and classified by other euphemisms which indicate an inferior rank.

When the children enter junior high school and high school, it dawns on some parents that their children are attending inferior or "bad" schools, while the white middle-class children attend "better" schools and "better" classes.

Finally, they may realize that their children are "losing heart" and dropping out of schools or getting an inferior diploma or being sent to vocational schools where they finish the learning of a trade which takes them nowhere. All these inequities can be seen in reports now available which indicate clearly these facts. (Richard J. Margolis, in "The Losers"—a report on Puerto Ricans and the public schools, written for Aspira, Inc., of New York in 1968; Richard Greenspan, in "A Story of Educational Neglect, 118 non-English-Speaking Pupils in New York City Public Schools," a study conducted for the Puerto Rican Forum of New York City in September 1970; and investigations conducted by the United Bronx Parents in New York City.)

INEQUITIES IN SOCIETY AT LARGE

In addition to the problems mentioned regarding the Puerto Rican children, there is a need to study the gross inequities found in the whole educational system and in the society at large. In a society where you have a multiethnic, biracial element which is polarized to a great extent, the society has within it the characteristics creating a nonlearning situation because of prejudicial perceptions and racist attitudes which might not always be projected or presented on a conscious level.

In that situation, the children become stigmatized to such an extent that they accept an inferior rank or role in society. They need only to see the sustaining symbols in their surroundings. Indeed, only white Americans seem to succeed—in school, their teachers are, by and large, white—in health, their doctors are white.

In other professional areas, people of stature are white. If they get in trouble, their lawyers are white; their judges are white. All of these make the children feel that people within their group cannot and are not capable of success and, furthermore, that the only positive role in America is the white role.

EFFECTS OF RACISM AND CULTURISM

Summing up what has already been stated, at the expense and danger of repeating myself, and in order to underscore how children have been affected, directly or indirectly, it should be evident that (1) intellectually and educationally the damage caused by racism and culturism can be translated into low reading scores, high dropout rates, placement in inferior classes—where Puerto Rican children cannot achieve, poor evaluation by psychologists, and many other educational deficiencies; (2) socially and emotionally this damage is translated into poor self-concepts, feelings of inferiority, high rates of mental illnesses, high incidence of drug abuse, high delinquency rates, and other social and psychological maladies; and (3) economically the damage can be seen in the high rate of unemployment found among the Puerto Rican youths of working age at the present time. One needs only to read the New York Times daily to become aware of these inequities. In addition, there is the fact that these damages have created a vacuum in terms of the number of professionally trained Puerto Ricans so direly needed to upgrade our community, a fact which also prevents the making of "positive" images which would hopefully motivate and stimulate Puerto Rican children to attain higher educational goals.

This must change. The children are denied effective educational instruction and a meaningful self image; and, unfortunately, the professionally trained adults of their world such as teachers and others are denied equal employment, sustaining the feeling that they must be inferior.

Unless these two models, racism and culturism, are changed so that children perceive themselves in a positive light, so that children become proud of what they are, until the teachers and other social practitioners respect children for what they are and perceive them as able to learn, until the liberal-speaking people step aside and allow the entrance of the Puerto Rican into well-paying jobs, until the Puerto Rican is assigned a place where he can attain, the problem of inferiority will prevail.

These changes must begin to take place in the educational arena first.

I respectfully urge you, as responsible legislators, to help the Puerto Rican to receive equal treatment in education.

Thank you for having given me the opportunity of addressing you today.

Senator MONDALE. Mr. Aquino, we are most grateful to you for that testimony.

What specific steps could be taken or required to be taken that you think would be of help in dealing with these racial ethnic perceptions, which persuade the young Puerto Rican child early in life that he is not going to make it? I understand you were once with the school system so you know about the testing.

Professor AQUINO-BERMUDEZ. Yes; I was. Other people will talk more extensively about that point but I would begin by saying that you have assumed one position that I quite do not agree with you. It is not only the Puerto Rican child perceiving himself as a positive well-developed individual. It is that we must deal also with racism in white America so that people can begin to perceive their racism even when they are not aware of it.

LANGUAGE AND CULTURAL PROGRAMS FOR ALL STUDENTS

I would recommend two things, to begin with: That more money be available, for example, for bilingual programs where respect for language is developed for all, for everybody across the board, so that good relations can be established.

The second thing that I would recommend is that all schools require that the Puerto Rican experience be included as a positive experience for all Americans.

For example, cultural programs and other programs that will present the Puerto Rican in a positive light for everybody because, as you well know, America has taken groups of people in here and nothing has been done. People have been messed up, thrown to the dogs, sort of, and so forth and so on.

I think that it is high time that in a new world and in a new era where the United States is claiming equality for all that equality take place.

Senator MONDALE. What you say is undeniably correct. Yet it is criticism which has been directed at the school system for a long time.

Professor AQUINO-BERMUDEZ. Well, the school system happens to be the weakest link. Everybody blames somebody, even within the school system. The junior high school teacher blames the elementary school teacher and down the line.

I think we have to begin dealing with the whole social structure. I think we have to take a chunk at a time. I think the school being a second socializing agent in society it should be held accountable. It should begin with kindergarten being aware that Puerto Rican children are not inferior.

Senator MONDALE. I am trying to figure out how you make the system respond. As you say, when you heap these criticisms on the system, fingers can be pointed in many different directions.

Professor AQUINO-BERMUDEZ. I would say that we are using, again, the euphemism, the system. If you will define it for me, then I will tackle the situation. I am directly saying, I am not saying "system," I am talking directly of a situation. I am saying that the U.S. Senate and legislators can mandate certain programs, too.

Other legislation that has been passed has been passed in such a faulty language to satisfy everybody, because nobody wants to step on everybody's throat. You have had here a hypocrisy that has to begin to be broken down. If we release programs for the Puerto Ricans, let us have programs for the Puerto Ricans.

If we release programs for the blacks, let us have programs for the blacks. We are living in a world where we are sending men to the moon. It makes me vomit when I think that a man goes to the moon and right here on terra firma we are not able to deal with our problems.

We are saying, yes, you know, somebody ought to, these poor children are being killed, people use all kinds of epitaphs to blame the educational system. Yes, the educational system is bad. I am not saying that it is good. I am saying that somebody ought to put a fire under it to get it going.

RECOMMENDATIONS FOR LEGISLATION

Senator MONDALE. If we were to draft an amendment which would act as such a catalyst, what should be its provisions?

Professor AQUINO-BERMUDEZ. That monies are allocated so that you can begin to bring in innovative programs. Some of the licensing procedures in some of the states are horrible and they are not realistic. When monies could be provided the way they are provided for in title I to have a group of people, an interested and committed group of people who will begin to deal with the problem in specific areas. Some exploratory work should begin to be done and evaluated.

The problem is that at the present time everybody jumps into the pot, grabs the money and there is no evaluation. We need to have evaluation. We have enough material, enough studies at the present time, to indicate what are the steps that have to be taken.

No action is taken. In the meanwhile the Puerto Rican is being, as my students would say—and excuse me for the expression—"screwed up," you see. We have begun dealing with these facts and hitting it head on. Not by "I cannot do this," "I cannot do that." Every time you take a step somebody is going to claim, "Well now, you are stepping on my toes." If toes are to be stepped on now, I say let us have those toes stepped on until people understand that we have to communicate.

Senator MONDALE. Very well.

Senator MONDALE. Mrs. Evelina Antonetty, Executive Director of the United Bronx Parents, you may proceed.

STATEMENT OF EVELINA ANTONETTY, EXECUTIVE DIRECTOR, UNITED BRONX PARENTS

Mrs. ANTONETTY. Thank you, Mr. Chairman.

What are the facts about the educational achievement of the Puerto Rican students in the New York City school system?

The board of education does not release achievement data by race. However, in district 7 in the Bronx, where 65 percent of the children are Puerto Rican, 73 percent of them are seriously retarded in reading.

Although 25 percent of the public school students are Puerto Rican, only 3 percent of the students who received academic diplomas from our city high schools last year were Puerto Rican.

I must explain this to you because the board of education sometimes tells us that 75 percent of the students graduate with academic diplomas. What happens is that they figure if four are left and three graduate, that is 75 percent. They don't say how many are dropouts.

DISCRIMINATION AGAINST PUERTO RICAN TEACHERS

What are the facts about the discrimination against Puerto Ricans in our New York City school system?

It is difficult to show cold facts which illustrate the bias against the Puerto Rican pupil. But it is easy to show the discrimination against the Puerto Rican educator as he tries to find a place for himself in this school system.

In 1969–70 the board of education spent over a quarter of a million dollars in title I funds to "recruit and train Puerto Rican teachers." A grand total of 125 Spanish-speaking teachers were recruited from Puerto Rico. Of this total, only 27 were licensed. According to the board of education office of personnel the other 98 candidates could not complete the application and testing process.

New York has 55,000 teachers; only 350 of them are Puerto Rican. New York has 1,000 guidance counselors; only 10 of them are Puerto Rican. New York has 1,700 assistant principals; 10 of them are Puerto Rican.

New York has 950 principals, but as of now we have only four Puerto Rican heads of school, and all of them are in an acting assignment.

Remember: New York City has 250,000 Puerto Rican pupils.

Senator MONDALE. There isn't a single Puerto Rican principal in the school system?

Mrs. ANTONETTY. I did not hear you, sir.

Senator MONDALE. There isn't one permanent Puerto Rican principal in the school system?

Mrs. ANTONETTY. That was Mr. Matthews. Since then he has become——

Senator MONDALE. There are four?

Mrs. ANTONETTY. That is, acting.

Senator MONDALE. There is not one permanent?

Mrs. ANTONETTY. There was Mr. Matthews. Since then he has become the one exception, a district superintendent.

You also must remember that New York City has 250,000 Puerto Rican pupils.

FUNDS ALONE INEFFECTIVE

All the money in the world will not solve the problem of the Puerto Rican child in the New York City school system.

New York City is now spending over $1,600 per pupil each year on education. That is more than most suburbs. Last year district 7 received an additional $1,271,000 in title I funds and $561,000 in State urban aid funds. And our children are still as far behind in reading as ever before.

As long as the money continues to go from the Federal Government to the board of education bureaucracy, which has miseducated our children for all these years, the money is wasted. That bureaucracy is biased against our educators and equally blind about our children.

COMMUNITY CONTROL

The problem is not our Puerto Rican children. The problem is a system of education which squeezes and manipulates and destroys our children. The Federal Government must stop subsidizing this bungling, biased bureaucracy. You must give our communities a chance to educate our children.

I would like to read an excerpt from a book which has been written by my training director. I am not trying to promote the book. It is a very good passage here:

In New York City parents are officially invited to come to school and confer with the teachers twice a year. If a child is having trouble in school, his parents may be asked to come in for an additional conference. These parent-teacher conferences ought to result in greater understanding and cooperation between the child's family and his school. Unfortunately, this rarely happens.

As United Bronx Parents we conduct parent education classes. In the fall before conference time we hold discussion with many parents, urging them to visit teachers, suggesting they talk to children first, and prepare a list of specific questions to ask each teacher. After a visit to I.S. 38 in the Bronx one mother brought in this report:

"I attended a conference with my boy's teacher. Miguel's English teacher gave him an F. When I asked why, he told me Miguel did very poor in some tests. I told him that my son told me about him not checking homework and not explaining the lessons clearly and how my son disliked that class. The teacher tried to change the subject, telling me the remarks he made on the report card that Miguel is a boy of great value. I asked him what he meant, because I knew of my son's value, but that would not help his English. His math teacher did not invite me to sit down. He was doing clerical work and he stood up and told me Miguel was a fine boy. When I asked about math, he showed me the record. But he was looking at another boy named Miguel.

"I told him. He then said he was sorry, but he had 200 children during the day and some of them were Miguels. We then discussed my son and he assured me that Miguel was doing fine work."

Now this goes on constantly with the Puerto Rican families.

Senator MONDALE. In other words, in the first case they flunked the child and finally got to a conference?

Mrs. ANTONETTY. Right. But in the second case, the teacher did not even know which Miguel she was talking about.

Senator MONDALE. He had too many of them.

Mrs. ANTONETTY. Yes, he had too many Miguels. We are going to have to name them by Miguel I, II, III, and IV. Usually what they start doing to the parents is that they go into the schools and they are told how gorgeous and beautiful their children are, but they never tell them how they are doing in reading.

TEACHER INSENSITIVITY

Comes May and they tell them that their child is failing, but they never told their parents before that. This is what the parents have to contend with. Most of the teachers do not relate to the students. Many of them come from middle-class families, they are white. The student does not see himself in the classroom. They are destroyed in many instances, especially when the teacher says, "Reading a funny book, only stupid people read funny books."

The child then remembers that his father picks up a funny book once in a while. This means that this goes to the child's father.

Miguel since then has become a drug addict. This is the saddest part of it, that our children are pushed out of school and they become the drug addicts and the dropouts from the school system.

Senator JAVITS. Mrs. Antonetty, I am sorry I had to be at another meeting of the Foreign Relations Committee this morning.

I gather you were in the midst of your testimony.

Mrs. ANTONETTY. I was almost through.

I just wanted to call your attention to a graph which we have done regarding how the Puerto Ricans fare in the New York City school system.[1]

You notice the great number of students we have as compared to principals, as compared to assistant principals, as compared to teachers, guidance counselors. Even in the paraprofessional and the school lunch personnel, which is nonprofessional, you see we are not doing too well. We somehow are not even seen. We are invisible.

I would like to call the committee's attention to that.

Then on the next page you have a study made by the Puerto Rican Forum on Personnel in the New York City school system.

If there are any questions, I will be glad to answer them.

Senator JAVITS. Thank you, Mrs. Antonetty.

I know you as a very intelligent woman and a real leader in the educational field.

---

[1] The graph can be seen in committee files.

Mrs. ANTONETTY. Senator Javits, I just hope that this is not just another futile attempt at something. I would like to see something really done about our children because we are losing them too rapidly.

In Benjamin Franklin, 14 students graduated with an academic diploma last year. We cannot afford this any longer. It is our future that is at stake. I call it genocide as it is now.

LEGISLATION LIMITS

Senator JAVITS. Mrs. Antonetty, I want to ask you a question or two.

As a practical matter, you understand the limitations of what can be done in the Congress. Let me get your observations on that.

Obviously these are terribly depressing figures and bear out everything that you conclude about them; as it is, it is the last chance for a tremendous number of children. We appreciate that very deeply.

Now, the Federal Government is not in a position to actually go in and take over the school system, actually appoint teachers, appoint principals, take over the teaching of children. This is the primary responsibility of the State of New York and the city of New York. What we can do is devote a certain amount of money to material improvements in the system.

Now, would you be able to tell us how you think money could be used in the New York City school system in order to improve these conditions? Because that is the only thing we are going to have an opportunity to do, to wit, appropriate money.

FEDERAL MONEY MISDIRECTED

Mrs. ANTONETTY. Fine, except that, as I said in my statement before, if you continue to pour that money through the local boards of education, for instance, the New York City Board of Education, you are not going to have any result because as it is I will compare it even with title I where there is no evaluation, nothing is really happening, but that money has lined the pockets of the teachers some more and the children are still the same. The same teachers who are teaching the children during the day get the jobs after school. Really, it is not accomplishing anything.

Children in my own district, district 7, so much money poured in the district, it is like a gargoyle; you keep pouring money in there and nothing has happened. The children have retardation of 3.1, the worst district in the city.

It is not the money. The money is going in. It is whom you are giving the money to.

Senator JAVITS. The money is going in now, let us say, from Federal sources. We are appropriating certain large amounts of money to New York under the elementary and secondary school programs and other programs.

We are talking about more money in order to deal with the racial isolation of the school—now, do you wish to tell us that no more money is needed?

Mrs. ANTONETTY. No. What I am trying to say is where you are buying is the wrong place to buy. I think you perhaps can make the

Puerto Rican community responsible for the money to see that the money is used to educate its children by giving it directly to the Puerto Rican community, to the Puerto Rican organization and not to the board of education which doesn't know what to do; there is no evaluation of these programs and nothing is really happening.

I think that you, too, will have to have some sort of evaluation process where you will see that the money is really being used for the purpose it was set up for.

COMMUNITY INVOLVEMENT

Senator JAVITS. You believe that could be done through the Puerto Rican organizations.

Do you believe it is also possible to do it through a Federal department like the Commissioner of Education?

Mrs. ANTONETTY. It could be done if they deal directly with our community.

Senator JAVITS. Just so long as it is not the same board of education which is administering the situation now; is that right?

Mrs. ANTONETTY. Which is bungling the situation right now.

Senator JAVITS. Bungling; right.

Now, suppose it was possible under the poverty program or a special program like we are considering to get money to a particular community group, let us say the United Bronx Parents, suppose we could really fund your organization, let us say $500,000, what would you do with that?

Mrs. ANTONETTY. I need more than that to set up a whole bilingual district.

Senator JAVITS. What would you say you need?

Mrs. ANTONETTY. I would need a high school, for instance, like the high school of science. I would call it bilingual high school of the city of New York. I would need a whole bilingual district.

BILINGUAL DISTRICTS

The Bronx, you know, is the capital of the Puerto Rican community. We are in there and we are the majority. We should have districts which are completely bilingual so that our children do not get lost. I think we could do wonders with such a district; our children would not get lost. We would not have so much drug addiction.

Senator JAVITS. Now, if you had such a district, that would result in drawing some thousands of children out of the New York City school system; is that right?

Mrs. ANTONETTY. Well, we have 250,000. We have a great number to choose from.

Senator JAVITS. I say you would be drawing some thousands out.

Mrs. ANTONETTY. Right.

Senator JAVITS. Should not the school system run that bilingual institution?

Mrs. ANTONETTY. They are doing so badly right now.

Senator JAVITS. They have failed?

Mrs. ANTONETTY. They have failed at practically everything they touch. Even when they are not failing, they don't recognize their own gains and they don't follow through on them.

Senator JAVITS. Mrs. Antonetty, suppose you had the money, do you think you could successfully make a contract with the New York City school system?

Mrs. ANTONETTY. It is very hard for me to talk about "supposing," and it is very hard for one to praise ourselves, but we have not failed in anything we have undertaken yet. We have been successfully organizing parents and successfully training parents to be more effective in their schools. Right now, we have started a training session of 100 parents. We have 265 and more coming every day. So that, I feel that we are capable of running a school system.

We would, of course, call on everybody in the community who is knowledgeable and who has the desire to see our children go forward.

Senator JAVITS. Now we have elected school boards in New York. Did your organization run any candidates in those elections?

Mrs. ANTONETTY. We certainly did not. That is the whole fallacy. They have no power. The policy is still controlled by the ones on Livingston.

SCHOOLS BOARDS POWERLESS

Senator JAVITS. Livingston street, for the record, being the Board of Education of New York.

Mrs. ANTONETTY. That is right. It is the citadel of the board of education.

We did not take part in those elections. However, that does not mean that we are not out on the street making sure that those who got elected, even though they don't know what they are doing, begin to function the way they should, begin to demand powers.

Senator JAVITS. But you did boycott the election?

Mrs. ANTONETTY. Yes; we did.

Senator JAVITS. Thank you very much. Mrs. Antonetty. This is very helpful to us in deciding what to do about this question.

Mrs. ANTONETTY. Thank you.

Senator MONDALE. Mrs. Antonetty, did you prepare these figures broken down by districts showing the number of children?

Mrs. ANTONETTY. Yes.

Senator MONDALE. If you have no objection, we will include these figures in the record following your statement.[1]

Mrs. ANTONETTY. Whenever you need any figures on the New York City's school system, we are glad to give them to you. We have them all.

Senator MONDALE. We are most grateful to you. Thank you very much.

Mrs. ANTONETTY. Thank you, Mr. Chairman.

(The position paper follows:)

POSITION PAPER ON THE MISEDUCATION OF PUERTO RICAN CHILDREN ON THE MAINLAND (U.S.A.)

(Presented by Mrs. Petra Valdes)

The present educational systems on the mainland are almost totally failing children of Puerto Rican extraction. Not only are they failing to educate our children, a serious enough situation, but they are also miseducating them.

The first charge—failure to educate our children—is well founded and documented by a number of studies and statistical data. For example, there was an intensive study of the experiences of the Puerto Rican children in the public

---

[1] See Table I, p. 3736.

school system of New York City. The result of the study was published in a document, titled *Puerto Rican Study 1953–57*, which not only clearly showed the poor educational achievement of the Puerto Rican pupils but also included twenty three (23) specific recommendations to remedy the problems.

In May 1968, Aspira, an organization vitally interested in Puerto Rican affairs, conducted a nationwide conference to determine the status of the education of Puerto Ricans on the mainland. One of the documents that it analyzed, utilized and compared with updated material, was the previously mentioned *Puerto Rican Study 1953–57*. It was indeed frustrating to note that eleven years (1957–1968) after that study, the participants of the conference could only present a similarly discouraging picture. Obviously, the powers-that-be had not seriously utilized the document and/or considered or implemented any of the recommendations. In fact, the Aspira conference indicated that the educational situation of the Puerto Rican child was becoming progressively worse.

Data of 1963 drawn from the New York City Public School System is very revealing. Let us analyze the following statistics:

	Number	Percent of total school population
Total	244,458	
Puerto Rican pupils—		
In elementary schools	147,000	20
In junior high schools	52,437	18
In academic high schools	29,908	
In vocational high schools	12,869	23
In special high schools	2,244	29

DIPLOMAS GRANTED TO HIGH SCHOOL GRADUATES, NEW YORK CITY, 1963

	Number of diplomas	Academic diplomas		Vocational diplomas
		Total	Percent	
Puerto Rican	1,626	333	1.6	1,215
Afro American	3,434	762	3.7	2,672
Others	33,244	19,636	94.7	13,608

These figures have a critical significance for the Puerto Rican community. They indicate a high rate of dropoutism and a woeful amount of under representation in the academic high school. This is further highlighted when the importance of the academic diploma for entrance into college is considered, as the lack of an academic diploma means almost total exclusion from the higher educational systems.

Data publicized by the New York City School System itself indicates that the same trends are continuing. In pointing out the data, reading scores of the Metropolitan Achievement Reading Tests, April 1968, we show that in *all* grades our children fall below both the city and national mean and norm.

Grade	2	3	4	5	6	7	8	9
Normal average reading score (nationwide norms)	2.7	3.7	4.7	5.7	6.7	7.7	8.7	9.7
New York City mean reading grade report	2.7	3.7	4.7	5.7	6.8	7.1	8.1	8.9
District mean reading grade report:								
Districts:								
1	2.3	3.0	4.0	4.9	6.2	6.4	7.2	8.4
2	3.0	3.8	4.6	5.6	6.5	6.5	7.1	8.8
4	2.5	3.2	4.1	5.0	5.8	6.1	6.7	7.6
7	2.3	2.8	3.8	4.4	5.1	5.5	6.4	6.9
12	2.2	3.0	3.9	4.8	5.7	5.6	6.4	7.2
14	2.2	3.0	3.9	4.5	5.2	5.8	6.8	7.2
15	2.3	3.1	4.1	5.0	5.7	6.0	6.8	7.4

Source: Board of Education, New York City Bureau of Educational Research.

In a quick survey, we can see the following:
1. In grade 2 the pupils are on the average three (3) months behind the city mean.
2. In grade 4 they fall an average of 6.4 months behind.
3. In grade 6 they fall an average of 10.6 months behind.
4. In grade 8 they fall an average of 13 months behind.

If the national norm were used, the discrepancy would become even greater in grades 7, 8, 9.

It is most important to note that in all of the data presented above, Puerto Rican pupils rated C to F in the language scale *are not included* since they are not prepared to take the Metropolitan Reading Achievement Test. For the uninitiated, the language scale (A-F) is as follows:

A=Speaks English like a native
B=Speaks English with a foreign accent
C=Speaks English well enough for most situations met by typical native pupils of like age, *but* still must make a conscious effort to avoid the forms of his native tongue. Speaks hesitantly upon occasion
D=Speaks English in more than a few stereotyped situations, but speaks it haltingly at all times
E=Speaks English *only* in stereotyped situations
F=Speaks no English

There is a very significant number of pupils who fall in the D-E-F category as evidenced by the following statistics:

LANGUAGE SCALE RATINGS AND PERCENTAGE OF PUPILS IN SCHOOL SYSTEM

School group	Rating A–B	Rating C	Rating D–E–F	Total (percent)
Elementary	53.9	23.6	22.5	100
Junior high school	74.6	16.4	9.0	100
Academic high school	78.7	13.9	7.4	100
Vocational high school	82.2	15.9	1.9	100
Special school	71.0	15.3	13.7	100
Citywide	63.5	20.2	16.7	100

In all fairness to the school system, it must be admitted that it made some feeble attempt to tackle the linguistic barrier problem. It established English as a Second Language Program. However, this program has not been successful. In spite of the fact that it has existed for many years, it has not solved the educational problems of the Puerto Rican and other Spanish speaking children. This fact has been well documented by the April 1969 report on the Non-English Speaking Pupil given by the Puerto Rican Forum in New York City.

We think that we have adequately shown the first part of our charge, which is that the educational system has failed to educate the Puerto Rican children. Let us consider now the second part of the charge which revolves around the miseducation of the Puerto Rican pupil.

The educational process includes much more than curricula, books and methodologies employed in teaching the contents of the various textbooks. A most important aspect of the educational process is dependent upon attitudes.

The professional staff of the schools and the students differ in many ways. Some of these differences include: Levels of aspiration and expectancy; experiential backgrounds, social values, customs and mores, communicative and linguistic approaches and difficulties; systems of behavior and attitudes; a lack of mutual understanding, acceptance and respect; feelings of superiority/inferiority toward different groups; distorted self images and stereotypes of others; unsubstantiated opinions/beliefs of the capabilities, knowledge, skills of members of certain ethnic groups.

Each of the above mentioned items usually leads to a negative attitude on the part of the educators (predominantly Caucasoid teachers and administrators) toward the minority or Puerto Rican pupil. These attitudes cause the miseducation of the Puerto Rican pupil. They make him feel inferior and create within him a negative self image. They cause him to question and spurn his native language and rich cultural heritage. They foster negative thoughts, feelings and behavior toward other members of his own ethnic group. This is due in large part to the fact that he seldom, if ever, has in the school a successful ethnic model to emulate since practically all of the teachers/administrators are not members of the minority or Puerto Rican ethnic group. In addition, the teachers/administrators generally *expect* the pupil to achieve at a low level. This feeling is transmitted to the pupil who then behaves in the expected manner.

We have reached a point on which many factors converge. Some of these factors are the following: New decisions must be made to secure truly equal educational opportunities for all members of our ethnic groups; more effective remedies must be found if we are to properly educate the children of minority groups and to conciliate the Puerto Rican community. We have to seriously question the power establishment's lack of sensitivity and/or misunderstanding of the critical nature of the problem.

We must begin to recognize that the language instruction of Puerto Ricans on the mainland is a very serious one. Therefore, new approaches and methods have to be found in order to bridge the gap between the native English speaking and the non-English speaking child. The question is no longer: How can we teach and impose English as rapidly as possible on the child? No. The question is: How can we insure a high level of educational achievement of the Puerto Rican child? This achievement must, at least, match that of the norm for all mainland pupils.

One way to accomplish this task is to seriously examine the bilingualism approach to teaching. We have tried to drive this point home before. During the first city-wide conference of the Puerto Rican community called by Mayor Lindsay of New York City, there was an indication of the deep seated resentment and indignation toward the educational situation of the Puerto Rican on the mainland. The group submitted thirty-two (32) recommendations to the Mayor. The institution of a bilingual approach and ethnic heritage programs was part of those recommendations. The bilingual approach not only develops and preserves the knowledge of Spanish among Puerto Rican children, but it also serves as a vehicle and means of providing, in the native tongue, subject matter instruction that will raise the levels of achievement of the pupils.

More bilingual schools should be established, especially in areas where the greater percentage of the pupils are Spanish speaking dominant. In addition, there should be, immediately, implemented the teaching of Spanish.

Other means by which the educational achievement of the pupils may be raised are as follows:

1. Terminate, immediately, the discriminatory practices of children and schools as a way of differentiating minority group pupils from those of the majority group.

2. Enact and *enforce* legislation which will end discriminatory practices involved in the recruitment, employment and upgrading of educational personnel. The key to this problem is the *enforcement* of the laws, rules and regulations.

3. Insure the hiring of *qualified* rather than merely certified personnel. For example, the Board of Examiners in the New York City School System through its certifying procedures, actually prevents the hiring of a host of highly qualified persons.

4. Make a careful review and revision of the College Entrance Examination Boards. Admission to college must be considered a *right*, to be enjoyed by all, and not a privilege.

5. There are hundreds of thousands highly qualified Spanish speaking and Puerto Ricans here on the Mainland. Many of them cannot serve in our schools due to the "certification game." These persons must be utilized even if it is necessary to set up intensive/extensive training programs for them to meet the artificial and meaningless certification criteria.

The Puerto Rican community, like other minority groups such as the Afro-American and Indian, has grown restless. Students have begun to engage in militant demonstrations and protests on the junior high, senior high and college levels. Soon, the presently exempted elementary school level will probably be included. The students, all ages, are rebelling against the degrading and academically meaningless experiences they are forced to undergo in the schools. They refuse to participate in and give lip service to a dehumanized system that leads to the vicious cycle of poor education, poor jobs, poor housing, poor health, poor self-images, high crime rates and wasted human life. Frankly, ladies and gentlemen, I do not blame them. Do you? If not, I implore you to do something about it.

Senator MONDALE. Our next witnesses are a panel of students, former students and parents from the city of New York.

Would the panel please come up to the witness table?

You may begin as you wish.

Mr. NEGRON. First, I would like to know how many Senators were supposed to be involved in this and how many of you are Senators.

Senator MONDALE. The two of us are Senators, even though a lot of people would disagree. The people behind us are staff members.

Mr. NEGRON. Am I correct in believing that there were supposed to be 15 Senators present at this hearing?

Senator MONDALE. No. While we have 15 members of the committee perhaps eight or 10 different committees meet at the same time and we have to spread ourselves very thinly.

Mr. NEGRON. Then I guess I will have to believe that you are the only two concerned about the Puerto Rican problem in education.

Senator JAVITS. I think, sir, if you will forgive me, that is not true.

Mr. NEGRON. You are not concerned?

Senator JAVITS. We are deeply concerned, but we are not the only two. There are other colleagues who are also concerned but there are simply——

Mr. NEGRON. I can only go on the basis of what I see. I see only two Senators.

Senator JAVITS. We might as well say you are not concerned about something that is happening in New York because you are in Washington today. That would not be true.

Others of our colleagues are engaged elsewhere in very important work for our country.

Mr. NUNEZ. There was an article in the New York Times which indicated that the aides actually run the Senate.

I would like to ask, respectfully, where are these aides? They do exist? And they are being paid with Federal money. It should be the responsibility of the Senators to make sure the hearings are covered; otherwise, they should give up the office.

Senator JAVITS. The aides are here and everything that is said and done here will be available completely to our colleagues.

Mr. NUNEZ. Can I make a request on the part of the panel that the aides of the respective Senators please be introduced? I realize you have a nameplate which says Senator Javits, and you know my name. I would like to know who is responsible and who are the aides assigned present here for each Senator so that I will be able to report to my constituency in the Puerto Rican community that something is going on.

Senator MONDALE. Will one of the staff members please prepare that list for them? We will submit that to you.

Mr. NUNEZ. Thank you. I think that is a great respect to the Puerto Rican community to let us know when you call us from the community that you are at least here to listen to us as individuals.

Mr. NEGRON. I would like to add that during the time the first speaker was giving his story as a witness there was a conversation going on with Senator Mondale and somebody else. I don't like to see that going on. I demand your attention.

Senator JAVITS. Gentlemen if you will allow us, we would like to go ahead with the hearing.

Could we call on Miss Rodriguez, the first one in line?

Will you be good enough to give us your views?

STATEMENT OF MISS DORIS RODRIGUEZ

Miss RODRIGUEZ. I think I am being cheated out of my education because they don't treat us equally in the schools.

I am in a vocational high school and they want us to go out to work or to a 2-year college, not to a four. How would you like your kid, whether he is black or Puerto Rican, when it is Christmas vacation, that the teacher kisses all the whites but the Puerto Ricans and black she kisses them with "yuk," like she doesn't want to kiss them.

I think we are being cheated. All they teach about is Americanism. Why don't they bring Puerto Rican teachers from Puerto Rico? The United States has enough money to bring them over here and let them teach us our own culture.

We need more black and Puerto Rican teachers because the white teachers are influencing us and discouraging us from our education. I don't think that in my class I would ever like to be a teacher.

Thank you very much.

Senator MONDALE. What year are you in school?

Miss RODRIGUEZ. Third year.

Senator MONDALE. The next is Miss Lopez.

STATEMENT OF MISS AGGIE LOPEZ

Miss LOPEZ. What I was going to say is that in my school they do have Puerto Rican teachers but they have about five of them and they are in the non-English department. We don't learn anything about our culture like Doris said before.

The Puerto Rican teachers that we do have in the school system are sold out. They sold out to the white people. They are just like the white teachers. What is the use of having Puerto Rican teachers that are sold out already?

Senator JAVITS. Thank you very much.

STATEMENT OF FRANK NEGRON

Mr. NEGRON. What I am about to read is my own experience in the school system.

I grew up in a home where the only language ever spoken was Spanish, where the most educated person in the family was my mother who attended school in Puerto Rico and went to only the eighth grade.

By the time I started school, the only English I knew was the little I picked up on television or from some of the neighbors where I lived. Learning for me was always a problem. The teachers could never give me the individual attention I needed in order to learn something at least once a week.

The number of pupils in the class was always more than the teacher could handle. Once a day for about an hour I would be pulled out of my class and taken to another class with a teacher who spoke an unusual Spanish. She helped me learn a little but 1 hour a day was hardly enough to help me keep up, with the rest of the class. That program was teaching English as a second language.

CLASSES IN ENGLISH

Quite naturally, after a long time of learning very little, listening to meaningless lecture and debate in a foreign language and watching the teacher create unfamiliar writings on the blackboard, being bored in school was nothing new, and now to escape the boredom, I finally developed an interest in drawing.

I became so good at it that the teacher would always have me working in the back of the room on a "project" that always involved drawing. Now school had a new meaning to me, a place to draw and to develop my skills in drawing.

I drew my way right through every test and every grade until in the third grade I was sent to this Museums Art School in Brooklyn, near Eastern Parkway, to get expert instructions in drawing. To my knowledge, all expenses were paid by the school (attended P.S. 287).

I keep going there until about a year later my mother began to realize that I wasn't learning anything about reading or anything similar. She stopped me from going to those art lessons and complained to the principal of the school.

NONCOMPREHENSION

That year I was left back and was put in a special class that was supposed to help me in my reading, most of all. I still had trouble because the teachers had a hard time getting across to me.

As time went by, I would always take notes and kept a very neat book and pretended to know what was going on in class, making believe I understood what the teacher was talking about. And, although I exposed my lack of knowledge every time the teacher would call on me to read or spell something, the fact that I had not learned anything didn't mean much to the teacher; she passed me anyway because I was sweet and cooperative.

Naturally, I played right into the hypocrisy of the educational system.

Junior high school was not much different except for the fact that you had a better chance of learning something because of the number of teachers involved in your education. In the seventh grade, I had gotten left back again because I had failed my midterms. Now, how can you try to convince me of anything about equal education in New York City school system when I, an innocent Puerto Rican child with a little English as a second language was left back twice because I was not given an opportunity to learn with and from my own peers?

Now, I didn't even want to go to school. School was a place to build your hopes and have them destroyed at the end of each school year. Later on, I quit school and, as the years went by, I experienced all those things you run into when you are too young to get a decent job and too old to go back to school and live in the ghetto.

I smoked pot like it was nothing; it kept me happy. I had tried just about every kind of drug there was, including junk—heroin—for 2 years.

Realizing how everything seems to work in a monopoly, I became a rebel. I reinforced my justification as a rebel when I saw one of my own people put together a type of educational program needed for the Puerto Rican child and it was used by the system to pacify the people and then to criminally repress and hinder the education of my people as in the experimental school district in the Ocean Hill-Brownsville area that was stopped because it was so effective and, of course, other racist reasons.

All existing educational programs that are supposedly to help the so-called Spanish-speaking youth are either too passive or too expensive and never deal with the real needs of the people. I don't expect much to come out of these hearings because I have lost all faith in the American way when I realized that you failed me and therefore became a rebel.

So, if you expect to stop producing guys like me, you better start approving plans that would allow those elements among my people who can deal with the real needs and don't let these hearings be another appetizer before you eat your turkey.

Senator JAVITS. Thank you very much, Mr. Negron.

Mr. Nunez?

STATEMENT OF ANGELO NUNEZ

Mr. NUNEZ. Yes.

I am going to go into my personal experiences. I also want to make some significant points because I am going to emphasize the high school education which is very decrepit.

First of all, from the beginning school is supposed to be an educational experience where learning occurs. In this country, learning occurs in English. If you do not speak English, tough luck.

One of the bad problems, or I won't even question whether it is bad because my people do retain the native tongue, is that our Puerto Rican community is a Spanish-speaking community. In our homes, we retain our language and we live and function every day in our language, Spanish.

Now when we enter school we are right then from that moment at a disadvantage because we cannot read the books in English. We cannot learn how to do arithmetic because we can't read the problems. In order to be able to gain this educational experience, you must know the language. Now, many solutions have been presented as far as educational learning to improve. One is bilingual education.

BILINGUAL INSTRUCTION "TOKENISM"

I would like to make aware to the Senate committee in many cases the bilingual education is a farce. In district 14, there are as many bilingual teachers in school for 80 percent of the Puerto Rican population as there are librarians. It came out to an average of one teacher per school. This one teacher is supposed to give these students an adequate background, adequate education, adequate information in order that they may come up to par with the other students.

No one can tell me that one teacher who also has the responsibility of putting on the Pan American Day parade, acting as interpreter, can educate 1,000 students or any fraction of that which may need the services. This is just tokenism, something which will not solve the problem.

Another concerns the educational system, itself.

It is not open, it is not viable for new ideas. Only by having a big fight and rioting and nearly burning down a school can new ideas be introduced to the Board of Education of New York City. This is very obvious with the local school boards which were started by the actual community and degerated down to the extent where they have very little power except over what to serve for lunch. The staff also presents a problem..

DISCRIMINATION BY BOARD OF EDUCATION

Now, I am not going to say here that I believe they should all be Puerto Rican or that they should all be black, but right now the Human Rights Commission of New York City is investigating the hiring practices of the board of education for a very specific reason. There is an absence of minority black, Puerto Rican, Orientals in there. And this is a commission of the U.S. Government. This is not a commission by the community. It has become pretty obvious that there are racist tendencies in our boards of education.

Now we will go down to our education. In high schools, as Mrs. Antonetty said, 3 percent of the Puerto Rican population graduates with an academic diploma. An academic diploma is usually what is required to get into college to get further education. When our students are graduating with general diplomas, vocational diplomas, technical diplomas, commercial diplomas, certificates of attendance, that is not getting education.

Like I am walking in here today, that is what they do. It does not seem apparently the high schools are looking for any solutions, either.

On November 17 a document was printed by Mr. Zack who did research work and Mr. Don Grew of the board of education in the high school division, in which they listed priorities for the education of our students, things that were needed, and the No. 1 thing was security for us. More policemen in our schools to protect the kids. to keep in school, to keep the people out of school, not to improve the education.

TESTING

Now our high schools are in very sad shape, especially for the minority students. There is one thing that you must all be aware of since most of you, I am sure, are college graduates. There is something called the college entrance examination test. SAT achievement tests, which are made up of two parts: mathematical and verbal. Now, as you know, probably when you took some when you were in high school, it comes with great difficulty to people who speak English as their native tongue to achieve scores that are considered good. That would be 600, 700. When you don't know the language and when you graduate from the twelfth grade with an eighth grade reading level you cannot take this test and hope to even score a 300 which means you are not going into college unless you are shoved into some community college because you are a minority student.

You know, just as they like to say in the high schools, they don't get the education. It starts from the very beginning and just continues like a snowball going downhill, gathering strength, gathering size, weakening the knowledge of our students. Now we are very well aware of this situation and something must be done.

Now, the testing practices are also very, very racist. I was a very fortunate student. I went to a public school in a predominantly black neighborhood. Since I was able to get a score on my third grade EQ test they transferred me to what is known as an SP class, special progress class, which gives accelerated work in a white community. They don't have these classes in the black communities mainly because the students are not up to par. So, I have been able to so-call make it in our educational system. Now I attend a specialized high school, Brooklyn Tech.

There is one thing that must be very clear. These problems are everywhere in our educational system. In the school I go to, there are about 6,000 students; 160 are Spanish names. There are about 500 black students. All the rest are white. I am not saying that there are racist tendencies because I am in no position to accuse people of that. But from these figures it seems very apparent to me that there is something lacking in the educational system for a Puerto Rican student and a black student and something must be done. Believe me, if something is not done, something worse could happen.

The students are in a position now where they are fed up with their educational system. Incidents like George Washington, Benjamin Franklin, are going to happen more and more. More actions of rioting are going to occur in our schools; it is very apparent. The students are fed up with the hiring practices.

UNQUALIFIED TEACHERS

You know, it is ridiculous when you go into a Spanish class and you have a teacher there who teaches it because they have had 2 years of Spanish or you go into a Latin American study class or something like that, which is not even given in half of the schools where it ought to be given, and the teachers who are teaching it are history teachers who took two courses in college in Latin American studies.

Another thing which is very severe, and that is the thing where Puerto Rican students give you great difficulty in taking their own native tongue into their schools. I am a student who, when I was in junior high school, they told me I could not take Spanish. Why? Because my class that I was in was taking Italian and French. At the same time, there were courses going on in Spanish where I could have easily sat in but, no; I have to take French or Italian.

When I went to my high school, I went to my speech department. I asked them for language could I take Spanish. "Well, have you taken it in junior high school?"

I said no; they would not let me.

"Well, you cannot take it in high school because you did not take it in junior high school."

FUNDS FOR COMMUNITY PROGRAMS

Through student activities, a lot of these things have been changed. I think it is about time that the Federal Government started earmarking funds, not to go to the board of education and be derailed with a nice executive report showing where the money is to be spent, and don't tell me that the Federal Government cannot earmark the money because you can. You do it with highways, you do it with many other programs.

Earmark it for constructive community involvement, community-linked bilingual education programs. Get involved with the local people in the community, find out what our complaints are. You should not have Senate hearings where I have to get an invitation by special delivery mail in order to come down here and tell you the problems because there are many people who are more capable than I am who don't even know these hearings exist and are not able to file their complaints with you.

If you are going to be a representative government of the people, whether they be black, Puerto Rican, Italian, Irish, or whatever they may be, you are going to have to be responsive to them. Not when you call a hearing and you select a few people who you feel are going to give you all the answers because, believe me, the problem in our educational system is much more deep than what I or he or anyone else back there sitting can give you the answers.

The New York City educational system is a failure. When teachers give students a 55, it is really not a mark on the students; it is really on the educational system. They wouldn't even try to let the students mark them because they would be downright failures.

Thank you.

Miss LOPEZ. My French teacher last year—she taught us French for 2 years. Now we are so far behind that we don't even learn anything in our French class. She is absent half a year and we don't learn anything.

Since we wanted to change to Spanish, they told us, no, that we already know Spanish, as they say, but we don't. We wanted to learn our language and they would not let us. Like the French teacher, she was absent half the year and then she did not even know French. Everything she taught us was half wrong and we never learned anything in French.

PUERTO RICAN TEACHERS

Senator JAVITS. Miss Lopez, you said you did have some teachers of Puerto Rican extraction in the school, but they had "sold out." I would like you to explain to us what you mean by "sold out."

Also whether you found that their teaching was more satisfactory than that of the white teachers? Did they speak in Spanish? Did they really do what a bilingual teacher is supposed to do?

Miss LOPEZ. They don't teach us Spanish, just for the people who don't understand English. What I mean by "sold out" is that they act so much—they try to be so much like the white teachers that they are categorized as white people.

Senator MONDALE. We have a rule in these hearings that there are not supposed to be any outbursts. I recognize the intensity of feeling being generated but I would ask you to restrain yourselves.

Senator JAVITS. Would you answer that question? Notwithstanding the fact that you feel that they sold out, as you say, nonetheless would you still prefer to have the teacher who is of Puerto Rican extraction than the teacher who is not?

Miss LOPEZ. Yes, I would rather have a Puerto Rican teacher than a white teacher, because I feel more at home with her, more eager to learn from my own people, knowing that they have experienced what I have.

Senator JAVITS. Thank you very much.

Miss Rodriguez, you wanted to say something?

Miss RODRIGUEZ. Is that objectionable to express feeling?

Senator MONDALE. I was referring to the applause in the back.

Senator JAVITS. Mr. Negron, I was very much impressed with the literate quality of the paper you read, considering the fact that you dropped out of school and had gone through such terrible agony and difficulty. Did you write that paper?

Mr. NEGRON. Yes, I did.

Senator JAVITS. How did you get so competent in the language?

Mr. NEGRON. Self-education. What I know I have learned in the streets. What I am capable of I have gained in the streets.

IQ TESTS

I want to mention some other things also. I have been pretty much involved in community things for over three or four years now. One thing that I recall from my own educational experience is the type of IQ test that is given to you when you are six or seven. At the time I did not know what they were.

I believe they are Wechsler IQ tests and the standard Binet test which is given in English to Spanish-speaking children and that determines the placement, usually in a CM, child with mental retardation.

Now those files stay with the child for a period of something like 7 to 15 years. That automatically handicaps the youth in anything that might come down as an opportunity for the Puerto Rican child.

Also I think that if I had a Puerto Rican teacher, maybe a few Puerto Rican teachers, they would not only be a motivating factor, but I am sure they would have dealt with some of my cultural needs, would have let me know something about my history, let me know about the long years of rebellion for independence in Puerto Rico that was never taught to us in junior high school or in high school.

They would have dealt with my problems of communication and perhaps I would have been able to get a more decent education.

INSTRUCTION IN ENGLISH

Senator MONDALE. You said that you spoke Spanish at home. Your first days in school, I gather, you were taught by white teachers in English?

Mr. NEGRON. That's right.

Senator MONDALE. This is an experience, of course, that I never had and I don't know what it is like, but I would gather that there was a total lack of communication. Could you try to explain to me what that is like when you go to a school and are taught by someone in a different language? What happens?

Mr. NEGRON. I tell you what happens. You feel like you do not even belong there. You wonder what you are doing there. Yet your mother makes you go there. You try to explain to your mother what is going on. You try to explain to your mother you do have a problem in communication, but you still have to go to school.

It is frightening and, believe me, it is really boring.

Senator MONDALE. You did not receive any bilingual education or training at all in your earlier years at school, is that correct?

Mr. NEGRON. One hour a day in elementary school.

Senator MONDALE. In your first year you did get some training in English, is that right?

Mr. NEGRON. No. It started when I finally got to the second grade.

Senator MONDALE. The first year you had no assistance whatsoever?

Mr. NEGRON. None.

Senator MONDALE. Would you say that your language problem prevented you from learning much of anything.

Mr. NEGRON. I didn't learn my A B C's until I was in the third grade and I did not even know that too well.

Senator MONDALE. Was this true of most of your classmates?

Mr. NEGRON. That's right.

Senator MONDALE. What did you do then? You have someone speaking to you in a foreign tongue and you don't understand it. What do you do? Just sit there?

Mr. NEGRON. Try to develop an interest in something else. In my case I developed an interest in drawing and the teacher would always have me in the back of the room keeping me busy so I would not interfere with the process of education of the kids who could learn.

Senator MONDALE. So while they gave you something to distract you, you were not part of the learning process?

Mr. NEGRON. That's right. Otherwise I would be very uncooperative. I would interfere with any of the educational process in the class and I would stop the teacher from teaching. The teacher would either hit me on the head or send me to the principal's office. I would be sanctioned in some way.

Senator MONDALE. Would any of the others comment on this situation? What happened to you the first day you went to school?

Miss LOPEZ. I didn't want to go because I saw everybody was so light, all the teachers were talking English so rapidly. I knew English when I was small, but not very well. But I learned.

Senator MONDALE. So, you had some small understanding of English, but not enough to follow?

Miss Lopez. I followed, but I still——

Senator Mondale. Did you have any bilingual training in the first year?

Miss Lopez. No.

Senator Mondale. Did you have white teachers?

Miss Lopez. Yes, every year.

CLASSROOM DIVERSIONS

Senator Mondale. So your experience was that you just sat there?

Miss Lopez. No, I used to do other things. Maybe I used to get a pass to go to the bathroom and stay there a half hour.

Senator Mondale. What else would you do because you weren't learning anything?

Miss Lopez. Not in the first grade.

Mr. Negron. Play in the halls.

Miss Lopez. Since there was nothing else to do, I used to mark up the walls.

Mr. Negron. When I was not doing artwork, I was fighting. I guess at the time I didn't realize it might have been my retaliating against the system, you see. As a matter of fact, I was often sent to the dean's office my first year in junior high school for fighting.

Miss Lopez. When I was in the fifth grade, a teacher of mine—I guess she took a dislike to me and she slapped me, so I defended myself and then I was the one who got in trouble. I was going to be suspended, but then I explained. They made me get out of school for 2 days. This was only in the fifth grade.

She took a personal disliking to me and she slapped me.

Senator Mondale. Would you comment on this situation?

Miss Rodriguez. When I went to school, my mother tells me I didn't want to stay there. "Look, all these ladies with blond hair, skinny. I am used to seeing you. You are fat and you are never dressed."

When I went to school, I saw these ladies with bleached blond hair. Now even today the teachers "cut us loose." What I mean by that, when we ask a question, they call us "dumb" or "stupid" and they don't answer us. When they address themselves to the white kids, they address them differently. To us they say—like to the white kids they say, "Oh, you didn't understand it," but to us, "I don't know what is the matter with you, are you dumb?"

Where I was, this boy that the teachers were always talking about, one day he was so mad he raised his hand. He wanted to know about Puerto Rico. The teacher sent him down to the dean. What do you think about that?

Senator Mondale. Have you ever had a Puerto Rican teacher?

Miss Rodriguez. No.

Senator Mondale. Never?

Miss Rodriguez. No.

Senator Mondale. Did you ever get any bilingual education when you first started? Did you get any help at all with the English language?

Miss Rodriguez. No. The only thing I got was Spanish and it was taught to me by an Italian teacher.

Senator MONDALE. You got Italian Spanish?

Miss LOPEZ. Yes, and my class was split up in a French group and Spanish group. Not one single Spanish teacher is Puerto Rican or from a Spanish-speaking country. I want to bring out another point.

SPECIAL SCHOOLS: NOT POSSIBLE FOR NON-ENGLISH SPEAKING

There is a special high school, the Bronx School of Science. That is a school where it is supposed to be for smart children. So far in these past 4 years only about 10 students from our school have gotten in.

Senator MONDALE. How many are in the school?

Miss LOPEZ. Two.

Senator MONDALE. Only about 10 students you know have been transferred to the special school.

Miss LOPEZ. In the past 4 years have graduated to that school. That is not from our learning. It is from what is being taught. Everything that we are being taught in the sixth grade they are being taught in the fourth or fifth.

Senator JAVITS. Have either of you ever been given a course in Puerto Rican history or culture?

Miss LOPEZ. No.

Senator MONDALE. Culture?

Miss LOPEZ. No.

Senator MONDALE. Art?

Miss LOPEZ. No.

Senator MONDALE. Never?

Miss LOPEZ. No.

ENGLISH AT HOME

Mr. NUNEZ. I am in a precarious situation because my parents were faced with the problem that they are faced with now. In my household the one thing that was bad, and I regret it now, is that English was always spoken because my parents always told me if I were to get an education, that I would have to be better than anyone else.

So, for that reason I pursued it. I am more articulate, but I am in a position of being like a Philadelphia lawyer in many cases to students who are not as fortunate. For that I have been reprimanded.

One good example was that we have in my school, which is like Bronx School of Science, a specialized school, we have a very serious problem about getting minority students in general in the school. It appears that these kinds of tests they give, there are no marks and everything is kept secret. It is like college admissions.

The only one who knows what is going to happen is the administrative assistant in charge of admissions and a few deans. If you are lucky enough, you can get in there and look over the forms.

Through pressure I have become very active in my school. I have had access a few times to see which students are coming in. You know, the minority students who are coming are in the same position I am. You do not see students in my school who cannot speak English articulately. There is no conceivable possibility for a student such as he who never learned English and never had a good background to get in the school.

When I took the test to get in, they have vocabulary words this long. Even T didn't know them. When I learned, I learned in my special progress class, phonetics, which is not taught to regular students.

Students who do not have a good solid understanding of English will not make it.

Senator MONDALE. In other words in your home they spoke English?

Mr. NUNEZ. Yes, in my home the situation was where my family has been in this country for a long time and my parents were faced with the problem and I can give you an example. They did not know how to ask to go to the bathroom in school, situations like that. They knew the problem that was entailed in not learning the language.

The system when I went, which was in 1956, was not in any way reciprocal or open arms to these problems. You either knew it or you didn't. I was in a position where I was lucky enough to know it. So I did not run into those difficulties.

PUERTO RICAN HISTORY AND CULTURE

Senator MONDALE. Have you ever taught Puerto Rican history or culture?

Mr. NUNEZ. I have been fighting for that for ages. There are only a few Puerto Rico study lessons in the city and those are where students went to strike and threatened to do physical damage to the plant.

In the school I have gone to nothing involving Puerto Ricans has ever been taught. The nearest thing I have got to Puerto Rico up to this year when we got something was Pan–American Day. No such thing as Puerto Rican studies.

I am now taking a course in Puerto Rican studies through a community organization at St. Francis College.

Senator MONDALE. Have any of you been taught by a Puerto Rican teacher?

Mr. NUNEZ. Never.

Miss LOPEZ. I had one Puerto Rican teacher and she was a very sick person. She left the school. I guess another reason she left is because she was not allowed to teach everything she wanted to teach.

Mr. NEGRON. One of the things I want to point out, one of the illnesses that I feel the system is responsible for among black and Puerto Rican children, like I recall when I was in school we used to make fun of each other's parents when they came to school simply because all the heroes we had seen were white. The cop, the crossing guard was white, teachers were white, the principal was white. To us on the television, the Lone Ranger, all you heard was white.

Naturally, when your parents came up, we made fun of them, not realizing what we were doing. It just goes to show that the system has not provided the education that we need to feel proud of our culture. As a result we made fun of each other's parents.

I myself hated it when my parents came to school for that reason.

Miss RODRIGUEZ. I have learned some of my culture from the Aspira Federation. I have asked my social studies teacher can they teach Puerto Rican culture that I am supposed to do on my time?

Mr. Nunez. When she says, "I have learned culture from the Aspira organization," which is a citywide organization, we have been fighting to very little avail, although we have done a few things in certain schools through pressure. I want to bring out one point that must be brought out.

WHITE EQUALS SUCCESS

It not only deals with education, but everything in this country, and that is the bleached white attitude in the educational system. Up until this year—I have not seen the new toys, but you notice in the kindergartens they have these hand puppets. One is a cop, one is a doctor, the other is a nurse. You look at these puppets. You notice they are all as white as the paper here.

Even though it may not be obvious—it is obvious, but it may not be the first impression—if you look at this, you begin to wonder what about all the black Americans, Puerto Rican Americans, orientals, what do they do for a living? They don't tell you that the reason why they can't show Puerto Rican teachers—first of all, that is the first stimulant to really castrate the mental attitude of students.

They have not given you the correct approach, that in America you can't make it unless you are white, unless you fit in the system. You don't see too many Puerto Rican doctors.

Any day you want to take a look, I will mail you a copy of El Diario-La Prensa. You can look at a column that big of doctors. You tell me how many Puerto Ricans or blacks you are going to see because we don't exist and we don't exist because we don't get the education to get the chance. If this is supposed to be a committee on educational opportunities being equal, believe me this committee had better be expanded and you had better put in a lot of money, because you are going to have to rebuild or revise the present educational system or restructure or give remedial lessons to principals who at this present state have reached the stage where they think they can no longer learn, most of them.

WHAT MUST BE DONE

You will have to start from scratch and rebuild not only your physical plants, but your textbooks, your educational process, your syllabuses. Otherwise this problem will continue.

Right now we are here relating the problems. The kids who are in school now may not come here. They may take matters into their own hands.

Mr. Negron. Like the rebels.

Miss Lopez. I want to tell you that I am in an SP class, a special progress. In that class we are learning now what pupils in the so-called white communities have been learning maybe the year before. We are supposed to be special progress.

If you want to call that "special progress," we are behind what the white people are learning. How many Puerto Ricans are up there, I would like to know.

Miss RODRIGUEZ. That is what I wanted to know.

Senator MONDALE. How many on the staff? We have none.

Mr. NUNEZ. We have one Puerto Rican Congressman, that is it.

Mr. NEGRON. I have one more comment. The IQ oral test that determines the learning ability of Puerto Ricans should be given in Spanish or not at all. I think you are going to have to start some bilingual paraprofessional training programs. Also, community control of all schools, because we find that the hiring practices are not on merit, but on seniority. They are not always the best qualified.

Also, we would be able to get some black and Puerto Rican teachers in the schools and you get the parents involved. That in itself would be a vehicle for motivating the youth involved.

Senator MONDALE. Thank you very much. I deeply regret that we can't take more time.

Senator JAVITS. Mr. Chairman, may I say before the witnesses leave, that I think one thing they have demonstrated is that there is no brain drain from the Puerto Rican community. They are all bright, on the ball.

I can assure you that your words have been put in the right place. We will do our utmost to be of help. Any details of whether you are right or wrong about a given subject are immaterial. The point is that massive structural reorganization of education for this group is essential.

We will do our best to help.

Senator MONDALE. Thank you very much.

We will next hear from parents and former students.

If you will proceed in whatever order you wish.

STATEMENT OF MRS. CARMEN ARROYO (AS RELATED BY INTERPRETER)

Mrs. ARROYO. My name is Carmen Arroyo.

Senator MONDALE. Proceed to make your statement.

Mrs. ARROYO (through interpreter). She is the mother of six children and her children are all attending the public school system of New York City and three of them previously had attended the public school system in Puerto Rico.

The first horrible experience that I had with the public school system was when my daughter, who is now 13 years old, but at that time she was 7, came home and the full hand of her teacher was marked on the child's cheek. When I went to the school to inquire what had happened, I went up to the teacher, a white young lady, hair falling down to her waist, who seemed to look at me as if I were a pig.

"LACK OF RESPECT"

She said that my daughter was lacking or not showing the proper respect to her, that my daughter did not behave and that every time she was reprimanded, this lack of respect was shown by her not looking into the teacher's eyes, looking directly into the teacher's eyes, but looking at the floor.

This is a custom, a cultural behavior pattern, and they taught us through years of tradition that when our superior is talking to us or reprimanding us, as a sign of respect we look down and we do not look the person in the eye unless we are directly speaking and holding a dialog with each other. Although it was a bad experience, now looking back at it, I think it was fruitful because it taught me that the American teachers do not teach the children respect or how to respect other individuals and that at the moment what you do learn is that you learn to talk back and be disrespectful to the person.

Today that child, 13, is a good student and I hope with God's help that she might be able to go to college if we can break down the barriers and the walls that now do not permit children from the Puerto Rican community to be educated so that they can attend the higher education institutions just like the white students.

One of the bad experiences that we have in the Puerto Rican community is that when we want to go back to Puerto Rico and take our children with us so that they can go to college down there, they find it impossible to enter the University of Puerto Rico or any other university on the island because they have not been taught Spanish here within the school system and they have become illiterate in both languages, English and Spanish, and they have not been taught anything about their own background.

So they go back with a very definite bad self-image. How do you expect a mother, who cannot communicate with you, as you see, in English properly when I go to school to communicate with the teachers and the principal within that school when none of them can speak Spanish, none of them can communicate with me, I cannot communicate with them except through an interpreter that edits and editorializes and tells me exactly what the teacher wants me to know, not what I should know.

FAMILY PROGRAMS

We need programs for the Puerto Rican family so that we can learn what happens within the school, how the school is structured, and so that we can really find out when we sign a paper what we are really signing for. I don't think that the money that is funded for the educational system should be handled by the same people who teach our children during the day.

What they teach our children is exactly what they want our children to learn and how they want our children to turn out. So that later on in life these children cannot grow up and take their rightful position as leaders or directors within that system and become their bosses.

Senator MONDALE. Thank you very much.

STATEMENT OF MRS. MARIA VALDOQUIN (AS RELATED BY INTERPRETER)

Mrs. VALDOQUIN. I would like to talk specifically about my school. It has 1,700 pupils and 80 percent of them are Spanish speaking. I am the PTA president of that school. I have been the PTA president of that school for the last 3 years.

LANGUAGE BARRIER

I think that at this moment parents are coming much more into the schools, visiting the schools, and it is not because they don't care about the education of the children, but because of the language barrier that they find difficulty. When they come into the school, the principal talks English, the social worker talks English, the guidance counselor talks English. This leads to a lack of privacy because they do not know how to go about resolving their problems.

They cannot communicate directly with the person so that there always has to be a third person present, and that third person then becomes knowledgeable about the private matters of this family and this child.

According to the principals and the teachers our children don't learn because we speak to them in Spanish at home. I have a son whose reading level is above the grade average, much higher. I feel that this is because I have taught him at home to be proud of his own people, his own culture, and I have always talked to him in Spanish and taught him the language.

I had a very funny experience happen. I went to a school to visit and the teacher told me that my daughter spoke English very well and this showed that I constantly must be speaking English at home, because how else was my daughter going to be learning this language?

I believe that if my children were taught in a bilingual program, they would learn both languages and they would learn the other academic subjects more rapidly. If the Puerto Rican child is pushed and oppressed in the school because he constantly speaks Spanish and he is constantly reprimanded for that and he is pushed to speak English, this builds a whole complex, a negative complex about his own language and his own culture, and this does not let him learn.

Senator MONDALE. Let me ask one question.

When your children first went to school, they did not speak English, is that correct?

Mrs. VALDOQUIN. Yes.

Senator MONDALE. What did they talk to you about? Did they ask for help? If so, what went on in the family when they brought this problem home?

Mrs. VALDOQUIN. They always said the teacher told them that I should help them with the school work.

Senator MONDALE. So this probably injured the attitude that the child had for her when she could not help when he needed her.

Mrs. VALDOQUIN (through interpreter). No, because she helped them and she helped the daughter, but she helped them in Spanish and she helped them to learn Spanish and all the other academic subjects in Spanish.

STATEMENT OF GERALDO SANCHEZ

Mr. SANCHEZ. My name is Geraldo Sanchez. I come to you as a father of four children and also as a Puerto Rican. I also come to you as a PTA president.

I will ask you one question. Are you really ready to help us Puerto Ricans after 70 years, or is this another of your exercises in futility?

If your answer is "yes," then help us Puerto Ricans in New York City by finding ways to make the State of New York or the city of New York abolish their New York City Board of Examiners.

We do not believe that the city needs this board. The board of examiners, as you, Mr. Javits, know, was set up by the State when there was no such thing as a New York State Education Department of Examiners.

The State has set up basic standards and qualifications for teachers and supervisors, but New York City has never changed the system. We all know what is wrong with the board of examiners. Many a story has recommended the abolition of the board, but nothing has been done.

Let us do it now and you will be helping the Puerto Ricans in New York State. If you want to help us, give us more bilingual schools. Give us some of the money you send to the welfare treasury of the city of New York. Give this money to the community corporation for them to create bilingual districts, districts controlled by the real community, by parents of the children of the community and not by somebody in downtown city hall, but by us who care for our children.

NEED FOR PUERTO RICAN TEACHERS

We are really interested in this education. Help us by putting in more Puerto Rican teachers as principals and supervisors, so that their children can learn by their example and they know someday they can become principals and teachers.

The Puerto Rican children do not see enough Puerto Rican personnel in places of authority in the school system of New York. No wonder they feel rejected. They are not encouraged to have ambition to follow the steps of great men, and we have great men—Betances, DeDiego, Munoz, and Mario Valdosa, our greatest teacher.

All of this the children should know.

You say you want to help us. This is your opportunity to do the right thing for us, who are denied the constitutional rights that your country gave us on paper in 1917. Let us start a new beginning and let it start with our children really through education, positive action. You have the power and the means.

Let us use it for the benefit of our children and our country.

Thank you.

Senator MONDALE. Thank you very much.

STATEMENT OF RALPH ORTIZ

Mr. ORTIZ. I will speak on three subjects: one as a student in the New York City school system, as a parent, and as a community worker.

When I was in school, I never saw a bilingual teacher. I never was taught Puerto Rican history. The lunch was garbage. When you went to the lunchroom you saw peanut butter sandwiches. If you hit somebody with it, you might give him a fracture, the thing was so hard.

I went upstairs to my classroom hungry. I went home to a cold building, no steam, no hot water. My family was very poor. The only one who worked in my house was my father. We have a family of seven.

My mother used to go to school. She could not relate herself at that time in good English. So my mother could understand when I had some problem I couldn't relate to teachers.

One, the racist attitudes that teachers had at that time. I am talking about 15 years ago, maybe more. They had me the majority of times going to the principal's office for monitor. I didn't have any choice. One, I am a Puerto Rican.

Second is who the hell I am. As a child I had a good memory. I remember a lot of black and Puerto Rican parents used to come to school and try to speak to the principal. The principal could never see them because he was in a conference. The conference means that he was eating lunch. Then if the father or mother wanted to see him, his attitude was to threaten him with the police department. So the parent went home.

I went to junior high school. I never finished high school. I was wondering why kids in my class never knew how to read and write year after year. We never saw Puerto Rican culture books at that time.

They came out with a high school diploma, but they could not read or write their names or read a book. Now Federal money goes into New York City. The whites are qualified. They went to school.

Now how a person could give a person a diploma without having an education. I propose that there should be an investigation in that—I don't care if you look back 20 years—where the money has been going. The State and the city put money in schools. These teachers were qualified and licensed by the State and city. There is no action taken.

When a licensed person gives a diploma to a black or Puerto Rican child, he gets away with it. As a parent I have six children. One of the schools is in district 7, P.S. 51. The reading level there is so bad I think it is 7 percent in the sixth-grade level could read. That is seven kids out of a hundred. It all depends on how many kids they have in the sixth grade level.

COMMUNITY ACTION

The first time I got involved in a community thing was when the principal of that school a couple years ago had his own way. The school was dirty. When the parents used to go there and ask questions why their children were not learning to read, there was no answer. The principal had been smacking kids and using nasty words—"you black bastard," "you spic."

So the community got together. We gave them due process the way the union states. Due process came. They had a district office, you went in there. After all the meetings and hearings they found the principal was doing these things, in other words. What happened was the community took action where he slapped a black child in the face. That is when the community got outraged.

I don't think anybody in the school system has a right to lay hands on a black or Puerto Rican child, any child. I don't give a damn who they are, white, Chinese. So, we took action.

We got rid of the principal. In midsummer the superintendent of the district tried to get him back in that school, the community found out and took action again. With all the due process we gave him, they tried to stick him back in the same school. In other words, the community did not have a say-so, the parents that go to that school don't have a say-so.

The principal could go around slapping the child, kicking him and doing all this kind of brutality to the child, but the Puerto Rican has no right to take over.

PRACTICE TEACHING

You know that in New York when a teacher comes out of college, gets his license, they go on a 3-year probation. That means they go anywhere to teach education. The majority of them are sent to the ghetto area. The reason is that they have to get 3 years' experience.

For 3 years they practice on our children, the next year they are transferred to a white district. What happens then? In 1968 you have 100 teachers coming into the district and in 3 years they are out. A hundred or 200 teachers come out of school, they practice on our children and they go away. And they are teaching nothing to our children.

As a community person I work with a lot of kids. I get involved. I will give some examples in some schools. The guidance counselor, I never saw one yet that is Puerto Rican or Spanish speaking. When a Puerto Rican teacher is in the school and he is the only one in school and it is 80 percent Puerto Rican, they put him in as a dean because he could relate to the children.

After his experience in college, he should be teaching rather than being a dean.

During the school strike 2 years ago a lot of teachers of Puerto Rican descent, Spanish speaking. supported the community. What happened? The union after the strike was over came back into the school and the pressure was on from the principal all the way down. They couldn't function.

The White teachers got together and there were as many as one or two Puerto Ricans in that school and they had no choice but to leave that school and go to a different State or keep on getting a nasty attitude from their colleagues. I don't think that is right.

The board of examiners is all white. They talk about action. I know a lot of Puerto Rican teachers that come from Puerto Rico that go for their licenses. Because they have had some action, they don't get their license. But if you are going to come like that—I don't go down to the southern schools down South, the southerners talk a different way. I can't understand their English.

They come to New York for the pay and they get a license. You have teachers that are supposed to be math teachers and they are teaching English and the kid gets behind. The same thing with science or anything else.

The lunches again. I would like to see some of my native food in the school system. I don't know if there should be a special grant on that. If the whites want to eat white food, that is their business. If the blacks want to eat soul food, that is their business. If the Puerto Ricans want to eat their own food, I think they should relate to that.

HOME ENVIRONMENT

The majority of the people in South Bronx are on welfare, taking public assistance. They live in disgusting homes, with rats, roaches. A lot of them get lead poisoning, their minds are affected by that. They don't have the clothes. The ones that have them just wear them day-in and day-out.

They live in cold buildings. A group like the United Bronx Parents teach these parents their rights in the schools. They teach them how to go to schools and ask questions. A lot of the parents don't have that kind of education, because they are from Puerto Rico, different parts, Santo Domingo, Cuba, so they have a language barrier there. They can't express themselves.

We have an office. They come with problems, we solve them as best we can.

The schools that we have are overcrowded. If they are approved in 1970 and they are supposed to be opening up in 1973 and the population of that school is 1,500, 3 years later the population doubles. That means that the school is overcrowded.

The majority of our kids go half sessions, some a couple of hours. A lot of them are turning into dope fiends, drug addicts. They drop out of school, they have nothing to live for. They can't relate in school because there are no bilingual teachers or principals, assistant principals, guidance counselors.

PUERTO RICAN PROFESSIONALS

If you put more Puerto Rican professionals in schools, the kid could look at them and say, "I am going to be one of those." But now they don't have them in the school. If they do, they have only one. If he wants to relate to the kids more, then the rest of the teachers are trying to find out why. If he is Puerto Rican, then the pressure starts coming in if he does a good job.

I think there should be money, especially for the South Bronx or the city of New York, if you want to put it like that, for people who don't have money to send their kids to school.

I think that is it.

Senator MONDALE. Thank you very much. I regret that I am not going to have a chance to question the panel. Unfortunately it is 12:30.

As so often is the case, we have run out of time. We have two further witnesses.

Senator JAVITS. I would like to thank the witnesses who have gone to great personal trouble to come here. I might say in courtesy to the ladies who spoke in Spanish, I speak a little Spanish and I understood what you said in your own language, but I don't speak it well enough to engage in this kind of conversation.

We are very deeply aware of the problem. Senator McGovern, who is chairman of another committee, and I were in the South Bronx recently. We are working now in an effort to remedy those particular conditions in the South Bronx which are the worst of any except Bronxville in New York, and I think anywhere else in the country.

It is unbelievable, unbearable. Senator Mondale is a man of great humanitarian interest. I can only assure you that we will do our utmost not only to get money, which I think we can get, but to exercise our influence by the use of the money on many of these conditions which you mentioned.

I would like to say to all the parents that I believe that the Puerto Rican community will turn out to be the salvation of New York, because it is the most likely to become the soonest a very productive economic group. But we must make that possible in this way through schooling and other things.

I am very appreciative of your coming here. I just want you to know that you are not dealing with people who are ignorant of the problem or even people who have lived above the problem. I have lived in just the circumstances which you have described. I know them well.

You are helping us to move the Congress to do something really big in this field.

Senator MONDALE. Thank you very, very much for your help.

Our next panel consists of Mr. Luis Fuentes and Mr. Luis Mercado. Both are principals, I gather, in the New York school system.

Senator JAVITS. I must ask you to excuse me while you are testifying. I have to leave. I am due at a caucus of all the Republicans to try to do these very things that you are urging us to do. I will stay as long as I can, but I don't want you to think that I am being impolite if I leave.

STATEMENT OF LUIS FUENTES

Mr. FUENTES. The suffering of the Puerto Rican student in the foreign, cold, and alien classroom environment is an experience that few of you have shared with me or with some of the other people in this room, as Senator Mondale pointed out a little while ago. This child doesn't understand what is going on. This child can't share his own experiences or share in the experiences that other children are sharing in, or the relationships that they happen to be developing together in the classroom.

ISOLATION OF PUERTO RICAN STUDENT

Equally sad is the fact that no one understands what the child is saying, his needs are neglected, his wants go unfulfilled. His ideas, his fears, his customs, his traditions are forgotten. This youngster eventually winds up in the corner of the room with a picture book, as one of the young men pointed out earlier this morning, with orders to learn English, sometimes emphasized by a well-insulated perpetuator of Anglo culture, who thinks that the child can learn English best if the teacher continues to yell louder and louder in English.

Finally, this is the youngster who finds himself isolated in a crowd of 20 or 30 other youngsters and this then becomes the breeding ground for boredom and frustration, and in many instances going beyond, because it also becomes the significant breeding ground for hatred, hatred for the system that has deprived him so severely.

Statistics prove that too few of us have been successful in coping with this educational system which is typical of the "warm welcome"

—I say that in all sarcasm—extended to our youngsters in our schools. Those of us who do make it through the system, the few of us that do, do so because we have learned to ignore the subtle and the overt bigotry; in order to do this you have to be an exceptional individual, and exceptional we are indeed.

But for each one of us who has been successfully brainwashed, and I say that, too, with sarcasm, there are thousands who have been less fortunate or perhaps by some measure, depending on which side of the fence you are looking at, have been stronger in resisting the Anglocizing process.

ANSWER IS BILINGUAL, BICULTURAL EDUCATION

But they join us and we join them in treating with cynicism this so-called democracy and its promise to educate. The sad part about it is that we know at least one of the answers and it has been emphasized here this morning more than once. Our children must be taught not only by teachers who make our children feel welcome and comfortable, but by educators who can understand the child and talk with him and talk with his parents, an educator that will by example, by his mere physical presence give him at least one professional aspiration.

The answer, gentlemen, is a bilingual, bicultural education conveyed and transmitted by bilingual-bicultural educators, an individual possessing these qualities and selected by the community.

Shortsighted educators have labeled those of us that suggest such a program as separatists, but what could be more horrid than the alternative of loneliness, seclusion and isolation? That is what is taught to most of our youngsters in classes today, not only in New York City, but everywhere else where the Puerto Rican finds himself uprooted.

The bullet or the piece of shrapnel that has claimed the lives of many of our young men who are fighting on foreign shores for democratic principles did not ask that young Puerto Rican how little or how much English he knew. The figures in our educational situation and in our educational system speak for themselves and the sound they are making is loud and clear. There are all too few bilingual educators in the city of New York and that is not by mere accident.

In a system that has 65,000 educators where we can only claim a representation of one-tenth of 1 percent, this is no mere accident. The deplorable conditions that prevail in an American city the size of New York with a population of 1 million Puerto Rican citizens and 1 million other Spanish-speaking citizens from 21 other Spanish-speaking countries is preposterous. A powerful and determined force has created this condition and has maintained this unnatural proportion.

OFFICIAL DISCRIMINATION

The only way that a teacher can come into the New York City school system is by way of the New York City Board of Education. Obviously the board of examiners, which is their main arm for keeping us out, has maintained this unnatural proportion. They are joined in this conspiracy by the powerful and infamous United Federation of Teachers, and the equally infamous Council of Supervisors.

The art of saying one thing while doing another is a skill they have highly developed, agreeing with us that there are not enough qualified bilingual educators, while at the same time they are the ones who control the factors, the process and the machine that guarantees that no more than one out of 200 Spanish-English-speaking educator candidates make it through the screening process.

BILINGUAL EDUCATORS AVAILABLE

It is a known fact there are at least 5,000 qualified bilingual educators in the city working outside their profession.

Senator MONDALE. How many?

Mr. FUENTES. 5,000.

Senator MONDALE. You are speaking of Spanish bilingual?

Mr. FUENTES. Yes.

Senator MONDALE. How many bilingual educators educated in Spanish and English are in the public school system teaching courses for which they were trained?

Mr. FUENTES. Approximately 250 in the classrooms.

Senator MONDALE. The public school system employs a total of 250 Puerto Rican teachers.

Mr. FUENTES. That is correct.

Senator MONDALE. Not all of them are bilingual?

Mr. FUENTES. Unfortunately if you have a Spanish surname in New York, you are automatically Puerto Rican.

Senator MONDALE. So that that figure would not reflect the true number of Puerto Rican teachers?

Mr. FUENTES. Yes, sir. Most of these 5,000 qualified educators are working in fields other than education. Many of them have many years of teaching experience. Quite a few of them have state certification, but they have been rejected by the board of examiners because they have accents or they failed to write in a particular English sentence fashion.

Spanish is their main language. Because they are fluent in Spanish is the basic reason why to us they are in heavy demand. But in New York City the examinations are conducted only in English and this year the city has administered for the first time what they are calling a bilingual classroom teacher's examination. Some of us really believed that one of our problems was soon on the way to solution, but most of us knew better.

The contention of the majority of us was confirmed when the examination was actually produced and administered and turned out to be basically another exercise in English with only two questions dealing with Puerto Rican history or culture.

An examination supposedly intended to bring in more active Spanish-speaking teachers turned out to be another frustrating exercise in futility and another way of keeping them out of the system. Dr. Scribner, the newly appointed chancellor of education, has dared to speak out against these injustices and inequities exercised by the board of examiners.

Because he has done this, his resignation has been demanded. They are claiming that he is talking contrary to the State Constitution or the state law, and that he is being led by militants and vigilantes, two words in our community that mean parents.

In Ocean Hill-Brownsville and at P.S. 155 we have demonstrated over the past 3 years that even when funds are not available, if dedication is there, if community involvement is for real, if our real objective is to help our children, then with eagerness and with ideas we can cast aside money and do what has to be done to further improve the educational opportunities for our children.

In that area a handful of Puerto Rican educators—I managed to get seven out of the 200 I sent to the board for examination—a handfull of educators, mostly Puerto Ricans, and a handful of parents joined hands to find ways to help our children succeed.

FIRST BILINGUAL SCHOOL

Forty percent of our school is Puerto Rican. The majority of our parents are black. It was by working with the blacks, who joined us, that we were able to achieve some of the successes that were not available to us under the white power structure. We did commence the first bilingual school in New York City.

The results? Well, our holding power is 95 percent, because kids are learning and parents know it. Our attendance is running something like 98 percent, because children are enjoying the experience of learning and because they do want to go to school. Most significant of all, our children are reading. They learn to read first in Spanish and are gradually phased into English as their English vocabulary and experience is expanded.

By the sixth grade, I am happy to tell you, they can communicate effectively in both languages. In our school all children can talk with teachers. Parents can talk with teachers. Parents can help their children with their homework, at least with the Spanish portion of it. Because of it, parents are taking an active part in all phases of school activities.

Our children are proud of eating rice and beans. Our children are equally proud of talking Spanish and English. Our children have learned about Puerto Rico as well as about Minnesota, Texas and New York. They have learned about George Washington and Albizu Campos.

Our bilingual teachers have learned a great deal of English and English-speaking teachers have for the first time an opportunity to learn a great deal of Spanish.

Gentlemen, the need for bilingual educators is obvious. The only way to bring bilingual teachers into the classroom is to abolish, remove or eradicate the board of examiners, the group that has persistently blocked the entry of these much-needed educators that will benefit our children.

DETERMINED PARENTS

Let us face reality. There are 250,000 ignored Puerto Rican youngsters in that city. They are there whether you like it or not, but there are 1 million parents determined to see to it that they get an education, the education that you promised them, the education that they are entitled to.

We have listened to too much rhetoric. We have gotten promise after promise and excuses galore. We have waited patiently. We have waited too long. We are ready to act. We want you to join us.

Let me point out one thing that might be of particular interest. Perhaps Senator Javits can clarify this a little bit. I understand that there is legislation in Washington and in Albany for the purpose of funding Yeshiva religious schools. I would like to state at this time that as important as this is to the Jewish community, the perpetuation of its ethnic group, its culture, its language, we want no more and no less to perpetuate our language and our culture.

Thank you.

Senator JAVITS. Mr. Chairman, let the record show that I know of no legislation which the witness described other than some special appropriations in foreign aid which don't even help the schools in this country. But I will look into it based on what the witness has said.

Mr. FUENTES. It has taken the shape of released time in New York City.

There is talk about funding it in Albany.

Senator JAVITS. This does not concern the Federal Government.

Senator MONDALE. When were you hired as principal and where?

Mr. FUENTES. In 1967 I was hired, first, by the people of Ocean Hill-Brownsville, then by the New York City Board of Education.

Senator MONDALE. Were you then the first Puerto Rican principal in history in the New York City school system?

Mr. FUENTES. Yes.

Senator MONDALE. I was impressed by what I think is a brilliant statement.

Mr. FUENTES. I was born in New York City of Puerto Rican parents. My father was a Spanish-American veteran serving in the U.S. Navy. I had the good fortune of having had the experience of teaching in Georgia, in Florida, California, and Long Island. After leaving New York I joined the Marine Corps. I hasten to add that in every place I have been I was never asked what my nationality was except in N.Y.C. I enjoyed being a principal in a rural white Georgia school without being labeled a Puerto Rican principal. I am more proud of the fact that I was selected by the people in Ocean Hill-Brownsville than I am of the fact that I was the first Puerto Rican Principal in New York City.

(Complete statement follows:)

PREPARED STATEMENT OF LUIS FUENTES

One thing that distinguishes the New York City educational system from all others is its immensity. Other big-city systems have many of the same administrative shortcomings—inbreeding, over-centralization, buck-passing, over-conformity to rules, crisis management and insulation from parents—but none of them on the same scale.

School officials desperately need more explanations for their failures and more suggestions for reversing such failures than they have received thus far. Some are beginning to realize that time is running out on them and that they had better reform the system quickly before the ghetto unrest leads to rioting and demands to take over the schools, and the white middle class exodus contributes to the final downfall of big-city public education.

The temptation in diagnosing how the schools have failed is to search for scapegoats. Actually, the entire institution of public education is to blame, as are the present conditions of urban life that it confronts. This system cannot work if the bureaucratic structure is not radically altered. State education laws, traditions, rules, and interlocking administrative relationships victimize everyone who comes into contact with the system—parents with legitimate complaints, people applying for teaching licenses, city officials developing community renewal programs, publishers struggling to get their textbooks and readers into the classrooms even after the teachers and principals have accepted them, teachers, principals and children waiting months to receive needed supplies from headquarters. To maneuver through the bureaucratic maze of the New York City school system takes more patience and political connections than most people ever hope to have. In this kind of institution it is almost impossible to innovate. Policy statements are only the beginning of the process. Those who make decisions, even if they are eager for reform, must negotiate with the professional staff to secure compliance with their directives. They must secure efficient coordination of the actions of all units carrying out plans and they must provide rewards and punishments that will ensure compliance, institute performance measures, and evaluate how the plans actually worked. Legal and bureaucratic constraints, however, limit the power of the chancellor and the board over the headquarters and field staff, and reforms mandated from above are seldom carried out as they were intended.

Therefore, gentlemen, we are talking about a school system that is typical of what social scientists call a sick bureaucracy. Caught up in this maze of bureaucracy, injustice, and malpractice are the 1.3 million youngsters in public schools, 55% of whom are black or Puerto Rican. The needs of the Puerto Rican community and its 250,000 children are what we are addressing ourselves to this morning. I must point out that all of the children are the victims of this bureaucratic illness. There are approximately 65,000 professional educators in the City of New York. No more than $\frac{1}{10}$ of 1%, or approximately 250 are educators of Puerto Rican ancestry (born either in Puerto Rico or the U.S. mainland). There are approximately 960 elementary schools in the City of New York. There is not one licensed elementary school principal of Puerto Rican ancestry in any of these schools. For that matter, nor is there one in any of the city's Junior High Schools or High Schools.

The Board of Education, the Board of Examiners, the C.S.A. and the U.F.T. would have us believe that the reason for this is that ours is a recently arrived group. While this migrant factor may be true, there are other reasons for the severe and obvious absence of Puerto Rican personnel. Collusion between the Board of Examiners, the C.S.A. and U.F.T. to deliberately use the examination process for the deliberate purpose of screening out qualified candidates is something many of us have been confronted with. In the past three years, at least 500 qualified candidates of Puerto Rican ancestry have applied for teaching licenses before the Board of Examiners. They have reported numerous cases of intimidation and outright indications of racism. Perhaps one of the most classic of these is the story of Antonia Pantoja, the keynote speaker yesterday and the founder of Aspira. Mrs. Pantoja had her hopes to teach Puerto Rican youngsters in New York City destroyed by what the Board of Examiners referred to as an "accent" that would prevent her from successfully teaching the children. Ironically, Mrs. Pantoja was competent enough to teach teachers at Columbia University but incompetent by Board of Examiner's standards to teach youngsters she felt she could benefit the most.

Mr. Hector Roldan, presently a teacher at P.S. 25 in the Bronx, could tell you a little bit about the negative questions. He was asked what he would do after force-feeding a student on free lunches. Unable to fail Mr. Roldan in the interview because of the hostility he showed to the interviewer, he was indeed failed on the written part of the examination. He was told that he made 22 errors. A careful review of Mr. Roldan's paper revealed only two mistakes. As his principal, I brought the matter to the attention of the Board of Examiners and refusing to acknowledge their error, they suggested that Mr. Roldan present himself for re-examination. Having taken the second exam, the paper was immediately destroyed when he turned it over to the examiner and he was told on the spot that he passed.

Early in 1968, as principal of P.S. 155 in Ocean Hill-Brownsville, I received authorization from my Unit Administrator to do some recruiting in Puerto Rico. A letter was circulated by the U.F.T. stating that I was in Puerto Rico recruiting teachers for my school and for the bilingual program to take jobs away from American teachers. There are many other instances of racism. For example, ESL (English as a Second Language) teachers are still being assigned to classes made up of Spanish speaking children. Only one out of every 200 ESL teachers can communicate with a child in his native language. It is still the belief of most city educators that these "gringos" with their limited bag of techniques and their inability to communicate with the child are a panacea for our problem.

Even in the face of the much heralded Bilingual Act under Title 7, arrangements are being made to circumvent the law by placing ESL (non-Spanish speakers) people as teachers in bilingual classes. As an excuse, the system is saying that bilingual educators (fluent Spanish speakers) are difficult to find. Dr. John B. King, former Deputy Superintendent of the New York City schools, presently Supervisor of Education at Fordham University, has stated that there are at least 5,000 Spanish speaking qualified educators in the City of New York working as waiters, social workers, ambulance drivers, factory workers, many of whom have attempted to return to the work for which they prepared themselves professionally and have either been turned away by examinations given totally in English or because of the well-known fact that they did not stand a snowball's chance have never gone before the first inquiry step.

In 1969, the most incredible act of racism was implemented. Qualified professional Spanish speakers, with many years of preparation and experience, were hired as bilingual professional assistants to do everything that teachers are called upon to do. However, since this was carefully labelled a training program, they were mandated to attend, without remuneration, evening courses in English. Their pay was $5.00 per hour. (New York City gringo teachers are paid $10.15 per hour.) The same year saw the withholding of certificates of competency for anyone with a Spanish surname or with a trace of an accent. However, American-born educators found it easy to apply for and receive this same certificate of competency. This year the system is eagerly promoting a bilingual examination for teachers of elementary grades and another bilingual examination for teachers of early childhood. This examination is 75% in English and only two questions have to do with Puerto Rican culture. The Board of Examiners is hell bent and determined to do exactly what the U.F.T. letter of 1968 said, in order to keep out Puerto Rican educators. I suggest to you, if this committee has the political influence and is seriously concerned with equal opportunity for all youngsters and seriously determined to avoid an uprising of a rejected people, that the following recommendations be strongly supported:

1. The City of New York, in order to meet the needs of its 250,000 Puerto Rican youngsters, each in varying degrees of knowledge in Spanish or English, must infuse at least 10,000 bilingual educators.

2. We further recommend the abolishment of the Board of Examiners, at a savings of 3 million dollars to the city annually. Supportive evidence and references are to be found in the recommendations contained in the Bundy report, Commissioner of the New York City Human Rights Commission, The New York Times editorials of October 1970, and the New York City Master Plan.

3. We recommend State Certification as the only criteria necessary and acceptance of reciprocal New York State Certificates with the certificates of Puerto Rico.

4. New York State legislation is necessary in order to eliminate the Board of Examiners. You gentlemen can bring all pressure to bear upon the Governor and the legislators to bring about the demise of the Board of Examiners.

Senator MONDALE. Mr. Mercado.

STATEMENT OF LUIS MERCADO

Mr. MERCADO. I will read my statement and then I will answer any questions.

I am Luis Mercado, Puerto Rican Community Principal at P.S. 75 Manhattan, 735 West End Avenue, New York, N.Y. 10025. Student population, 1,038. Ethnic breakdown: 45 percent white, 35 percent Puerto Rican and Hispanic, and 18 percent black.

I am a Puerto Rican survivor. It is difficult to explain how I have managed to survive in my 32 years in public education. But I have and I will never surrender. I submit that I have gone to public school in New York City since the age of 4. I spent 8 years in elementary school, 2 years in junior high and 4 years at the Bronx High School of Science. Four years at City College of New York, B.A. degree, graduate studies in sociology; M.A. equivalent and becoming a school teacher in October of 1958 are evidence of my survival.

Many people ask how Mercado in his ten years of elementary school classroom teaching was able to maintain his hope, faith and respect for all our children's ability to learn? My answer is that I have always been proud to be a Puerto Rican and this has helped me. Despite all the putdowns, pressures and attempts to process me, the system has failed. They know, I know and my fellow Puerto Rican survivors (mi raza) here know, that more help is coming as we realize how we have squandered the untold human resources available through an emphasis on the strengths of our minority group values.

OFFICIAL OPPRESSION

Our schools have failed. Our schools are damaged. Our Puerto Rican children are being destroyed. The opportunities must be taken by Puerto Rican peoples to defend our children. The New York City educational system is guilty of complicity in a process which has destroyed the self-image and identity of hundreds of thousands of our children.

Puerto Rican professionals have been harassed, intimidated, purged, weeded out, discarded and prevented from teaching and from supervising the education of our Puerto Rican children. Our Puerto Rican children are the hostages of an unfeeling, unsympathetic homicidal system. This system's sole purpose is to keep Puerto Ricans in their place as inferior second-class citizens.

My own struggles against this perverted unsound educational system and its professional bureaucracy becomes a case history for those of you who wish to understand our peoples' struggle against the educational oppressors.

I believe there is an arrangement operating in the New York City educational-political system. It is based on cronyism, political patronage, corruption and the spoils system. It involves individual members of the New York City Board of Education, the administration at 110 Livingston Street, the Board of Examiners, the Office of Personnel, the Council of Supervisory Associations, the Elementary Principals Association, the Assistant Principals Association, the United Federation of Teachers, and other groups.

Its purpose is to deny equal educational opportunities and professional advancement for Puerto Ricans as teachers or supervisors. This informal arrangement has the support of members of the educational establishment on the Federal, State, and city levels. Puerto Ricans are virtually excluded from jobs or any role, influential or otherwise, in these bureaucracies.

On the basis of my own personal experience in 1969–70, may I state these facts:

1. It is a fact that there are about 490 teachers of Puerto Rican ethnic background in a total teacher population of 65,000 teachers in public schools in New York City.

2. It is a fact that today there are five community principals, all of them acting, who are Puerto Rican, out of a total of 969 in New York City.

3. It is a fact that out of 2,039 assistant principals in New York City ten are Puerto Rican, and these are all acting or temporary.

4. It is a fact that the New York City Council of Supervisory Associations (Board of Examiners) has attempted to remove me as community principal of P.S. 75 Manhattan four—yes, four times—in the first two months of my service which began September 9, 1970. This is an average of once every two weeks.

5. It is a fact that the Council of Supervisory Associations prevented me from assuming the principalship of P.S. 75 Manhattan from April 1, 1970 to September 9, 1970 through court actions against the community, the superintendent and the local school board.

6. It is a fact that Deputy Superintendent Lang, New York City Board of Education denied payment of my teacher's salary during two months and is still denying payment of my principal's salary.

7. It is a fact that Deputy Chancellor Anker and Deputy Superintendent Lang refused to honor a title VII Federal job commitment from July 1, 1969 to September 9, 1970 that ensured my title as Project Director and my salary at $18,000 by "Building Bilingual Bridges," a bilingual education pilot project on the Lower East Side of Manhattan.

8. It is a fact that I have made complaint against Deputy Chancellor Anker and the Board of Education with the New York City Human Rights Commission, charging him with discrimination based on my ethnic origin due to their refusal to honor the terms of my contract.

9. It is a fact that Puerto Rican children and their parents and professionals are being excluded from participation in the title VII building bilingual bridges project by the combined efforts of the educational bureaucracy and its consultants, in violation of the 1964 Civil Rights Act.

10. It is a fact that representatives of citywide Puerto Rican organizations, Aspira and the Puerto Rican Forum, a meeting was denied with the community superintendent of district 2, Elliot Shapiro, to discuss this dangerous situation.

11. It is a fact that we in the Puerto Rican community hold Dr. Elliot Shapiro and the Community School Board of District 2, New York City, personally accountable for the denial of basic human rights to our people.

12. It is a fact that Mrs. Jean Narayan, program officer, U.S. Office of Education, bilingual programs, title VII, made libelous and totally incorrect statements about me personally and the building bilingual bridges project in order to deny Puerto Ricans their rights,

remove Puerto Rican professionals and destroy my career. Dunlap Associates is also involved.

1. I accuse Deputy Chancellor Irving Anker, Deputy Superintendent for Personnel; Theodore H. Land and Dr. Elliot Shapiro, superintendent of district 2; Joseph Steinman, office of business affairs; Helene Lloyd, assistant superintendent and others as being willing accomplices of the Council of Supervisory Associations' continuing efforts to control and oppress the Puerto Rican and Spanish-speaking Spanish-surnamed children living in New York City.

2. I accuse the above of trying to destroy my career.

3. I accuse the New York City Board of Education and the New York City Board of Examiners of pursuing enrollment and qualification standards unlike those applied to cities in New York State and cities throughout the country in order to exclude Puerto Ricans from professional employment.

4. I accuse the New York City Board of Education of having the worst record in the United States of America in terms of employment of minority group members in professional capacities.

5. I accuse the board of education, 110 Livingston Street, and the board of examiners of having the worst record of any major city in the nation in its record of promotion and providing opportunities for Puerto Rican supervisors and teachers.

6. I accuse the educational bureaucracy of having a dismal record and reputation for identifying school leadership, improving standards and finding Puerto Rican candidates to meet them.

7. I accuse the New York City Board of Examiners of discouraging Puerto Ricans from entering the educational system.

8. I accuse the New York City Board of Education and Board of Examiners of having examination procedures for initial appointment as a teacher or supervisor as serving no useful purpose.

9. I accuse the Federal Government of not vigorously enforcing the Equal Employment and Opportunities Section of the 1964 Civil Rights Act.

10. I accuse the members of the New York City Board of Examiners and the Council of Supervisory Associations as having mutual interests which eliminate Puerto Ricans from the hiring and selection process.

11. I accuse the Board of Education of Puerto Rican elimination on the basis of its own census, the statistics for which show that less than 1 percent of the Puerto Ricans in public schools are professionals. In June of 1970 there were only four Puerto Rican principals —three of them acting principals—in the entire City of New York.

12. I accuse the Federal Government of discriminating against Puerto Rican children in its distribution of title VII ESEA funds for 1969–70. Out of a total of $20 million, we have received one-half million, or one-half of 1 percent.

13. I accuse the New York City Board of Education—Board of Examiners of poor minority hiring practices which discriminate against enrolling Puerto Rican teachers and official supervisors in the public school system.

RECOMMENDATIONS

1. A congressional investigation of the hiring practices of the New York City Board of Education and the Board of Examiners.

1.1. The relationships between members of the Board of Examiners and the Council of Supervisory Associations must be investigated to determine the extent that mutual interests play in the hiring and selection process.

1.2. Evaluation of enrollment and qualification standards as compared with those of New York State and of other cities throughout the country.

2. The Federal Government must finance educational programs leading to the enrollment of potential teachers and supervisors.

3. An investigation of the attempts on the part of agents of the United States Office of Education to discourage the rise of Puerto Ricans in leadership positions in bilingual education and in public education in New York City.

4. A vigorous enforcement of the 1964 Civil Rights Act with emphasis on the provisions for equal education opportunity.

5. An investigation of the ESEA Act, title VII Building Bilingual Bridges as to whether the current practices, excluding Puerto Rican children as well as professionals, is a violation of equal educational opportunity and endangers Federal funding.

6. We recommend basic reforms such as the elimination of the New York City Board of Examiners examination and licensing procedures so as to protect the basic rights of all Puerto Rican citizens to equal employment opportunities.

I am submitting for the Congressional Record the following documents: (1) My statement; (2) statement of Parent Association President from New York City; (3) New York Times Article, November 3, 1970 "Three Principals Here Shun Formal Tests" and press statement "Three Community Principals"; (4) report to the Parents Association on P.S. 75 on Case Concerning the Appointment of Principal to P.S. 75 Manhattan; (5) Letter to Dr. Elliot Shapiro; (6) Letter to La Mia Buying Club; (7) U.S. District Court, Southern District of New York, *Boston Chance and Louis Mercado, et al., plaintiffs,* v. *The Board of Examiners;* (8) Parents Association Newsletters 1, 3 and 6; (9) Press statement, June 18, 1970; and (10) Letter to Lang, October 4, 1970.

Senator MONDALE. I will accept those documents and make them part of our committee files.

SUCCESSFUL BILINGUAL PROGRAM

You made reference earlier to efforts at quality bilingual cultural education, which I gather is under your direction, in which you said you only have a 5 percent rate of dropouts, 98 percent attendance, which is phenomenal, I think.

What would be the standard truancy rate?

Mr. FUENTES. In our particular school four years ago there was 65 percent average daily attendance.

Senator MONDALE. So this is really phenomenal.

Mr. FUENTES. Interestingly enough, sir, no. The figures I was quoting pertained to Puerto Rican students. But it is having an effect on the rest of the school as well. We are predominantly a black school, 60 percent. We have been able to achieve a kind of relationship that has had connective good results throughout the entire school. We are up to 85 percent average daily attendance throughout the entire school.

Senator MONDALE. This program is being conducted within this public school, is that correct?

Mr. FUENTES. Yes, sir, without funding.

Senator MONDALE. Do you get any Federal bilingual money?

Mr. FUENTES. No, sir.

Senator MONDALE. You are doing it with your existing funds?

Mr. FUENTES. Yes. We applied for funds, but we were denied funds. In fact, our program has been denied existence by the Board of Education because it did not come from them, it came from us, the community.

Let us not forget that. If anything comes out of Ocean Hill-Brownsville, it is not supposed to have merit. At least this is the thinking of the bureaucracy in New York City.

Senator MONDALE. Pardon my ignorance, the name of your school, P.S. 155, is certainly not a warm term.

Mr. FUENTES. We have another name for 155. It is Nicholas Herkimer, whoever the hell he was.

Senator MONDALE. This is a program which you instituted in your school?

Mr. FUENTES. I did not institute it, sir. The community instituted it. I had to listen to what the people were saying, what their problems were, as a community-selected principal and in an experiment that was community-oriented, I listened to what the people were saying. As an experienced educator, I implemented the kind of programs that would complement what the people wanted.

Senator MONDALE. How many children are in that program?

Mr. FUENTES. In the program itself?

Senator MONDALE. In the bilingual program.

Mr. FUENTES. The bilingual classes are actually one class at each grade level, a total of six classes with an enrollment of 30 in each class. That is a total of 180.

BILINGUAL ALTERNATIVE

Senator MONDALE. You are not reaching all the Puerto Rican children, are you?

Mr. FUENTES. No, sir. All the Puerto Rican children and all the Puerto Rican parents are not interested in bilingual education.

Senator MONDALE. This is an alternative?

Mr. FUENTES. It is an alternative.

Senator MONDALE. How many years have you had that program in operation?

Mr. FUENTES. Three years. We are going into our fourth in January.

Senator MONDALE. So that at your school when a child arrives from a Puerto Rican Spanish-speaking background, there is an option for that child to get bilingual education?

Mr. FUENTES. That's right.

Senator MONDALE. In how many schools of your kind in New York City is that option available?

Mr. FUENTES. I believe it is only a total of three, if I am not mistaken. Certainly not more than four.

Mr. MERCADO. Are you talking about classes or schools?

Senator MONDALE. Schools which offer this kind of quality sensitive bilingual education.

Mr. MERCADO. In terms of quality I will say Mr. Fuentes is correct. However, there are throughout the city bilingual classes that are being formed, not bilingual subject schools.

Mr. FUENTES. Unfortunately too many of our so-called bilingual schools and classes are being conducted by gringo teachers. A gringo teacher is an American individual whose first language is English and then he acquires Spanish. He may be able to communicate, but he can't relate. That is the quality that is missing.

AVAILABILITY OF BILINGUAL TEACHERS

Senator MONDALE. Do you have any difficulty finding qualified bilingual educators?

Mr. FUENTES. No, sir, I had no difficulty in finding them. The difficulty was in getting them through this horrendous process of examination, the board of examiners. The board of examiners seems hell bent and determined to screen our people out of the system.

You know, it is an old story. Let one Puerto Rican in, they all want to come in.

Senator MONDALE. I greatly regret it is 1:05. We have one further witness. I am most grateful to both of you for your testimony.

Thank you very much.

Mr. FUENTES. Thank you, sir.

Senator MONDALE. Our final witness is the President of Aspira. Thank you for your patience.

Mr. NUNEZ. It has been a long morning.

Senator MONDALE. You may proceed as you wish.

STATEMENT OF LOUIS NUNEZ, PRESIDENT, ASPIRA OF AMERICA

Mr. NUNEZ. I just want to make a few comments. I know everyone is getting a little tired of hearing so many speakers.

I think these hearings have been a historic occasion for the future of our community. Unfortunately, I did not see much publicity on it. This morning, for example, I read the Washington Post and the New York Times, and both of them had a cover front-page story, on the fact that there was a plan afoot to reduce the years spent in colleges from four years to three years. That is an idea that has been around with us for some time. I sometimes wonder how the press, the media, assesses the value of news stories.

We are talking here about a community of 2 million people and I estimate that 90 percent of our young people are failing, failing in the system. The educational system does not work. I think it is a national crisis, really.

Senator MONDALE. I despair over this. We had similar hearings on the educational problems of Mexican Americans, who comprise the second largest minority, 6 million. The TV cameramen broke their legs trying to get out of the room when we turned to the subject. I decided that the fastest way to empty a hearing room was to announce hearings on Mexican American education problems.

But I have now found a way to clear a hearing room even faster, and that is to discuss Puerto Rican education problems.

It is a scandal. Here you have two million Americans involved from all these figures and data. It is just an unbelievable tragedy. How are we going to generate the public support that we must if the American public through their press won't even listen to the problem? I don't have the answer to that. I just despair over it.

Mr. NUNEZ. You have heard a lot of anguished statements today. You have heard statements of despair. I think you must understand that our community is despairing. It is sick and tired of what is going on. We who try to present a more reasonable light on some of these problems find out in reality that these problems do exist. The educational system does not want to work effectively with our young people.

I would like to enter into the record a report that Aspira commissioned several years ago entitled "The Losers," which is a composite report of the conditions that Puerto Ricans face around the country. We retained a special education writer to do this, named Richard Margolis. So far as I know, it is the only report that looks at the educational situation of Puerto Ricans on a national level. I think it would be interesting for the committee to have that.

Senator MONDALE. We will include that in the record following your testimony.

Mr. NUNEZ. Fine.

I come to you this morning to talk about two major points. Before I get into them, I recall this morning Senator Javits indicated that there were many issues that were being presented for which the Federal Government did not have a direct responsibility.

I would point out to you that you do have a direct responsibility over the functioning of the administration of the Office of Education and the Department of Health, Education, and Welfare.

NO PUERTO RICANS IN POLICY POSITIONS

There is not one Puerto Rican in the Federal Government at the present time in a policymaking position in any area that I know of. This is on a national level.

In the New York region, the northeast region of the Department of Health, Education, and Welfare, I understand that they have three professionals working, three Puerto Rican professionals, out of 450. These people are in minor slots.

So that, I think the Government has to become more and more concerned with the involvement of our people in the decisionmaking process. This has not occurred, unfortunately.

Two points I would like to cover. One is the issue of the college student, the Puerto Rican college student. I would like to quote briefly from my paper which brings to light this situation because I think it is an interesting phenomenon.

THE EMERGENCE OF A PUERTO RICAN COLLEGE POPULATION

In 1963, there were no more than 300 Puerto Ricans entering college in the United States. In 1970, the entering class numbered more than 5,000 Puerto Ricans. There may now be over 7,500 Puerto Rican students attending over 125 colleges around the country. The statistics are, by necessity, estimates. They are based primarily on our direct knowledge of the situation at Aspira and the fact that we have helped about 3,000 of these young people enter college. No government agency or school system has yet to assume the responsibility for tracking the educational progress of the 1,500,000 Puerto Ricans who live on the mainland.

Significant progress has occurred in the last few years. But, this progress should be measured by the reality that no more than 5 percent of Puerto Rican college-age youth are moving on to higher education. This compares to 45 percent for the general population, and about 15 to 20 percent for the black community.

THE SURVIVORS

This new population in higher education comes to the university with some very special problems and concerns. They are all concerned with the fact that they are the survivors—and I believe you heard that phrase used quite often—this is what we are talking about; we are talking about the survivors here of an educational system which has succeeded in eliminating 50 percent of their group before they completed high school. They are all concerned about the extent of racism in our society.

In a group with a varied racial background, sometimes white, sometimes black or, more commonly, some shade in between, they struggle with racial identity and its consequences. They are also concerned with the future status of Puerto Rico and the questions of the time—whether "Puerto Rico is a slave colony of the United States," or "A showcase for Democracy."

They enter college in a period of general disaffection with the university, its purpose and role in our society. They make increasing demands for courses and programs in the field of Puerto Rican studies and at the same time are anxious that their education pay-off in a job which will break the bonds of poverty.

To appreciate the full weight of the impact this group will have, consider this: There are, right now, as many Puerto Rican students in college as there are college-educated members of the entire Puerto Rican community. Obviously these concerned and troubled young people will have the skills and discipline needed to "make it." They will also have—at least many of them will have—the determination to improve the lot of their own community.

The statistics on college achievement are worth looking at if we are to not be lulled into a false sense of satisfaction. Since the entering class of 1963, there has been almost a 17-fold increase in Puerto Ricans going on to postsecondary education. The figures are: For 1970, 5,000; 1969, 1,700; 1968, 1,300; and 1967, 1,000.

Our studies show that half again as many Puerto Ricans drop out or interrupt their college careers as the general college population.

TWO TO ONE ODDS AGAINST COMPLETION

I should like to interpret that—and, again, bear in mind that only 5 percent of our high school graduates ever make it to college. What it means is that those few who have survived the public schools, who have overcome the language barrier, who have somehow found the money, or who have convinced their families to forego the income they could produce, face odds of 2 to 1 against completing college over the next four years.

I submit that my community cannot afford these negative odds; and, as I am sure you believe, neither can this country. Of course, this belief rests on a very basic American notion. It is that education for the individual is his best passport out of poverty. For our community as a whole, I believe that our richest resource for achievement lies in the young people of the community, itself.

Many of the speakers today and yesterday have pointed out in rather depressing details the plight of our community, the total breakdown in the educational system as it pertains to Puerto Ricans. I would like to think ahead, what are we going to do about this? What can we do about this? What are some possible alternative strategies that we can adopt to deal with these problems?

One, I look at this group of college students and tying in with what I read this morning in the Times about the three years, why couldn't a group at such a college, a sort of emergency college youth corps, be organized to immediately tap into this youth resource, these young college students to start working for our community, benefit our community?

RESOURCES FOR THE COMMUNITY

Senator MONDALE. Most of those college students are bilingual, aren't they?

Mr. NUNEZ. Yes.

Senator MONDALE. They could go back and help work their way through college.

Mr. NUNEZ. I think they should get college credit, get a year's college credit for doing a service of direct benefit to our community.

Senator MONDALE. That is what the Teacher Corps is about.

Mr. NUNEZ. The Teacher Corps, I believe, is composed of people who have already graduated, are already in the system.

What I am advocating is put to use some of these young people while still in college.

Now, we work with young people. We have been working with them for the last 9 years. We find that people are despairing. Young people want to do something. If they are not going to do something constructive, they will turn to the more radical, the militant, because there is no incentive for them to do anything in the structure. The structure keeps them out effectively.

These youngsters are the survivors of the process. They feel guilty. They feel they want to do something. There is an enormous increase in the aggressive instincts of these young people. They want to do something and there is no outlet for them. So, I think something has to be done.

This is a new college community for us. It is pitiful in comparison with the total community but it is a start. But we do have some significant human resources, young people whom we can immediately put to work.

PARALLEL EDUCATIONAL SYSTEM

Now, aside from that, we at Aspira have for the last year been working on what we call the Aspira complementary comprehensive educational system which is an attempt to develop a parallel structure for our community. Rather than us being a supplementary service, we should as a community-based organization begin as an equal component in the educational process in our community.

What I am indicating this morning is that I don't feel that the public school system as it exists today can any longer function, for our community, for any youngster in the inner city. The system is based on white middle-class values and it just does not work for our people. It does not work with Chicanos; it does not work with blacks, American Indians. This is a fact.

We do spend a lot of time doctoring the system, trying to make it work better. One, we have the problem of entrenched bureaucracy; people don't want to change. They are living off the system. They don't want to change anything.

What I am advocating is that we develop some complimentary services. What type of service am I talking about? I am talking about tutoring services. I am talking about counseling services. I am talking about developing courses on the culture and history of Puerto Rico. The community continually demands this of the Board of Education.

What is the result? Grudgingly, they offer it, if they offer it at all. It also happens only after the students practically threatened to burn down the buildings.

Rather than getting into that stress, why don't we adopt a process of contracting out some of the services and give it to someone who wants to do it, who is committed to do it, and let the student take that type of service in a community-based organization.

EARLY CHILDHOOD EDUCATION

Senator MONDALE. What about the opportunity for early childhood efforts; for community-based organizations to become the contracting parties for early preschool training programs? I don't mean programs which intervene at age five, where Headstart begins, but age two, where you could work with children on nutritional problems, health problems and bilingual problems. Wouldn't that be a hopeful strategy?

Mr. NUNEZ. I agree that we should work at all levels, but I do think that the kind of educational policy focusing on preschool early childhood is wrong in the sense that I don't give up in our community.

The fact that our youngsters are dropping out of high school, are not completing even junior high school in some of the cities around the country, does not mean that they are finished. I have known people completely uneducated by the system, who through personal efforts have gone back and finished.

I am not prepared to write off all the young people in the schools, the junior high school students, high school students, and say we have to start off in the preschools because everything else is so bad off. As a matter of fact, the city university this year has taken in students who obviously, although they have a paper indicating that they have a high school diploma, by no stretch of the imagination would you consider them high school graduates. There is an expectation and a quiet confidence that they will be able to help them to become effective college students.

As a member of the board of higher education, we have had this dialog for 3 years, back and forth, what to do. The themes have been repeated constantly throughout these hearings, one saying that it is not the responsibility of the University to concern itself with the problems of the high schools. We decided it was the responsibility of the university to begin to salvage Puerto Ricans who otherwise would never go to college, we could not wait for the high school system to straighten itself out.

What I am indicating is that a complimentary system of education is an immediate possibility, that we can start in the next year developing these complimentary services that have to be recognized as another component, another input into the educational process.

INDEPENDENT COMMUNITY SYSTEM

Now, I am not talking about contracting services from the board of education to a community-based group. I think that process is all wrong and that is what goes on, to some extent. I am talking about an independent system of community-based educational services that are directly funded.

What I am trying to indicate at the moment is that no matter how much we improve the school system, how much we try, we need the community-based component to succeed with this community. This is what is lacking in the present system.

We have to have more bicultural educators, we need more effective bilingual education. The implications of bilingual education have not even begun to be assessed.

There was a study commissioned by the Office of Education several years ago, "Bilingualism in the Barrio," which was a $300,000 study which concluded in the foreseeable future Puerto Ricans will remain a bilingual people. Has the educational thinking of the school system been affected by the study? Nothing happens to change the system. The studies are filed away.

Right now the only experiments involving bilingual education are in the elementary schools. If we are talking about a truly bilingual community, we are talking about having these courses in junior high schools and in the high schools and in the colleges. If we want to develop this, unless we are cynical and want to try some stopgap method, we must have more than 3 or 4 years of bilingual education and then go on to do something else.

ALLOCATION OF EXISTING FUNDS

I think the Federal Government can begin to take some leadership in this area. It does not really require even additional funds. There is a billion dollars that goes into title I, $300 or $400 million that goes into title III, moneys that are being poured into the systems to work with the disadvantaged. Now, part of that money, a significant part of that money, could begin to be turned over or earmarked for this type of services. It does not require an enormous sum of money.

The problem here is that we are talking about having an institution that the community recognizes as their own. The community does not have any confidence in the school system. It has no confidence that we are going to do something.

Senator MONDALE. We have talked about setting aside say, 10 percent of title I funds for directly funded community-based education, which would be distinct from the local education operation. We have heard pleas for this kind of management from the Mexican Americans. I think that is what you are suggesting.

Mr. NUNEZ. Yes; I think at least that amount.

Senator MONDALE. As a matter of fact, it is interesting that, by all odds, the best bilingual education programs almost always are programs that have been set up by the community-based organizations because they understand the language and are not devoid of culture.

On the Navajo Reservation, the Navajo Reservation Bureau of Indian Affairs said they could not teach children Navajo because there were no Navajos who wanted to teach. They did not want to teach in the Bureau's system. But when they set up a system of their own in Rough Rock, in 1 year they had more Navajo teachers coming out to the reservation to help out than the whole Federal apparatus had in the history of the BIA.

They wanted to teach in a system of integrity that they felt was sympathetic and enthusiastic about the Navajo language and culture, their own people.

Mr. NUNEZ. In a city like New York or in a city like Chicago or Philadelphia, I don't think the solution of our problem would be to set up a separate school system.

Senator MONDALE. The Rough Rock thing is a separate example.

But you could be, as you say, counseling, advising, outside bilingual education.

RELEASED TIME CONCEPT

Mr. NUNEZ. Yes; the concept of released time is appropriate here. Why couldn't the youngsters be allowed to take two hours to go to one of our centers to take history and culture? These things could be done.

What I am suggesting is that public schools as they are organized today don't have to remain that way. Something has to happen in this area.

I think the Federal Government can take an initiative in this. Obviously, it is not coming from the State governments; it is not coming from the cities. The educational bureaucracy is trying to hold on to what they have. They are paralyzed with the disintegration of the system and there are no new initiatives.

I think the community-based apparatus will do a lot to lessen the tension. The people will feel that they have a real stake in the system. Part of the system will belong to them. Now we see attempts to take over the system and the system is resisting being taken over. The present situation cannot go on any further.

(Discussion off the record.)

Mr. NUNEZ. When I quote statistics that 300 Puerto Ricans went to college in 1963, one can see that our community has grown from that period to now but not that much. Now we have 5,000 going. I am sure that even then in 1963 there were 3,000 or 4,000 youngsters who could have gone to college if somebody had sat down with them and said, you deserve to go to college, your marks are at the level you can go to college. That wasn't done.

SUCCESS FOR PUERTO RICANS VITAL TO NATION

Even the pathetic progress we have made, we have made through struggle; enormous struggle. The picture has been painted very darkly in the last several days but it is a dark picture, Senator. It is unfortunate that the Federal Government until very recently has not concerned itself with this. I think it is important. It is important for our Nation that our people succeed. We just cannot remain at the bottom as we have been and we cannot perpetuate our society, our community, at the bottom as it is now. Our community is not accepting that. It is awakening.

The concept of the Puerto Rican as being a docile Puerto Rican is ending. You have seen the changes today and it is mild. You should have had the hearing in New York.

Senator MONDALE. This was very easy today.

Mr. NUNEZ. The people are desperate. They are angry. They are injured. They have a right to be. The system does not work for us.

Senator MONDALE. Really, what we are talking about today, particularly what these young students testified to, is just as dramatic in its own way, just as destructive as, say, starving a child.

As a matter of fact, it is probably worse because it carries a personal insult. Hunger is a sort of neutral thing. Yet, the side does not seem to respond in an emergency sense, and it is an emergency.

When children are being systematically mangled, destroyed in this way, not given a chance, it is an outrage, an indefensible situation for a rich and powerful society like ours to continue it. It is not just those children.

COST OF EDUCATIONAL FAILURE

American society loses millions of dollars, if you just want to hear a commercial, billions of dollars worth of talent. I sometimes would like to have some economist figure out what it costs American society for every one point in an IQ that is lost through a bad school system. I bet you nationally it is $10 billion a point.

Many of these kids, as you know, are bright, full of hope and within 4 years they are candidates for subnormality. It has happened throughout the country.

Mr. NUNEZ. Senator, what you say is very true. I am trying to look for solutions. This is what I get paid for, to try to look for solutions.

The Office of Education has to straighten itself out about Puerto Ricans. I put in a proposal for a study on the emerging Puerto Rican college population. I put it in conjunction with the city university research foundation. It was turned down on the basis it was not basic research.

We traced the $10 million that comes into New York for research grants and not one community-based group gets any of that money. There is nothing in the law that prescribes it but the people who are working in the Office of Education, these departments, are the same people who are receiving the money on the outside. They know that in another few years they are going to go back to the college and be on the other side.

You say, well, couldn't a non-Puerto Rican understand the situation?

ADMINISTRATIVE INSENSITIVITY

I am saying that there has been developed in the New York State Board of Education and HEW an insensitivity on the part of administrators. We have good people; we are not ashamed of them; they have the academic qualifications; they are aggressive; they want to change things but they are completely destroyed by the system.

You just saw two principals here this morning. They are bitter men as a result of the fight they have gone through to break through the system. They reflected the despair in our community. If these two men are having all these difficulties in just doing their job, and there is every indication that they do the job 10 times better than the average principal in our city, what about the other people, the people who didn't graduate from high school? What are they supposed to do if these men are having the troubles that they are having?

I believe with you and the rest of the committee that you can develop new initiatives. There is a need for legislation here. I know the Federal Government has a commitment to the whole area but I don't think it has ever thought of it until very recently in these terms, that the community must be given a controlling role in part of the delivery of educational services.

Thank you.

Senator MONDALE. Thank you very, very much for a most useful statement.

I don't think you read your full statement. I have read it. So, let us put it in the record at this point.

(The full statement follows:)

PREPARED STATEMENT OF LOUIS NUNEZ

My name is Louis Nunez and I am the president of Aspira of America, a national, Puerto Rican non-profit organization with affiliate agencies working in the cities of New York, Chicago, Philadelphia, Newark and San ·Juan. The major purpose of our organization is to develop the leadership potential of the Puerto Rican community through education.

I am also a member of the New York City Board of Higher Education; the governing body for the City University of New York; a member of the Board of the National Urban Coalition; and the National Reading Council. I am also a member of the planning committee, task force on race and minority problems of the White House Conference on Youth. For the last 8 years I have been intimately involved in the development of educational and counseling programs at the high school and college level which will be of benefit to our youth.

I speak to you today concerning a new phenomenon in higher education, the emergence of a significant number of Puerto Rican students in colleges and universities around the country. In 1963 there were no more than 300 Puerto Ricans entering college in the United States. In 1970 the entering class numbered more than 5,000 Puerto Ricans. There may now be over 7,500 Puerto Rican students attending over 125 colleges around the country. The statistics are by necessity estimates. They are based primarily on our direct knowledge of the situation at Aspira and the fact that we have helped about 3,000 of these young people enter college. (No government agency or school system has yet to assume the responsibility for tracking the educational progress of the 1,500,000 Puerto Ricans who live on the mainland.) Significant progress has occurred in the last few years. But, this progress should be measured by the reality that no more than 5% of Puerto Rican college age youth are moving on to higher education. This compares to 45% for the general population, and about 15 to 20% for the black community.

This new population in higher education comes to the university with some very special problems and concerns. They are all concerned with the fact that they are the survivors of an educational system which has succeeded in eliminating 50% of their group before they completed high school. They are all concerned about the extent of racism in our society. In a group with a varied racial background, sometimes white, sometimes black, or, more commonly, some shade in between, they struggle with racial identity and its consequences. They are also concerned with the future status of Puerto Rico and the questions of the time—whether "Puerto Rico is a slave colony of the United States" or "A Showcase for Democracy." They enter college in a period of general disaffection with the university, its purpose and role in our society. They make increasing demands for courses and programs in the field of Puerto Rican studies and at the same time are anxious that their education pay off in a job which will break the bonds of poverty.

To appreciate the full weight of the impact this group will have, consider this: There are, right now, as many Puerto Rican students in college as there are college-educated members of the entire Puerto Rican community. Obviously these concerned and troubled young people will have the skills and discipline needed to "make it." They will also have—at least many of them will have—the determination to improve the lot of their own community.

The statistics on college achievement are worth looking at if we are to not be lulled into a false sense of satisfaction. Since the entering class of 1963, there has been almost a 17-fold increase in Puerto Ricans going on to post-secondary education. The figures are: for 1970—5000; 1969—1700; 1968—1300; and 1967—1000.

Our studies show that half again as many Puerto Ricans drop out or interrupt their college careers as the general college population. I should like to interpret that—and again, bear in mind that only 5% of our high school graduates even make it to college. What it means is that those few who have survived the public schools: who have overcome the language barrier; who have somehow found the money; or, who have convinced their families to forego the income they could produce, face odds of 2 to 1 against completing college over the next 4 years.

I submit that my community cannot afford these negative odds; and, as I'm sure *you* believe, neither can this country. Of course, this belief rests on a very basic American notion. It is that education for the individual is his best passport out of poverty. For our community as a whole, I believe that our richest resource for achievement lies in the young people of the community itself.

A word here about our experience with colleges is in order. Basically, there is room for our students in the country's college system. In 1963, there were fewer than four million college students. This year there were over six million. Clearly, ways are being found to make room for somebody. This same system which has expanded itself by 50% in seven years can and must redouble, and then redouble again within the next five years, its enrollment of Puerto Rican students. If it did that, where would we be? We might be just about on a par with the college enrollment of the black population today.

It must also be noted that the major increment this year in enrollment stems from the new open admissions policy of the City University of New York. We do know of some 125 other colleges, state and private, which have, during the past few years, accepted one or more Puerto Rican students. But, for the most part, the country's private colleges have yet to make the special effort needed in this area. The students do need help in reading and verbal skills. Again, the colleges have the capability for giving this help; and, when motivated or challenged or prodded, they do deliver.

Thus, what I am suggesting are two basic priorities to achieve more rapid progress: 1) Focus on the student's individual needs while still in high school and 2) follow through with the students in college itself.

The stakes here are very high. The young people in college—and I see this all the time—are determined to improve their community. If it isn't done systematically; if some orderly method for change isn't offered to them; if they can't work toward achievable goals, then they will follow some other route. Learning can be a dangerous thing. It may be a tool for building. Or it may be a weapon for destruction. I believe the students want to use their education constructively and there are ways in which this can be done.

What is the community the students want to work in and want to help? It is poor, fragmented and isolated. Over half of the Puerto Rican community in the continental United States is either below or just barely above the poverty level. Their educational level is the lowest of *any* ethnic or racial group in the communities where they reside. The students see with great clarity that this situation can and must change. We as a community must be given the basic assistance necessary to help ourselves. Through creative self help programs, we must be able to develop educational services that will change this. I would like to cite the case of the Puerto Rican Forum to illustrate the concept of creative self help.

Early in the 1950's a group of college-trained second generation Puerto Ricans organized an association to explore their individual experiences in "making it" in our society. They wanted to know whether they could be used to develop a broad program of service to the community. A volunteer group, it was some time before the ideas crystallized and a mode of operation developed. The conclusion that began to emerge was that if a community was to progress, it must begin to develop its *own* institutions and its *own* agencies to deal with its priority problems. The concept that those who had already broken through the poverty barrier had a responsibility to the less fortunate members of the group, became part of the working philosophy.

Although self help as a concept is an established feature of our community, it required a fresh perspective in the light of the enormous expansion of the government in the field of social programming. The Forum decided to create a private non-profit leadership development agency concerned with the development of a group of new leaders for our community. Youngsters would be aggressively recruited and trained, and an ethical commitment would be instilled in them to assist in the solution of the group's problems. The agency was developed and Aspira opened in 1961 in New York, supported by five foundations. In 1966, in keeping with its philosophy of creating new institutions in our society, the Puerto Rican Forum developed a Board for Aspira and spun it off as a completely independent agency.

Today this agency has grown to a national organization with five affiliate agencies. It has been the major factor in materially increasing the number of Puerto Ricans going on to higher education.

I think it is important to note that the agency was created by Puerto Ricans, is directed by Puerto Ricans, and serves Puerto Ricans, but is supported by the private sector, city and federal government, the Commonwealth of Puerto Rico, and the general community. One might raise the point how can this be considered self-help if the organization is essentially supported by outside sources. The crucial factors in this concept of creative self help included the following: a community group assessed its own needs, organized its own people, set forth its own programs, then went out and got the necessary funding and during the whole process maintained control over the institution.

I say to you today that one of the major problems in all of the educational support programs which the federal government has developed in the last few years is that essentially all of the funds have gone into an educational system in our inner cities that gives no evidence of making any significant progress to change the grim prognosis for our community. The current system of public education, as it operates in our urban centers, is unable to serve the special needs, interests, and problems of the young people it is meant to educate. Puerto Rican youth in particular are deprived of their right to adequate education by systems which seem to work effectively only for middle class whites.

Throughout the life of a young Puerto Rican he is frustrated at virtually every step in the education process. Non-English speaking children often receive academic instruction in a language they do not understand, and fall behind their classmates; Puerto Rican parents, caught up in the day-to-day struggle for survival, and awed and confused by the administrative maze with which the school system confronts them, fail to bring their influence to bear; school teachers, less than 1% of whom are Puerto Rican, in general look upon the Puerto Rican Child as a problem that they are barely trained to deal with.

Clearly the school systems have failed to effectively assist Puerto Ricans to make use of the educational opportunities as evidenced by the fact that nearly 50% drop out before completing high school in comparison to a national average of 15%. The established educational system, boards of education, the parochial school system, the colleges and universities have demonstrated no significant or effective commitment to the special needs of Puerto Ricans; they have shown no ability to create or carry out effective programs for culturally alienated groups and after years of abortive efforts, we have become convinced that the existing system is incapable of providing the educational services which will result in producing a generation of Puerto Ricans at the same educational level as the rest of society. The communities' lack of confidence in the system, the lack of commitment on the part of staff to significantly effect change, the rigid bureaucratic organizational structure, the rising demands for effective community participation make it mandatory that alternate strategies be developed.

Among some of these new strategies being proposed are those of performance contracting and the voucher system. Donald Rumsfeld in a recent speech eloquently pointed out the fear and hostility with which professionals view these new initiatives. He said, "In spite of our best efforts to date, the educational system remains relatively ineffective from the standpoint of the poor." Yet criticisms of the Office of Economic Opportunity's experiments in education have been voiced by some special interest groups. I doubt that these people speak for most teachers. The critics fear experimentation because it may call into question their dogmas and their orthodoxies. They seem to be embarked on a crusade to stifle efforts to gain new knowledge to improve. The defensiveness that has characterized the criticisms indicates all too clearly the need for new actors in educational policy planning roles.

Community based and controlled educational institutions which would offer certain educational services to Puerto Ricans could clearly be some of the new factors in the educational process. Let me cite an example. We at Aspira offer educational counseling services to high school students. Our experience over the last nine years indicates that the young people that come to us show no evidence of ever being counseled or that if they were, it was almost always negative. Why couldn't this service be officially turned over to an organization such as Aspira which has demonstrated its effectiveness in this area. Rather than our services being supplementary and grudgingly acknowledged as an incidental contributor, these services could be seen as an integral and complementary part of the established system.

I wish to be very clear on this point; I do not advocate the elimination of the public school system as it exists today. What I do say is that education has gone beyond the pupil-teacher relation and that in the myriad special areas such as counseling, tutoring, parental involvement, special courses on Puerto Rican culture, leadership development, that a community-based group could do a much more effective job. At the very least we would know when we are failing; something the educational system itself has yet to face up to.

I think also of this new emerging Puerto Rican college population and its vast potential for our community. These thousands of motivated young people could be tapped even while still in college to begin putting in time working on behalf of their community.

Everyone is concerned with youth today and its increasing radicalism, but aside from the Peace Corps and the Vista programs which appeal to middle class youth, no real thought has been given to the emergence of this new minority youth group. Young people want to feel that their efforts count, that they will not have to go through a mind dulling apprenticeship before they can do significant work of value to their community.

I would suggest also that the present organizational structure for the delivery of educational services, with its rigid requirements as to who is able to teach and counsel are not sacrosanct and that they developed out of a need to protect the people in the professions. The requirement that someone possess at least a bachelor's degree to teach in the public schools and that one have an advanced degree to teach on a·higher level have not been of any apparent value to our community. Of course I realize that we will not be able to change the nature of the educational bureaucracy overnight. What I am suggesting is that a parallel, complementary, community-based institution be developed to deliver certain crucial services and that perhaps they can do a more effective job.

New initiative must be taken to get away from the impasse we have reached in the school system. Programs should ultimately be judged on the basis of the final results. The present educational system does not work for our community. I would strongly encourage you to look to support initiatives such as those I have suggested today.

Senator MONDALE. Thank you very, very much, and the rest of you for a most useful morning.

We stand in recess until tomorrow morning.

(Whereupon, at 1:35 p.m., the committee recessed, to reconvene at 10 a.m., Wednesday, November 25, 1970.)

EQUAL EDUCATIONAL OPPORTUNITY FOR PUERTO RICAN CHILDREN

WEDNESDAY, NOVEMBER 25, 1970

U.S. Senate,
Select Committee on
Equal Educational Opportunity,
Washington, D.C.

The committee met at 10:25 a.m., pursuant to recess, in room 1318, New Senate Office Building, Hon. Walter F. Mondale (chairman of the committee) presiding.

Present: Senator Mondale.

Also present: Senator Schweiker.

Professional staff present: William C. Smith, staff director and general counsel; and A. Sidney Johnson, deputy staff director.

Senator MONDALE. The committee will come to order.

We are privileged to have Senator Schweiker from Pennsylvania this morning to introduce our first witness.

Senator SCHWEIKER. Thank you very much, Mr. Chairman.

I apologize for the delay. We are holding a Veterans' Committee meeting upstairs and I am a member of that. I will have to duck out of here later for that.

It is a real pleasure and privilege to introduce a Pennsylvania constituent who has been very active on bilingual group problems as posed by the Puerto Rican community in Philadelphia.

Mr. Ralph A. Franco has been a specialist in the Office of Intergroup Education, Community Affairs, School District of Philadelphia. He is very knowledgeable and expertise in this area. I welcome him to the committee and I look forward to hearing his testimony.

Senator MONDALE. Mr. Franco, we are pleased to have you with us here this morning.

STATEMENT OF RALPH A. FRANCO, BILINGUAL INTERGROUP SPECIALIST, OFFICE OF INTERGROUP EDUCATION, COMMUNITY AFFAIRS, SCHOOL DISTRICT OF PHILADELPHIA

Mr. FRANCO. Mr. Chairman and honorable Senators, it is indeed a great responsibility and privilege to come this morning to speak to you on behalf of my people from Philadelphia and its neighboring towns of eastern Pennsylvania.

It would be so good to be able to speak about positive results to you at this time. It would give me a comfortable feeling to say to you that the Puerto Rican children are learning so much in our public schools and that they are fast becoming part of the American dream, whatever that is.

It would be great to be able to say that our children love school and remain there from kindergarten to college, because the school system is doing so much for them.

Yes; it would be nice to be able to say all that ·but, gentlemen, I cannot, because the opposite is the truth.

ECONOMIC FACTORS

Education and training determine skills marketability; while interrupted education is an individual and family problem, it has implications for delinquency, employment, and social welfare services. (Burton Weisbrod, "Prevention of School Drop Outs", *Measuring Benefits* of Government Investments, ed. by Robert Dorfman (Washington, D.C.: Brooklings Institute, November 1963).)

A low level of education can be correlated with a similar level of employment and income. The 1960 census showed the Puerto Rican population of Philadelphia as having the highest level of unemployment, the lowest level of income and the lowest level of education of any racial or ethnic group in the city.

DEMOGRAPHIC INFORMATION

Only 9 percent of the Puerto Rican population over 25 had finished high school as opposed to 24 percent for the black population—in the United States, 70 percent of the population graduates from high school. Median family incomes can be similarly compared. Puerto Ricans earned an average of $3,435. Blacks earned a median family income of $4,248. (Arthur Siegel, Harold Delans, Loyal Greer, *Puerto Ricans in Philadelphia* (Philadelphia: Commission on Human Relations, 1959).)

Philadelphia has been the home of 71,200 Spanish-speaking people as of September 1, 1969. Of these, the reliable estimate of Puerto Ricans is 65,000. (Charles Unanue Associates, *The Spanish Speaking Market in the United States* (New York: unpublished market study, 1970) exhibit III. Information on estimates was gathered from telephone conversations with Mr. Unanue, personal contacts with Mr. Luis Diaz-Carlo, late of the Puerto Rican Forum in New York City, and personal contact with members of the Philadelphia Puerto Rican community.) The median age of the Puerto Rican population in New York is between 20.5 and 21 years. (Charles Unanue Associates, *The Puerto Ricans of New York State* (New York State Commission in Human Rights, 1969).) There is no reason to assume it is any higher in Philadelphia.

It is probable that the number of Puerto Rican children of school age is much higher than 7,021—it is close now to 8,000—the figure given by the school system for Spanish-speaking students in the public school system during the 1968–69 school year.

LOW ENROLLMENT, HIGH DROPOUT RATE

The parochial school enrollment for Puerto Ricans is small, probably under 2,500. The exact figure is either not compiled by the diocesan school system or unavailable to the public. So far as eligibility is concerned, probably a full third of the Philadelphia Puerto Rican population should be in school. They are obviously not. This, coupled with a drop out rate of 65 percent among Puerto Rican students, paints a dismal picture for the educational enfranchisement of Philadelphia's most alienated community, the Puerto Rican students. (Direct Communication with Dr. Bernard Watson (former Deputy Superintendent of Policy and Planning) in an interview for the Community Relations Service, United States Department of Justice, August, 1969.)

The aforementioned data gathered by Mr. Alex Vasquez, a planning specialist in the Planning Office of the Philadelphia School District, is reliable and exact. I must add that by working in the past as a minister and teacher in Lancaster, by visiting and keeping in touch with colleagues and friends in Reading, Bethlehem, West Chester, Coatsville, I have seen that the lot of the Puerto Rican and his schoolchildren is exactly the same there as in Philadelphia.

The Puerto Rican population in Lancaster, Pa., has grown tremendously in the past 5 years. I have been informed by sources there that it is over 5,000. There are no Puerto Rican teachers in the schools and no special programs, but problems that the school officials seem unable to solve.

Bethlehem has a Puerto Rican population of 8,000, the largest minority group in that city. Nine hundred children are enrolled in the public schools and there is one Puerto Rican teacher in the system.

The other cities already mentioned have the same number of Spanish-speaking people in some smaller or larger number. All have the same common problem in the schools. The school officials and teachers are desperate because they are not prepared to teach these recently arrived "foreign children." They fail to understand their own American history. The school districts are failing these children, because they are trying on them the same old methods that have failed English-speaking children.

LANGUAGE BARRIER

Imagine the situation of children who cannot speak the language used as the teaching medium. The child newly arrived is tested in a foreign language (English) and is given objects to identify that he has never seen before in his life. The language barrier becomes the first obstacle.

Due to the fact that the child cannot communicate in English, he is branded as retarded, slow learner, uncooperative, et cetera.

Senator MONDALE. Would you yield there?

Senator Schweiker, we have two distinguished Spanish-speaking educational experts. We have several but two of them, one is Dr. Palmarez from California, a Mexican American; the other is soon to be Dr. Martinez, who is completing his work at Harvard.

Both gentlemen spent several years in grade school in the subnormal class. Martinez was in a dumb class for three years.

This underscores that here are two geniuses, really, who, because of language difficulties, were rejected by their school systems and dumped into dumb classes. It is easier to handle such a child by putting him in a dumb class.

Proceed.

TEACHER ATTITUDES

Mr. Franco. Teachers become upset because of the language barrier, frustrated, and many times get angry at the child because he sits in the classroom and vegetates. One principal was so angry that he said right out to some of his colleagues, "Who the hell sent for them? They should stay where they belong."

It is fortunate that I wasn't around there at the time. It is hard for teachers to realize that without the knowledge of the language it is hard to communicate.

Teachers' expectations and attitudes have been the cause of many children to drop out. After a while, teachers don't expect these children to learn much and that's exactly what happens. They may learn the language and speak English fluently and still the teachers' expectations are very negative.

Many counselors call in the pupils and their advice most of the time is to forget about college, to go out and get a job because they will never make it in college.

I can cite here an interesting case of a high school girl who graduated with very good grades. Her counselor took the college application that we gave to her and the thing disappeared so that when it was time for her to go to Temple University she didn't have an application. We finally got an application and she is in college today.

MELTING POT CONCEPT

The old concept of the melting pot is another arm of destruction for the Puerto Rican in the schools. Teachers and administrators have the already stale idea that once in America you must become an American, whatever that is. Becoming American to many is to forget your native culture, language and identity and be whatever the rest of the people are. In many cases, it is impossible to find out what they are.

We Puerto Ricans are very proud of the fact that we are Puerto Rican Americans and want our children to be both and be the better for it.

The disease of racism in the mainland has taken its toll among our children and adults, for that matter. Our children come from an environment of mutual respect and warm feeling toward everyone regardless of skin color, religion or political background.

In Puerto Rico, we have all shades of skin color; yet we are not black, white, red, or any other color; we are Puerto Ricans, members of the human race. But as soon as we come to the mainland which is our country, in the space for race they put an "X". To some, we are nonwhite; to others, we are nonblack. Pray tell what do they want us to be?

Our children in the schools are very upset by the treatment full of racial prejudice they receive by both black and white teachers. I must say that there are exceptions.

In many schools, English as a second language has been taught to help the children who do not speak English. In many cases, depending on the dedication and preparation of the teacher, the pupils have been helped tremendously. In other cases, I have observed the children pick up the badly used phrases that the teacher may use in Spanish from time to time and the child comes out with a confusion of languages that it is very hard to know whether he is speaking English or Spanish. The English as a second language program is funded by the title I Education Act.

The most widely accepted theory to better educate the Spanish-speaking child, and the one we have put our hopes on is the concept of bilingual education. That is teaching the child in both his mother tongue—in this case, Spanish—and in the newly adopted tongue—English, in our case.

PHILADELPHIA BILINGUAL EDUCATION PROGRAM

Under title VII, various school districts have received Federal funds for the experimental stage of the program. The only district that receives such fund in Pennsylvania, to my knowledge, has been Philadelphia. No other place gets it. Here the program is looked upon favorably and the first year's research has shown that the program may be successful.

Many parents, administrators and even teachers are still confused as to the philosophy of the program. You see, not much information has been given to these people about these bilingual programs. Many old-timers, firm believers of the melting-pot concept, are against it. In Philadelphia, the grassroot parents have not been involved in the bilingual program.

The parents must be fully informed and involved to have this worthwhile effort have the success we expect it to have.

In many cases, the programs are monopolized by a central foreign language office and the personnel involved may not be as trained and qualified as they should be. Usually, they are run by English-speaking Americans, who do not allow qualified Puerto Ricans to use their experience for fear of losing full control of the bilingual programs.

There is a change of history these days and it is time that the Puerto Rican educators, themselves, be involved in the education of our children. There is too much "hands off" policy by the white establishment, and everyone else wants to run the program of educating our children, leaving out the Puerto Rican educators.

By the way, now everyone is an expert on bilingual education; everybody is writing about. I won't go into that any further.

In some cases, the people involved in the development of curriculum and materials for the bilingual programs have no qualifications to be in such positions, but the directors, hoping to save money and to avoid competition by experts, hire such people, paying them a low salary, thus damaging the progress of the children who should get the full benefit of the programs, still throwing the old dry bone so that the Puerto Ricans can entertain themselves while the money is going some place else.

LACK OF LOCAL, STATE AND FEDERAL REPRESENTATION

Puerto Ricans have been left out, not only city and statewide, but also nationally at the Federal Government level.

In the State of Pennsylvania, in Harrisburg, there is not a single Puerto Rican in the Office of Education, the department of public education, nor do we have a Puerto Rican in the Office of Human Relations.

In the Office of Health, Education, and Welfare, we have no Puerto Ricans employed. There was one in the Office of Education, the only one they hired and because of the lack of funds, he was laid off. As soon as funds are diminished, the first ones to go are the Puerto Ricans.

A Committee of Mexican Affairs was set up some time ago. After much hollering by Puerto Ricans of the eastern seaboard, the name was changed to Committee of Spanish-Speaking American Affairs. There hasn't been much change since the office of migration, education, et cetera have staffs with other Spanish-speaking people and the Puerto Ricans have been left out.

RECOMMENDATIONS

I recommend the following:

1. That one or two Puerto Ricans be employed by the Office of Education in Washington, D.C., and please do this before a big demonstration group comes here and starts screaming. The Puerto Ricans don't like to scream. We don't like to speak dirty but I think we are running out of patience. Even a minister has to say hell and damn and worse from time to time. We are running out of patience.

2. That a committee be set up to check the bilingual programs and keep directors and personnel in line with recommendations and guidelines set up by the Federal Government governing those programs.

3. Provide Federal funds under title VII for cities with a large number of Puerto Rican students which are not receiving funds at this time, and need the programs badly.

4. Provide funds for the creation of teacher-training institutes for English-speaking teachers with Puerto Rican students in their classes, so that they may learn how to handle these children and teach properly.

5. The directorship and supervision of federally-funded bilingual programs be in the hands of qualified Puerto Ricans and not in the hands of people from the white establishment, or the black establishment, for that matter. It should be in the hands of the Puerto Ricans because we should have a say in the education of our children.

6. Put pressure on school districts who are receiving Federal funds for programs to set up local offices of Puerto Rican affairs so that the Spanish-speaking community may become involved in the education of their children, and that other departments may not become the clearing house of Puerto Rican education in those districts.

7. Put pressure on local districts receiving Federal funds for bilingual programs to set up an office for the operation of those programs instead of having them as a sideline of other offices within the central district office.

In Philadelphia, the Foreign Language Office is the clearing house for the education of the Puerto Rican children. The director is a good lady, director of the pilot program, director of the continued education program. She is director of everything. She has a few Puerto Ricans working for her instead of working for the Puerto Rican children.

Senator MONDALE. Thank you very much for a most useful statement, and most specific recommendations.

Senator Schweiker?

Senator SCHWEIKER. Mr. Franco, how long have you been associated with the Philadelphia situation, either in this capacity or some other way?

Mr. FRANCO. I started first in Lancaster and I spent 5 years there. Then I moved to Philadelphia and I have been in Philadelphia close to 6 years. In Philadelphia, I have served both as a minister, a social worker, and now in the capacity of bilingual intergroup specialist in the school system, working both with the community and the school administrators.

Senator SCHWEIKER. How long have you been in this position as a specialist?

Mr. FRANCO. I have been in this position close to 3 years now, sir.

PROGRAMS IN ATTITUDE AND APPROACH

Senator SCHWEIKER. You have been in Pennsylvania and working closely with this problem for some years. Do you see any change at all in either the attitude in Philadelphia or the approach or have you still a long way to go? How much progress since you started are we making? I gather we have a long way to go from what you have said in your statement. I must say it is a good statement and I concur with it and I hope the committee will take your recommendations and incorporate them in their report. I think they are very good.

But, have we made much progress at all in Philadelphia, or not?

Mr. FRANCO. To say that we have not made progress would be a lie. We have made some progress. It has been a small step that the teachers who are involved in the education of Puerto Rican children have accomplished through great efforts.

The pilot school, the research done in this past year has shown that the program can be very successful. However, more information has to flow from the central office to the parents of the children, even to the principals in the schools. I am called from time to time by principals asking me, "Franco, do you know what is going on because we don't?"

You see, this is something new. In order to be successful, we have to educate and set out some kind of instruction to the English-speaking principals and teachers involved in the program. But our hopes are in the program now because I think it is going to work.

Senator SCHWEIKER. Did anybody hold your position before you assumed it as specialist, or was the position set up with you?

Mr. FRANCO. This position was set up by the superintendent of schools; the office of community affairs was set up about 5 years ago. I got in the office as a miscarriage of nature, so to speak. Up to this point, it is very hard to try to communicate with people, because with the establishment when you have an accent that puts you out on a limb; it does not matter how much education or how much expertise you have, as soon as you open your mouth and you show that you have an accent, the administrators become at least hesitant to really let you be involved in policymaking.

Senator SCHWEIKER. What do you have to work with presently in Philadelphia? In other words, in your job as a specialist, what tools have they given you to work with, what do you have, if anything?

Mr. FRANCO. I can work directly with the district superintendents where they have a large number of Puerto Rican children. Also, I am working with the principals. I am setting up staff development conferences for the teachers involved. I also have taken on to myself to keep in touch with the different experts nationwide so that I can take expertise into Philadelphia. I also have the community.

We intend to educate the Puerto Rican community to stop being so passive and so docile and come out and start asking for what is theirs. I am working on this level with the community, giving them the information that we have about the programs in their schools, also with the young people.

Those are my tools.

PUERTO RICAN TRAINED BILINGUAL TEACHERS

Senator SCHWEIKER. What about bilingual teachers with Puerto Rican training? Do you have any of those in the public school system or the parochial school system?

Mr. FRANCO. Yes, sir; we have some of those with the career ladder program. Some teachers have been trained; teachers with a high school diploma and 2 years of college, and above have been placed in the classrooms to teach Spanish-speaking children. They have been accredited by the State. They have an emergency certificate and they are still working towards their bachelor degree, and others are working toward their master's.

Also, I have been going to Puerto Rico and different places, trying to steal already qualified teachers to help us in the system.

Senator SCHWEIKER. How many teachers would you have in Philadelphia that would fit this category, roughly?

TRAINING INSTITUTE

Mr. FRANCO. From the so-called bilingual institute, the career ladder program, we have 60 teachers; 20 that were trained last year, and 40 that were trained this year.

Senator SCHWEIKER. How many do you think you should have to do the job right?

Mr. FRANCO. We should have these teachers there but we should also have at least 50 fully qualified teachers who are fully bilingual, who know the culture of these children so that they can continue to work as teachers and also move into administrative positions because at this point we don't have any Puerto Ricans as principals or superintendents or anything else, only teachers.

Senator MONDALE. Would you yield?

Am I correct that one of the problems in bilingual education is that many outsiders do not realize that a language is also a culture?

When you train, for example, a white person to be a bilingual teacher to an all-Puerto Rican class, she may learn the language but she may not be able to relate because she doesn't understand the culture that is wrapped up in it. So, a lot is lost in the process.

So, I would like to ask, if I might follow up Senator Schweiker's question, how many of these people being trained do you think are capable, really capable?

Mr. FRANCO. The 60 that have been trained?

Senator SCHWEIKER. Who can relate to the culture and the whole problem.

Mr. FRANCO. Yes; they can because the career ladder program was aimed mainly at Puerto Ricans and people with a Spanish-speaking background. In that program, we have Puerto Ricans, Chileans, using the Latin American background. The majority of them are Puerto Ricans.

It seems that the other ones can come in and really take in the culture of the Puerto Ricans and they are relating, they are relating very, very well to the Spanish-speaking children. I am talking about the 60 that are involved in this career ladder program.

Senator SCHWEIKER. This program that you described, where is that operating?

Mr. FRANCO. That is operating in Philadelphia.

Senator SCHWEIKER. Who set that up?

Mr. FRANCO. That was set up by the office of foreign languages in the school district.

Senator SCHWEIKER. How long has that been operating?

Mr. FRANCO. Two years. It is federally funded. This is also another program from the office of foreign languages. District 5, being the largest district Puerto Rican-wise, close to 2,000 to 2,500 are involved in these special programs.

Senator MONDALE. So that, well over half of the children are not getting any help at all?

Mr. FRANCO. That is right.

Senator MONDALE. What happens to those kids?

Mr. FRANCO. Well, they just vegetate around and usually by the time they become 14 and 15 and 16, they are still in the fourth or fifth grade; they decide that there is nothing for them in the school system, and it is best to drop out and find a job—$30, $40, $50 a week for them is better than just sitting in that classroom with a teacher that cannot communicate with them.

MANY BILINGUAL PROGRAMS INEFFECTIVE

By the way, the reason I am pleading with you to check the bilingual programs is because the continued education program under this bilingual umbrella is providing education for junior high school Spanish-speaking children and high school Spanish-speaking children but many times the materials set up are not adequate and even though they may be in the program they tend to go in the mainstream of the dropouts.

Again, I don't want to condemn this too much because this has been in operation only 2 years, 1 full year, and the beginning of the present school year. We have to give it a chance, but we must have other experts involved there, possibly Puerto Ricans, to help set up a good curriculum and provide good teaching materials.

I am sorry to have to give you such a long answer.

Senator MONDALE. Now, your second recommendation calls for a committee to check on the bilingual program. I believe I am correct that there is a national advisory committee on bilingual education in the Office of Education today.

Are there any Puerto Ricans on that committee, on that advisory committee?

Mr. FRANCO. There is one.

Senator MONDALE. Thank you very much.

Mr. FRANCO. Thank you so much for the opportunity to appear before you.

Senator MONDALE. Our next witness is Mr. Hernan LaFontaine. the first president of the Puerto Rican Educators Association, who. I understand, is the principal of the bilingual school, P.S. 25. I hate that P.S. 25. Can't they call these schools something else?

STATEMENT OF HERNAN LaFONTAINE, FOUNDER AND FIRST PRESIDENT OF PUERTO RICAN EDUCATORS' ASSOCIATION, INC.

Mr. LaFONTAINE. The reason we call it that is that it was the first one in the city and in the northeast region. Perhaps it was a lack of imagination but it does describe the school.

Senator MONDALE. You may proceed as you wish.

Mr. LaFONTAINE. During the past few days, you have heard from a number of my colleagues and fellow Puerto Ricans regarding the tragic situation in which our Puerto Rican community finds itself. It is clear from their testimony that Puerto Ricans have been relegated to the lowest level of economic, social and educational poverty.

Coming from "El Barrio" or Spanish Harlem in New York City, I have survived through the painful realities of this poverty. Being a professional educator now, I am witnessing an equally painful reality of educational failure.

EVIDENCE OF EDUCATIONAL SYSTEM'S FAILURE

The most distressing aspect of the system's inability to educate our Puerto Rican pupils is the ubiquitous evidence that equal educational opportunity is not being provided to our pupils. The massive retardation in academic achievement, the astronomical dropout rate, the inability to provide effective programs to overcome the language barrier and the very small percentage of Puerto Ricans going into college are all manifestations of the inequality of educational opportunities.

At the very least, it is suspicious that in a vast public school system of over a million students, it is the Puerto Ricans who are constantly at the bottom of every aspect of educational progress.

There is no doubt that there is a myriad of factors contributing to this tragedy. We can mention the harmful effects of negative attitudes on the part of teachers, supervisors and other school personnel, the overt and subtle racism practiced in the schools, the rigidity of a bureaucratic and impersonal structure, the dehumanized and insensitive nature of such a vast school system, the lack of appropriate and effective programs and materials and the lack of Puerto Rican personnel to provide appropriate role models for the children.

All of these are certainly crucial factors affecting our children.

However, today I would like to focus on the effect of financial resources on education. I want to make it clear that I do not by any means consider that money is the panacea to all of our educational problems. And, yet, it is obvious that many educational improvements and innovations require additional financial support for effective implementation. Many a sound and promising educational idea has been aborted because of a lack of adequate funds.

I especially want to discuss some of the problems which we have been concerned with regarding the financial support of education for the Puerto Rican child.

Since the days of Sputnik I, we have seen an unprecedented nationwide interest in education followed by equally unprecedented injections of massive amounts of money for education. The questions which come to mind quickly to anyone investigating this issue are: (1) How much money should we spend? (2) Are we getting our money's worth in educational productivity?

Theoretically, the answer to the first question should be that we must spend as much as is necessary to provide for all of our educational needs. Practically, we know that the answer to this question depends greatly on how well we are using the funds already allocated to education.

We cannot continue to demand more and more money without making an accurate assessment of the impact of existing funds on the improvement of education.

In New York City, the public school system receives large amounts of money from a variety of sources and we still don't seem to be satisfied with the results of the programs funded from these sources. During the 1969–70 school year, approximately $174 million were available from Federal sources and more than $72,400,000 from state sources. This is in addition to the $1.6 billion already in the overall expense budget from city tax levies.

We have to admit that these are very large expenditures, but we also have to ask what proportion of this amount is directed to and received by the 250,000 Puerto Rican pupils in our schools, including the 118,000 pupils who are classified as non-English speakers.

These data are difficult to obtain and I have had to carefully review the board of education's summaries of funded projects to determine approximate figures.

Senator MONDALE. Would you yield there?

I asked yesterday for estimates from some of the witnesses from New York City as to what percentage of Puerto Rican children were not proficient in English.

Would you say that classification of non-English-speaking students is low, that a much higher number, in fact, would have substantial difficulty with the English language when they come to school?

Mr. LaFontaine. This is a fairly accurate figure. Actually, that 118,000 pupils includes other students who are not Puerto Rican.

Senator Mondale. In other words, .there would be Mexican Americans, Cubans, et cetera, also Puerto Ricans. So that, of the 250,000 Puerto Rican students, maybe 100,000 are proficient in English, in the English language?

Mr. LaFontaine. Roughly, because it comes out roughly 95,000 or so Puerto Rican pupils.

Senator Mondale. That is a much higher percentage of English-speaking Puerto Ricans than I had thought was the case.

I asked this question. It was a little difficult question. What percentage of the Puerto Rican children entering the first grade are proficient in the English language?

Mr. LaFontaine. That is a little different.

Now, in the first grade, for example, in my particular school we have students coming in who are mostly proficient in Spanish. We, of course, have to classify the children by language dominance because of the nature of the program. We find, for example, that our students are approximately 85 percent Puerto Rican and out of that I would say that more than 50 or 60 percent are dominant in Spanish.

Now, some of them know Spanish and English but are still more proficient in Spanish and others speak only English.

Senator Mondale. Given a classroom of teachers in English, what percentage of the Puerto Rican children are from a linguistic point of view ready to learn; in other words sufficiently proficient in English, so that it is not a barrier to them?

Mr. LaFontaine. I would say that would be a negligible percent.

Senator Mondale. That is the point.

So that, maybe 5 percent are ready to move right along?

Mr. LaFontaine. Right.

Senator Mondale. We had four students here yesterday from New York City. Of the four, only one had grown up in a Puerto Rican family which spoke English and he felt he was proficient in English when he started school. The other three had had no English.

Mr. LaFontaine. Right.

I might add, linguistically speaking, that the child who comes to school when he is 6 years old has had 6 years of communication in Spanish. He certainly cannot be expected to be at the same level as one who has had all his background in English.

Senator Mondale. Right.

PERCENTAGE OF FUNDS FOR SPANISH-SPEAKING

Mr. LaFontaine. Of the State funds allocated to New York City under the Office of Urban Education quality incentive programs, approximately $881,000 were earmarked for programs specifically designed for Spanish-speaking pupils; that is, bilingual programs, ESL, Puerto Rican history and culture, language division, et cetera.

An additional $1,254,000 were allocated under the urban education community education centers for similar programs. The total of

$2,134,300 represents only 2 to 3 percent of the entire urban education state aid of $72.4 million.

Of the Federal and special State funds, we counted approximately $2,580,000 earmarked for programs for Spanish-speaking children. This is roughly one to one and a half percent of the total allocation.

Don't forget, we are talking about a student population which consists of some 22 percent Puerto Rican pupils.

Looking at the statistics for the distribution of city funds, we find that the per capita costs vary tremendously from district to district and even from school to school. Unfortunately, again we find that schools with high percentages of Puerto Rican pupils generally have the lowest per capita costs.

I would like to underscore one specific area of educational funding since it is of special interest to me professionally, and it affects our children very directly. I am referring to bilingual education.

TITLE VIII, ESEA

The Bilingual Education Act, or title VII of the ESEA, was approved by Congress in January 1968, but it wasn't until late in 1968 that appropriations were actually authorized. This delay meant that programs could not begin until September of 1969. Meanwhile, the experts' recommendation of a need for approximately $40 million to establish such programs was virtually ignored.

Senator MONDALE. Is that a national figure?

Mr. LaFONTAINE. National.

Senator MONDALE. When we extended the ESEA Act, Senator Javits, myself and Senator Yarborough increased it to $80 million. I think at the end of the act we had it up to $250 million. But we are appropriating clearly under the authority.

Mr. LaFONTAINE. Yes; the authorization is much higher than the actual appropriation. In fact, I mention here the final appropriation amounted to a ridiculous $7.5 million for the entire nation. Of this total, about 18 percent went to programs designed for Puerto Rican children in cities across the Nation. In New York City, only two projects were funded for a total of $369,000.

My own personal experience with title VII as implemented through the New York City Board of Education has been most disappointing.

To begin with, I literally had to submit my own individual proposal directly to the U.S. Office of Education to assure that someone would read it. A cover letter from the superintendent of schools was obtained and sent later, after it was apparent that our proposal would be considered.

Since then, numerous problems have arisen because of administrative difficulties at the central board of education headquarters. Requisitions for books and supplies have been erroneously returned many times; little or no central accounting has been kept by central headquarters, and a general state of confusion has existed regarding all fiscal matters related to the title VII projects.

This week, on Monday, as a matter of fact, after one and a half years of operation under title VII, I was assured that virtually all of these problems would be resolved in the immediate future.

This situation is just one of many problems we are concerned with regarding the whole area of educational funding. Generally, we can indicate that there aren't sufficient funds allocated for education as a whole. The reduction of funds for title I programs drastically affected our Headstart programs and the number of paraprofessionals working in the classrooms as educational assistants.

I have already indicated that the distribution of those funds presently available is clearly inequitable and does not reach our Puerto Rican student population. As we saw, this applies to Federal, State, and city funds.

METHOD OF DISTRIBUTION

The method in which Federal funds are distributed is also unsatisfactory. In New York City where a decentralized system is supposed to be in operation, the bulk of Federal funds is still controlled by the central board of education.

In many cases where funds have ostensibly been decentralized, the central board virtually mandates the continuation of programs which have been centrally operated. This immediately reduces the actual amount of money with which community districts can establish their own programs. In other cases, such as my own title VII project, the administrative bureaucracy of central headquarters creates so many problems that one must summon all of one's energy and patience to keep from becoming totally demoralized in the process of overcoming all of the obstacles.

The problems of improper timing and of delays in receiving approvals for grants pose another difficulty which exists at all levels and which causes untold waste. It is not unusual to be informed that a particular proposal must be written and submitted within a week. Immediately, everyone involved is pressed into a superhuman effort in order to meet the deadline.

More frustrating, however, is the fact that after submitting the proposal, many months may pass before notification of approval or disapproval is received. Too often, approval is received long after programs are scheduled to begin, causing delays and extreme confusion. Personnel cannot be hired, materials cannot be purchased and, worst of all, students do not receive the services intended for them. When approval is finally received, the last minute planning and hurried decisions which are made lead to a disorganization which results only in inefficient and poor quality programs.

UTILIZATION OF FUNDS

Another significant problem is related to the actual utilization of funds. Of course, we have all heard of gross malpractices in the use of Federal funds, such as the construction of swimming pools for middle-class schools with money earmarked for disadvantaged children, but many of the malpractices are far more subtle.

Supplies which arrive after programs have been terminated usually do not reach the intended target group. Money which is specifically allocated for books for non-English-speaking pupils is distributed under limitations which actually negate the very purpose for the allocation of the funds.

An example here is the fact that we were prohibited from buying library books in Spanish because they were not on the "approved" board of education library book list. All of my letter-writing and telephoning to rectify this situation was in vain.

A drastically more serious incident occurred when I first organized our bilingual school in 1968. A proposal for a comprehensive research project which I had submitted—again under last minute pressure—was finally approved in May of that school year. Mind you, this was submitted in August. I got the approval in May.

I notified both the New York City Board of Education and the New York State Department of Education that because of the extreme delay in receiving approval of the proposal, I planned to implement the project the following school year. In spite of the fact that the State department of education agreed to carry over the funds into the next fiscal year, the New York City Board of Education refused to allow this modification.

After many heated discussions with central headquarters personnel, I was informed that the money was being utilized for other purposes. To this day, I still do not know where or how this money was spent. Considering that the project was budgeted for over $100,000, I must maintain that this action was tantamount to grand larceny.

ACCOUNTABILITY

Certainly, if we are going to expect any improvement in our schools from the input of massive funds, then we must at least see to it that these funds are used properly. Strict attention to the concept of accountability is especially essential today.

Accountability is also necessary in the area of community participation in matters related to funding. Most government guidelines regarding funding include some provisions for community advisory committees or other similar groups. Unfortunately, it appears that the term "advisory" usually means that these groups have no real authority to participate significantly in making decisions. They may suggest, recommend and advise, but they may not decide what direction the education of their children will take. This apparently is only for the "experts" to decide.

In New York City where the Puerto Rican community has been struggling to achieve community control, it is particularly important that funding procedures be carefully monitored and, hopefully, strengthened to insure a meaningful role for community residents.

PUBLIC INFORMATION REQUIREMENT

Some of the problems which I have already mentioned come about because not enough information is conveyed to those individuals and groups with the greatest need to know. The extent and the nature of the available financial resources are generally unknown to teachers, principals, parents and community groups.

I believe that a wealth of innovative ideas can be found among all of these people who are in daily contact with children and who are intimately familiar with their problems and their needs. Therefore, these persons should be aware of the many possibilities for supporting and implementing any sound educational program which they may design.

At present, the whole realm of educational funding is a mysterious and complex system which sometimes does and sometimes does not treat them kindly. Without exaggeration, there are many principals who walk into their schools in September to discover that they have been "blessed" with a funded program. And shame on them should they dare to refuse such beneficence. In the meantime, many community groups are searching desperately for funds to establish exciting and valid educational programs in and out of the schools.

I hope that I have been able to describe at least some of the problems with present funding practices. These, of course, affect all schools and all children, but they have a particularly devastating effect on our Puerto Rican pupils in New York City and in other cities across the nation.

From these problems, we can suggest that special emphasis be placed on the following recommendations:

RECOMMENDATIONS

1. Federal and State granting agencies must make every effort to insure that a higher proportion of available funds are earmarked specifically for Puerto Rican pupils.

2. In New York City, provisions should be made to allow for the allocation of funds directly to community school districts.

3. Granting agencies must insist on strict adherence to guidelines for accountability of funds. Provisions should be made for followup action on the proper and efficient use of funds.

4. Granting agencies and school districts should be made accountable for the efficient and expeditious processing of proposals and funds.

5. Present regulations should be modified to allow for community participation at the decisionmaking level.

6. Procedures for publicizing the availability of funds should be revised to assure a broader dissemination of information.

EQUAL JUSTICE

May I conclude by saying that the Puerto Rican community in one sense is indeed very wealthy. That is, in spirit. And we are going to use this wealth to create more wealth, that of educational excellence. The financial resources we seek are merely a vehicle for the attainment of this excellence. But we come before no man with hands outstretched. We ask only for that very elusive "equal educational opportunity."

In the words of a famous Puerto Rican leader: "Yo no pido que me den. Solo que me pongan donde hay."

Senator MONDALE. Can you give me a little bilingual help on that?

Mr. LaFONTAINE. It simply means, "I am not asking to be given anything; I just want to be put where the opportunity is."

Senator MONDALE. In other words, the issue is not charity but justice.

Mr. LaFONTAINE. That is right.

Senator Mondale. Tell me a little bit about P.S. 25. How many students? What percent are Puerto Ricans?

BILINGUAL SCHOOL

Mr. LaFontaine. We have approximately 900 students. There are about 85 percent Puerto Rican pupils. The other 15 percent are black pupils who are in the program to learn Spanish as a second language.

Senator Mondale. Is that a special school dealing only with bilingual education?

Mr. LaFontaine. That is right. The entire school is a bilingual school.

Senator Mondale. How did you happen to set up a separate school for this purpose?

Mr. LaFontaine. It comes from a demand from the community, basically. We have been involved for many years in educational activities in New York City and every conference dealing with education of Puerto Ricans generally came up with a recommendation that our children should be taught in Spanish as well as in English so that in the South Bronx the community residents and leaders, parents, got in touch with the superintendent of the district, Dr. Barnard Freedman, made this kind of demand, and he in turn asked the community, the local school board, which also approved, and the school was established. That was in May of 1968.

I was selected to head that school, to organize it. It just so happened that there was a building available which was going to be an annex of a new building that was set up so that we took that building and we set up the entire thing from scratch.

Senator Mondale. Does this include grades 1 through 12?

Mr. LaFontaine. Kindergarten through sixth.

Senator Mondale. Now, this has been in process now for two years?

Mr. LaFontaine. That is right. We are starting off our third year.

Senator Mondale. Can you tell us how this arrangement is working, in your opinion?

MEASUREMENT OF SUCCESS

Mr. LaFontaine. At this moment, I can just give you a subjective opinion. You see, for example, several evidences. One, the children are anxious to go to school. The attendance figures are the highest in the District. This past month was 90 percent.

Senator Mondale. What is the city-wide average?

Mr. LaFontaine. I don't know.

Senator Mondale. That is clearly over the city average?

Mr. LaFontaine. I would say so.

This is one indication that the children want to come to school. They enjoy being there. There is a minimum of disciplinary problems. Every school has some problems but we certainly don't have the kind of thing which occurs in many other schools which actually interfere with instruction.

Senator Mondale. How many of the instructors are proficient in bilingual education?

Mr. LaFontaine. The entire staff is bilingual; everybody.

Senator Mondale. What percentage of your faculty are Puerto Rican?

Mr. LaFontaine. I would say there are 28 Puerto Ricans out of about 50 on the staff.

Senator Mondale. Do you have white teachers who are in your opinion, competent bilingually?

Mr. LaFontaine. Yes. The 28 Puerto Rican teachers are those who have come from Puerto Rico or maybe from New York City or from other places. Then we have other teachers who are also native Spanish-speaking individuals from other countries.

Then we have native English-speaking teachers who are proficient in Spanish.

That is, all of the staff has had the kind of experience somewhere in their background which brought their proficiency in a second language well beyond the level of just school learning.

Senator Mondale. Now, you went through the public school system in New York State, I assume?

Mr. LaFontaine. That is right.

Senator Mondale. Did you begin school proficient in English.

Mr. LaFontaine. No; I spoke Spanish. I learned the alphabet in Spanish. My mother taught me the alphabet in Spanish. When I went to first grade, I had to begin to learn English.

Senator Mondale. Did you have bilingual help?

Mr. LaFontaine. No. But I might point out that for every individual like myself I can easily point to another 50 or 100 who don't make it, who turned out to be dropouts and junkies and several of my personal friends who died of drug addiction at an early age.

MOTIVATION

Senator Mondale. The reason I was asking that question, was to find out whether you could compare the environment for motivation to learn in this bilingual education system with the experience you had when you started without bilingual help?

Mr. LaFontaine. I think personally that I would have been far better off in a situation which we have today, with bilingual education. The children come to our school and they know; they get the feeling of what it is to be Puerto Rican. They can look up and see a teacher who is Puerto Rican and a nurse and a secretary and the principal.

When someone tells them, listen, Sonny, you can make it in this city, then they can see that there is some truth in that, that maybe there is some hope; whereas the past has been the kind of thing where people can tell them, "Yes; you can make it," but all they saw were the bus boys, elevator operators and everything else. Children are human beings and they know when they are being lied to.

So, this kind of situation is an improvement just in the whole question of self-image and cultural identity.

PUERTO RICAN CULTURE AND HISTORY

Senator Mondale. Do you teach courses in Puerto Rican history and culture?

Mr. LaFontaine. In the school; yes. We make it part of the social studies curriculum.

In addition to this, there is a whole flavor throughout the school which gives this sense of identity to the pupil.

Last year, I remember that we had a new admission coming in; a little boy came in with his mother. They had some questions that had to be answered so they brought them into my office. This little boy from the island of Vieques in Puerto Rico, which is even smaller than Puerto Rico—came into my office, in which I happened to have several photographs of different places, different towns in Puerto Rico. One of the little photographs was of Vieques. So that, while the mother was talking to me, he looked up on the wall and he saw this picture of his home town in the office of the Principal of a school in the biggest city in the country, and so on. He just couldn't hold himself. He said:

"Mama, mira, un retrato de Vieques." "Mama, a picture of Vieques"; and he just burst right out.

When he left that office, he walked out with his head high and chest out and I know that child had a good feeling about the school just from that one incident.

So that, there are many things that have happened that are kind of intangible incidents but which have a tremendous effect on the children.

ACHIEVEMENT

Senator Mondale. Do you have any preliminary data on achievements?

Mr. LaFontaine. The only thing we have roughly is the cooperative Inter-American tests which are generally given to non-English-speaking pupils, not all the time and it is not the best test. It was standardized; the norms were developed in the southwest for Mexican American children. For the moment, it is the only thing we have so we are using it.

We looked at the scores. Those children took the test last year and they scored on the 72nd percentile as an average which I think is fairly good as a beginning.

Senator Mondale. What about the children's learning rate in terms of becoming proficient in the English language? Would you say they are becoming more quickly proficient in English than had they not had bilingual help?

Mr. LaFontaine. This is our contention in this kind of program. You have to understand the pedagogical background of bilingual education. There are many different kinds of motivation for establishing bilingual education: political, cultural, all sorts of things. Some of the programs which are going under the title "bilingual education" are not bilingual education at all.

ENGLISH/SPANISH PROFICIENCY

There is a difference between transfer and maintenance types of programs. Some go from one language to the other. Others maintain both languages.

Our particular program, the idea of it is that we want the students to become proficient in both English and Spanish, and we have the theoretical model developed which allows for these children to get instruction in the second language at an increasing rate as they go through the grades.

Now, that means that when they start they will start with 95 percent of the instruction in the native language and five percent in the second language and then 15 and 20.

We do not then insist that the children begin to learn to read and write English immediately because language is not learned that way. So, they must first begin to understand and be able to speak English. This we do in the kindergarten, in the first grade.

Then, depending upon the children, they begin to get the instruction in reading of the second language. In the meantime, they have already begun to develop mastery in the native language so that they can get subject areas, science and math and so on, in their own language, get these abstract concepts while they are developing mastery in the second language.

So that, around the second grade or so, these children begin to get into the reading of English.

Senator MONDALE. Do you expect the children to be at grade level in understanding English by the sixth grade?

Mr. LaFontaine. Yes.

Senator MONDALE. Do you have reason to believe that you are accomplishing it?

Mr. LaFontaine. Yes; I do. Right now, we are looking at the second grade which is the first grade which has been in the school since their entry into the school, that is, this is our third year. They started in the kindergarten; they are now in the second grade. These children seem to be achieving quite well.

If this rate of growth continues, I would anticipate that they will be on level in the sixth grade.

Senator MONDALE. This is a broad, sweeping question that probably can't be answered, but how many of the tragic failures that we have been told about in Puerto Rican education could have been avoided had this kind of quality bilingual education been available to all Puerto Rican children? What kind of changes would you have anticipated?

Mr. LaFontaine. I would say that we should be able to get something like 80-something percent. Let me say why.

If we look at just the normal bell curve for any group, we find a normal distribution of intelligence and success and what-not. If we look at a curve for the Puerto Rican population, we are skewed way over to the left, way down here with the underachievers and failures and everything else.

Assuming we have this kind of quality programs, we should be able to straighten out that curve and have a normal curve just as any other group would, given the right kind of opportunities.

FUNDS VERSUS COMMUNITY CONTROL

Senator MONDALE. You make one point about money and yet it seems to me you come down a little harder on the responsiveness of the institutions. You describe your frustrations with the New York City School Board and the bureaucratic efforts there. This is not a fair question, but if you had to choose between full community control of the money now being spent to educate children in the Puerto Rican areas of New York City, or substantially increased funding with the present framework of control, which would you accept?

Mr. LaFontaine. This is not difficult. I think it would be full community control. It is a very simple matter. There is money available and we know how to use it but we have to get our hands on it.

Now, at this moment, I am operating on a $300,000 project for this title VII fund. I worked very hard to get that money. I don't want somebody downtown telling me that I can't do this and I can't do that because of all sorts of administrative redtape down there.

At the same time, in the local community where there are parents and other community leaders who know what the needs are, we can sit down together, and we do, and we can plan what we want for our children. We know how to use the money.

If there are community people there who feel we must have bilingual education, they come and get me and say, "You are the professional. We will get up $300,000 to set up a program"; I will do it and we can do it successfully, because there is nobody downtown who knows any more about setting up a bilingual program than I do. I am not being immodest but this is a reality.

Senator Mondale. I can't imagine why they would resist such an effort.

CUMBERSOME SYSTEM

Mr. LaFontaine. I don't know whether it is a resistance. I think it is an inability to actually carry out what they are supposed to be doing. It is such a vast system when we talk about 1 million pupils. They have units over there that are supposed to be specifically for accounting. Last year when it came to submitting the new proposals, we had to give them the figures for their reports.

So, what do I need them for if I am going to be doing their job? It should be the other way around. They are supposed to be providing supportive services.

Senator Mondale. What percentage of the Puerto Rican children attending the first grade in New York City receive even a minimally adequate bilingual education program?

Mr. LaFontaine. In 1969 and 1970, there were two projects funded under the Bilingual Act. One was my school which we started with some 800-some pupils. The other one was a Chinese-Spanish-English program which was predominantly Chinese.

So, in effect, we were at that time servicing just the pupils in my school.

This year, there are four more projects under title VII and gradually there are other attempts being made to provide bilingual education with other funds.

What bothers me is something which was mentioned previously by Mr. Franco, that some of the people who are jumping on the band wagon, so to speak, don't really know what they are doing. It may turn out that when they do not succeed, then every one is going to say, "See, bilingual education is really not the solution after all."

Senator MONDALE. That is where community control comes in. Members of the local community would be more sensitive to the need of the children.

Mr. LaFONTAINE. I believe so.

Senator MONDALE. Thank you very much, Mr. LaFontaine, for a most excellent presentation. I am most impressed by what you are doing at P.S. 25.

Mr. LaFONTAINE. Thank you very much.

Senator MONDALE. Our next witness is Mr. Ortiz. We will take a slight break before he commences.

(A brief recess was taken.)

Senator MONDALE. You may proceed, Mr. Ortiz.

STATEMENT OF ANGEL ORTIZ, PUERTO RICAN FORUM, PROGRAM DIRECTOR

Mr. ORTIZ. My name is Angel Ortiz.

I don't have a written statement because what I have to say is very brief. I was asked to say it by the group that was present here yesterday.

After the feeling of elation and of satisfaction with the way the hearing went yesterday, we went over to the Office of Education for an appointment with the Deputy Commissioner, Mr. Muirhead. The feeling of satisfaction ended right there.

We went there more or less to discuss with Mr. Muirhead, a policymaker within that office, certain of the problems and desires that we had as a community, as a nationwide community.

LACK OF REPRESENTATION : OFFICE OF EDUCATION

Again, as we sat down, the group begin to present their case as to the plight of 5 million Puerto Ricans, close to 6 million Puerto Ricans, in the United States, and the lack of representation within the policymaking positions, not only of the regional offices of education but of the national office right here in Washington.

Obviously, there was an agenda prepared for us, but one thing we did not want was an agenda that had been prepared for us because we had our own agenda.

When Mr. Muirhead began belying the past efforts and the failures of past efforts in title I, title III, and title VII, and how these efforts were going to become much better in the near future, that the past wrongs were going to be righted and right now there are definite regional committees being set up to review the guidelines that had previously been in effect, when we said that we were not represented in those regional committees that were reviewing these guidelines and again these regional committees that were reviewing guidelines are merely advisory and not decisionmaking committees, we went into the aspect of the running of the Office of Education here and the personnel within it, the lack of Puerto Rican personnel in it, not only in the professional ranks but in the policymaking ranks, they were totally nonexistent, at that point Mr. Muirhead came in and gave us the bureaucratic run-around that there is an office set up to which we can send résumés of qualified Puerto Ricans that we think should be hired.

Again, we told him that we don't want to send résumé because probably the Office of Education has a file, a whole closet full of Puerto Rican résumés that nothing has been done about. We said, "You have to make positions and those people who have been in charge of recruitment of personnel should be fired because of the total lack of performance in doing their job."

At that point, a lady from within our group made a statement and at that point Mr. Muirhead in a very patronizing way insulted her in the way he referred to her. We asked for an office of Puerto Rican affairs at the assistant deputy commissioner level. He said he cannot talk about those things because these are things that they have to decide upon.

Again, the Puerto Ricans became frustrated; anger came out; and they just walked out of the meeting room.

We just told him, "You are coming again with the same rhetoric as before."

"We are doing the best we can. As vacancies open up, we will try to fill them."

We said, "No; that is not the case."

The insult to the lady was the last straw.

Again, this, I think, exemplifies the arrogance, the institutional arrogance, with which Puerto Ricans are treated here in the national office, the regional offices and so on.

PUERTO RICANS: INVISIBLE MINORITY

The total invisibility of our community is also evident. We are powerless in that our desires as such do not have to be taken into consideration.

I think yesterday was much more real for me in that office than the hearing because we are not going to be dealing with Senator Mondale. We are going to be dealing with the bureaucrats within the Office of Education. These are the people who will be implementing whatever comes out of the Senate. And whatever highsounding philosophy comes out of the Senate, as we can see with the 1964 civil rights law, usually gets stuck and becomes nonfunction as soon as it gets into the hands of the bureaucracies out there.

I think we need political pressure; I think we need political power. Puerto Ricans as such do not have it politically in terms of voting numbers and so on. I think we are developing it. But it is evident that other actions like that with the microcosm of the Puerto Rican community that we had there because we had professionals, grassroot leadership, parents, students, when they see this type of thing, just like the students told you before, power can also be gotten in other ways, through fear, fear of what your actions are going to be.

I think this is what came out of there. That anger is still there. It has not received an expression. I fear what type of expression it would receive during the coming year if no action is taken to have these people become responsive, Deputy Commissioner Muirhead, the incoming Commissioner Marland.

Again, we have very definite requests that we made of him. I think these requests are the ones that we should begin to discuss. There are 650,000 Indians; they have been decimated down to that number; but there is still a Bureau of Indian Affairs.

The blacks have gotten their attention within the bureaucracies in Washington.

OFFICE FOR PUERTO RICAN PROBLEMS

What we are saying right now here, let us begin at the national level with the Office of Education and begin setting up an office, an assistant commissioner with a staff and a budget, to deal with the problems of the six million Puerto Ricans in the United States.

Senator MONDALE. I can't disagree with you.

We just had a report released yesterday prepared by five outside organizations which had monitored the expenditure of $75 million being spent for quality integrated education in the present emergency. This report documented wide-spread violations of the law including the diversion of money to obviously segregationist institutions. These abuses are occurring in the face of not only legal prohibitions but also a clear sense of the intentions of Congress expressed in its debate over conditions which apparently the Department of HEW decided should be disregarded. Your experience is not unique.

That is not a very helpful comment. But we had similar testimony from the black community, Mexican American community, the same kinds of problems. I think your trouble now is to get a bureau of Puerto Rican affairs. If the BIA is an example, it will be 100 years before they ever hire a Puerto Rican.

Mr. ORTIZ. Right.

Senator MONDALE. I think we ought to send his testimony to the Commissioner-designate and ask for his comments before he is confirmed. We asked him some questions about Spanish-speaking employment in the Office of Education. The other day I asked those questions. I would like to get those answers before we act on his confirmation.

It seems incredible to me that in the Department of Education there isn't at least one top, high-level Puerto Rican educator, at a minimum. The same for Mexican Americans.

Mr. ORTIZ. I think in the whole Office of Education at the low levels there are two or three, at the most.

Senator MONDALE. That is right. You are talking about the second team. I mean on the first team, the people who get to go to the meetings where the money is dished out; that is the meeting you want to go to. The others are a lot of fun but the one that really counts is that one.

Mr. ORTIZ. Right.

Senator MONDALE. Your frustration is well understandable to me. Thank you very much.

Mr. ORTIZ. Thank you, Mr. Chairman.

Senator MONDALE. Our final witness this morning is Mr. Frank Negron, Assistant Director, Center for Urban Education, New York City.

STATEMENT OF FRANK NEGRON, ASSISTANT DIRECTOR, CENTER FOR URBAN EDUCATION, NEW YORK CITY

Mr. NEGRON. I'm afraid that the subject matter that has been discussed in the past 3 days has not attracted the attention of the

T.V. media. I thought for certain we would have coverage on the last day, and that is why I wore a blue shirt.

Senator MONDALE. I finally put on a white shirt; I gave up.

Mr. NEGRON. As you mentioned yesterday, if you wanted to clear the room of newspaper people or television cameras, all you would have to do is indicate that a hearing on Mexican Americans or Puerto Ricans was being conducted and they would vacate the premises quickly.

Senator MONDALE. It has not failed yet.

Mr. NEGRON. I am wearing several hats this morning, Senator. At this point, I am speaking to you as the chairman of the Education Committee of the Puerto Rican Forum which was the committee that helped to coordinate the speakers for these 3 days of hearings before the Senate select committee on equal educational opportunity.

Senator MONDALE. For which we are most grateful.

Mr. NEGRON. I would like to recapitulate the presentations made by the previous speakers.

FIRST PUERTO RICAN EDUCATION HEARING

Before making it though, I would like to, here and now, congratulate you and Senator Javits for initiating these hearings. Never in the history of the Puerto Rican community have we had the opportunity to present in a clear, concise and dramatic way our educational needs to a select committee of the U.S. Senate.

Senator MONDALE. I was wondering about that. There has never been a hearing before the Senate?

Mr. NEGRON. That is right, in spite of the fact that many of the speakers were rather cynical about the hearings and had to be convinced to participate. We knew that as responsible legislators, you and Senator Javits had a commitment and a desire to see that the educational needs of our people were brought to the attention of the law makers.

I can't tell you how excited we were in knowing that this was being made possible. We are very happy that we have had this opportunity.

Senator. MONDALE. We get into a peculiar situation.

We are even afraid to call hearings because the community feels that it is being used; it doesn't expect anything to happen. Yet, if we don't at least begin the process of making that kind of record, how are we ever going to make progress?

The figures, information and personal portrayal of experiences, this is the first time we have heard about it. It is the first time I had heard about it. I certainly am not going to say that there are any saviors around here, but without this record I don't know how we could do it.

Mr. NEGRON. That there was a lot of suspicion and people felt, well, what is the use of going down and speaking; it is just going to be one of those things where you sit down and they listen to you and nothing is done. It goes no further than the congressional record. But, let me continue with this brief presentation.

In the past 3 days, you have heard from a number of responsible and knowledgeable students, parents, community organization rep-

3832

resentatives and public school personnel from all over the country on the genocide that their school systems are perpetrating on the Puerto Rican child. The picture that they have presented to you is not a pretty one, I admit, but the facts are undeniable.

Because of this, there exists today an uneasy calm in the Chicago, Boston, Philadelphia, New Jersey, and New York Puerto Rican communities. Do we have to destroy the institutions of learning in order to underscore our plight or is there another way out of this dilemma? I think there is.

The answer is in your hands. Through the legislative process, we can avoid the collision course that two million Puerto Ricans are on as a result of the system's refusal to provide them with equal educational opportunities. Many excellent suggestions have been made to this august body of legislators by the more than 21 speakers that have participated in these hearings.

RECOMMENDATIONS

The following are the major recommendations, and there were many, as you well know, Senator.

1. A closer look at the New York City School System into which the Federal Government is investing over $100 million yearly of title I moneys. This is true even though we have an 85-percent-dropout rate in our community which, by the way, indicates a clear violation of the 1954 Civil Rights Act.

Now, in lieu of this, it has been suggested that the funding go directly to the local school communities, leadership development programs and community education institutions.

Recommendation 2: The appointment of a Puerto Rican Assistant Commissioner, with an appropriate staff, of course, within the United States Office of Education, to deal with the educational needs of our community.

The final recommendation: That there be an increase in appropriations for bilingual and bicultural programs.

Senator, I would like to now switch hats. I am now the assistant director of the Community Program Division for the Center for Urban Education.

PARENTAL INVOLVEMENT

The previous speakers had very little to say about community programs geared towards benefiting not only the Puerto Rican child, but also his parents. My feelings is that the program which I am about to present can be implemented in most communities of the United States.

The Center for Urban Education (CUE) is a nonprofit organization supported by the U.S. Office of Education under title IV of the Elementary and Secondary Education Act. Its main goal is to improve education for city children. It does this by offering programs and activities in which people from communities and schools can work together so that children may benefit.

The Center for Urban Education is firmly committed to the concept that the equality of educational opportunity for Puerto Rican and other minority and disadvantaged Americans can be fully realized when there is widespread citizen participation in the planning, policy decisionmaking, staffing, and execution of the public educational programs in each community.

In order that many more informed citizens, among the Puerto Rican and other disadvantaged Americans, now living in our urban communities, may become more actively and effectively involved in the efforts to improve the quality of education for their children, the Center for Urban Education has established in two large, predominantly Puerto Rican Communities in New York City community learning centers.

COMMUNITY EDUCATION

These centers are functioning in both the South Bronx and the Williamsburg section of Brooklyn. Their primary purpose is to help these communities realize the educational goals and aspirations of their resident citizens. These centers provide the kinds of community educational opportunities through program design and execution, that the public schools cannot provide under the atmosphere of citizen distrust, feelings of alienation and community tensions and conflicts between the minority, disadvantaged and the public education establishment.

Moreover, the community learning centers, under auspices of the Center for Urban Education, is viewed by the program participants as a neutral site for local residents to acquire the necessary skills, knowledge, and understandings about the public schools, which they can employ to help peaceable and constructively to improve the quality of education for their children attending public schools.

Senator MONDALE. Mr. Negron, I have read the full statement.

The reason I interrupt is this: There are two Senators on the floor that want to change the name of Cape Kennedy to Cape Canaveral. I think you would want me over there to fight that. I have been asked to come over and participate.

What I suggest is this: That we place the remainder of your written testimony in the record.

(The remainder of the testimony of Mr. Negron follows:)

The Community Learning Centers are not just an "outside-of-school" site for resident citizens to acquire knowledges and skills relative to educational affairs and their schools, but they are viable institutions of continuing educational service, places where reflection, instructions, information, and planning for intelligent action and interaction between the schools and the concerned citizens of the community are integrals of daily life.

The viability of the Learning Centers, in the Puerto Rican Communities of the South Bronx and Brooklyn, is evident from their enthusiastic and full participation in three programs sponsored by the Center for Urban Education: The Educational Leadership, Parent Participation Workshops, and School-Community Seminars Programs. In each of these programs, Puerto Rican and other disadvantaged citizens are sharing staff positions as trainers, administrators, and secretaries. Puerto Rican fathers and mothers are trainees in each program. The preliminary studies and reports concerning the effectiveness of these programs, clearly indicate a growing success in the training and instruction received by the participants. Both the parents and school officials are beginning to utilize these skills and knowledges in working cooperatively on problems confronting the schools in the Bronx and Brooklyn.

Citizen participation, therefore, in urban education is perceived to be a wise and feasible goal when a vehicle of a Community Learning Center, with an appropriate program stratagem, is provided for the local citizens to cross the bridge to their public education institutions, to render assistance based on increased knowledge and understanding, and equipped with the skills to improve the quality of their children's education.

LEADERSHIP POTENTIAL

Mr. NEGRON. The point I am trying to make here is that there exists a need for community programs that can help develop the leadership potential and the educational know-how of the parents.

Senator MONDALE. These are what the witnesses have asked for.

Mr. NEGRON. Yes. As a matter of fact, this was initiated by me in 1968 when I was the deputy commissioner of the mayor's Office of Education Liaison.

Senator MONDALE. If you have any more specific details of how these programs are working, you could submit them for the record.

Mr. NEGRON. I gave you some materials on Monday. Included were the basic program plan and the description of the program. I will be happy to leave you seven additional copies.

Senator MONDALE. Let us excerpt that and make it part of the record following your testimony.

Mr. NEGRON. Fine. I would appreciate that. I feel that this is a worthwhile project, whether done by CUE or any other institution. It is something that is viable and helpful to the communities.

Senator MONDALE. Thank you very much for your testimony, for the work of your organization, and for your help in setting up these most useful 3 days of testimony. Now it is up to us to do something about it.

Mr. NEGRON. Yes, and we are depending on you and Senator Javits. We feel that these hearings will help to publicize our educational needs. We have tried everything to help our children obtain the education that they are entitled to, but the system just won't permit it. Your efforts on our behalf will bridge the gap which exists between our community and the society as a whole.

Senator MONDALE. Thank you very much, Mr. Negron, for not only the testimony but the spirit in which you have presented it.

We stand in recess, subject to the call of the Chair.

(Whereupon, at 12 noon, the committee recessed, to reconvene at the call of the Chair.)

APPENDIX

NEW YORK URBAN COALITION, INC.,
New York, N.Y., November 18, 1970.

Re Education of the Puerto Rican
Mr. WALTER F. MONDALE,
Chairman, Select Committee on Equal Educational Opportunity, Washington, D.C.

DEAR MR. MONDALE: Enclosed please find statement which I wish to appear in the Congressional Records in reference to the Hearing of the Minority Council to the Senate Select Committee on Equal Educational Opportunity—Education of the Puerto Rican on November 23, 24 and 25th.

Very truly yours,

MANUEL DIAZ, Jr.,
Vice President.

[Enclosure]

[MEMORANDUM]

NOVEMBER 19, 1970.

To: Minority Council of the Select Commission
On Equal Education Opportunity U.S. Senate I.
From: Manuel Diaz, Jr., Vice-President, New York Urban Coalition.

It has long been apparent to me and to my colleagues that this nation is not living up to its liberal rhetoric. Liberalism in fact has become a largely procedural matter, a way of living by the rules; mutually administered, of compromising, of abiding by the status quo and abiding by the outcome.

The consequence, of this policy, throughout all aspects of functioning is reflected in the lives of the poor and of our minority groups. Our Puerto Rican population is one of the best examples of the dysfunctioning of our liberal rhetoric. All aspects of life which guarantee and reinforce human dignity, barely exists for the major portion of the Puerto Ricans. It is public record that the income of the Puerto Rican male head of a family is still at the bottom of the economic ladder, that the Puerto Rican child in the public school system still trails his black or white counterpart with regard to achievement and reading level, that the dilapidation and deterioration of housing in the areas where Puerto Ricans live continues at an accelerated pace, that in the administration of justice through our courts, full equality eludes and evades the reach of the Puerto Rican and that in economic development the community has yet to make significant gains.

There should be no question as to our capability. When we look to Puerto Rico we are policy makers, educators, architects, politicians, brick layers, construction workers, etc. Yet we look at the record here in terms of achievement and we see relatively little in roads and the future looks bleak. In Senate Hearings before the Special Subcommittee on Bi-Lingual Education May 18, 19, 26, 29 and 31, 1967, Nathan Brown, the then executive deputy superintendent of schools in New York City was questioned by the late Senator Robert Kennedy, as to the number of Puerto Rican teachers in the school system. He responded "no more than one percent". On the question of principals although Senator Kennedy had the percentage of 0.6 percent there was no Puerto Rican licensed principal. The record now reads, one licensed principal and 0.4% of 969, in acting positions. No Puerto Rican occupies any of the topmost policy making positions, that of chancellor or three deputy superintendents. In the 1968–69 school year Puerto Rican pupils accounted for a total of 21.5% of the school population;[1] A mere drop in the bucket. When we consider the magnitude of the problem it is clear that the bucket has a hole in it.

---

[1] Analysis of Puerto Rican and Black Employment in NYC Schools—Richard Greenspan (Puerto Rican Forum).

During the Hearings, before the Subcommittee on Executive Reorganization of the Committee on Government Operations United States June 11 and 12, 1969, Establishing an Interagency Committee on Mexican-American Affairs, the Honorable M. Montaya, U.S. Senator from the state of New Mexico, indicated, in his statement, an amendment which "would merely ensure that the Inter-agency-Committee is meant to serve and meet the problems of all Spanish-speaking Americans be they Mexican-American, Puerto Ricans, and all other Spanish speaking or Spanish surnamed Americans residing in the several States and the District of Columbia."

I also had the privilege to testify before this committee and express my concerns and those of some of my colleagues. In my testimony it was indicated that "at the inception of the Interagency Committee on Mexican-American affairs, I welcomed the establishment of the Interagency Committee on Mexican-American Affairs. I welcomed the establishment of that committee but raised a series of questions which are still questionable. One point is specifically relevant to the hearing on the education of Puerto Ricans, my concern that this committee deal with the problems of all Spanish-speaking people. Although the committees name has been changed to date there is no Puerto Rican representation.

The point that must be stressed is that the blight of the Puerto Rican is public record. If facts and rhetoric are to mean anything they must be demonstrated by action. That means the appointment of Puerto Ricans, to policy making positions on all levels of governmental structure, federal, state and city, for it is pressure and political structure, federal, state and city. Pressure and political power, in the final analysis determines how our children will be educated. Therefore, it is imperative that at all levels of decision making Puerto Rican representation be involved in order to articulate and pressure (demand) for fundamental change in our communities.

The New York City school system is a case in point. It has successfully excluded our professionals, our parents and our children. Our children are not learning. The public education system by its own records cannot defend its productivity both quantitatively and qualitatively. We get demonstration projects and schools to administer as acting administrators with insufficient funds. This is not enough.

Only a program for change in the school system itself, can begin to address our specialized problems. If it becomes necessary to abolish the present Board of Education to achieve these goals, then we, must be prepared to support this move. The federal government must provide larger sums for Bi-Lingual Education programs. (A minimum of 300 million dollars for New York City). However, the largest commitment is to develop methods to employ Puerto Ricans at all levels. Dr. Scribner, in directing himself to the issue of Teacher recruitment indicated, "There is no more important decision for a school board than the selection of the people who will teach and manage its schools, and I believe strongly that no school board can logically be held responsible for the end result if it lacks the power in the first instance to hire, unhindered, the best leadership it can find. . . . No one is against merit; no one is for favoritism. The point is that merit is not the exclusive possession of the present licensing system. It is, I believe, perfectly possible to devise other methods of selecting staff which retain the principal of merit and yet eliminate the rigidities and inflexibilities which, in my opinion, render the present system no longer workable".[2]

I support this position. It is only when we can view differences as positive and consciously endorse varied educational directions to meet these differences, will we begin to develop meaningful new avenues for change. It is only when rhetoric is endorsed by commitment and concrete action that it has a purpose.

[2] Excerpt of an address given by Dr. Harvey B. Scribner, Chancellor of the Board of Education of the City of New York on Tuesday, October 27, 1970 before the New York Society for Experimental Study of Education at the High School of Art and Design.

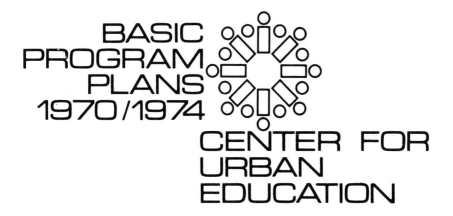

BASIC
PROGRAM
PLANS
1970/1974

CENTER FOR
URBAN
EDUCATION

Contents

Part 1

Overall Goals and Strategies

NATURE OF REPORT

This document, the Basic Program Plan, presents the major long-and-short-term programs of the Center for Urban Education. It explains the reasons for their selection, the expected outcomes, the strategies and procedures, the work schedule and the projected costs. It also describes key aspects of CUE structure, management, and program operation.

The Basic Program Plan aims to provide in a single document a unified view of CUE's activities for the next five years, and thus to enable annual modification of activities against a backdrop of comprehensive planning. In describing each program, we have reviewed the evidence of need, described the work in progress, indicated how the capabilities of the CUE organization will be utilized in planning future development, and finally, set our standards for evaluating the success of each program.

GOALS

In the two-year period since publication of our Basic Program Plans for 1968, the trend to decentralization in urban school management and operations has accelerated sharply. Decentralization is now a fact of life for the nation's largest school system, where state law has institutionalized local community control of New York city schools.

This development, which both reflects and foreshadows similar events elsewhere in our country, is central to the context for CUE planning for the period 1970-74.

From its inception CUE has been engaged in the work of seeking solutions to problems in urban education. Our goal has been and continues to be: the improvement of teaching and learning in the schools of our cities and their suburbs.

1

Experience has convinced us that educators do not yet know how best to educate the urban young toward literate and socially concerned adulthood, and that citizens and students in turn do not yet know how best to shape educational affairs in ways that will benefit them most.

The resulting gap between school performance and community expectations will continue to widen during the 1970's unless significant adjustments are made between the practices of educators and the needs of those they are employed to serve. This evolving demands that an educational laboratory such as CUE should develop new orientation, new knowledge, new skills. Many of the old formulations of objectives will be revised; many of the traditional relationships among teachers, supervisors, parents, and students will be transformed.

Our role, as we see it for the next period, is to sustain and deepen those efforts that would strengthen the quality of teaching in the urban settings, and at the same time strengthen the ability of parents and community to share effectively in the conduct of educational affairs.

To this general end we have devised several strategies and designed specific programs.

STRATEGY

CUE's chief strategy in reaching its stated goal is based on the assumption that no reform within urban schools will produce the changes desired in education unless better transactions among teachers, parents, and students are developed. These transactions, which are at the present time often misguided by conflicting or poorly understood social values, can be reshaped and harmonized only by changing the ways in which authority and responsibility are shared among teachers, parents, and students.

CUE has previously invested its resources in several approaches to the solution of urban educational problems (see Appendix B). For example, it has conducted a great number of studies and planning projects designed to provide *compensatory* education. It has participated in *teacher-training* programs and in the design of improved teacher-training techniques and materials. And, it has sponsored the largest longitudinal field experiment in *early reading instruction* in the history of American education.

These studies and projects, despite their practical worth, suggest that, essential as desegregation, good compensatory instruction, teacher training, and the improved teaching of reading are, *it is the fundamental structure* of urban public education that must be redesigned if there is to be any significant education gain. A context must exist within which teacher, parent, and student an all share in determining both the ends and means of growth and learning. Such transactions, which will be on the increase as decentralization spreads, will require an informed professional community on the one hand and a concerned and informed lay community on the other.

To meet the needs of this emerging situation, CUE has made its main strategy the design, field testing and wide dissemination of *a series of alternatives to conventional modes of school-community interaction within cities and suburbs.* This strategy calls for an approach to the school-student community triangle on all sides. Formal education is on the brink of a vast transformation, with the walled-in school itself becoming but one among many diverse educational options.

2

Reflecting the CUE strategy, the overall themes which unify all of its programs are the themes of *effective citizen participation* and *literacy through social education*. What are the civic responsibilities of principals and teachers? How and in what respects shall school staff members be accountable to members of the community? What does *literacy* mean to the urban poor? What part shall parents and taxpayers play in fixing educational, curricular policy and in insuring responsive practice within the school? How can they strengthen their own ability and the ability of their children to participate effectively in both school and society? The answers to these and other questions are basic to both citizen participation and literacy through social education. The following sections will describe and define the two themes, in order to make clear the main angles of approach taken by the CUE programs.

CITIZEN PARTICIPATION

There must be no mistake about the intent of CUE's thrust in the area of citizen participation. In an age when such words as "citizenship," "civic," "social," and "community" have been abused and debased, when they have been converted into slogans or distorted within schools as terms for narrow codes of conduct and discipline, and when they have been appropriated by diverse political interest-groups at large, we must here specify what we mean by "citizen participation." Participation is the noun for which "to partake of," is the verb. One participates by taking one's part. This is what we intend. The citizenry of a democratic society is by definition a participative citizenry, since democratic processes presuppose and require a full sharing of powers and responsibilities. Central to democratic thought is the conviction that it is the participation that educates the participants; hence the belief in the vital necessity of both.

Applied to urban public education, this concept of participation implies that since a school, reflecting the larger society, is a pluralistic institution, the decisions affecting it should be shared appropriately by administrators, teachers, students, and members of the surrounding adult community, including parents (but not restricted to them). The boundary between such a school and its community, while real, must be extremely permeable and subject to constant relocation or alteration in the service of community interests and needs.

Some of the recent research on aspects of citizen participation, along with experience with urban renewal programs, anti-poverty community action programs, model cities programs, and community control movements within big city education, has led many social scientists, government officials, and educators to conclude that citizen participation in social and educational policy defeats "the instrumental goals of policy reform and implementation." (For an excellent analysis of the literature and viewpoints, see Jon Van Til and Sally B. Van Til, "Citizen Participation in Social Policy: The End of the Cycle?" *Social Problems*, Vol. 17, No. 3, Winter 1970.) The Center for Urban Education is convinced that this interpretation, left to take its evolutionary course, could prove fatal to democratic government in general and public education in particular.

What must be recognized is simply that certain modes of citizen participation have failed either to involve citizens effectively or to result in improvements in public policy and practice. Obviously, if we continue to use these same modes,

3

repeated failures will continue to evolve. It is imperative that, instead, we must work to develop modes which insure a *fully democratic urban pluralism*. In the case of urban public education, CUE believes that this requires the development of means through which the learning interests of the minority poor may be accommodated without precipitating the power of the bureaucratized and unionized public school establishment against them so that educational change is stalemated. As the Van Tils point out for social policy in general, "The alternatives to such institutional innovation would appear to be repression or rebellion." So, the alternatives to effective citizen participation in urban public education would appear to be the garrison school or a revolt of both students and taxpayers.

LITERACY THROUGH SOCIAL EDUCATION

To be an effective citizen in an advanced industrial, urban society is to be *well informed* as well as concerned and involved in public affairs. Literacy is an educational objective in its own right; what is more, it is clearly a skill of critical instrumental utility for the achievement of most other educational aims. From its beginnings, CUE has invested heavily in research and development efforts to resolve the problems of defective instruction in beginning reading in urban schools, and of cumulative illiteracy among urban elementary school children.

In its current work, however, CUE stresses literacy *for* civic competence, in the conviction that this combined objective will contribute to the goal of literacy *in ways that go beyond rudimentary cognitive skill*. The conviction stems from our discovery that an abundant, rapidly improving variety of methods for teaching reading are available and are beginning to be adopted by urban school systems. In a few years, the challenge of ensuring the child's right to read will become the challenge of enlarging and enriching the social and personal meanings taken from the printed page. Hence, "literacy through social education" as CUE defines it, means:

> . . . the acquisition of those special cognitive skills that are necessary for the comprehension and utilization of concepts of civic participation, and involvement in the process of changing one's environment.

> . . . the strengthening of those attitudes and understandings that are constructive and action-oriented, as an important basis for an urban child's development into an effective, concerned, and participating adult.

SUMMARY STATEMENT

Keeping in mind the above goals, strategy and themes, it should be clear that CUE's programs have been chosen because they are important to the future of urban education, and to the general quality of life in any urban society of the future. Every family, every community, and every school contributes in every generation, for better or worse, to the preparation of literate citizens for participation in the democratic society of the next generation's history. Within public education, however, concern about this contribution has been left, for the most part, to academic definers of the social studies. Now and from now on, however, the collective efforts of citizens to identify and solve or ameliorate urban social and environmental problems must be supported by more and better contributions from many more sources, if the quality of civic effort is to be strengthened.

4

It should be understood that the plans contained in this document are subject to continuing study and review by CUE. Modifications will be made whenever they are deemed desirable or necessary by the Board of Trustees and the Director.

There will be many reasons for periodic modification. First, the *funding decisions* of the U.S. Office of Education and other agencies, including state and local public agencies, foundations and firms within the education and publishing industry, will have profound impact on plans for program activity. (The Basic Program Plan does not distinguish, for example, between sources of support, although some components of both programs are supported by federal funds and others by private funds. Revisions made as a result of funding decisions will be reflected in the annual report prepared each September).

Second, the continuing *experience of the staff* and the program advisors to the Center may modify *The Basic Program Plan.*

Third, historic changes in our milieu may expose new opportunities or close off lines of intended action, thus recommending or requiring alterations in resource allocation or emphasis.

This document and its successors should be considered as an updating of prior long-term plans (see e.g., *Basic Program Plans*, 1968-1972) taking into proper account the various economic, social and professional changes that must or should affect CUE and other similar institutions.

While the efforts of CUE continue, as of 1970, to be mostly regional in focus, *national* extension is beginning to evolve. CUE has exchanged many products with other regional laboratories and R & D Centers. It has collaborated directly with Research for Better Schools, Incorporated, in Pennsylvania and New Jersey, and with the Central Midwestern Regional Educational Laboratory in Tennessee. It conducts an information exchange program in collaboration with National Urban League, among the chapter affiliates of the League, throughout the cities of the United States. It has cooperated vigorously with the State Education Department of New York. During 1970-74, CUE will continue to implement existing plans for increasing its product dissemination and expanding the scope and depth of its cooperative activities with other agencies responsible for the management of urban educational services.

Much of the work described in this document has evolved through pilot projects undertaken on a small scale from 1966 through 1968. CUE's program efforts have narrowed since 1965 from about 34 discrete pilot projects to two major programs each with its several components. New pilot projects, not described here, will be expected to spring up from year to year, and parts of current components will, doubtless, be discarded.

The next section shows how the two main programs, set up to carry out the goals and strategies of CUE, will reflect the above policies. They comprise Part II of this report.

Part 2

The Programs and their Components

As has been seen in the general introduction, CUE continues to work towards the end of achieving a better urban educational system, one which will reflect a fully democratic pluralism in society, and will have as its outcome the development of better learning and teaching in metropolitan schools and communities. For CUE believes that educators do not yet know best how to educate the urban young, and also that citizens and students do not know how best to participate in shaping urban education in productive ways.

The Center for Urban Education will accordingly allocate its resources and technical skills for 1970-74 within a unified programmatic aim: *its object will be to research, design, field test, disseminate and institutionalize products that will improve the scope and quality of literacy and civic participation among educators, community residents, and youth, especially those of the urban poor in large metropolitan areas of the U.S.* Its main strategy, as explained above in Part I, is to emphasize and expand the alternatives for effective transactions among the above three groups of people, as they interact to improve urban education. This aim and strategy will be developed by setting up a series of experiments in community education and in literacy through social education. Out of these experiments will emerge the *products* to be field-tested, replicated in other settings and institutionalized as innovative improvements in urban education in the U.S.

The programs are divided into two categories of endeavor; one is primarily community-based and one is school-based. The several component parts of each are described individually in the pages that follow.

Both programs develop their products collaboratively, working together and with public school staff, students, community leaders and parents towards

6

common ends. Both are therefore scheduled to overlap in the research, development, diffusion and dissemination processes.

Products developed in one major CUE program are planned to be relevant or adaptable to the purposes of the other program. The ways in which this is to be done will be explained in detail under each separate component heading below. Neither program limits itself to a specific type of citizen participation, student learning or teacher behavior. Instead, the products are to be developed for use in a host of settings and for a variety of purposes. The products, in other words, are not to be tied to the service of one cause within any one neighborhood, school region or state, but are to serve as models that are capable of modification to fit changing conditions in changing times and other places.

THE COMMUNITY LEARNING CENTER – A NEW CONCEPT

The central vehicle for carrying both of CUE's programs into the field is the establishment of a CUE-Community Learning Center. This Center, planned and established by CUE with full community cooperation and endorsement, is located in a strategically important spot in a given neighborhood area. It is, therefore, a community-based operation, carrying out its activities outside the school, but designed (after working with school youth, teachers, administrators, and school boards in the area,) to carry its ideas, participation and influence into the school establishment. It likewise provides a place where movement may take place in the opposite direction, that is, from the school into the neighborhood. It is geared to offer teachers and administrators an opportunity to learn more about the culture and needs of the community, and to serve as a place where they may meet with their "clients", (parents, community leaders and youth,) in an informal and mutually beneficial setting.

CUE plans that each Community Learning Center shall eventually provide this service beyond the immediate neighborhood, extending either by means of its programs or by the establishment of other Centers (or Mobile Unit Centers,) into other neighborhoods, regions or districts of the large metropolitan area. Like all of the CUE Program components, the concept behind the Community Learning Center is that it shall represent a model or sample framework which may be replicated in slightly adapted form in other urban settings in the nation after its purposes, its structure and its management procedures are field-tested, evaluated and found to be valid by the CUE experiments. Eventually the CUE part of the Community Learning Center would disappear as such, since its goal would be to become completely institutionalized in the community, and to operate without the guidance or support of CUE.

The CUE-Community Learning Center is planned to be considerably more than just the place where various activities and programs will take place. It is, first of all, the central mechanism for the integration of CUE's school and community programs. Next, it is a resource center for the community on questions and problems relating to educational affairs. But beyond serving as the means whereby CUE's programs will become effective, the CLC is also an important entity in itself. The creation of a viable Community Learning Center is an essential end product which may be made available to other urban settings.

There are in existence at the present time two CUE-Community Learning Centers; one is in the South Bronx, and the other is in Brooklyn. A description of

7

the various activities and programs now taking place in the CUE-Community Learning Centers will be found in the accounts of the program components that make use of the Center's facilities.

SELECTING PROGRAM COMPONENTS

In selecting specific components for development within our programs, the above general aims and concerns are combined with other, more technical consideration. The broad programmatic objectives, while indispensable, are too general to do more than guide the desired direction of effort. Below, we cite the *main guidelines* used by the Center for Urban Education to select program components.

1. *Participation.* Any acceptable component must manifest CUE's major concern for improving the quality of joint participation between school and community.

2. *Need.* The component must also hold promise of meeting a need of high intensity within metropolitan area schools and communities.

3. *Yield.* The component must demonstrate longer-term as well as short-term benefits that result from its establishment — to stimulate its adoption outside the range of the original experiment.

4. *Scope.* The component must develop products which can be adapted and used in a variety of settings and under various auspices. While the initial activities may originally be concerned with a particular age group, grade level, or occupation, they should, in subsequent phases, be expandable or adaptable for use by other persons or groups, in or out of school settings.

5. *Collaboration.* Each component, and the development effort entailed in its creation, must permit and promote a wide range of cooperative activities with other components developed under CUE with other program goals.

6. *Engineering.* The product development process projected for each component must be one that makes room for a balanced sequence of steps ranging from research to design, to field testing, to training and dissemination. This sequence must include a stage in which educational outcomes are empirically specified.

7. *Cost.* The component must be of a kind that can make a significant impact on urban education *within* the estimated dollar resources of the Center for Urban Education.

Citizen Participation Program

The Citizen Participation theme of the Center for Urban Education is served by neighborhood level, community-based research and development activities. These are designed to generate products that will improve the scope and quality of citizen involvement in urban educational decision making and practices.

It is a matter of common knowledge that students and parents are making demands upon the school system that it cannot now meet. Most, if not all, of these demands are an outgrowth of increased knowledge and increased political awareness. The demand is for the school system to educate children, regardless of their diversity, to the maximum capacity of each individual and to meet the needs of a changing society at the same time. Most urban educational systems have not been able to respond successfully to either of these challenges.

The Citizen Participation Program sees itself as a facilitator of change, a catalyst but not a direct agent in this capacity. In this role, we have made assumptions which underlie our present and future community research and development plans and programs. These assumptions are: that urbanization will continue, that the need to keep abreast of technological changes in society will increase; that the democratic way, including the principle of democratic pluralism, will continue to be aspired to and thus must be incorporated in action.

Therefore, any CUE program concerned with the goal of improved citizen participation must focus on two areas; first, to clearly analyze and understand the existing educational structure; second, to mount research and development programs which reflect and answer community needs important to the changing of that structure.

Activities scheduled for the 1970-74 period are organized into four components of one Citizen Participation Program. The first of these, Leadership Training, aims to develop products and procedures for the continuous improvement of the quality of lay leadership in local educational affairs. Through training, parents in poverty neighborhoods are prepared to play an informed and positive role in shaping school policy and services to meet the needs and interests of their children and their community as a whole.

The second, Parent Participation Workshops, is aimed at involving parents in the day to day curriculum of the neighborhood elementary school through sustained educational encounters between parents and educators.

The third component, School-Community Seminars, serves similar objectives but concentrates on designing materials that will sensitize educators to the concerns of parents and children. All three components are connected with evaluation research and with long-term community studies of attitudes, population trends, and the educational adjustments of families in transition out of the ghetto.

The fourth component, Library Services, will provide the resources for specialized library and support services important to the above components, as well as giving special courses of training which will help adults develop reasonable competence in appropriate library and research techniques.

9

CUE's Citizen Participation Program should result in more than measurable improvements in the quality of school-community relations within poverty areas of the cities and their suburbs. As these relations are strengthened, CUE expects to clearly demonstrate that pupil achievement will improve; school services and particularly curricular programming will change in the direction of fulfilling local needs and interests more precisely; and, in combination, mechanism for peaceful yet substantial change in urban public education will be developed.

These outcomes depend for their realization upon concommitant fulfillment of the objectives of CUE's Literacy through Social Education Program, for it is through the activities of this second endeavor that the curriculum of the neighborhood schools served by CUE-Community Learning Centers will be revised experimentally. Therefore, the activities of the two programs must be closely interwoven if curriculum change and pupil learning are to be included in the list of expected outcomes from improved participation.

Leadership Training

REASON FOR SELECTION AND DESCRIPTION OF PROGRAM

The *Leadership Training* program is of major importance in carrying out CUE's central strategy of trying to improve the ability of educators and citizens to work together contructively. This program trains citizens for leadership roles in educational affairs. Through such training, CUE aims to strengthen the ability of community residents to share effectively in the educational process. Parents and other citizens who try to participate, but are unaware of the complexities involved and lack information and problem-solving skills, are frequently frustrated and defeated. The result is that the school system suffers the loss of their potential contributions. If the Leadership Training program is successful the school as well as the parents will benefit, and students and society will be the ultimate recipients.

The immediate, short-run objective of this program is to help the community develop a cadre of citizens who will understand the structure of public education and the roles that community residents can most effectively play. To this end, a training program was begun in 1969 in communities with high proportions of Puerto Rican and black residents in the city of New York. Trainees were selected from among applicants recommended by citizens, school administrators, community school board members, and by community agencies and organizations. Each cycle of the program operates for 15 weeks, with a minimum of nine hours of training per week, six hours devoted to classroom discussion and three hours to field work by the trainees.

The training is conducted in groups of a maximum of 25 trainees. Each group is led by one professional trainer and two skilled community residents who serve as assistant trainers. The training employs a variety of techniques such as role playing, small discussion group meetings and a study of condensed reading materials. The sessions are conducted (and all materials are prepared) in both Spanish and English. All sessions are conducted at Community Learning Centers.

Approximately 70 percent of the training sessions are devoted to analysis of the school system and the roles parent and community leaders might play in its functioning. Topics include the following:

The history of community participation in the schools.
Analysis of the 1969 decentralization law.
Functions of community school boards.
The Central Board of Education and its relationship to the community school boards.
The election process for community school board members and how to organize for election.
Educational problems of schools in the local area.
The school site selection process.
Statistics on schools in the local area and how to interpret them.
Special school programs, especially bilingual education.

The role of paraprofessionals.

The public school curriculum and who determines it.

Parent-teacher relations and parent-school relations, with emphasis on how to keep informed on school affairs.

Problems and the role of the Parent Association in school-community relations.

EXPECTED OUTCOMES

Two principal outcomes are expected. The first is the development and training of leaders who can help improve communication between the community and the school. The second is development of a replicable curriculum package and training model for community leadership programs. Preliminary evaluation of the pilot phase and first year of this program indicates that the program is motivating individuals into action, that graduates of this program are more optimistic after the program than before about the chances of improving the school system by constructive, peaceful means, and that graduates find school personnel *easier* to deal with and more open to them than before they enrolled in this program.

It is expected that the program will have a multiplier effect in each community: the trainees can effectively broaden the base of community support and educational leadership through training other community residents and stimulating further community development around school-community relations. Evaluation of the program to date has provided evidence of this positive effect.

NEXT STEPS

The curriculum is being revised, based on the experience of the program to date and CUE's evaluation of the program. A training manual is also being written, detailing procedures that have been used successfully in each part of the curriculum.

In addition, a seminar will be initiated for graduate trainees that will serve as a forum for airing school-community relations problems. This seminar grows out of the need and the desire for further work expressed by the graduates of this past year's program.

EXPORTABILITY

Since basic need in virtually any community of the urban poor is for skilled, informed, indigenous leaders, this program's curriculum for training approach should be of value in urban communities throughout the country. CUE plans to assure further refinement of this program by applying the experimental design to several other urban and suburban communities in the New York area as part of its five-year development procedure.

INTERRELATIONSHIP WITH OTHER CUE PROGRAMS

This program is a central step in CUE's efforts to bring about more effective citizen participation in educational efforts. Therefore, all programs and studies feed into it, informing the curriculum, the training, and the approach to the school and the community.

The School Attitudes Study provides basic information regarding the community and school-community relations, and the Black Suburbanite Study

12

points the way to new areas and new problems where the Leadership Training program could be of value.

The Parent Workshops and the School-Community Seminars are parallel efforts to this program, each of the three focusing on a different aspect of the same problem and the same goals, all three taking place in the Community Learning Center, and all three making use of and contributing to the Library. The Leadership Training program also provides the basic personnel to manage the Community Learning Center, which, as has been indicated, will eventually become a fully community controlled and operated institution.

The activities of the CUE school-based development program will benefit from a knowledge of procedures, expressed needs and actions taken by the Leadership Training program. A close liaison will be maintained with a representative from the latter group.

School Attitudes Study

REASON FOR SELECTION AND DESCRIPTION OF STUDY

This study attempts to discover how urban public schools maintain or lose the credibility and acceptance given to them by their adult constituency. The aim is not to legitimate an unreformed system that is in reality no more responsive than it was before. Rather, the aim is to enlighten professionals and citizens on how best to open schools to citizen influence in order for the schools to achieve and merit the support of parents, students, and taxpayers.

As was stated in Chapter I, the outcome of the Center for Urban Education's efforts should be more effective and more responsive education systems in urban settings. The School Attitudes Study is an integral part of that effort because it explores and analyzes the underlying forces that have produced the crisis of confidence in our urban schools.

The central questions in the study are the following: To what extent are attitudes about the legitimacy of an institution related to its effectiveness? To what extent are clients' perceptions related to objective measures of such effectiveness? To what extent is the openness of an institution to client influence (actual or potential) related to the legitimacy clients accord it? To what extent is the openness of an institution, as perceived by clients, related to any objective measure of openness?

Using descriptive data for all elementary schools in New York City, we selected a sample of 64 elementary schools stratified on the basis of ethnicity and socioeconomic status. A total of 960 mothers of children who attended these schools were interviewed in the spring of 1970.

In the first year of this study, the broad framework was conceptualized; relevant literature was reviewed; background demographic work was completed to serve as the basis for sample selection for current and future work; instruments were developed and refined through pretesting, and the parent interviews were completed. Data are being analyzed, and an initial report on the findings of the first phase of data analysis will be completed by September 30, 1970.

EXPECTED OUTCOMES

Aside from providing definitive answers to the central questions cited, this study should enable CUE program developers to definitely determine at what points interventions might be most productive for different subgroups of the population. More importantly, this study should throw light on the kinds of changes that must be made in the schools if the crisis of confidence is to end without repression or rebellion.

NEXT STEPS

A thorough analysis of the data from the parent interviews is the next immediate step. Additionally, in the fall of 1970, members of our staff plan to conduct interviews with school personnel in each of the 64 schools and with community leaders in these neighborhoods. The data from this second phase of interviewing

14

will provide information about interrelations between parents' and school personnel's perceptions and various objective indicators of the prevailing situation.

EXPORTABILITY

The findings, and recommendations flowing from them, should be valuable to researchers, developers, lawmakers, and concerned citizens.

INTERRELATIONSHIP WITH OTHER CUE PROGRAMS

As a part of the Center's efforts to build a base of knowledge that would help close the gap between the school and the community, this study will provide some of the knowledge and insights needed. Since the study has gathered such extensive data on the perceptions and attitudes of parents and school personnel, the information gained will be useful in the construction of curricula for the Parent Participation Workshops, the Leadership Training program, and the School-Community Seminars.

Parent Participation Workshop

REASON FOR SELECTION AND DESCRIPTION OF PROGRAM

The Parent Participation Workshops program is designed to encourage constructive interaction between school personnel in urban areas and poor minority parents. Research indicates the value of parents' awarenesss of what goes on in the schools, of their own unique role in their child's educational development, and of the social values they feel that schools should foster. Therefore in order to encourage parents to become actively involved in their children's total education (nonschool as well as in-school), CUE has established the Parent Participation Workshops. Through this program, CUE will assist parents to develop skills and techniques that will enable them to work more effectively with schools and to understand (and, if necessary, change) their children's learning environment. CUE views these workshops as a necessary part of its efforts to improve student performance and to insure effective citizen participation.

In the spring of 1970, CUE initiated its first program for Puerto Rican and black parents of fourth-grade children from nine schools in the South Bronx. After nine weeks of discussions and training in leadership skills, conducted in the Community Learning Center, each parent conducted her own workshop sessions with a small group (10 15) of parents she recruited from her own school. Twenty workshop sessions were conducted in each school. Once a week, each of the group leaders returned to the Community Learning Center for a review and evaluation of the problems and progress of the workshops and for further training. (In all, the group leaders attended 26 sessions at the Community Learning Center). Approximately 140 parents participated in this program.

To accomplish the Center's long-range goals of productive civic participation and increased literacy through social education, objectives of the Workshops are:

1. To encourage parents to increase and make effective their contacts with school administrators, board members, and teachers to the end that both groups may better understand what each wants from and can bring to the school experiences of children.

2. To better inform parents of what takes place in the schools and why.

3. To help parents understand the unique educational role of the home.

4. To encourage parents towards greater observance of their children's learning, so they can better recognize and appreciate the strengths and weaknesses of their children's performance.

5. To help parents to become better informed about the educational resources and services available to them in the community.

6. To provide parents with opportunities to interact with other parents concerning mutual interests and needs, in order to develop strategies for change.

7. To provide parents with a problem solving methodology.

16

EXPECTED OUTCOMES

The short-run outcomes expected are:

1. Greater parental contact with school administrators, school board members, and teachers.

2. Increased parental understanding and use of the educational and other resources and services available to them in their community.

3. Improved home resources (e.g., greater language interaction with children) and a heightened awareness and increased use of resources in the home.

4. The production of a replicable parents' curriculum, a trainers' guide, and a parents' manual.

For the long-run, this program has been designed specifically so that parents in the poor urban areas may further their children's educational progress and, at the same time, may themselves become informed citizens able to participate in the restructuring now taking place in urban education.

Preliminary evaluation of the program indicates that the Parent Workshops have uncovered potential parent leaders among a group of women who were ordinarily uninvolved in educational affairs. Observations showed that parents who have often been called apathetic, indifferent, or hostile turned out to be merely lacking in confidence and/or opportunity. According to CUE's evaluation, the pilot phase of this program has already begun the process of helping such parents discover their own competence.

NEXT STEPS

The next development in this program component is an expansion of the 1969-1970 Parent Participation Workshops, carried on as noted above in schools of the South Bronx. During the past year, the program dealt primarily with existing school curricula, investigating ways in which it could be supplemented in the home. This phase of the program is now being evaluated with a view to further amplification.

The Community Learning Center was the main vehicle for fielding the Workshops and will continue to be so. Workshops also extended into the actual schools of the districts involved; this aspect will also be continued. Parents will be able, therefore, to have close contact and interaction with their children's schools and teachers and with other parents who share intimately their own experiences. At the same time they will benefit from the independence and broader focus of being part of the Community Learning Center experience.

Although no formal participant-developed manuals were written during the 1969-1970 Workshops, the program defined recruitment procedures, identified interest and needs of participants, clarified the role of the group leader, produced a body of training procedures and organizational structure suitable for and acceptable to participating parents, and established working relations with school personnel. These experiences will serve as the base for building further stages of the Workshop Program.

In the coming year we shall establish workshops in two economically depressed areas — one in the South Bronx (continuing our program of 1969-1970) and one 17 in Brooklyn. The Group Leaders who will participate in the Parent Participation Workshops will represent 9 schools. Through discussion of local school and community problems and utilization of local resources, the Group Leaders will develop and expand the list of previously developed strategies of problem solving that resulted from 1969-1970 Workshop experiences. This training information will be shared with the parent participants in small workshop groups.

The Center will provide the appropriate consultants, specialists in curriculum, housing, health, nutrition, and consumer education. With their assistance and the help of the CUE staff members, participants will generate materials that will ultimately become the home curriculum. There will be 12 training sessions for Group Leaders and 30 sessions for parent participants.

EXPORTABILITY

As a result of the full-scale experimental program, the CUE staff will have produced a Parent Participation program complete with training and parent manuals for utilization in other areas throughout the country. It should be useful to other parent groups, to those wishing to institute Community Learning Centers and to officials charged with implementing decentralization plans.

INTERRELATIONSHIP WITH OTHER CUE PROGRAMS

As with the other community programs, the Parent Participation Workshops program is enhanced by being a part of the Community Learning Center as explained above.

The Community Learning Center will also be strengthened by the Parent program if the parent comes to recognize that his hopes for his children are central to the guidelines for the Community Learning Center. CUE believes the parent will recognize this as he gains understanding of his role in the education of his children. Then he will also perceive that whenever all community parents can interact effectively with professional school personnel, they are helping to insure that the schools truly reflect community needs.

The relationship of the Parent Participation Workshops to the School-Community Seminars is discussed under the Seminars section. As in the case of the Seminars, the findings of the School Attitudes and Black Suburbanite Studies will be incorporated into the material used for discussion in the program. Parents will be able to compare their attitudes with others and to sharpen their understanding of what it is about the schools that affects those attitudes. This is a necessary step before constructive participation in civic and social change can occur. A look at what other parents are doing — i.e. those in suburbs, who have similar problems, but more fully developed local-control mechanisms — will suggest opportunities and pitfalls in educational participation. The Black Suburbanite study will also underscore the importance of state and federal roles in educational policies and will do so in a manner no recitation of laws and directives could accomplish.

What is learned from the program and from the parent manuals will become part of the rich empirical foundation of the LARC program, and LARC will, simultaneously, provide curriculum material for the Parent Program.

The Library Services program is doubly important to the Parent Workshops. Many parents are able to attend meetings only if child care services are provided.   18

The program can then reach families with young children who will benefit both from the library program itself and from their parents' opportunity to take part in the Parent Workshops. Parents themselves will also have at hand library materials vital to the successful pursuit of their program.

Much of what the parent participants in the program will discuss and experience will parallel the concern and interests of their children. The program will provide an opportunity for making CUE's school-based curriculum a vital part in meeting the need for home-school congruence in interests and social aims. The school program itself will study the parent curriculum manual for clues to its own greater relevancy in the lives of urban children.

School-Community Seminars

REASON FOR SELECTION AND DESCRIPTION OF PROGRAM

As part of its effort to improve the ability of educators and citizens to transact in productive ways, CUE has designed and initiated a series of meetings (seminars) among principals, community representatives, and teachers who serve as union chapter chairmen. These seminars, which take place outside of the school, focus on topics that are at the heart of the present crisis separating the school from the community. The following list of problems that have created the need for this program make up the agenda in these seminars:

Decentralization and the struggle for self-definition by Community School Boards.

Federal grants that mandate local community involvement.

Increased demands on the part of local community people for accountability in education.

The growing militancy and power of unionized teachers.

The failure of traditional solutions to long-standing educational issues.

The pilot phase of this program was conducted in the spring of 1970 in the Community Learning Center in the South Bronx. There were 52 participants — 26 principals and 1 assistant principal, 22 chapter chairmen, and 3 members of the Community School Board. There were 15 seminars, held once a week. Consultants were available at nine of the sessions; CUE personnel conducted and led the other six sessions.

The concept of the Community Learning Center is especially important to the success of the School-Community Seminars program. The seminars are deliberately planned to take place away from the physical symbol of the school authority, in a location where community representatives can feel free from the possible intimidation of the official school establishment and where school personnel should be better able to see the new community board structure and local demands as extensions of the traditional American belief in the policy-making responsibility of the citizenry. The Community Learning Center admirably fulfills this requirement of the program.

Evaluation of the 1969-70 seminars indicated that the politically neutral locale of the Community Learning Center is highly desirable. In addition, the attendance of a number of community people greatly enhanced and opened up discussions. The 1970-71 phase of the program, therefore, will expand the activities involving the seminars more closely with the Learning Centers and will recruit a larger number of interested community representatives.

EXPECTED OUTCOMES

We expect this program to improve school-community relations as a result of the following changes in which professional school leaders will:

1. Redefine their roles and their relationships with pupils, parents, and other community residents.

20

2. Become more responsive to the problems, needs, and aspirations of the communities which they serve.

3. Develop new approaches to dealing with their constituency.

At the same time, community representatives will:

1. Redefine their relationship with school personnel.

2. Clarify the needs of their communities.

3. Develop workable approaches for achieving their goals.

Finally, we expect to develop, as a result of this program, a replicable curriculum and training manual on school-community relations.

NEXT STEPS

Participants will be selected on this basis: 18 principals, 18 chapter chairmen (United Federation of Teachers), 18 community persons, representing the Community School Board, parents, and community leaders.

The activities and tasks (and the skills and competencies for performing each task) that participants will perform in each of 15 workshop sessions will be specified.

Materials and methods will be developed for a plan of instruction intended to affect those skills and competencies. This will include further review of the literature and use of the data derived from the first cycle of the program.

EXPORTABILITY

The third year of the program will see the dissemination of curriculum and training materials to urban areas outside New York City. Evaluation of that work will result in final packaging of manuals and materials in time for general use by the following school year.

INTERRELATIONSHIP WITH OTHER CENTER PROGRAMS

The integral role played by the Community Learning Centers in the School-Community Seminars has been discussed above. It should be obvious that the seminars themselves will, in turn, enhance the validity of the Community Learning Center as a valuable and legitimate vehicle for community-school relations improvement and restructuring.

The seminars are intimately interwoven with other Community Learning Center based programs. The community participants will, in all likelihood, be selected from among people who have previously participated in Leadership Development and Parent Workshop programs, insuring seminar members who possess skills required for effective and knowledgeable participation.

The School Attitudes and School Innovations Studies will feed their findings into the Seminar program, giving an empirical base to discussions and manual materials. The Black Suburbanite Study findings will suggest areas of discussions and possible innovation in School-Community interactions.

Black Suburbanite Study

REASON FOR SELECTION AND DESCRIPTION OF STUDY

Population studies show that blacks are moving to the suburbs at a greater rate than whites, and demographers are predicting a continued significant increase in nonwhites in the suburbs for the 1970s. Though there is much in the literature about blacks in white suburbs, few studies focus on the effects of this population movement on the suburban and urban educational systems. CUE is conducting an exploratory study to determine the impact of suburbanization of blacks on our school system.

By isolating those factors which contribute to the success of multi-racial school districts, this study will provide valuable data for school officials, lawmakers, and citizens involved with decentralization and community control.

For 1969-70, CUE conducted open-ended interviews in two suburbs in the New York metropolitan area. One community has a majority of black residents, and the blacks are predominantly middle class but with a sizable minority (about 30%) on welfare. The second community has a minority of blacks, and the blacks are predominantly middle and upper-middle class. The respondents included people from the community and people from the school system, (blacks as well as whites,) people who lived there a long time, and blacks who had only recently moved in. Special care was taken to include low-income blacks. The interviews ranged from 30 minutes to two hours. We are now analyzing the data we have gathered.

EXPECTED OUTCOMES

1. A published document with an analysis of the background data on the two communities and including a demographic report to document percentage increases of black population in suburban areas.

2. A published report with recommendations for full-scale research and developmental programs along these relevant themes:

   (a) Curriculum changes and additions, including both the role of the student body and community in planning changes, and the effect of such changes on the student body.

   (b) Methods of teaching of reading.

   (c) Effect and influence of organized groups (social, religious, educational, political) on decision-making within the schools.

   (d) The governmental and institutional context of surburban education. This category includes such matters as: welfare policies, tax laws, funding levels, the governmental structure, and conflicts between tax-paying home-owners and low-income renters.

There are several immediate uses to which the information gathered will be put:

1. Dissemination to suburban communities beginning to experience increases in black population.

22

2. Dissemination to governmental officials to whom its findings will be of value in planning money allocations and formulating public policy.

3. Use by CUE program developers as source material in citizen participation programs.

4. Use by CUE program developers as source material in preparing materials for literacy education.

NEXT STEPS

Based on our exploratory study, we project an experimental survey of selected communities representing both urban and suburban schools, black, white, and integrated, for comparative purposes and meaningful data analysis. The survey should provide definitive answers to many questions arising from the increasing black suburban population. Schools in the suburbs will be able to use these answers in planning their programs and in providing quality education for all their clients. Since many whites view the influx of blacks with alarm, facts are needed to plan appropriately for changes.

EXPORTABILITY

As we have indicated above, the products, programs and documents generated by the study and the projected survey should be of value to both urban and suburban schools experiencing change in the makeup of student populations. Legislators, educational program developers, government agencies, and researchers will find the research valuable to their work. Many programs may be more readily tried and innovations dared when evidence of the effects of change is available.

INTERRELATIONSHIP WITH OTHER CUE PROGRAMS

The Black Suburbanite Study is relevant to CUE products and program development. It will provide information on which CUE's new school-based materials can be built. Parent Participation Workshops and the Leadership Training program should incorporate into their curricula the findings and insights of the study. Both community people and school personnel should be helped to see what factors operate for successful community change. Resistance to change is often lessened by seeing what others have done.

Library Services

REASON FOR SELECTION AND DESCRIPTION OF PROGRAM

Library Services will play a vital part in CUE's overall effort to strengthen community participation in educational affairs. Through the Library Services program, CUE will provide the resources for a specialized library as well as bilingual instruction in its use.

Community persons enrolled in or graduates of CUE's Leadership Training program, School-Community Seminars, and Parent Participation Workshops need to acquire the technical know-how and experience to search independently for information concerning new problems or situations on the school scene. To properly develop leadership roles, community residents also need to learn the uses of a library, the types of information stored there, and how to get at this information. The Library Services program is designed to meet these specific requirements.

The Community Learning Center, as the site for CUE's community programs, constitutes a logical setting for the creation of a library specializing in materials related to school-community issues. Its location in the heart of the target community is an added advantage.

The parents in the Community Learning Center programs would of course prefer to have their preschool children cared for near them rather than at distant day care centers. An "on site" child care service in a library setting fulfills this desire. This service provides, for example, a place for young children to have supervised play, to look at books, hear stories, and learn about the pleasures of books and literature at an early age. The library will thus double as a facility for a child care service and a learning resource center.

EXPECTED OUTCOMES

The adult participants will develop reasonable competence in various library skills and research techniques. They will become familiar with new equipment designed for libraries.

The training sessions and seminars, as well as post-training community experience, will be enhanced by trainee access to and use of library resources.

Preschool children of participating parents will receive a variety of enriching experiences through books and play.

Finally, through the establishment of an adult collection of relevant paperback books, magazines, and newspapers, parents and other residents will become more aware of what books and libraries have to offer them in the way of pleasure as well as information. The Library Services in the Community Learning Centers, it is hoped, will encourage parents and children to become more involved in self-education, thus enriching their contribution to the community.   24

NEXT STEPS

The CUE Library Services program will provide, in an appropriate location in each Community Learning Center:

1. Library materials (including relevant films and filmstrips) to support current programs and dealing with the following subjects:

The community (South Bronx and Brooklyn)
The history and culture of Puerto Ricans, blacks and other ethnic groups
Local school systems and decentralization
Social services in the community

2. Facilities for children's library services and child care, including the following:

Films and filmstrips
Records
Educational games
Children's literature relevant to the various ethnic groups and cultures
Appropriate children's furniture

3. Instruction in library techniques by CUE's qualified library staff in such basic library skills as use of the card catalog, indexes, and reference materials.

4. A curriculum and training manual based on the library skills instruction in both English and Spanish.

Library programs can be made operative by the fall of 1970, and then offered on a year-round basis.

INTERRELATIONSHIP WITH OTHER CUE PROGRAMS

An introduction to the library and instruction in basic library skills will be incorporated into the training sessions of all CUE community programs. Additionally, the child care services will enable parents to participate in Community Learning Center programs they might not otherwise attend.

Literacy Through Social Education

The theme of Literacy through Social Education is served principally by CUE's school-based instructional development program, which is called *Social Participation through Understanding and Reading* (SPUR).

It consists of a series of program components engineered to result in substantial improvement in the scope and quality of student literacy through social education and in the effectiveness and relevance of teacher performance in an urban setting.

SPUR is designed to reinforce and parallel the Citizen Participation Program with which it works collaboratively in the process of developing useful products and innovational educational procedures.

While the main developmental setting for SPUR is the public school in the same neighborhood where the Community Learning Center is located, its instructional products are designed to stimulate teacher and student toward fuller, more meaningful participation in the community at large.

Because the majority of children who will attend public school in the 1970's and 1980's will live in an urban environment, the SPUR program is designed to help them to develop the skills which will enable them to cope effectively with the problems and promises of urban living. SPUR is built on the philosophical premise that the structure of society and its institutions are built and shaped by man, and that the local citizenry have the power to reshape their environment.

The school climate of the 1970's will reflect the pluralism of culture and values which will be found in the school population. This is a fundamental change from the previous emphasis of the "melting pot" concept which sought to minimize cultural differences among children. The richness of the varied backgrounds of the American public school population will be used as asset to create a more vigorous social educational curriculum. The National Council for the Social Studies has stated succinctly the goals of an expanded Social Studies Program:

> Education of the 70's and 80's must be aimed at equipping individuals to anticipate change and to develop the cognitive structure, analytical skills and affective responses which would seem to be functional in coping with a continually changing social environment. [National Council for the Social Studies, 39th Yearbook, 1969, p.34.]

The target population for the SPUR Program is the economically deprived minority groups of the metropolitan areas. The program will be developed and pilot tested in selected public schools in the New York Metropolitan area with student populations reflective of this target goal. The major portion of the pilot testing will be conducted in schools in the same New York City public school district which have been selected for the location of the CUE-Community Learning Centers.

The SPUR Program will generate three major kinds of products: instructional materials for students and teachers, informational materials for school principals and administrators, and parent-community involvement materials. 26

The Social Education Program, within the five-year period of this basic plan, will develop these product materials into a learning system for elementary school children in grades four through six. This development would constitute a major step towards achieving a longer-term, overall goal: the construction of a pre-kindergarten through grade twelve curriculum in Literacy Through Social Education.

The outcome of such a program would be the development of children into adults who are confident of their ability to participate effectively and intelligently in the societal decision-making processes which affect their destiny.

Social Participation through Understanding and Reading (SPUR)

REASONS FOR SELECTION AND DESCRIPTION OF PROGRAM

CUE's *Social Participation through Understanding and Reading* program (SPUR) is an action-oriented program that relates the school experience of urban, economically-deprived children directly to the local community and the larger society in which they live.

Its aim is twofold:

    1. to develop in children of the middle grades the ability to read critically, as a major tool to understanding material in community studies

    2. to equip them with the skills, knowledge, and attitudes they need to participate in and effect change in community life

The program thus is a major arm of CUE's effort to achieve literacy through social education.

Social education in the context of the SPUR program denotes student involvement in civic activities in ways that go beyond traditional boundaries of social studies. First, in contrast to the passive learning about the community process, as is the rule, the students in this program will be actively engaged in community life through projects, interviews, reporting, and research — outside of the school as well as in it. Second, the students will have an opportunity to improve their reading skills in specific ways that are most appropriate to the action-oriented curriculum that they will pursue. For the term "reading" here does not mean participating in reading drills in isolation from relevant life experiences. In pursuit of understanding, the student will be dependent upon reading to acquire, evaluate, and assimilate important information. He will need instruction in a wide range of reading skills in order to understand the content and material basic to his mission.

The content and materials of most social studies programs now used in classrooms are designed for the suburban or rural child. These programs, therefore, do not tap the natural experiences of the lower-class child, nor reflect how he views the world and its problems. In general, there are few models or situations in these programs that appeal to him sufficiently to help him grow intellectually and emotionally.

Evidence that this situation can be changed by an action-oriented approach is documented in our three years of experimentation with the *Planning for Change* curriculum, the forerunner to the expanded SPUR program (See the September 1968 Center for Urban Education *Basic Program Plans* for a brief history of *Planning for Change*.) A main thrust of this program was based upon Coleman's research finding, now widely acknowledged, that poor children need to develop a sense of control over their environment. According to his report, the child who perceives that he can change or affect his environment tends to achieve more in the school setting.

Designed for 4th and 5th grade inner-city youngsters, *Planning for Change* was received with widespread enthusiasm by school administrators, teachers, parents,   28 and students in New York City and, in adapted versions, in suburban schools. Teachers saw the program as possessing considerable potential for a total elementary and, eventually, secondary urban education scheme.

The underlying philosophy of the program is that the urban environment is the product of man's decision and as such can be changed by man. The program affords the child opportunities to rediscover his neighborhood and his city. The action-oriented assignment prepares the child to participate in the process of change. Thus, what goes on in the classroom becomes relevant to everyday life. The SPUR program is designed, therefore, to provide the child with appropriate environmental encounters and with the level of reading competence that will enable him to develop his potential as a socially useful member of society.

PROJECT I: SPUR Instructional Modules

The SPUR program will develop teaching modules covering such topics as Health, Drug Addiction, Pollution, Occupation, Sanitation, Environmental Ecology, Aesthetics, Crime, Cultural Diversity, and others. These will be developed in terms of concepts that have been chosen as being basic to a meaningful social studies curricula.

The activities included will involve an action-oriented, inquiry mode in which students and teachers do such things as:

identify problems
explore value implications
establish problem priorities
explore methods of investigation
collect and analyze data
arrive at conclusions
make decisions
act on decisions

Concept Development

The teaching strategies of the SPUR program will be organized around a framework of selected concepts which are developed spirally and sequentially. This approach has been adopted in line with the current movement in curriculum reform in social studies initiated by Taba, Fenton, Morrissett, Price and others. The focus on concept development will assist students in shifting away from dependence on memorization and the study of isolated facts. The use of selected concepts will, instead, provide for the study of facts, events, and phenomena that may be grouped together to explain various events and trends. Stress is placed upon the development of the student's cognitive powers. The use of the conceptual approach permits the development of an action-oriented program in which students develop generalizations as a result of varied experiences, as they proceed through the specified curriculum stages.

Wherever possible, existing instructional materials will be used in the SPUR program, to amplify or illuminate the basic conceptual scheme. The SPUR program will organize its instructional modules around concepts of which the following are examples:

Conflict. It is essential that students develop into adults with positive healthy attitudes that will enable them to cope with the various types of conflicts they will encounter at different levels of development. They should also be helped to acquire effective patterns of conflict resolution.

29

Power. If the student is to develop into a person who can effectively plan for and help effect positive change, he must understand the nature of the power relationships within his society. He must understand the use of the various types of power: social, economic, and political, and the relation of power and its lack to intergroup conflicts, social controls, and social class conflicts.

Habitat and Environment Control. A major aim of this program is to develop within the student an awareness that he is able by his own actions to effect some change in the environment in which he lives. The concept of habitat is vital to this curriculum in that it is through the development of this concept that the student will grow to understand that man's habitat has always been subject to changes made by human action.

The Role of the Teacher
As can be seen, the teacher is a key person for the realization of the program. He is not cast in the conventional role of purveyor of knowledge but as a vital facilitator of the learning process. He must be carefully trained in the mode of inquiry approach. He also must become familiar with a wider range of reading skills, so as to teach them not as isolated skills but as integral parts of social education. Above all, the teacher should become acquainted with the life style of his students. To assist the student in behavioral changes, the teacher must appreciate the student's ethnicity and environment.

Since the intervention is to be primarily through the teacher, the program will specify not only the behavioral objectives for the students but also behaviors required of the teacher. Among them, as already mentioned, are: greater differentiation of instruction, including the use of the inquiry mode; the use of learning activities which involve the children with problems of the community; interaction with parents and community; and emphasis on reading skills. The teacher will be given help in locating, analyzing, and selecting instructional material, avoiding dependence on a single text as the basis for instruction.

Based on the rationale and strategy above, the SPUR program will expand the present CUE *Planning for Change* program into an elementary grades 4 through 6 school social education program. It will provide for the development of those cognitive skills, knowledges, concepts, and values which would enable the urban student to actively engage in the processes by which social change is effected. Essential to the development of these perceptions and capabilities is the acquisition of reading skills commensurate with the demands of the program.

In addition to the development of modular units and other materials to form a complete social education curriculum for grades 4-6, the SPUR program will include a strong component in reading instruction.

PROJECT II: The Readers
High pupil interest in the *Planning for Change* curriculum indicated excellent potential for motivating students to improve their reading skills. Experts agree that reading proficiency increases with training in the techniques needed for reading different kinds of subject matter.

Studies by Shores, Artley, McMahon, Smith, Robinson, and Hall further support the conclusion that in addition to instruction in general reading, there is definite need for instruction in the reading skills peculiar to each field. Social   30 education calls for skills in critical reading based on the need to read with an attitude of inquiry, to evaluate, challenge, and decide upon truthfulness, bias and authenticity.

A survey of materials currently on the market, and those projected in publishers' lists of future publication, indicates that there is a serious lack of social studies material designed to improve the reading skills required by most social studies curricula.

The SPUR program therefore projects the creation of a series of readers that will:

1. reflect themes of interest and value to the modern student in a pluralistic, urban society;

2. help the student to develop the specific reading skills necessary for understanding and processing the information he needs to use as a participating citizen.

It must be emphasized that this is in no wise a program of beginning reading. Many inner-city schools throughout the nation are already working with experimental programs on that level. Therefore, this program focuses deliberately on the intermediate grades, the grades in which reading problems begin to multiply, in part, because of the sudden increase in the subject content. There has yet been no concerted, systematic attack on the reading problems arising out of the need to read different types of material for different reasons.

Tales of Your Cities Readers

As has been shown above, the lack of relevant and contemporary reading materials for our target group makes the provision of such materials an urgent matter. CUE's series of readers will be titled *Tales of Your Cities*. Selections will be fiction, poetry, and non-fiction, chosen for literary value and for themes related to key concepts underlying social education. These would reflect children's needs; for example, the need for fun and self-discovery and the need to cope with economic and social realities. The emphasis will be on understanding and appreciation of individuals and groups in multi-cultural, urban settings.

The readers will be designed for students in grades 4-6, and will include selections suitable for three reading levels: easy, average, and more mature. Suggestions supplementing each selection would cover such activities as role-playing, simulation-games, and exercises in critical reading skills.

Photographs and drawings related to the text, as well as illustrations featuring students' work, will be incorporated into the finished product.

The series would be specifically constructed to avoid the problems commonly ascribed to social studies reading materials, with special attention paid to correlating the selections with specific skills. The student volumes would be supported by teacher's guides indicating appropriate teaching strategies for achieving both effective social education understandings and an increase in reading efficiency.

We project that students using the *Tales of Your Cities* readers will manifest a higher level of learning in these areas: inter-group understanding, social geography and history, and general and specialized reading and comprehension skills.

31

Teachers using the readers and the manuals will be greatly assisted in their efforts to provide the type of specialized instruction needed for reading in the content areas.

PROJECT III: Measurement and Testing

On both the curriculum modules and the readers, segments of the SPUR program will pay special attention to assessment of pupil change. Since the Literacy through Social Education Program is designed to modify the student's attitudes, knowledge, and skills, it is obvious that different types of measurements are required.

Attitudes are generally measured by a self-report procedure which directly asks the student's opinion, with the result that surface opinions are tapped. However, a well-constructed questionnaire can reveal basic changes in attitudes. Changes in attitudes may also be reported by the teacher.

Knowledge is best measured by a test. Objective tests, while useful, are likely to be too specific; therefore, in the SPUR program they will be used in conjunction with short essay questions. The effort will be to gauge the student's understanding of the subject matter rather than his knowledge of definitions of terms. Part or all of the test results will be communicated to the pupils early in the year as a means of guiding their learning processes.

Skill is best measured by having the student perform a sample task. Written tests of skills will be used where appropriate, but it is expected that more complex skills will be measured by having the students solve problems orally or perform a task related to the instruction. Again the pupils will be informed early of the performance expected of them at the end of the instruction.

An additional measure of class development can be obtained by collecting notes on critical incidents. In this technique, a record is kept of outstanding event of individual or group behavior in the area of social education.

All of the above techniques, with the possible exception of complex skills tests, will be used by the teacher in the SPUR program to assess the progress of the individual student for the purpose of individualizing instruction and assigning grades. In addition, the combined results can give a picture of class performance.

Assessment is thus viewed as an integral part of instruction. In addition to providing data on pupil progress, it informs the teacher of her class needs and the pupil of his goals. CUE staff will prepare the necessary questionnaires, observation and teacher-report instruments designed to measure attitudinal and behavioral change. These will be incorporated into the program as part of the teacher's manual.

The following guidelines will be used in constructing reading achievement tests. As much as possible, these will avoid the objectionable features of published instruments.

Every attempt will be made to have the test content (pictures, words, and story themes) reflect the language and experience of the students for whom they are designed.

The format of the tests will be as simple, straightforward, and consistent as possible to facilitate understanding of the test tasks and directions by students whose experience with standard English might be limited.

32

Reading tests will be limited to curriculum-related tasks and skills. They will not attempt to cover general learning ability or intellectual functioning, although these factors obviously can not be completely eliminated. Since many students fail to score on traditional tests even though they have mastered some low-level reading skills, the project tests will be constructed to include a large number of items at the easy end of the difficulty scale.

EXPECTED OUTCOMES

Products:

1. The construction of sequential instructional materials (modules and readers) that are related to students' needs and experiences and are designed to help them gain reading competence.

2. The development of a teacher training course of study to prepare teachers in this program to use the SPUR materials effectively.

3. The invention of measurement instruments to meet the special needs of the program.

Student Gains:

1. The acquisition of reading skills he needs for probing and solving social problems and working effectively with other people in probing and solving social problems.

2. The acquisition of some basic social concepts that form a basis for understanding many human relationships and human activities.

3. The acquisition of the knowledge he needs to help him affect change in his environment.

4. The development of a sense of self-worth and a sense of control over the shaping of his life and his environment.

Teacher Gains:

1. A better understanding of each student, and the student's environment.

2. Greater involvement in preparing student for social reality.

3. Improvement in teaching performance and teaching methods.

NEXT STEPS

Product Development. With the assistance of curriculum consultants and/or writers, CUE will design the following materials for the SPUR program:

1. Modular units (e.g., special units on drugs, air pollution, aesthetics and others) emphasizing relevant content and action-oriented procedures.

2. *Tales of Your Cities* Readers which will contain a variety of literary selections and a social studies reading skills program.

3. A *Teachers Guide* which will contain specified teaching strategies, student behavioral objectives, suggested learning activities, with community program components and en route evaluative instruments.

4. Reading tests which will contain two batteries: a pre-reading battery for use prior to the start of reading assignments; and an achievement battery for use when the students have mastered decoding skills.

5. A *Staff Development Guide* which will consist of a pre- and in-service course of study for teachers in the program.

Field-testing. Experience with the *Planning for Change* curriculum has demonstrated the advisability of taking important preliminary steps before   33 installing this program in schools. First, CUE will plan to choose schools in terms of student and parent needs. Schools will be selected in areas where parents of the students are engaged in CUE *Citizen Participation* programs. Next, CUE will seek the cooperation of the local school superintendent, principals, teachers and parents (through such organizations as the PTA). Orientation sessions will be conducted at which all parties concerned will have an opportunity to react to the SPUR program concepts and instructional materials. At first the program will be field-tested in a very limited number of schools in order to provide the most intensive training, observation and feedback. After the initial feedback, prompt revisions will be undertaken and the program will be installed in a much larger number of schools so as to include a more representative cross-section of students and teachers. At the time of the field-testing, an evaluative component will be mounted and directed at the three major areas of the program: student, teacher and instructional materials.

Dissemination. After the pilot tests and revisions, the SPUR program will be ready for widespread dissemination to other urban areas in need of this type of program.

EXPORTABILITY

The problems confronting educators and citizens in New York City are endemic to the American urban context in the 1970s. The solutions generated by CUE's SPUR program should be of value to educators throughout urban America. This is particularly true since these solutions will have been worked out not only in the classrooms, but also in tandem with citizens in CUE's Community Learning Centers. The solutions, therefore, will have been tested in the most appropriate (and challenging) context.

The solutions generated by this program and the base of knowledge created will materialize in the following products: a set of instructional materials to be used in the instructional modules; a teacher's guide on the use of the materials; a teacher training manual, and a series of readers. The existence of these products will greatly facilitate the exportability of this program into other settings for further refinement and additional expansion to fit specific local needs.

INTERRELATIONSHIP WITH OTHER CUE PROGRAMS

All CUE programs and studies will feed into the SPUR program. The SPUR Curriculum, the approach to the parents and students, the preparation of the reading series, and the training of the teachers can benefit from the knowledge and insights derived from the other CUE programs and studies. The chart at the end of this chapter graphically illustrates how one component from the Civic Participation program may be interrelated, and how such a collaborative approach can heighten the value of all CUE activities.

Since SPUR relates school learning directly to the community life of the student, contact with the community in and through the programs taking place in the Learning Centers will be essential to personnel preparing materials for SPUR. To take two examples, the Leadership Development Program, for one, will have citizens and community leaders at the Learning Center discussing community life. A member of the SPUR writing team preparing materials for the curriculum

34

modules will be in attendance at sessions of the Leadership Development Program to keep abreast of community concerns. And the Parent Participation Workshop will have hard-to-reach parents at the Learning Center discussing school problems of their children. Here again, the scheduled presence of SPUR staff at these sessions will allow them to gather valuable insights about community life and then transfer them directly into program materials for teachers and pupils, as part of the SPUR programs.

Similarly, the SPUR program feeds into the programs going on in the Community Learning Centers. Through SPUR, students will be solving community problems and acting on their own decisions. Past experience with *Planning for Change*, in which similar activities originated, indicated that what students come up with can be of benefit to the adults engaged in programs at the Community Learning Center. The benefits, of course, can be multiplied if the adults engaged in those programs are the parents of the pupils in the SPUR program.

Language Acquisition Resources Center (LARC)

REASON FOR SELECTION AND DESCRIPTION OF PROGRAM

LARC is a home-based program designed to facilitate the development of communications skills for young children from infancy through five years. The program consists of parent-child language interaction activities which coordinate with and give practice to the child's natural course of language learning. These activities may be used wherever parents and children (or parent surrogates and children) meet together: in community centers, Head Start programs, or in baby sitting arrangements; they are planned to serve as prototypes for language curricula in each of these places.

LARC is designed to meet three specific needs converging on the field of education: the burgeoning concern for the potential of learning during early childhood, the role of home environments in shaping early experience, and the demand for new service personnel to direct and carry on educational efforts, in early childhood programs.

The program content focuses on language acquisition because learning how to read and write ultimately depends on perceiving the efficacy of communication. For most people, with the rare exception of a Helen Keller, this occurs through experience with the spoken word. The spoken word, however, cannot be considered apart from its context: the activities, places, and persons which shape its meaning. It follows that the form and function of oral speech will differ according to the environments in which they occur. Therefore, arranging a child's environment and his social interaction with peers and adults to maximize the opportunities for language usage becomes the pivot on which the structure of the LARC program turns.

The program makes no assumption of cultural deficit for any child or group of children. It is not constructed as a remedial tool. Dialects are viewed as different rather than deficient models of communication. Since a dialect is regarded as a rule-governed language like any other, children are not corrected for their use of it. Instead, both mothers and children are encouraged to explore correspondences of syntax and meaning in standard and non-standard speech. It is further maintained, however, that the close approximation of some dialects to standard English can make the latter harder to learn as a second language — if the former are constantly disparaged — because of memory interference in trying to keep separate the related aspects of grammar.

Thus, of course, the child who does not speak standard English is at a disadvantage in the classroom. Keeping this in mind, LARC will determine how emphasis on the co-existence of standard and non-standard forms affects later school performance. The use of a curriculum which allows mother and child together to gain expertise in standard English, without devaluing the use of dialect, may further the acceptance of dialect itself as a teaching tool. Moreover, such a curriculum can ultimately provide a great continuity between the speaking environments of home and school.

36

This approach to language acquisition is an important first step along the path to a general state known later as "literacy." As such the LARC program is appropriately designated as one of CUE's most significant programs under the *Literacy Through Social Education* theme although for reasons of its utilization of a community-based site of operation it also qualifies as a *Civic Participation* entry.

During 1969-70, LARC has been conducted in an inner-city housing project in Bridgeport, Connecticut. Through this program CUE is creating a new professional role, that of Language Counsellor, and providing the training for it. Chosen as the candidate for the first stages of the Language Counsellor Training was a young woman from the neighborhood, who worked with a group of mothers and children under supervision of CUE personnel. Together, they refined and administered the Home Curriculum working individually and with small groups of children, ages six months to two years.

The LARC effort is now being partially supported by the Model Cities Agency of Bridgeport. But their funding, while indicative of their high interest and approval of the project's potential, is very limited and short term, extending the program only a few months beyond the pilot stage financed by CUE.

Results so far achieved appear to indicate that, on both a theoretical and a practical basis, the LARC program has value since it offers, first, a thorough and effective series of activities for strengthening the young child's acquisition of language, a skill basic to his later success in or outside of schools, and second, a means of administering it which involves the unique skills of parents and/or a specially trained community person, the Language Counsellor. It is a program that can be institutionalized by a large or small community without costly delay or prodigious effort. This has happened because LARC applied significant research findings in a creative but practical and realistic way.

EXPECTED OUTCOMES

The following achievements are seen to be reasonable outcomes for the LARC Program.

1. A systematic, structured curriculum of language acquisition will be developed for children of 6 months to 6 years of age.

2. Children undergoing this program will acquire language in a manner that is more relevant to their needs, environment, and their own rates of progress.

3. Parents will be able to guide their young children in a home-based program of specific activities which will enhance their children's earliest acquisition of language.

4. The position of "language counsellor" will be created, as a new service role to education, to act in either a school or community setting to administer the program to children and/or teach parents how to administer it.

Three specific products result from the Program:

The curriculum for parents and young children, consisting of a series of guided activities covering all speech skills possible, at various stages of child development.

The training course of the Language Counsellor.

Measures of language acquisition on which the curriculum is based.

37

LARC differs from other contemporary offerings in the field of early childhood language development through its triple-pronged approach — work in the home, work on the delimited area of language functioning, and work with children from early infancy to five years of age.

NEXT STEPS

In the next phase of development, CUE plans to expand the pilot state of the LARC program, locating it in the two New York Community Learning Centers where it may become an ongoing part of community activities. In addition, efforts are being made to develop other sites in which the LARC Curriculum may be replicated and refined. For example other Model Cities settings, as well as those in which State Education departments work with CUE, are logically locations in which to establish the program next.

The phase of development will be as follows:

The refinement and expansion of the Language Counsellor Training.

The refinement and expansion of the Child Curriculum for the LARC program.

The refinement and expansion of the Home Curriculum and Activities for Parents.

Development of Testing Measures to be used with the Child Curriculum.

As may be expected, the processes involved in development will comprise full field testing and evaluation of each phase. Details are explained in the work schedule and budget section. (see appendix)

EXPORTABILITY

Because of the extreme importance of language acquisition in the field of early childhood education, the LARC program would seem to have significance for use in many other settings and locales besides the urban one. As has been stated above, LARC finds its usefulness "on-the-scene"; that is, in any setting in which the mother-and-child relationship may be utilized to the ends that the LARC program is especially designed for. Therefore, after being tested and validated, LARC could find much usefulness in public and private Day Care Centers, in Housing Project activities, or as part of many State or Federal supported programs focusing on early childhood education. Both suburban and rural communities will find the LARC program as relevant to their needs and interests as it was to the urban setting out of which it was developed.

INTERRELATIONSHIP WITH OTHER CUE PROGRAMS

As an example of how the LARC program might become accessible to parents through interrelationship with other program components, the following procedure has been specified for involvement with the Library Services program. Mothers interested in LARC activities would first serve with the day care unit for a minimum of three months on a part time basis. They would receive instruction in "basic service skills" which would include such activities as meeting with parents and children, collecting data on family experience, and observing the child's development. Then they would begin a closer involvement with other

38

aspects of the LARC program, such as observing the child's language/and the parent's language, learning the importance of language interaction, observing motor directed and verbal directed language, understanding the child's comprehension and production of language, learning and the modelling of language behaviors.

Each parent would work with three children in specific areas of language function, as well as carry out with one family an initial set of procedures designed for home usage.

Evaluation measures would be designed to assess changes in language patterns of the children in the day care center, of the children's families, of the trainees who work with the children, and of their own families.

Children who are brought to the Community Learning Centers for day care service will become prime clients for enrollment in the LARC program, since LARC is designed to be carried on within the Community Learning Center. In addition, the Parent Participation Workshop program will serve as a direct extension of the LARC curriculum into the homes of the participating youngsters, and will provide access to selected mothers who may wish to undertake the Language Counsellor Training Program themselves. In addition, LARC will be useful to the School Community Seminars Program, as it will serve to allow educators to become more familiar with the important phases of early childhood language acquisition and should stimulate interest in the eventual institutionalizing of parts of the LARC approach into kindergarten or other school based programs.

Adoption of Innovations Study

REASON FOR SELECTION AND DESCRIPTION OF STUDY

This study was undertaken in order to explore, identify, and document the characteristics and processes common to the adoption of innovations by school systems. Its aim is to discover the best ways to put innovative solutions and approaches into practice. Since dissemination and diffusion of new approaches are essential to the success of the Center's work, this study is a logical adjunct to all of the Center's research and development efforts. It should enable us to shorten the time between product development and program outcomes, and acceptance in the schools.

Unlike numerous other innovation studies which focus on the characteristics of those who adopt innovations, this study takes a more pragmatic approach and focuses on those aspects of the diffusion and acceptance process *over which the disseminator and innovator have control*. To this end, CUE has identified two innovations which have been adopted, at least on a trial basis, by the New York City public schools. CUE personnel are now conducting case studies of (1) the process whereby these two innovations were adopted initially and (2) the process of diffusion -- or failure of diffusion -- to other schools and school systems. Through open-ended interviews with leading participants in the adoption process, the study attempts to document and analyze the processes and characteristics (of the innovations) which have led to the adoption or rejection of the new approaches.

For the first year, CUE has accomplished its aims in regard to one of the innovations. The acceptance process has been reconstructed, and a list of characteristics of the innovation has been drawn up. As a result, several tentative hypotheses of the nature of the relationship between the characteristics, the process, and the initial adoption of the innovation have been formulated. In addition, CUE has begun to explore conditions that would explain why this innovation, although apparently successful, has not been widely disseminated.

EXPECTED OUTCOMES

The short-run objective of the study on Adoption of Innovations is the completion of a set of identified innovation and dissemination characteristics presented in the order of their importance and impact on the acceptance process. More importantly, the information and insights derived from this study should permit the researchers to work with program developers and help them mold programs and products so as to facilitate the adoption of the programs and products.

NEXT STEPS

In the second year, this exploratory process for the second innovation will be completed and next steps for both will be undertaken. These steps include the testing of the conclusions and hypotheses from the first year's work. In addition,

40

four more innovations will be selected, including those that contain characteristics which specifically correlate (positively or negatively) with the characteristics found to be useful or harmful in the exploratory study of the first year.

EXPORTABILITY

The findings and recommendations of the Adoption of Innovations Study should prove valuable to R & D Centers and regional laboratories throughout the country. Research and development are worthless without dissemination, diffusion, and, in the case of products, adoption. Beyond that, the study should pave the way for a new approach to the dissemination of innovations. The old approach — concentrating on the characteristics of people and institutions that adopted or rejected innovations — too often fostered a self-defeating outlook. CUE's new approach is based on a recognition that even the most rigid institutions . do adopt innovations. This new approach, therefore, challenges inventors and innovators to try harder to get their ideas adopted in the so-called rigid institutions, which may, after all, be the places where innovations are needed the most.

INTERRELATIONSHIP WITH OTHER CENTER PROGRAMS AND STUDIES

The Adoption of Innovations Study is an important part of CUE's efforts to solve one of urban education's major problems, namely, that educators do not know how best to educate the young. This study should help to break the log jam that prevents good ideas from reaching the classroom.

Since CUE's aim is to improve the ability of educators and citizens to interact in productive ways, the citizens who participate in our programs (Parent Participation Workshops and Leadership Development Program) should profit from this study. For they need to become better acquainted with the best ways to introduce new ideas into the school system.

SAMPLE DIAGRAM OF CUE'S COLLABORATIVE PRODUCT DEVELOPMENT

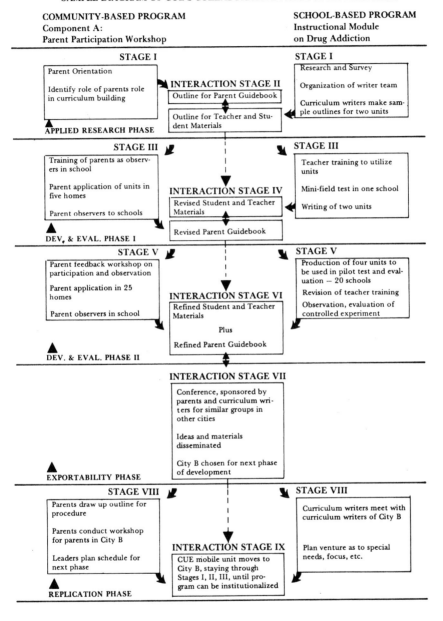

COMMUNITY-BASED PROGRAM
Component A:
Parent Participation Workshop

SCHOOL-BASED PROGRAM
Instructional Module
on Drug Addiction

STAGE I

Parent Orientation

Identify role of parents role
in curriculum building

▲ APPLIED RESEARCH PHASE

INTERACTION STAGE II

Outline for Parent Guidebook

Outline for Teacher and Student Materials

STAGE I

Research and Survey

Organization of writer team

Curriculum writers make sample outlines for two units

STAGE III

Training of parents as observers in school

Parent application of units in five homes

Parent observers to schools

▲ DEV. & EVAL. PHASE I

INTERACTION STAGE IV

Revised Student and Teacher Materials

Revised Parent Guidebook

STAGE III

Teacher training to utilize units

Mini-field test in one school

Writing of two units

STAGE V

Parent feedback workshop on participation and observation

Parent application in 25 homes

Parent observers in school

▲ DEV. & EVAL. PHASE II

INTERACTION STAGE VI

Refined Student and Teacher Materials

Plus

Refined Parent Guidebook

STAGE V

Production of four units to be used in pilot test and evaluation — 20 schools

Revision of teacher training

Observation, evaluation of controlled experiment

INTERACTION STAGE VII

Conference, sponsored by parents and curriculum writers for similar groups in other cities

Ideas and materials disseminated

City B chosen for next phase of development

▲ EXPORTABILITY PHASE

STAGE VIII

Parents draw up outline for procedure

Parents conduct workshop for parents in City B

Leaders plan schedule for next phase

▲ REPLICATION PHASE

INTERACTION STAGE IX

CUE mobile unit moves to City B, staying through Stages I, II, III, until program can be institutionalized

STAGE VIII

Curriculum writers meet with curriculum writers of City B

Plan venture as to special needs, focus, etc.

PROGRAM PLANS FOR 1972-74

Particular activities ongoing during 1970 and next steps to be taken during 1971 on each program component have already been described. What of the steps projected for the next three years? This section offers a general strategy for the long term activities of CUE.

1972 – REPLICATION AND COST ANALYSIS

By the end of 1972, all projected products and procedures contained within a model Community Learning Center will have been fully field tested and evaluated two or more times. in the Center's Southeast Bronx and Brooklyn neighborhood field units. The comprehensive curriculum for a school-based program of social education will not have been completely developed editorially, but enough elements will have been fielded and evaluated to enable the Center to make 1972 the year for assessment of the *relative cost effectiveness* of a model Community Learning Center.

This means that during 1972, CUE will attempt to answer the question: how much would it cost to field a Community Learning Center within a poverty neighborhood in any American city or suburb? In addition, what would its existence and operation yield per dollar in terms of improved school-community transactions, improved lay leadership, and pupil achievement in literacy and social knowledge?

Previously projected research and development operations would be recycled continuously, of course, as basic studies, materials design, and field trial become routines integrated into the functioning of the Community Learning Center itself. The new activity for the Center for Urban Education would be to lay a basis for widespread dissemination of the model, as part of cost analysis. Another part of 1972's effort on behalf of planning for future dissemination will be to plan and arrange for the introduction of one Community Learning Center in a medium size city (80,000 to 400,000) and one in a suburb adjacent to a large central city.

1973 – INFUSION OF NEW PRODUCTS; MARKETING OF PRESENT PRODUCTS

During 1973, all phases of R & D projected for 1970-1972 will continue. On the basis of cost analysis and the beginnings of modification of the model to fit varied community settings during 1972, efforts in 1973 will be given over to *packaging* and planning for the *marketing* of the Community Learning Center and its products.

Collaboration with the media and education industries will be intensified, and cost analysis will continue but with emphasis given to cost dimensions of package production and distribution. Market-oriented research on the question of demand in American cities and their suburbs will be undertaken, as will an effort to analyse the requirements for the cultivation of interest through publicity and information exchange.

42

In order to strengthen the overall quality of the ingredients, CUE will attempt to'incorporate early reading instructional materials, multicultural materials and bilingual instructional products into the model during 1973. These elements will not be designed by or at CUE, but will be imported on a contract basis from cooperating universities, laboratories, and publishers. Explorations toward this end have already begun in 1970, incidentally; the process will continue indefinitely. But 1973 is scheduled to be the year by which definite decisions for such component parts will be made, and in which new contracts with such institutions as the above will be undertaken.

1974 – DISSEMINATION AND INSTITUTIONALIZATION

A major new objective of the Center during 1974 will be to install Community Learning Centers in at least *ten* poverty neighborhoods in cities and suburbs outside New York City. These will not be funded by the Center for Urban Education; rather, they will be purchased contractually by localities or groups and agencies within localities. Thus, 1974 is the culminating year in this program plan – the year when both demand and effectiveness can be demonstrated on a substantial scale.

The model Community Learning Center was designed originally to channel the forces of change which will continue to sweep across the face of urban public education throughout the 1970's. Sociologically, the decline of public confidence in education and the progressive disorganization of the urban polity suggest that any model of reform must be flexible enough to be adapted to a variety of conditions.

Therefore, the programs and products generated inside the model must remain replaceable and infinitely modifiable. To this extent, advance planning, while essential, cannot become too firm to allow swift alterations to be introduced.

3884

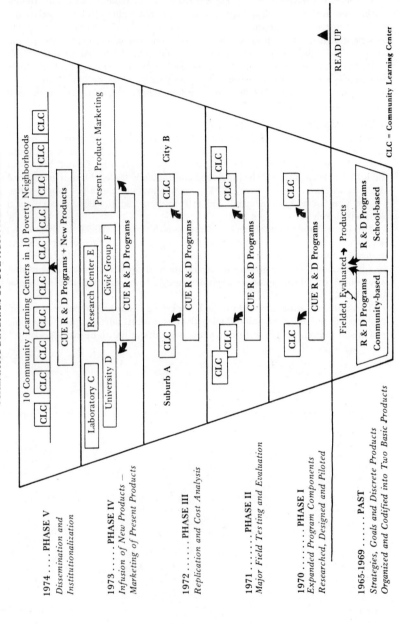

SCHEMATIC DIAGRAM OF CUE ACTIVITIES 1970-1974

10 Community Learning Centers in 10 Poverty Neighborhoods

CLC CLC CLC CLC CLC CLC CLC CLC CLC CLC

CUE R & D Programs + New Products

Laboratory C   Research Center E   Present Product Marketing

University D   Civic Group F

CUE R & D Programs

1974 . . . . PHASE V
Dissemination and
Institutionalization

1973 . . . . . PHASE IV
Infusion of New Products —
Marketing of Present Products

Suburb A   CLC   City B   CLC

CUE R & D Programs

1972 . . . . . . PHASE III
Replication and Cost Analysis

CLC   CLC   CLC

CUE R & D Programs

1971 . . . . . . PHASE II
Major Field Testing and Evaluation

CLC   CLC

CUE R & D Programs

1970 . . . . PHASE I
Expanded Program Components
Researched, Designed and Piloted

Fielded, Evaluated → Products

R & D Programs   R & D Programs
Community-based   School-based

1965-1969 . . . . . . PAST
Strategies, Goals and Discrete Products
Organized and Codified into Two Basic Products

READ UP

CLC = Community Learning Center

MATRIX OF DEVELOPMENT OPERATIONS

Year & Activity	Basic Studies and Product Research	Field Trial and Evaluation (See Note)	Cost Analysis and Market Analysis	National Distribution
1970				
Citizen Partic.				
Leadership	X	X2		
Workshops	X	X		
School Seminar	X	X		
Social Education				
SPUR	X	X2		
LARC	X	X2		
Library	X	X		
1971				
Citizen Partic.				
Leadership	X	X3		
Workshops	X	X2		
School Seminar	X	X2		
Social Education				
SPUR	X	X3		
LARC	X	X3		
Library	X	X2		
1972				
Citizen Partic.				
Leadership		X4	X	
Workshops		X3	X	
School Seminar		X3	X	
Social Education				
SPUR		X4	X	
LARC		X4	X	
Library		X3	X	
1973				
Citizen Partic.				
Leadership		X5	X	X
Workshops		X4	X	
School Seminar		X4	X	
Social Education				
SPUR		X5	X	X
LARC		X5	X	
Library		X4	X	
1974				
Citizen Partic.				XX
Leadership				X
Workshops				X
School Seminar				X
Social Education				XX
SPUR				X
LARC				X
Library				X

Note: Numbers X2, X3, X4, and X5 indicate cycles of field trial and evaluation.

Part 3

Decision and Support Structure

BACKGROUND

The Center for Urban Education was founded in February, 1965. Funded initially by grants from five foundations, and then funded by the United States Office of Education as a research and development center during 1966, CUE functioned as an inter-university consortium, with much of its program subcontracted to the participating, governing eight-member colleges and universities. The main emphasis of its work was on fundamental and applied research into urban education. (See Appendix B for Bibliography.) Development, while important, took second place. However, during 1966, it became apparent that CUE could more efficiently solve the problems of urban education if it pursued a different line of effort. It became evident that a development-oriented regional laboratory would better serve CUE's initial objectives, and make a more significant contribution to the solution of urban problems. Accordingly, in March, 1966, the Board of Trustees decided that "the overall developmental objectives of CUE as a regional laboratory would be to initiate and promote through research and development, and to change, through cooperation, the policies and practices of urban education."

There was no change in CUE's Charter from the Board of Regents of the State of New York; only a change of emphasis in operational strategies. Instead of a broad-gauged cluster of research projects, CUE sought to increase its practical contribution by narrowing its focus. CUE's role as a consortium of universities was reduced. The Board of Trustees was enlarged so as to make its membership more representative of the region and more inclusive of individuals, lay as well as professional; basic research was also cut back.

44

In this final part of *The Basic Program Plan*, the decision structure and support structure of CUE are described. These structures have changed in response to developing experience ˘over the five years of CUE's existence, and they will doubtless evolve continuously between 1970 and 1974.

BOARD OF TRUSTEES

The Board of Trustees of the Center for Urban Education operates in accord with By-Laws established under the founding Charter from the Board of Regents of New York and under the educational corporation laws of the State. (See Appendix A for Charter.)

Membership on the Board of Trustees is fixed at the Annual Meeting of the Board by election from a slate presented to the Board by its Nominating Committee. Since 1968, the Board has included from 17 to 19 members nominated as individuals but reflecting in their diverse affiliations and occupations the categories of officers of institutions of higher education within the New York metropolitan area, and persons prominent in civic and community affairs within the same region. At the Annual Meeting, the Board of Trustees also elects a Chairman and Vice Chairman, and, as officers of the corporation, a Director and Secretary-Treasurer. The Director is under the By-Laws, also a member of the Board of Trustees. The Board of Trustees meets five times a year as a committee of the whole. Its Executive Committee of five Trustees meets at periodic intervals. All members of the Board are welcome to participate.

The Board is responsible for the determination of *fundamental policy decisions* governing the funding, program, personnel, and affiliation of CUE. On questions of work in progress and the review of future program efforts, the Board receives reports via the Director from the *Ad Hoc* Program Advisory Committee, a body of eight to twelve expert and objective educators and social scientists who are appointed by the Director to consult regularly with CUE's professional staff.

MANAGEMENT

The programs and staff of CUE are managed by the Director, the Deputy Director and the Program Directors.

The Director is responsible for overall leadership of the program and staff. His office includes a Planning and Review Coordinator and an Assistant to the Director. His chief responsibility is to mold and specify programmatic objectives within CUE's general mission; to subject these objectives to review, modification and approval by the *Ad Hoc* Program Advisors and the Board of Trustees; and to insure that all time and effort within the staff are directed toward fulfillment of these objectives. The Director is also responsible for the cultivation of resources which can be put to use in achieving programmatic objectives.

The responsibilities of the Deputy Director parallel those of the Director in effecting programmatic objectives. The Deputy Director, whose office includes an Administrative Assistant, is also responsible to the Director for those aspects of the work delegated to him. Officers in charge of staff offices (Business, Training, Editorial, Technical, and Site Coordination) are responsible to the Deputy Director, who is accountable for overall management of the Program Services Division. These arrangements may be modified where new tasks and changing assignments require.

45

The Deputy Director now serves as Secretary-Treasurer of the Board of Trustees. It is his responsibility to maintain effective communication with the Board on all matters, including legal counsel and fiscal review.

By direction of the Board of Trustees, both the Director and the Secretary-Treasurer have signatory power for the making of contractual arrangements and for authorization of expenditures.

Each Program Division is managed by a Division Director, who is aided by an Assistant Division Director. Management is differentiated from the functions of research, development, dissemination and evaluation, which are carried on in a climate of professional autonomy and under the direction of designated senior staff within each Program Division. A Division Director is responsible for projecting Centerwide objectives in terms of resources that include professional assignments. He is responsible for monitoring program performance, advance planning, and continuous modifications or work efforts within his Division. He also shares responsibility for the quality of joint efforts with other divisions and offices within CUE and with other agencies and groups participating in CUE's programs.

PROGRAM PLANNING AND REVIEW

The machinery for program planning and program review is concentrated in the Office of the Director, but its operation is shared with many groups and individuals inside and outside of the Center. The diagram on the next page indicates the sources and channels through which advice and planning flow.

Individuals and groups not on the staff but participating in CUE programs communicate suggestions to CUE staff. These are developed into more complete recommendations by the Program Division Directors and their staffs and then submitted to the Assistant to the Director. The task of the Assistant to the Director is to help insure that basic questions are answered. She provides aid and written guidelines to this end. When the proposal has reached a formative stage, the Assistant to the Director shares it with the Management Group, which includes the Director, Deputy Director, Division Directors and Business Manager. It is also shared with the elected Program Staff Advisory Committee, whose chairman sits with the Management Group. When the proposal has reached a stage of more complete formulation, it is shared with the *Ad Hoc* Program Advisors. The Board of Trustees entertains new program proposals when the time for policy determination is at hand; that is when costs, funding sources, time schedules and the relation of the new work to standing objectives have all been specified fully.

The review process operates in the following way. First, the schedules that have been established in each annual report permit the Planning and Review Coordinator to keep a record of work in progress, through the receipt of periodic progress reports from supervisors, as well as through direct discussion. The Coordinator also schedules review by the *Ad Hoc* Advisors and by USOE consultants who are employed to make annual spring reviews of work accomplished.

BUSINESS MANAGEMENT

The Business Office functions as one of the CUE's support structures. Administrative controls and fiscal reports enable the Program Divisions and Staff   46

Offices of CUE to attain their objectives within the framework of the various contractual obligations that CUE enters into.

The Business Manager is responsible to and reports directly to the Deputy Director. His responsibilities include budgeting, purchasing, contracting and disbursement of funds. In addition, they include the maintenance of records affecting personnel time and effort, payroll, fringe benefits, and plant maintenance and communications facilities.

BUDGETING

1. In consultation with the Program Directors, budgets are prepared as required to insure the inclusion of all anticipated costs, the reasonableness of these costs, and the relationship to CUE's overall dollar projections.

2. Monthly budget reports, including expenditures and obligations, are issued for each program unit as a basis for assessing future actions and commitments in the light of the current status of the budget for each project. These reports also enable management to evaluate the progress of each project in consideration of the rate of expenditures as they relate to the projected budgets.

3. A quarterly budget review of the entire program is made, thereby permitting the re-allocation of funds among CUE's programs as requirements increase or diminish during the course of their implementation.

PURCHASES AND COMMITMENTS

1. All requirements for goods and services are reviewed by the Business Office to determine their applicability to specific budgets.
Purchase orders are issued for the procurement of all materials and supplies.

2. Letters of contractual agreement are entered into with all consultants, both individual and corporate. These agreements spell out consultants' obligations according to time and effort, specific results expected by CUE, and details of remuneration.

3. In all sub-contracts which are executed, there is included a detailed and specific "scope of work," as well as the applicable provisions which are part of the base contract supplying the funds. Adequate provisions for fiscal reporting and control are also included.

4. Disbursements are made only for those items having prior approval, on advice from authorized personnel of receipt of materials or completion of services contracted.

PERSONNEL

1. Agreements entered into with professional personnel provide for individual responsibilities of time and effort, work assignment, remuneration, and rights of CUE to publish findings or produce materials.

2. The services of support personnel are secured by the Business Office when the needs arise. Timely transfers are made in the interests of need and maximum utilization of the support cadre.

3. The Fringe Benefits Programs are administered by the Business Office.

OTHER SERVICES

Assignments of work space; maintenance of offices and facilities; control of program and office equipment, including property inventories; coordination of meeting facilities; purchase, control and distribution of office supplies.   47

3890

COMMUNICATIONS

Assignment and control of telephone equipment; control of mailroom facilities. Maintenance and control of all duplicating equipment and facilities.

EDITORIAL MANAGEMENT

The Editorial and Marketing Office is set up in such a way that it may be of maximum service to CUE from the inception of a program idea or project until a tested product emerges and dissemination is undertaken. All publications are planned by the originating program division in close collaboration with the Editorial and Marketing Office. This early consultation and aid is seen by both the operating division and staff office as a most important component in the generation and dissemination of CUE products. All CUE publications are also subject to the application of editorial control of policies by this office. (These policies are set forth in the Administrative Manual).

Related to this process, the Editorial and Marketing Office manages, as a service to the program divisions, a constant flow of information regarding relevant programs, projects and instructional products being produced in experimental or commercial form by agencies outside CUE. In this way, CUE program planners receive early guidance on their product output, and avoid costly waste of time and effort.

In addition to these services performed for CUE itself, the Editorial and Marketing Office serves as the *disseminator* of all CUE information, maintaining a publication schedule for the issuance of reports, monographs, books and other documents. This Office also disseminates information of interest to the general public via a newsletter, press releases and other services designed for various communications media.

It is also the responsibility of this Office to search out and provide avenues by means of which the CUE developed products may be more widely distributed, once they are in final form. Therefore, the Office maintains continuing liaison with appropriate commercial firms, such as educational publishers and others interested in instructional materials, and makes arrangements by which CUE products may enjoy national distribution and use in schools and communities.

SITE COORDINATION

CUE maintains a liaison position within the laboratory to assure continuing relationships between itself and State Departments of Education in urbanized states.

CUE also engages in cooperative relationships with other laboratories. For instance, the Individually Prescribed Instruction program, developed by Research for Better Schools, has been implemented by CUE in the New York Region. The *Instructional Profiles*, for another example, a CUE component, has been used by the Central Mid-Western Regional Educational Laboratory. In order to meet the needs of clients, the Site Office works to extend these relationships by actively seeking products developed by other laboratories, and by bringing them to the attention of CUE sites. Conversely, CUE's products are offered to other laboratories to utilize in sites of their choosing.

CUE's primary site for field testing of its products is the group of varied inner city areas of New York City. These will continue to receive the largest share of   48

3891

CENTER FOR URBAN EDUCATION
HEADQUARTERS TABLE OF ORGANIZATION – 1970

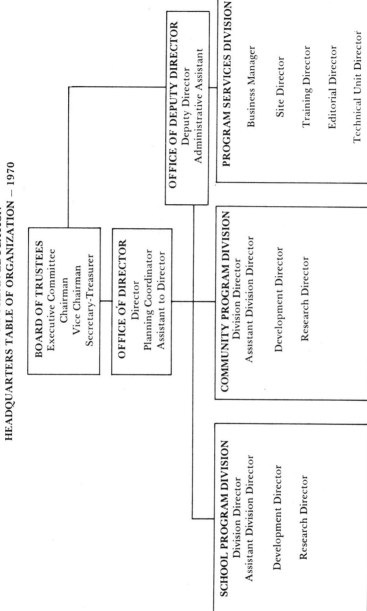

BOARD OF TRUSTEES
Executive Committee
Chairman
Vice Chairman
Secretary-Treasurer

OFFICE OF DIRECTOR
Director
Planning Coordinator
Assistant to Director

OFFICE OF DEPUTY DIRECTOR
Deputy Director
Administrative Assistant

PROGRAM SERVICES DIVISION
Business Manager
Site Director
Training Director
Editorial Director
Technical Unit Director

COMMUNITY PROGRAM DIVISION
Division Director
Assistant Division Director
Development Director
Research Director

SCHOOL PROGRAM DIVISION
Division Director
Assistant Division Director
Development Director
Research Director

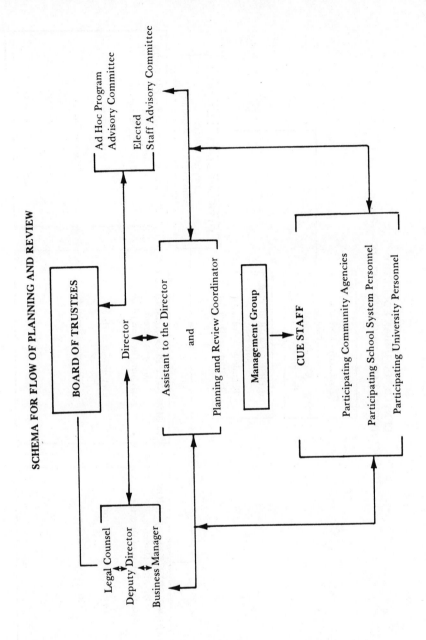

SCHEMA FOR FLOW OF PLANNING AND REVIEW

attention. The thirty newly decentralized districts in New York City will serve as a continuation of 1969 – 1970 relationships developed with Bridgeport Connecticut; Red Bank, New Jersey; and Glen Cove, Wyandanch, and Harrison, New York. These serve as the basis for future efforts to expand relationships with other urban sites in the implementation of CUE programs.

Good relationships with community school boards, boards of education, superintendents, principals, teachers, and parents must be established if CUE programs are to make an appreciable impact.

The development of mutual trust and confidence between persons or groups using CUE's products and CUE itself has been a matter of prime concern. When a program is brought to a site, initial approaches are made to the local school superintendent, who, if he approves, helps CUE to secure the approval of the local board of education. The Site Coordinator plays a key role in the process by visiting, conferring, and building a solid working relationship. He will also be active in the diffusion phase, when the program is passed on to the schools. For example, the Site Coordinator will meet with each principal and seek his cooperation. The Site Coordinator will also continue to act as liaison for training programs developed for teachers using CUE materials.

CUE has been interested in the use of its programs in a variety of sites. This inclusion of different types of geographic areas, of groups of varied ethnic backgrounds, and of diverse socio-economic groups will continue in the 1970-74 projected program.

CUE's overall goal in developing informed, concerned, and active citizenship is achieved through development, field testing and evaluation of programs in both curriculum and community development. Local school districts in large cities, small cities and suburban towns form the network of sites in which programs are developed and refined. The Site Coordinator acts as liaison in assessing the worth of programs. He also works closely with those responsible for teacher training and research in guiding field trials and evaluation.

TECHNICAL OFFICE

The Technical Office is one of CUE's support structures. Its internal operations are performed by three sections. The principal administrative responsibilities are borne by the Director of the Technical Office, who is responsible to and reports directly to the Deputy Director. He coordinates the work of all service units and the substantive programs which develop within and outside each unit. The main sections are: Survey Research, the Information Center, and the Mobile Unit. All three sections work in close cooperation. Their activities sometimes overlap, and personnel assignments are frequently interchangeable. For example, for information retrieval purposes, the Information Center and the Research Section work in close coordination; the Mobile Unit utilizes the resources of the Information Center.

As each substantive project is developed, the appropriate Director appoints a Study Director who works in conjunction with the Director of the Technical Office and the Section Supervisors. They unite in an effort to plan and execute the kinds of field data-gathering, library research, analysis, or developmental operations which will resolve their R & D problems.

49

SURVEY RESEARCH SECTION. The survey Research Section performs multiple functions. It is organized into eight sub-sections, which include the following: Technical Services Data Bank; Sampling and Statistical Services; Field; Coding; Data Processing; Public Opinion Polls; Content Analysis; and Evaluations.

The Technical Services Section studies and recommends computer utilization wherever necessary. It conducts colloquia where CUE research personnel and visiting scholars and technicians present methodological and substantive ideas. These, in turn, lead to discussions on research-related topics, and on the application of modern technology to the Center's diverse areas of concern.

The Data Bank takes care of the storage and retrieval of all data accumulated in studies conducted by CUE. It maintains an Instruments Bank, which stores all research instruments used in previous studies, and helps in the construction of new instruments. It also maintains a storage of accumulated Demographic Data, which is predigested so as to be of use to the Program Division Directors. An example of these data is the preparation of maps of the boroughs of New York, which show schools and school districts to which census data have been added and which are constantly being updated; e.g., according to racial, ethnic, socio-economic distributions, etc.

The Sampling and Statistical Section is responsible for the development and maintenance of mass, elite, and organizational sampling frames. Its work is determined by the intellectual questions and target groups involved in each project. It is also responsible for keeping track of methodological innovation and advances in the state of scientific survey research.

The Field Section is responsible for most data collection on New York area projects. Through its supervisory staff, it is responsible for recruiting and training interviewers or other field data collectors; for maintaining contact with a permanent interviewing staff; for consulting with Study Directors on instruments development and the field administration of instruments; for pretesting instruments; for making field assignments for all projects; for editing and validating completed work; and for evaluating interviewers.

Most of the members of field staff are qualified to conduct in-depth interviews. All members of the field staff are accustomed to conducting interviews with a wide range of structured instruments common to behavioral and attitudinal research. Interviewers are drawn from a variety of racial, ethnic, and socio-economic backgrounds; several are bilingual. While the personal interview is the characteristic technique of the field staff, it is also trained to be utilized for enumeration of units, acquisition of records, and observation of social interactions.

The Coding Section translates all field-gathered data into a form that is as empirical as possible, but is also compatible with rapid data processing. It also provides a final qualities control check on the work of interviewers. This section always works in close conjunction with the Study Directors, as well as with the Field and Data Processing Sections.

The Data Processing Section is responsible for all machine operations relating to the tabulating of data gathered by the Field Section and coded by the Coding Section. Its main tasks are: punching, verifying, reproducing, sorting and cleaning IBM cards, and tabulating results of the processing procedure.

The Public Opinion Polls group conducts all public opinion polls requested by the Project Directors of the Program Divisions. It coordinatesthe services of all sections during the periods in which public opinion polls are being conducted, and creates the quality control tests necessary to insure their successful completion.

The Content Analysis Section applies the most modern techniques in the field as it performs content analysis of the data gathered and processed by the pertinent sections.

The Evaluation Section, experienced in a complete range of evaluative techniques, serves an internal and external evaluation function for CUE projects.

THE INFORMATION CENTER. The Information Center, which includes the Library, Clearinghouse and Reference Services, performs special functions of information retrieval both inside and outside the Center.

The continuous reader service is particularly aimed at teacher education students, teachers already in schools, community groups, students in general, and parents involved in schools.

The tasks of background and literature research for all CUE projects are based on the retrieval capabilities developed within the unit and the system called TORSO (Technical Office Retrieval System Operation), specially designed for CUE.

The Information Center also regularly publishes bibliographies on pertinent subjects that are of great help to researchers, both inside and outside of CUE. It also has a phone reference service, a "hot line" on urban education questions.

This section concerns itself, too, with the provision of training in Library Services, with establishing libraries in the CUE Community Learning Centers and in other community centers, and with all activities related to the library sciences.

THE MOBILE UNIT. The Mobile Unit consists of buses of the type used by the public libraries and other mobile educational centers, and is furnished with the following audio-visual equipment: tape recorders, slide projectors, sound-film projectors, video-tape equipment, 16 mm. motion picture projector, publications, books, and magazines of special interest for the communities and various products designed by CUE.

This unit concerns itself with whatever programmatic extensions that will bring the versatile and adaptable capabilities of the unit into use with various Program Components. These comprise participation with the Literacy through Social Education Program as well as with the Citizen Participation Program, and involve the Training, Marketing and Editorial, Site Coordination Offices, and the entire Staff Services Division.

The CUE Mobile Unit is able to function as a Community Learning Center in physically limited locations. It provides the locale for community oriented actions, while also maintaining close ties between the community and CUE. In addition, it functions as a tool for the Literacy through Social Education Program in bringing to its target populations the products derived from SPUR, as well as from the Citizen Participation Program and its component programs. The Mobile Unit also helps to set up "mobile training sites" near public schools, not only within the city, but also in neighboring school systems in the metropolitan area.

51

TRAINING OFFICE

Instructional systems of any description ultimately depend on competent trained personnel for successful implementation. Depending on the nature of the individual product components of a particular system, such personnel may include teachers, school administrators, parents, paraprofessionals, school board members, and various other participants in the educational process. CUE's development efforts run the full gamut of personnel training requirements. Principal responsibility for the design and development of training programs is lodged in the Training Office.

Drawing on a broad current repertoire of training approaches, the Training Office attempts to provide optimal fitting of training strategies, modes, methods and materials to specific program objectives. In carrying out this work, Training Office personnel are guided by a process model which has been designed for training program development. The model includes: specification of instructional objectives in behavioral terms for both trainees and trainers; a general teacher behavior model; an analytical model for teacher behavior; content analysis of curriculum materials; evaluative criteria associated with behavioral specifications; formative evaluation modes; skill behavior practice modes, including live and video modeling, simulation exercises, role playing, and microteaching.

The goal for each training problem engaged by the Training Office is a series of portable, fully tested and complete training products. Such products consist of diversified materials and media that meet the requirements of different learning styles and contexts. In carrying out past program requirements, the Training Office has provided training and consultation in New York metropolitan area schools for hundreds of teachers, supervisors, and administrators, and has extended its reach as far as Nashville, Tennessee, as well as to other locations beyond the Northeast region. The Training Office has produced several 16 mm. sound films which have had wide national distribution in schools, colleges and community groups. It has also conducted research on the characteristics and conditions of teacher effectiveness in urban areas across the country.

During the past year, the Training Office has specified and acquired a sophisticated three-camera videotape recording system capable of producing switching, fading and other special effects. It has trained staff personnel in the application of this equipment in both studio and remote production. This system is being utilized to develop prototype models as required by current program plans.

The Training Office will function with the School and Community Program Division in the implementation of the projected five year development program. Emphasis will be placed on engineering training systems as they are required by the programs developed in these Divisions.

As has been noted in Part II of this document, the school program will place primary strategic emphasis on the modification of the behavior of such school personnel as teachers and supervisors to achieve the pupil performance objectives it has advanced. The community program, as well, stresses behavior modification through training in its several program formulations. In response to these requirements the Training Office will perform the work described below.

SPECIFICATION OF BEHAVIOR MODELS. Task analysis procedures are being employed in order to yield tentative profiles of knowledge and skill   52 requirements for personnel objectives in the various program designs. These profiles will provide the basis on which to make an adaptation survey of related literature, and to discover such behavioral research findings as are applicable to the tentative profiles. Then several prototype models are assembled and analyzed against the tentative profiles. Finally the models emerge as a series of coherent performance objectives stated in behavioral terms and accompanied by appropriate evaluative criteria.

DEVELOPMENT OF TRAINING MODELS. The behavioral models developed above form the bases for the development of training models. As above, adaptation surveys of the related literature, using synthesis and invention where required, form the bases for fitting the training modes and techniques to trainee performance objectives. Training models also specify trainer behaviors and provide enroute and terminal trainee assessment materials and techniques. A series of video taped films will be provided, showing models of selected teacher and student behaviors in sample classroom situations. Where applicable, trainee self-analysis techniques and procedures will be developed, as will simulation exercises, scripts, and microteaching.

FIELD TESTING. Formative evaluation will result from the field trials of both behavior and training model components. Process and material revision decisions will result from Training Office collaboration with both School and Community Division evaluation teams.

(Hon. Jorge L. Córdova, Resident Commissioner from Puerto Rico, subsequently submitted the following materials for inclusion in the record:)

HOUSE OF REPRESENTATIVES,
CONGRESS OF THE UNITED STATES,
Washington, D.C., February 2, 1971.

Hon. WALTER MONDALE,
Chairman, Senate Select Committee on Equal Educational Opportunity,
U.S. Senate, Washington, D.C.

DEAR SENATOR MONDALE: I want to commend your Committee for the time it has devoted during the recent hearings aimed at exploring the many educational problems of Puerto Rican children living in the mainland.

The hearings have presented, I believe, an idea of the difficult task facing those who are concerned with providing equal educational opportunity to all of our citizens.

In submitting the attached statement and additional materials, I am cognizant that they deal with the progress we are attempting to make in public education primarily in Puerto Rico. Witnesses before your Committee have devoted most of their time to describing educational problems in those areas of the mainland having significant numbers of school-age children of Puerto Rican origin and descent.

As Resident Commissioner from Puerto Rico to the United States, I represent of course, your fellow citizens living in the Island. Because of transmigration however, and the ease of movement between the mainland and the Island, the problems of educating our children are entwined with and inseparable from those of children on the mainland.

No matter where they live, our Puerto Rican young men and women know that a sound education is the first step towards economic progress.

Your committee is to be commended for exploring ways to increase the opportunities that, on occasion, have been denied our young. I want you and your colleagues serving on the Select Committee to know that we appreciate your concern.

Cordially,

JORGE L. CÓRDOVA.

STATEMENT OF HON. JORGE L. CÓRDOVA, RESIDENT COMMISSIONER FROM PUERTO RICO TO THE UNITED STATES

I am privileged to have this opportunity to submit my views and some brief recommendations which I hope will give your Committee some idea of the progress we are attempting to make in Puerto Rico in educating our young men and women. The addenda to my views are some descriptive materials prepared by our capable and imaginative Secretary of Education, Dr. Ramón Mellado. Eloquently, they describe the long-range goals we have set in Puerto Rico and they constitute our agenda for the Island.

I am aware that your Committee's concern has been primarily directed towards an examination of the educational systems of the various states here on the mainland which are faced with increasing populations of Spanish-speaking citizens. For this reason, it is not my intention to duplicate the expressions of concern given to your Committee by previous witnesses. Many of these citizens, particularly on the Eastern Seaboard, but also in the New England States, the Midwest and in other geographical areas of the mainland United States, are of Puerto Rican origin and descent. Others in this area of Spanish-speaking origin are Cuban, Mexican American, and from other places where Spanish is the primary language of instruction and usage. These hearings, directed as they are toward problems of Puerto Rican children in school, are a sound contribution to the still sparse body of knowledge which educators can use in attempting to meet the particular needs of children who may have language disabilities which impair the learning process or particular problems stemming from a bilingual, bicultural setting.

In Puerto Rico we have some particular problems which are dissimilar to those of the mainland. Among these, the most obvious one is that Puerto Ricans are not a minority on our lovely Island. It is not until they come to the mainland that our children experience the frustration and particular problems of coping with instruction in a setting where the English language may be unfamiliar, the teachers unsympathetic, and the educational system, in toto, with an attitude that strongly mitigates the individual aspirations of your fellow citizens.

As you already know, the ease of movement between Puerto Rico and the mainland results in transmigration of Puerto Rican families. It is not uncommon to find children abruptly placed in an educational setting and a learning environment which can be a new and unfortunately disastrous experience. We have made great strides in recent years in improving the teaching of English which helps Puerto Rican youngsters adapt to mainland living if they choose to come here.

But another problem exists in Puerto Rico because of returning families. For a variety of reasons, many return to Puerto Rico and have children educated in the mainland who speak and write English, but who have difficulty with their Spanish. This constitutes a reverse bilingual problem since the prime language of instruction in Puerto Rico is Spanish.

Our Department of Public Instruction has intensified efforts to reach these youngsters who comprise an estimated 10,000 of our total school age population of 785,000 within the public education system of Puerto Rico.

They are doing so in the belief, which I strongly share, that Puerto Rico can be bilingual and bicultural, retaining its Spanish language and culture and yet moving into the mainstream of our democratic system. As you have discovered during these hearings, my view is not shared by all and is a topic of discussion, disagreement, and a continuing controversy wrapped up in the whole question of the Island's status within the framework of the U.S. system of government. Spanish, as you know, can be the language of the child when he is with family and with peers: it is often not the language within a school setting. This aspect of bilingualism heightens the child's frustration and this set of hearings bears eloquent testimony to the very high dropout rate of Puerto Rican youngsters from schools in the mainland. Among the recommendations I endorse is my hope that the educational systems of the various states develop instructional techniques to serve the particular needs of the bilingual and bicultural child and adult.

The typical American school is one whose educational philosophy is monocultural and monolingual. Your Committee has heard about the particular needs of the many children of Spanish-speaking origin within that school. The typical American school can confuse economically deprived with culturally different. We know that there are many bright and perceptive youngsters who are considered retarded and dull by a non-Spanish speaking instructor. To help these children, I strongly recommend that your Committee devote some time to making the promise offered by the passage of the Bilingual Education Act realized. This legislation, Title VII of the Elementary and Secondary Education Act, has, for a variety of reasons, not been fully and effectively implemented, not only nationally, but in those states and communities with large Puerto Rican populations.

While I endorse increased appropriations for this measure, as other witnesses have, I consider them not the only answer. The Bilingual Education Act originated as a research and demonstration project. It is not to be confused with a categorical aid program that should be applied in every school district with Spanish-speaking youngsters. It was meant to be a vehicle to explore and test a wide variety of approaches in the broad field of bilingual education. These techniques, when properly evaluated, would then have become available to school systems, higher educational institutions, non-profit organizations, and all sorts of individuals and organizations serving Spanish-speaking communities.

It is a tragedy that this has not been done. For this reason I suggest that the Committee devote some time to exploring ways of making the Bilingual Education Act more effective, either through a continuing evaluation or through a thorough review of the legislative intent of the program, particularly whether it is being followed within the U.S. Office of Education.

Further, I recommend that the U.S. Office of Education intensify their efforts to train more educational personnel in bilingual teacher training programs. The Bureau of Education Professions Development Program of the Office of Education has been instrumental in initiating with my strong endorsement and cooperation an Island-wide effort to upgrade the whole spectrum of teacher training in Puerto Rico. On the mainland, I am hopeful that the programs which they already have are expanded to meet the pressing need for teachers who are bilingual and bicultural. I recommend this because the ease of transmigration, and the problems of a moving population, make it imperative that we help Puerto Ricans no matter where they live.

Another recommendation that I endorse deals with the young men and women who need particular occupational training to meet the needs of a changing economy. A simple problem of the teen-age Puerto Rican adolescent may be that he is not in school and, further, that the school does not meet his desire for vocational education and manpower training.

Your Committee's main concern is directed towards the educational system itself, but I am hopeful that realistic alternatives to schools that reject young men and women needing occupational training are developed. Perhaps we need the passage of a Bilingual Manpower Act, similar to the Bilingual Education Act. We must move to solve the problem of the dropout whom the school system may have rejected.

There is an additional problem which I would like to call to your Committee's attention. Title I of the Elementary and Secondary Education Act has set aside a program for children of migrant workers. If a Puerto Rican child moves, let say, from Pennsylvania to Connecticut, his school records may be in the National Migrant Transfer Record System. This system was initiated by imaginative officials of the U.S. Office of Education but, because of the legislative definition contained in the law, children who travel from Pennsylvania to Puerto Rico do not have transferable records between the different school systems. I call this to your attention since we are exploring ways for Puerto Rico to link in to the system and are hopeful that this is realized.

I appreciate the opportunity to submit this written statement and am taking the liberty of attaching additional materials describing education in Puerto Rico. Our society in the Island is moving toward "La Nueva Vida.," meaning, "The New Life," for all of our citizens. We know that education is a strong component of that goal, a goal that will hopefully allow our young citizens to become participating members of a democratic society.

Your Committee's efforts in moving in this direction are commendable.

THE PUBLIC EDUCATIONAL SYSTEM OF PUERTO RICO: ACCOMPLISHMENTS AND UNSOLVED PROBLEMS

SUMMARY OF THE EDUCATIONAL OBJECTIVES TO BE IMPLEMENTED, JANUARY 1969-SEPTEMBER 1970

Objectives

1. To expand the opportunities for vocational and technical education.
2. To improve the quality of teaching at all levels of the System.
3. To provide for the unemployed young people between the ages of 16 and 21 who are not attending school.
4. To eliminate the shortage of adequate educational facilities necessary for the school population. (Classrooms, textbooks, equipment and materials.)
5. To improve the administrative processes of the Department.
6. To formulate an educational philosophy for the Puerto Rican public school.
7. To improve the learning environment in all schools of the System.

STATISTICS ABOUT EMIGRATION COMPONENTS AND DISTRIBUTION OF FAMILIES BY INCOME LEVEL

A. NET EMIGRATION COMPONENTS (PUERTO RICO PLANNING BOARD)

Origin and destiny	Fiscal year		
	1967–68	1968–69	1969–70
Net balance	−18,681	+7,047	−44,082
United States	−31,891	−11,582	−74,529
Virgin Islands	−4,836	−1,043	+6,233
Foreign countries	18,046	19,672	24,214

B. DISTRIBUTION OF FAMILIES BY INCOME LEVEL

Income level	1963 Absolute Figures	Percent	1969 Absolute figures	Percent
Less than $3,000	295, 501	64. 1	244, 919	41. 8
$3,000 to $10,000	147, 059	31. 9	240, 232	41. 0
$10,000 or more	18, 440	4. 0	100, 781	17. 2
Total number of families	461, 000	100. 0	585, 932	100. 0
Family income average	$3, 273		$4, 815	

Statistics about the educational system of Puerto Rico, 1969–70

A. Enrollment

Enrollment of Public Day Schools	672, 299
Enrollment of Accredited Private Schools	88, 609
Total	760, 908

The total enrollment represents 82.5% of the population of school age in Puerto Rico (6 to 18 years).

Enrollment of vocational and technical programs (10,235 more than the previous year—Includes regular day school students and others)	182, 534
Enrollment of extension educational programs (approximately 500 youths and adults took courses in English—This total is not included in the regular day school enrollment of 672,299)	63, 711
Double enrollment (3 hours) in the entire day school system (1 teacher teaches two groups: 1 in the morning and the other in the afternoon) (percent)	6. 3
Double enrollment (4 hours—similar to 3-hour programs, but an additional teacher is added for every 2 teachers in a 3-hour program to give 1 hour more of class for each of the four groups) (percent)	4. 2
Interlocking enrollment (5 hours—one teacher and group use a room in the morning and another teacher and group use the same room in the afternoon) (percent)	24. 1
Single enrollment (6 hours—all-day programs) (percent)	65. 4
Average number of pupils per classroom teacher (percent)	30. 9

B. Personnel

Number of teachers	24, 251
Number of vocational guidance counselors (each having an average of 802 students)	304
Number of school social workers (each with an average of 1,400 students)	347
Number of school doctors	0
Number of school dentists	0
Number of school psychologists	0

C. Special schools

Number of vocational high schools (San Juan, Rio Piedras, Mayaguez, Ponce, Arecibo, Caguas and Bayamon)	7
Number of senior high schools with departments of vocational trades and industries (Aguadilla, Barranquitas, Cayey, Fajardo, Guayama, Rio Piedras (San Jose) and Utuado)	8

Number of technological institutes (San Juan and Ponce)_____ 2
Number of study and work centers (Rio Grande, Mayaguez,
Guayama, Juana Diaz, Arecibo, Utuado, and Yabucoa)_____ 7
Occupational or multiple skills center (San Juan (Buchanan),
Ponce, Mayaguez, Cidra and Yabucoa)_____ 5
Number of free schools of music (San Juan, Humacao, Caguas,
Arecibo, Mayaguez, Ponce)_____ 6
Number of visual arts schools (San Juan-Luchetti)_____ 1
Number of centers of handicapped students (Cantaño, Humacao,
Caguas, Coamo, Mayaguez, and Arecibo)_____ 6
Number of centers for the prevention of drug addiction and
delinquency (Rio Piedras, Caguas, Ponce, Arecibo, Mayaguez
and Bayamon)_____ 6
Special Study Center of Buchanan_____ 1
Specialized school in diemaking_____ 1
Center at Last Mesas for exceptional children in science and
mathematics. (The purpose of this center is to attract excellent
students to the teaching profession)_____ 1

D. Libraries

Number of School Libraries_____ 373
Number of Public Libraries_____ 43

E. Radio and television Stations

Station WIPR–TV—Channels 6 and 3.
Station WIPR–Radio.

F. Budget (1970–71)

Budget for current expenses, state funds_____ $223, 114, 735
Budget for current expenses, Federal funds_____ 41, 516, 242
Budget for capital outlay, state funds_____ 22, 020, 000
Budget for capital outlay, Federal funds_____ 4, 247, 080

Total Budget of the Department for 1970–71_____ 290, 898, 057
Annual per pupil cost (1970–71)_____ 342. 03

G. Holding power of schools

Of every 100 students who entered 1st grade in the public and
private day schools of Puerto Rico in 1953–54 :
    57.3 completed 6th grade in 1959–60.
    36.6 completed 9th grade in 1962–63.
    25.8 completed 12th grade in 1965–66 (4.8 received vocational
        training).
    5.5 completed university studies in 1969–70.
Out of every 100 students who entered 1st grade of the public
and private schools of Puerto Rico in 1958–59 :
    61.1 completed 6th grade in 1963–64.
    45.3 completed 9th grade in 1966–67.
    37.2 completed 12th grade in 1969–70 (10 received vocatiohal
        training).
    Between seven and eight will complete university studies
        in 1974 (estimated).
H. Average years of schooling completed (1967) Population 25 :
    San Juan_____ 7. 88
    Humacao _____ 4. 75
    Arecibo _____ 4. 74
    Mayaguez _____ 4. 74
    Ponce _____ 5. 49
    Island _____ 5. 96
I. Population 16–24 out of school and unemployed_____ 70, 000
J. Unemployment in island (percent)_____ 10 to 12
K. Population 1970_____ 2, 689, 932

THE EXPANSION AND THE IMPROVEMENT OF VOCATIONAL AND TECHNICAL EDUCATION IN PUERTO RICO, JANUARY 1969–SEPTEMBER 1970

A. Accomplishments

1. A five year plan containing guidelines for vocational and technical education has been drawn up in accordance with the new federal law governing this program.

2. A study of the present and future needs of the Puerto Rican labor market for trained personnel has been completed to enable the educators to expand and improve the vocational and technical curricula.

3. During the 1970–71 school year the course offerings of thirty academic high schools are being expanded to include a variety of vocational subjects for both boys and girls. By January 1971 about 2,500 students will be benefiting from these new opportunities to learn a trade, develop special skills, and at the same time fulfill their own aims and ambitions.

4. Six new Vocational and Technical Schools are either in the planning stage or under construction.

5. Educational Television. In January 1971, a new television program will enable adults to receive vocational instruction at home. On Saturdays, the vocational schools will provide follow up and enable interested persons to gain practical experience.

B. Unsolved problems

1. The demand for skilled workers far exceeds the supply. Educational facilities must be significantly expanded.

2. Excellent personnel are lured away by private industry which pays higher salaries. It is necessary to devise a new scale of remuneration which can both attract new teachers as well as retain qualified faculty.

3. Obsolete equipment in some of the schools needs to be replaced.

THE IMPROVEMENT OF THE QUALITY OF TEACHING

A. Accomplishments

1. Significant salary increases were given to secure and keep capable teachers.

2. Half-day sessions were reduced from 11.4% to 6.3%.

3. The requirements for graduation from high school were increased from 12 to 15 credits.

4. Significant revisions were made in the various programs of study.

5. Four hundred twenty-five bilingual teachers were prepared to take care of many English classes in the primary grades. Audiovisual equipment was made available for English language classes.

6. A new policy of promotions was established. Success in school work depends upon the achievement attained as a consequence of instruction. The requisite concepts and skills have been enumerated for all subjects at each level.

7. Three thousand one hundred additional teachers have enabled the school system to take care of the increase in enrollment, reduce the number on half-day sessions, reduce class size somewhat, and add three credits in the high school as requisites for graduation.

8. Sixty-one guidance counselors, 72 social workers, and 22 physical education instructors were added during the past two years.

9. The Educational Testing Service of Princeton has agreed to conduct a complete evaluation of the academic proficiency of the school children during the coming two years.

10. Team teaching in the high schools is giving more students the benefits of studying under exceptional teachers.

11. The annual expenditure of $287 per student was increased to $342.03.

12. The program of special education for crippled children was expanded through the appointment of 32 additional teachers.

13. The school library program was improved by the naming of 68 additional teacher librarians.

14. Six counseling centers for the prevention of drug addiction and delinquency were established.

B. Unsolved Problems

1. The insufficient number of classrooms in the high schools indicates that the number of students studying under the alternate enrollment plan will have to increase.

2. There is a serious shortage of well prepared teachers. Even now there are about 5,000 teachers who have only a provisional certificate. The universities are not preparing enough teaching personnel to meet the needs of the schools.

3. The budget has not appropriated sufficient money to create additional positions for vocational counselors, social workers, health, special education, fine arts, etc. Personnel in these areas are essential to adequately care for the school children.

4. There is a total lack of the services of doctors, dentists, phychologists and psychiatrists in the Department of Education. Whatever assistance is given is rendered by outside sources.

5. School textbooks, laboratory equipment, and school libraries are lacking in many schools.

6. Humacao and Guayama are the two regions still without counseling centers for the prevention of drug addiction and delinquency.

OCCUPATIONAL EDUCATION PROGRAMS FOR PERSONS WHO ARE OUT OF SCHOOL; OTHER EXTENSION PROGRAMS

A. *Accomplishments*

1. At present six Work-Study Centers care for 840 daytime students, and another is open in the evening for 150 part-time students.

2. In January a new Work-Study Center for 180 students will open in Yabucoa, and plans are under consideration for another in Aquadilla.

3. The Televised High School for Adults is a highly successful program whereby adults eighteen years old or older may study to fulfill the requirements for graduation.

4. New public libraries have been opened in Arroyo, Lares, Aguadilla and Ponce, and contracts for libraries have been let in Aibonita, Añasco, Guayanilla, Ponce and San Germán. The Carnegie Library in San Juan has been reopened, and a branch in Santurce has been established.

5. The Department of Justice has provided library service for prisoners.

6. A variety of experimental programs are being tried out to meet the needs of adults in the Model City sector, in rural areas, and for those who have had no formal schooling.

7. The services of WIPR–TV will be available for a greater part of the Island as soon as its antenna has been moved to Cayey. The equipment has been ordered to change the transmission of WIPR–TV from black and white to color.

B. *Unsolved problems*

1. Insufficient budget appropriations have prevented any substantial improvement in educational services for adults.

2. The extension of public libraries in various cities is being delayed because of financial problems on the local, commonwealth and federal levels, as well as through a lack of trained personnel.

IMPROVEMENT OF EDUCATIONAL FACILITIES AND EQUIPMENT

A. *Accomplishments*

1. The commonwealth appropriations for buildings has gone up from $11,311,500 in 1968 to $22,020,000 in 1970.

2. A division for taking care of the planning for schools has been organized.

3. An inventory of the needs for schools in each district for the next four years has been drawn up.

4. During the last two years the building program erected 1844 classrooms, 167 lunchrooms, and numerous basketball courts, fences, and pavillions.

5. The money spent on textbooks has gone up from $2,500,000 in 1968 to $3,500,000 in 1970.

6. Federal funds have procured high quality audiovisual and laboratory equipment for many schools.

B. *Unsolved problems*

1. Lack of classrooms: during the next 4 years, 7,000 classrooms must be built.

2. Vocational and Technological Schools: present needs require that the facilities be doubled.

3. Recreational facilities are needed in the majority of the schools.

4. Insufficient budget appropriations account for the lack of proper maintenance of school buildings.

5. The lack of fences around many school buildings makes it difficult to protect the property.

6. An additional $9,000,000 would be required to purchase the books and supplementary materials needed in the programs of study.

IMPROVEMENTS IN THE ADMINISTRATION OF THE DEPARTMENT OF EDUCATION

A. *Accomplishments*

1. Formulation of a four year plan for educational development in Puerto Rico.

2. Establishment of the office of internal auditor.

3. Establishment of the office of methods and procedures.

4. Establishment of the office of external resources (Federal Funds).

5. Establishment of a purchasing office to transact all business connected with the acquisition of books, workshop equipment, laboratories, and school supplies.

6. Establishment of the office of school planning.

7. Transfer of the construction of schools to the Department of Public Works.

8. Establishment of the position of Undersecretary of Administration.

9. The studies made by Clapp and Maine and those of the Bureau of the Budget concerning the Central Administration of the Department of Education are the sources of many of the recommendations already carried out.

10. The following new organizations have been established in the Department to democratize the system:

    (*a*) Commonwealth Board of Education.

    (*b*) Planning Board composed of the Undersecretaries, the Auxiliary Secretaries, and the Directors of the Educational Regions.

    (*c*) Consultative Committee on Vocational an Technical Instruction.

    (*d*) Consultative Committee for Title I, Law 89–10.

    (*e*) Consultative Committee for Title III, Law 89–10.

    (*f*) Consultative Committee for School Libraries.

    (*g*) Consultative Committee for Public Libraries.

    (*h*) Committees of Citizens in each school district.

    (*i*) Committees of Teachers in each school.

    (*j*) Committees of Students in the High Schools.

B. *Unsolved problems*

1. School construction does not keep up with the urgent needs.

2. Highly qualified administrative personnel are difficult to obtain.

3. The handling of money affairs of the Department of Education should be transferred from the Treasury Department to the Department in order to speed up the process.

4. School guards are needed to prevent the $350,000 damage that occurs annually in the schools.

PHILOSOPHY OF EDUCATION

The Secretary of Education is formulating a philosophy of education which he will submit to the teachers, the citizens, and to all people who may be able to offer suggestions for its improvement. It will then be submitted to the Commonwealth Board of Education for its final revision.

THE IMPROVEMENT OF THE ATMOSPHERE OF ORDER IN THE SCHOOLS

The atmosphere of order in the public schools has improved somewhat. However, there are teachers who take advantage of their position to influence students to follow particular political ideas; there are still foreign forces interfering in the educative processes; and there are still university professors making political propaganda in the teacher education programs. However, thanks to the maturity of the Puerto Rican people, it appears that better days are ahead.

RAMON MELLADO, *Secretary of Education.*

A PRELIMINARY PROPOSAL TO DEVELOP A PROJECT UNDER THE EDUCATION
PROFESSIONS DEVELOPMENT ACT (EPDA)

I. Background and initial steps

Since October 1970, staff members from the Bureau of Educational Personnel Development (U.S. Office of Education) have been meeting with representatives from the Department of Education and the University of Puerto Rico to assess the possibility of engaging in a mutually agreed upon effort geared to the enhancement of educational personnel dealing with children and communities of disadvantaged areas. These preliminary activities culminated in a week-long workshop held at the Holiday Inn (San Juan), from January 11 to January 15, 1971. During this workshop, representatives from the Bureau of Educational Personnel Development, the Leadership Training Institute (LTI), the Department of Education and the University of Puerto Rico had the opportunity to analyze and assess the training needs of the educational personnel of the Department of Education and the University of Puerto Rico, as specifically observable in three proposed sites, for the development of a proposal to face such needs. These sites are the Llorens Torres area, the Model Cities area and Bayamoncito Second Unit at Aguas Buenas.

After initial talks on the general Island wide needs on personnel training, the participants of the workshop were divided into seven task forces to identify the most urgent training needs in the proposed sites. These task forces worked under the direction of a LTI consultant. The task forces visited the sites to have a first hand view of the situations involved and be able to understand better the needs of each site.

Each task force presented a report indicating the training needs of each site. The representatives from the U.S. Office of Education and LTI were instrumental in the consolidation of the needs as presented by the various task forces as well as in the indication of proposed alternatives to focus on the needs. The workshop participants were then grouped into three groups with the responsibility to:

1. identify the highest priority needs of the sites
2. identify those needs that can be addressed to the EPDA
3. recommend alternative ways to satisfy the needs
4. recommend a team structure to handle the development of the project.

II. Highest priority needs selected

A. *Teachers.—*
Highest priority:
More intensive pre- and inservice teacher preparation which emphasizes development of:
  (*a*) more positive understanding of the community
  (*b*) greater sensitivity to children's individual needs
  (*c*) a wider, less textbook based repertoire of teaching strategies.
Better use of staff, support personnel, and auxiliary personnel; reduced turnover and absenteeism.

It would be expected that such preparation would be directed toward better use of staff, support personnel, and auxiliary personnel. Reduced turnover and absenteeism are expected outcomes.

B. *Pupils.—*Highest Priorities:
Meeting total needs of students, giving social, emotional, and health needs equal status with academic needs. Increasing basic skills and achievement in all areas. Providing early orientation to the world of work, offering much more extensive occupational training.

The above needs should meet other needs such as reducing the drop-out, absentee, non-enrollment and behavior problem levels.

C. *Curriculum.—*Highest priorities:
Curriculum must become far more responsive to the needs of individual students and groups of students; it must become individualized for each school and within each school. It should reflect:
  (*a*) Special needs of poverty students.
  (*b*) Cultural differences between students.
  (*c*) Concern for building every child's self-image.
  (*d*) Awareness of pupil mobility.
  (*e*) Use of new methods and materials.
A special effort is needed to introduce students to the world of work.

D. *Community.—*Highest priorities:

The community school concept should be developed at each school to:
(a) Foster the idea that the school belongs to its community.
(b) Encourage, develop, and involve community leaders and agencies.
(c) Get parent involvement in planning, implementation, and evaluation.
(d) Integrate adult and early childhood education programs into the regular school program.

The school should make every effort to raise parents aspirations and to give a realistic sense of hope.

The school needs to use community resources (people, services, industry), in the educational program.

E. *Organizational.—*
This section was discussed in three parts; site, state, and university.

The overarching need identified was: To increase cooperation, communication, coordination and to reduce bureaucratic "red tape" within and between all agencies and all levels.

1. *EPDA sites:*
Highest priorities:
To give each school, and personnel within each school, not only the freedom and right, but the mandate, to make decisions and to innovate; to thus provide a more flexible structure, curriculum, and atmosphere.

To de-emphasize certification and instead emphasize competence.

To create much more flexible classroom routines so students are seldom all doing the same thing at the same time.

To develop a more flexible and imaginative reward system which enhances the appeal of teaching.

To implement non-graded, continuous progress, team teaching philosophies.

2. Central Office—Region—District:
Priority needs:
To decentralize decisionmaking and increase communications.
To increase means for cooperation with the University.

3. University of Puerto Rico:
Priority needs:
To vastly extend the clinical, on site, applications of university resources.
To developed inservice training which is relevant to teacher needs and opportunities.
Also to increase the capacity to train teacher trainers, and to improve internal cooperation and communication.

III. Population to be served

It was agreed to focus the development of the project on three specific sites: Llorens Torres area, Model City area, and Bayamoncito Second Unit at Aguas Buenas. The schools involved are representative of low income, disadvantaged areas of the San Juan East and West and the Aguas Buenas school districts. A general picture of these schools is shown as follows:

School and level	Grade	No. of groups	Enrollment	Type of organization
Aguas Buenas school district:				
Bayamoncito elementary	K	2	450	Double.
	1	2	55	Do.
	2	1	47	Single.
	3	2	67	Do.
	4	2	73	Do.
	5	2	68	Do.
	6	2	76	Do.
Total			426	
Bayamoncito junior high	7	2	90	Do.
	8	2	75	Do.
	9	2	64	Do.
Total			229	

School and level	Grade	No. of groups	Enrollment	Type of organization
San Juan West school district:				
Hernández-Gae án elementary	K	2	52	Do.
	1	3	119	Do.
	2	4	134	1 group, single; 3 groups, interlocking.
	3	3	113	Interlocking.
	4	2	87	Do.
	5	3	116	Single.
	6	2	81	Do.
	(1)	1	19	Do.
Total			721	
Labra, Junior High	7	8	274	Do.
	8	8	242	Do.
	9	9	230	Do.
Total			746	
Cordero, Junior High	7	5	178	Interlocking.
	8	3	95	Do.
	9	4	120	Do.
	(1)	2	35	Do.
Total			428	
San Juan East school district:				
Rodríguez Cabrero, Elementary	1	3	119	1 group, single; 2 groups, interlocking.
	2	4	118	Interlocking.
	3	4	134	Do.
	4	4	136	Do.
	5	6	190	Do.
	6	7	235	Do.
	(1)	8	124	Single.
Total			1,056	
Power, Senior High	10	11	377	Do
	11	7	250	Do.
	12	5	172	Do.
Total			799	
Perú, Junior High	7	10	366	Interlocking.
	8	10	349	Do.
	9	9	284	Do.
Total			999	

School and level	Grade	No. of groups	Enrollment	Type of organization
Río Piedras A school district:				
Tokyo, Elementary_____	1	2	50	Do.
	2	2	48	Do.
	3	2	51	Do.
	4	1	43	Do.
	5	1	43	Do.
	6	1	36	Single.
	(¹)	1	18	Do.
Total_____			287	
Nemesio Canales, Elementary_____	K	2	52	Interlocking.
	1	6	236	Single.
	2	4	144	Do.
		2	74	Interlocking.
	3	1	34	Single.
		5	158	Interlocking.
	4	7	230	Do.
	5	6	194	Do.
	6	5	167	Do.
	(¹)	1	18	Single.
Total_____			1,307	
Pales Matos, Junior High_____	7	5	216	Do.
	8	5	167	Do.
	9	5	186	Do.
Total_____			569	

IV. Proposed alternatives

In order to face the priority needs shown before, the following alternatives are proposed in terms of possible program elements:

A. On-site University training:

Both pre- and inservice.

For trainers of teachers, administrators, teachers, student teachers, paraprofessionals.

Utilizing "master teachers", community teachers.

Group dynamics workshop for school-community personnel.

B. Community school concept:

Utilization of community persons as support personnel, teachers, trainers of teachers, advisory council, home liaison facilitators.

Integration of early childhood, regular, and adult education.

Day care program utilizing high school pupils.

Clusters concept: Spin-off services to feeder schools.

D. Individualized instruction:

Educational technology.

Special education techniques for the regular program.

Curriculum development involving specialist and teachers.

Geared to the child, his community and culture.

E. Autonomy and restructuring:

Modification of College of Education curriculum and admission policies.

Prolonged student teaching internship.

Commitment to follow up placement in school.

Creation of paraprofessional certification by Department of Education= also "Master Teachers" title.

V. *Organizational structure*

To develop both the preliminary or developmental phase and the operational phase of this project, the following structure is suggested:

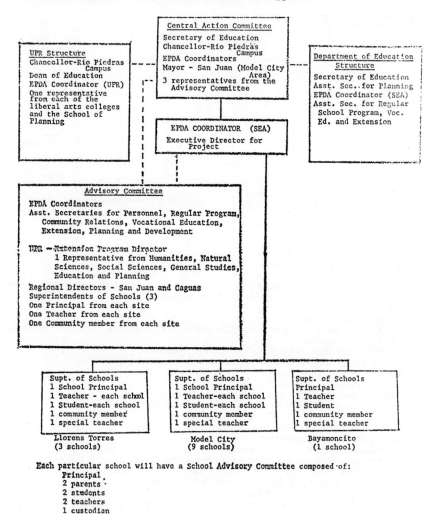

Each particular school will have a School Advisory Committee composed of:
- Principal
- 2 parents
- 2 students
- 2 teachers
- 1 custodian
- 1 lunchroom employee
- 1 local religious leader

VI. *Integrated design for process*

The various programs within the Bureau of Educational Personnel Development will attempt to satisfy the needs previously stated in an integrated effort.

Each program component will focus its resources so that an impact is produced in the community, the school personnel and the students involved. In this way, a working relationship of the various programs will be established.

The enclosed graph shows the working commitments of the various BEPD programs as follows:

1. Career Opportunities:
    (a) Pre and In-Service Training.
    (b) Teacher Mobility and Absenteeism.
2. Urban/Rural Development:
    (a) Individualized Curriculum.
    (b) Community Involvement.
    (c) Pupil Achievement.
    (d) Pupil Absenteeism.
    (e) World of Work—Occupational training.
    (f) Social, emotional, health needs of pupils.
3. School Personnel Utilization:
    (a) School Organizational Patterns.
    (b) Pre and In-Service Training.
4. Trainers of Teacher Trainers: (a) Increase capacity to train trainers of teacher trainers.
5. Pupil Personnel Services: (a) Social, emotional, health needs of pupils.
6. Special Education: (a) Attention to special education needs within the regular class groups.
7. Educational Leadership:
    (a) School Organizational Patterns.
    (a) Pre and In-Service Training.

VIII. Methods of coordination and integration of total comprehensive design

The coordination of the project will start at each school and the community will be involved as well as the school personnel. Schools will be represented at each site committee and by upward change of command, at the advisory and central committee (See Organizational structure). Meetings will be held periodically for a continuous planning and evaluation of the project. If necessary, advisors will be available to help in the process. New and creative methods of evaluation will be used. The committees at the University of Puerto Rico and the Department of Education will work separately as well as jointly, as the need arises in the design, implementation, evaluation and monitoring of the project.

A newsletter will be published periodically by the EPDA Coordinators to keep the personnel informed as to the progress of the project.

VIII. Budget

In order to provide for the necessary expenses during the development stage of this project, the following budget is presented: (January 15 through June 30, 1971)

A. Personnel services:

1 Department of Education coordinator ($1,260)	$6,930
1 University of Puerto Rico coordinator ($1,260)	6,930
1 Typist III ($330)	1,815
1 Typist II ($275)	1,500
Consultants	5,000
Total	22,175
Fringe benefits (retirement, social security, state insurance fund, health insurance)	2,000
B. Administrative expenses	500
C. Equipment, rental	2,000
D. Traveling expenses	2,000
Total	26,675

INTEGRATED DESIGN

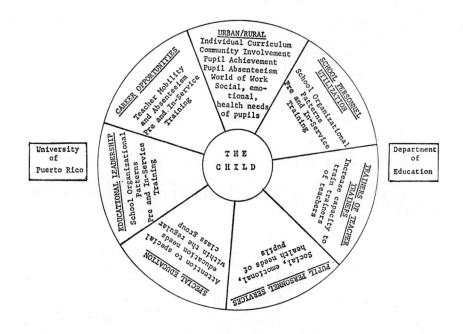

University
of
Puerto Rico

Department
of
Education

Community
Llorens Torres
Model Cities
Bayamoncito

Needs in schools was determined by task force groups

Teacher:
    More adequate preparation (Prof. Dev.).
    More stability:
        1. Less absenteeism.
        2. Reduced turnover.
            (*a*) Through promotion
            (*b*) Through quitting
            (*c*) Geographic transfer
    Better attitude toward the community.
    Larger number of teachers.
    Reduction or elimination of dysfunctional responses.
    Increased sensitivity to needs of children.
    Better staff utilization.
    More time for creativity and understanding of children.
    More and better trained support personnel.
    Diminish dependency on textbooks.
    Auxiliary personnel.
Pupils:
    Diminish dropout rates.
    Eliminate nonenrollment.
    Reduce under achievement.
    Basic skill development.

Reduce percentage in special ed. classes.
Reduce selection.
Meeting of total needs (physical, social, emotional).
Increased class participation.
Diminish problem behavior.
Reduce absenteeism.
More functional responses to their own problems.
World of work orientation.
Curriculum:
    Responsiveness to the characteristics of learners:
        (a) Mobility of learners.
        (b) Poverty (low income).
        (c) Cultural.
        (d) Self-concept (self-image).
        (e) More adequate methods and materials.
        (f) Other (?)
    Awareness materials for success orientation
    Consumer based curricular involvements.
    More individualized.
Community:
    Integration of adult and early childhood education programs into the regular school program.
    Encourage, develop, identify and involve community leaders and agencies.
    Present involvement in planning, implementation, and evaluation.
    Foster the notion that the school belongs to the community or a community institution.
    Utilize the community resources in the educational process (industry, people, services).
SEA—District—Regional—Commonwealth:
    More decentralized decisionmaking.
    Increasing ways and means for intra-department and interdependent cooperation.
    Increasing ways and means for University—Department of Education cooperation.
    Development of communication processes.
    Elimination of bureaucracy and red tape.
Organizational:
    Site—Reduction of self-contained and graded:
        Structureness (including promotion and retention):
        Intra-facing of programs.
        Educational programs.
        Intra agency.
        Diminish fixed class-organized activities in which all pupils in a class are doing the same thing at the same time.
        Flexibility of hierarchical Career Pattern.
        Flexible reward system (teacher pay, status, fringe benefits).
University:
    Increased capacity to train trainers of teachers.
    Improve inter-university communication and participation.
    Elimination of red tape.
    Flexibility of instructional methodology.
    Flexibility of admissions policies.
    Clinical application of university resources.
    More tr. professor involvement in decisionmaking.
    More student involvement in decisionmaking.
    Capacity to develop in-service training relevant to teacher needs and opportunities.
Materials:
    Need for instructional materials.
    More appropriate instructional materials (hardware and software).
    Better and more library resources.
    Facility for teacher production.
Equipment:
    More and better audio-visual.
    Specialized equipment.
    Better utilization of equipment.

Facilities :
    Adequate geographic location.
    More space :
        Classroom and other insite.
        Outside.
        Building.
    More specialized areas, library, lab, etc.
    Better upkeep (maintenance).
    Better custodial service (cleanliness).
    More flexibility for space utilization.
    More and better toilet facilities.
    Better construction and materials.
    More adequate non-instructional space (office, teacher rooms, storage, etc.).

TEACHER TRAINING NEEDS IN THE SCHOOL SYSTEM OF PUERTO RICO

(By Jesús Maurás Poventud)

This document has been prepared to provide data pertaining on the problem of teacher training for Puerto Rican schools.

It is well known that this topic has been widely discussed during the past years and will be subject of discussion in the years to come. Despite the progress achieved in the training of teachers, it seems that nobody is yet satisfied.

According to a study by Mr. Beresford Hayward, Consultant to the Department of Education, in 1958–59 we had 3,864 secondary school teachers, 2,120 (54.9%) of which held provisional certificates because of incomplete academic training. In the elementary school level, from 8,608 teachers 1,851 (21.5%) held a provisional certificate. This was so mainly because the 1950–1960 decade was characterized by a rapid expansion of the system and a critical shortage of teachers.

In 1957–58 the number of teachers increased to 12,500, of which 4,265 (37%) had a B.A., 7,750 (62%) had a normal diploma or less and 125 (1%) had a M.A. A total of 3,971 (31.8%) held provisional certificates because they lacked the necessary preparation of their particular field of teaching.

In 1965–66, the system had 17,431 teachers, 7,675 had a Normal diploma, and 441 had less than a Normal diploma ; 9,148 had a B.A., 166 had a M.A. and one Doctor's degree.

In August 1967, Dr. Pedro J. Rivera, Under Secretary of Education, indicated the need for better teachers. He said: "The needs for training teachers may be summarized under two categories: (a) a group of teachers who have not completed the necessary requirements, and (b) another group, that, after getting a degree have not kept in contact with the new developments in their major field and have not been able to keep up to date with research about learning . . ."

In August 1969 we had 21,750 teachers, from which 3,565 (16.4%) held a provisional certificate. The largest number of these provisional teachers were in secondary school level ; the junior high school had 27.9% in August 1967 and 22.3% in August 1969; the senior high school had 17.1% in 1967 and 13.7% in 1969. In the elementary school level the ratio was 8.4% in 1967 and 14.8% in 1969.

Data as of August 1969 reveal the following :
    1. In the elementary school level, 47.6% of the teachers of English did not have the required academic preparation to teach this subject.
    2. In the secondary schools, 30.2% of the teachers of English did not have the required academic preparation.
    3. In the secondary schools, 11.8% of the Spanish teachers did not have the required preparation.
    4. In the secondary level, 39.1% of the teachers of Science and/or Mathematics did not have the required preparation.
    5. In the secondary level, 20.0% of the Social Studies teachers did not have the required preparation.

Table No. 1 shows the professional growth of teachers in our system. in 1957–58 we had 4,625 teachers with a B.A.; in 1965–66 we had 9,148 ; in 1967–68 we had 10,968 and in 1969 we had 12,205. It may be observed that the number was tripled. However, the number of teachers with little academic preparation increased. In August 1965, we had 441 with a preparation below Normal diploma ; in August 1967 this number increased to 825. In August 1969, the number went up to 1,971 teachers, that is, almost five times in comparison to 1965.

In regard to provisional teachers, we had 31.8% in 1957–58. This situation improved during 1958–59 to 1965–66. In August 1966 only 13.0% of all teachers were provisionals. However, in August 1967, the number of provisional teachers started to increase. On that year, 14.4% teachers were professionals and in August 1969 it went up to 16.4%.

The situation has improved in the junior and senior high schools during the last few years, not so in the elementary level, where the tendency is moving to an increase in the number of provisional teachers.

Right now the largest percentage of provisional teachers is in the elementary and junior high school levels. We should insist, however, that the shortage of teachers with inadequate preparation has always been higher in the rural areas, both at the elementary and junior high school levels. In August 1967, 10.8% of the elementary rural teachers and 36.6% of the rural junior high school teachers were provisionals. In August 1969, 21.0% of the elementary rural teachers and 32.8% of the rural junior high teachers were provisionals.

TABLE 1.—ACADEMIC PREPARATION OF TEACHERS[1] AUGUST

	Less than normal	Normal	Bachelor of Arts	Master of Arts	Doctor	Total
Year:						
1957–58		[2] 7,750	4,625	125		12,500
1965–66	441	7,675	9,148	166	1	17,431
1967–68	825	7,215	10,968	253	1	[3] 19,460
1969–70	1,971	6,779	12,205	282		[4] 21,750

[1] Does not include educational administration personnel.
[2] Includes teachers with normal and less than normal preparation.
[3] Includes 198 teachers with nonclassified preparation.
[4] Includes 513 teachers with nonclassified preparation.

TABLE 2.—NUMBER OF TEACHERS BY SCHOOL LEVEL AND ACADEMIC PREPARATION, AUGUST 1969

	School level				
Academic preparation	Preschool	Elemental	Junior	Senior	Total
High school	3	70	24	58	155
Less than normal	14	1,324	282	196	1,816
Normal	200	6,126	377	76	6,779
Bachelor of Arts	15	518	881	460	1,874
Bachelor Elementary Education	108	3,973	378	92	4,551
Bachelor Secondary Education	10	329	2,154	1,569	4,062
Bachelor of Science	2	37	398	233	670
Bachelor plus 30 credits	2	224	441	381	1,048
Master of Arts	1	25	26	71	123
Master Elementary Education	4	32	4	7	47
Master Secondary Education		6	26	61	93
Master plus 30 credits		2	8	9	19
Doctor					
Vocational technician		1	9	2	12
Other [1]	3	122	227	149	501
Total	362	12,789	5,235	3,364	21,750

[1] Includes: Professional diploma, M.S., Master in School Administration and Supervision.

TABLE 3.—NUMBER AND PERCENTAGE OF TEACHERS BY TYPE OF CERTIFICATE, LEVEL, AND ZONE, AUGUST 1966

School level and zone	Type of certificate					
	Regular	Percent	Provisional	Percent	Total	Percent
Preschool	325	89.8	37	10.2	362	100
Urban	203	94.9	11	5.1	214	100
Rural	122	82.4	26	17.6	148	100
Elemental	10,890	85.2	1,899	14.8	12,789	100
Urban	5,367	92.6	432	7.4	5,799	100
Rural	5,523	79.0	1,467	21.0	6,990	100
Junior High	4,068	77.7	1,167	22.3	5,235	100
Urban	3,042	82.0	666	18.0	3,708	100
Rural	1,026	67.2	501	32.8	1,527	100
Senior	2,902	86.3	462	13.7	3,364	100
Urban	2,886	86.3	457	13.7	3,343	100
Rural	16	76.2	5	23.8	21	100
Grand total	18,185	83.6	3,565	16.4	21,750	100
Urban	11,498	88.0	1,566	12.0	13,064	100
Rural	6,687	77.0	1,999	23.0	8,686	100

TABLE 4.—ACADEMIC PREPARATION OF TEACHERS, AUGUST 1969

	Regular certificate	Percent	Provisional certificate	Percent	Total
A. Elementary school level:					
Special teacher of English	405	52.4	368	47.6	773
Other	10,810	87.4	1,557	12.6	12,367
Subtotal elementary	11,215	85.4	1,925	14.6	13,140
B. Secondary level:					
Special teacher of English	1,070	69.6	469	30.2	1,539
Spanish	1,095	88.2	146	11.8	1,241
Science and/or mathematics	1,243	60.9	797	39.1	2,040
Social studies	986	80.0	121	20.0	1,107
Other	2,576	96.0	107	4.0	2,683
Subtotal secondary	6,970	81.0	1,640	19.0	8,610
Grand total	18,185	83.6	3,565	16.4	21,750

A STATEMENT OF NEED FOR PERSONNEL TRAINING IN ADULT AND OUT OF SCHOOL YOUTH EDUCATION [1]

(Commonwealth of Puerto Rico, Department of Education, Education Extension Program, Hato Rey, Puerto Rico)

I. BACKGROUND DATA

General

In the course of its expansion and growth to meet the individual needs of the people and those of the society, the educational system of Puerto Rico has developed a subsystem to cope with some particular needs; namely, the development of the undereducated and the need to enhance the cultural background of the people through public library services and community education. We call this subsystem the Education Extension Program. It is one of the three instructional areas of the school system. As such it shares responsibilities with the Regular School Program and the Vocational and Technical Education Program in meeting the educational needs of the population.

During the last 70 years the public school system of Puerto Rico has been able to reduce illiteracy from 85 percent at the beginning of the century to approximately 11.5 percent at present. Coincidentally, this matches the present 11.5 percent unemployment rate among the able population. In spite of this

[1] This need has been succinctly stated by the Secretary of Education, Dr. Ramón Melado as one in a series f orecommendations addressed to high officials of the University of Puerto Rico on the subject of teacher training.

tremendous educational accomplishment excessive population growth has canceled part of the effort. In addition, a diminishing but still high dropout rate in the Regular School Program has increased the backlog of the undereducated.

At present around 768,000 persons 20 years of age and over a schooling below the 8th grade, while a total of 1,095,000 in the same age brackets have a schooling under the 12th grade. These figures would increase significantly if we were to include the out of school young population between the ages of 15 and 19. Thus, it has been estimated that the average schooling of the population is around the 6th grade with an enormous backlog among the out of school population who have passed the compulsory attendance age of 14 years.

To face its responsibilities the Education Extension Program includes seven subprograms: Basic and Secondary Education, English as a Second Language for Adults, Work Study and Job Corps Centers, Community Education, Public Library Services and Civil Defense Education for Adults.

Several of these programs are jointly funded by the Commonwealth and the Federal Government in the manner described below.

Adult basic education

The main purpose of adult basic education is the development of functional literacy to a level that will permit the students' reentry into the advanced general educational program or to enhance the employability and the earning capacity of those who choose to enter the occupational fields.

In 1969–70, basic education reached 19,238 adults. The budgetary appropriation was $1,155,515; the Federal grant, $648,000.00.

The Federal grant has enabled us to enrich the educational service through the recruitment of better teachers, the development and printing of suitable instructional materials, and through the establishment of new projects.

Adult high school education

Adult high school education reaches its clientele through different approaches; namely, evening programs operating under a semi-independent study basis, Saturday and summer courses, correspondence courses, and TV refresher courses for the High School Equivalency Test. Basic to the operation of the Adult High School Program is a testing service which encompasses placement and equivalency tests.

Over 19,500 adults and out of school youth were served in this program during 1969–70, while some 21,300 tests were administered through the adult High School Testing Service.

The operational expenses of this program amounted to $900,000 during Fiscal Year 1970.

It was totally Commonwealth funded.

Teaching of English as a second language to adults

The teaching of English as a second language enables adults and out-of-school youth to learn conversational English or to improve their knowledge of the language. It comprises formal, institutionalized instruction and extended teaching through television.

In 1969–70, 5,300 persons took advantage of the formal offerings of the program. The operating budget was $241,761.

No Federal funds were allocated to this program.

Work and study centers (Job Corps)

At present, seven Work and Study Centers are in operation. Two of these are Federally funded; namely, the Arecibo and Rio Grande Job Corps Centers with an enrollment of 310 students. The other five centers, located at Guayama, Juan Diaz, Mayaguez, Utuado and Yabucoa, are funded out of Commonwealth appropriations. The Yabucoa Center with a capacity for 150 students, was opened last October.

During Fiscal Year 1970 this program used Commonwealth funds in the amount of $1,020,088 and a Federal grant of $736,000,000.

Community education

The goal of community education is to impart basic teaching on the nature of man, his history, his life, his ways of working and of self-governing in the world and particularly in Puerto Rico. Motion pictures, radio, books, pamphlets, posters, and group discussions are some of the means used to attain this goal. The communities are stimulated to help themselves in the solution of their own problems, be these physical, social, or the like.

During 1969–70, the Community Education Program served 1,315 communities of which 1,147 were rural. Some 57,350 families and a total family membership of 338,200 persons were directly or indirectly the beneficiaries of the services rendered by the program.

Out of a total budgetary appropriation of $1,913,289.00, $689,789.00 were Federal funds.

Library services

Public Law 89–511 provides Federal funds for the expansion of public library services. It seems, however, that no funds will be available under Title II of the Law. During 1969–70, Federal funds in the amount of $257,616.00 and a Commonwealth appropriation of $644,486.00 were spent in the operation of the Public Library Services of the Department of Education. The curtailment of Federal funds will jeopardize the construction program of public libraries in Puerto Rico. Thirty-three out of the 78 municipalities of the Island still lack public libraries.

Civil defense adult education

Within the framework of the Extension Education subsystem, the scope of the Civil Defense Program is threefold. The system's contribution to civil defense is, first, an educational program through which the whole school clientele and the teaching and supervisory personnel are made aware of the implications of living in an era of nuclear power; second, it provides a protection program which includes planned ways and means to care for the immediate safety of all concerned; and third, it develops a coordination and service program to facilitate the use of the school buildings, their premises and related facilities in emergency situations.

Federal funds in the amount of $72,729.00 were used during Fiscal Year 1970. For 1971 the amount has been reduced to $20,000.00.

Future plans

Up to the present the Extension Education Program has attempted to expand its services with the available resources, focusing its efforts on the quantitative aspects of the program i.e., more youths and adults enrolled, more libraries opened, more communities served. We think that the time has come for a new thrust in development to bring about, not excellency, but some significant improvement in the qualitative aspects of the program.

In order to achieve the twin goals of further expansion and qualitative gains, the Four Year Plan for the Extension Program includes the following long range goals among others:

1. Curriculum revision and the development of the multimedia instructional system in which self-instruction will be an outstanding feature.

2. Revision and refinement of the testing system geared to the instructional materials system.

3. Improvement of the planning and overall program evaluation processes.

4. Improvement of the instructional materials distribution system.

5. Focusing of the local organization efforts in urban and rural adult education centers supported by an adequate transportation service.

6. Development of volunteer workers.

7. Development of a systematic and continuous training program in adult education for supervisors and teachers.

Much of the above development efforts will depend on the availability of resources through the increase of Commonwealth or Federal funds or a combination of both sources.

It should be emphasized that the Commonwealth's maintenance of effort in adult education has been both strong and continuous as shown by the figures on Appendix A for FY 1971, in which 70 percent of the funding comes from Commonwealth sources compared with 30 percent coming from Federal sources.

II. TRAINING NEEDS

General

The above data shows that adult and out of school youth education under the Education Extension Program of the Department of Education has become a $10 million enterprise with the enormous responsibility of reducing the educational backlog among the undereducated. This overwhelming task requires adequately trained personnel to provide for the special educational needs of this population.

Adult and Continuing Education has become the newest development in the educational field. This new frontier lends itself to promising innovations in its theory and practice and to the growth of a new body of professionals.

For decades the practice of transferring teacher behavior and relationships with children from the regular classroom to the adult teaching-learning transaction has been commonplace. In the present state of the art of teaching this practice is untenable.

Thus, there is a growing trend to establish the differences between the traditional fields of education for children, secondary school and college youth and the field of adult and out of school youth education. These differences cover the areas of goals, content, methods, techniques, materials, counseling and educational facilities. There are also differences in program organization and planning and in leadership training.

The problems of formal training in adult education has been a public concern for the past two decades in Puerto Rico. Up to the present, only three programs conducting adult education in Puerto Rico require from their personnel college training in this field. These are: Agricultural Extension, Cooperative Development and the Home Economics Program of the Department of Education. The University of Puerto Rico provides formal training courses in these three fields. However, no program exists to train public school *adult education* personnel. Other programs under the Department of Education and other public agencies engaged totally or partially in adult education must provide their own training.

Training interests areas

A research study conducted in 1965 among 24 public adult education programs showed that only 9.5 percent of the practitioners had taken college credits in the field of adult education and only 23 percent had received some form of in-service training.[1]

The previously quoted study found that adult education practitioners, including program administrators, reported high training interests in 10 different professional areas in the adult education field as follows:

1. Social Function of Adult Education.
2. Psychological and Sociological Passes of Adult Education.
3. Adult Education Methods and Procedures.
4. The Role of Content in Adult Education.
5. The Planning and Development of Adult Education Activities.
6. Personnel Recruitment and Training in Adult Education Programs.
7. The Recruitment and Participation of Adults.
8. Relationships between the Agency, the Adult Education Program and the Community.
9. Materials, Equipment and Facilities in Adult Education Programs.
10. The Administration and Supervision of Adult Education.

Personnel to be trained

Most personnel employed in the Education Extension Program come from the fields of elementary and secondary education. Some are unexperienced college graduates from non-professional fields who seek employment and are willing to join an extension program.

We have reasons to believe that the training situation found in 1965 among practitioners of the 24 adult education programs studied has not changed significantly by 1970.

Thus, it is estimated that from 1972 to 1975 the different subprograms under the Education Extension Program need to provide inservice training in adult education to the following categories of personnel: 2,348 teachers of basic and general high school education for adults, 236 supervisors, 175 counselors, 200 community organizers, 87 audiovisual technicians and 175 library specialists.

Training areas

If training interests can be considered indicators of training needs we could hypothesize that some training areas are more revelant than others for adult education practictioners. The following are possible alternatives:

---

[1] Marcano Blanco, Rafael, *Training Interests, Importance Given to Training and Other Related Factors in Adult Education in Public Agencies of Puerto Rico*, Indiana University, 1965, 194 pp.

Philosophy of continuing education

To develop among supervisors, teachers and other practitioners the understanding that the continuous cultivation of the adult mind is basic for the improvement of our civilization and the democratic way of life.

Adult psychology and formal learning
To impart knowledge about the maturing processes in the adult learner and

how they condition the educational program.

Community organization

To develop skills in the analysis of the structure of the community and the forces which operate in successful community organization conducive to adult learning.

Group processes in adult education

To develop skills for the most effective ultization of group forces in the learning process.

Methods and techniques in adult education

To impart knowledge and develop skills in the most innovative procedures and media to further individual learning and multi-group instruction in the adult learning center and other adult learning situations.

Administration and supervision

To develop skills in the planning, management and evaluation of the adult education enterprise.

These limited areas are suggested as alternatives to the larger core of professional content previously listed. They might be useful in the design and development of a general training model for practitioners in the Education Extension Program.

RAFAEL MARCANO BLANCO, *Ed. D.*
JANUARY 12. 1971.

APPENDIX A

EDUCATION EXTENSION PROGRAM OF PUERTO RICO—FUNDS ALLOCATED FOR FISCAL YEAR 1971

	Commonwealth		Federal		
	Fiscal year 1971	Percent	Fiscal year 1971	Percent	Total
Adult basic education	$676,682	50.6	$658,813	49.4	$1,335,495
High school adult education	789,750	100.0	0	0	789,750
English for adults	321,335	100.0	0	0	321,335
Work-study centers, Job Corps	2,211,899	71.9	862,000	28.1	3,073,899
Community education	1,257,991	59.9	840,000	40.1	2,079,991
Library services	1,027,616	71.1	415,878	28.9	1,443,494
Civil defense adult education	0	0	20,900	100.0	20,900
Program administration	269,246	100.0	0	0	269,246
Total	6,554,519	70.0	2,797,591	30.0	9,352,110

APPENDIX B.—TRAINING NEEDS IN THE EDUCATION EXTENSION PROGRAM, 1972 TO 1975

Professional categories	Number of positions, 1971 [1]	Estimated positions, 1975
Academic teachers	2,100	2,348
Supervisors	144	286
Counselors	60	175
Community organizers	24	200
Audiovisual technicians	10	87
Librarians	106	175

[1] Positions in each category available in each of the following programs: Adult basic education, adult secondary education, English for adults, work study centers (Job Corps), community education and public library services.

UNIVERSITY OF PUERTO RICO COLLEGE OF EDUCATION

THE COLLEGE OF EDUCATION: PRESENT NEEDS

The College of Education of the University of Puerto Rico has long felt an urgent need to satisfy the new and changing demands of the public school system and the demands of a dynamic Puerto Rican society.

Like any other institution of higher learning, here and in the U.S. mainland, the College of Education needs to redefine and renew old programs and practices and at the same time develop dramatically new and innovative problems of teaching and learning. It needs to focus on the new approach to the structuring of knowledge and must lead into the study and use of the various disciplines with emphasis upon fundamental methods of inquiring which should be in the main stream of the instructional program of the public schools.

I. NEED FOR CURRICULUM ENRICHMENT AND DEVELOPMENT

For almost four years now, the College of Education has been enbarked in a complete reevaluation of its curriculum. In order to cope with this great task it has faced the need:

(a) To improve the major disciplines of the curriculum and make these disciplines meaningful living experiences to learners.

(b) To consider the kinds of demands of our young people and the opportunities for greater service on the one hand, and a greater enjoyment on the other.

(c) To consider the particular situation of children and youths and the differences of their various schools in slum areas, large cities and wealthy suburbs.

(d) To consider the worth of teaching materials chosen in contributing to human values.

Through the above considerations our curriculum must develop a diversified program of teacher education and must enrich its offerings. Additional programs for pre-school education, special education, artistic education, vocational and industrial arts program, and other special programs must be provided in addition to the regular elementary and secondary school programs for prospective teachers.

II. NEED FOR CONTINUING EDUCATION

The College of Education needs to provide for the continuing education of teachers at all levels: College teachers and public school teachers. With the growth of innovating teaching strategies and materials it is imperative that all personnel dealing with the preparation of teachers be alert to the main problems of learning and teaching as well as how these are going to be coped with; since each academic area possesses its own unique objectives and content and the teaching learning process should be analyzed in terms of its relevance for teaching a particular subject. College teaching personnel must be familiar with the last trends and innovations in the field of teacher education and through its Graduate School the College of Education should assume more leadership in such professional training.

III. NEED FOR AN INSTRUCTIONAL MATERIALS CENTER

An instructional materials center is one of the most urgent needs that we are facing at present. It can provide opportunities for individual instruction of prospective teachers as well as for improving in-service education of teachers. More and more attention needs to be given to those teachers behavior that will insure student growth in performance. Some in-service teacher training activities used for inservice can be of value to prospective teachers. Additional activities for parents, administrators and teacher aids could be features of such instructional center.

IV. NEED FOR BETTER STAFF UTILIZATION

There is need for the establishing of supervisory unit or hours including several individuals with varying professional experience. College Supervisors, classroom teachers, student teachers and public schools administrative personnel can provide prospective teachers with rich and more meaningful professional experiences. Since education is becoming more and more a shared responsibility it is necessary that judgments and decisions be shared by all persons participating in the school system. The need for involving in planning and policymaking should be a feature of modern supervision. Thus, the University and the public school system should start as soon as possible a new kind of partnership in teacher education.

V. NEED FOR MORE FIELD WORK AND LABORATORY EXPERIENCES

The need to implement field work and laboratory experiences at an early stage of teacher education is very urgent to update professional education. With well designed behavioral objectives and an adequate set of performance criteria supervision teams can provide a solid professional training for prospective teachers which will result in a more effective professional training. If properly implemented field experiences will give prospective teacher the opportunity to—

(a) See more clearly the relationship between theory and practice.
(b) Gain a broader vision of the work of the teacher and the role of the school community.
(c) Grow in self analysis and self improvement.
(d) Develop a professional attitude that is a workable guide to action
(e) Formulate a more conscious educational point of view, and
(f) Seek increasingly better solutions to problems [1]

VI. NEED FOR MORE INVESTIGATION AND RESEARCH

Since it is an accepted fact that there is not a single method of teaching and learning it is also a fact that various theories of teaching will emerge. Hence the need for investigation and research in order to get new insights into children's behavior—teaching and learning process, effectiveness of teaching materials; teacher and pupil interaction, etc. Research and investigation should be a feature of the teacher education program. Early field experiences provide simple but excellent opportunities to initiate prospective teachers in the study of educational problems of their interest. A gradual up dating of such procedure will lead them into more sophisticated processes of investigation in more advanced levels of learning. In present graduate and undergraduate programs very little opportunity is provided to stimulate and conduct investigation research.

VII. NEED FOR UNDERSTANDING OF BETTER EVALUATIVE TECHNIQUES AND APPRAISAL OF THE TEACHING AND LEARNING ACT

At present the whole educational system lacks the professional personnel to offer guidance and direction in the use of proper evaluative procedures of the teaching and learning act. Except for some understanding on testing, all other evaluative procedures are often ignored by educational personnel. We have an urgent need for short seminars, workshops, advanced courses and other professional activities to provide most teaching personnel with the techniques needed for evaluation purposes. New programs and innovative ideas must be subject to constant evaluation so that the resulting products be incorporated as valuable means to the educational system.

VIII. NEED FOR NEW PEOPLE

The selection and recruitment of new people in the field of teacher education is another need of our educational system. The proper guidance at the high school and College freshman year with incentives such as scholarships; grants; internships, etc. may provide for a number of good candidates for the teaching profession. New teacher education programs are a good source for the recruitment of teacher candidates. At present we have been able to get some very good classroom teachers through some special programs, i.e., the Bilingual Program for Teachers of English; the Accelerated Program for Elementary School Teachers, both sponsored by the Department of Education, U.S. Federal Government; and the Teacher Training Program at the District of Guaynabo, sponsored at present by the University of Puerto Rico.

---

[1] Stratmeyer, Florence and Lindsay, Margaret. *Working with Student Teachers,* New York: Bureau of Publications, T. C. Columbia University, 1958. p. 401.

A variety of new programs like the ones mentioned above will bring new people to the teaching profession. Retention of such people is the challenge that the whole educational system must face. The initiative, creativity, and enthusiasm exhibited by these prospective candidates has to be fostered and stimulated by giving them new insights and greater knowledge of the teaching profession.

The above mentioned needs are not an exhaustive list, but they certainly are the most pressing. Adequate funding, better physical facilities and more equipment along with better trained personnel are needed in order to be able to meet those needs.

More than anything else, we need all the enthusiasm, involvement and commitment of the people who are in some way involved in the teaching profession. We will move as far ahead as we really want to move.

(Presented by Dr. Aida S. Candelas in representation of Dean José A. Cáceres at the joint seminar of the U.S. Office of Education, the State Department and the University of Puerto Rico.)

TEACHER TRAINING NEEDS IN VOCATIONAL AND TECHNICAL EDUCATION IN PUERTO RICO

Today, more than ever before, since the establishment of vocational training in the schools of Puerto Rico the professional development and improvement of vocational educators, at all levels, is being considered as a major goal in the total public educational system. It is, of course, a national problem and we are well aware that it is of particular importance in Puerto Rico.

The dramatic changes brought about in the economy and the social life of the Island, due to the industrialization program initiated some twenty-five years ago, and still under way, has required the preparation of large numbers of vocational and industrial arts teachers, guidance counselors, and other supporting personnel, to serve the growing needs for manpower development and training under the Department of Education in the vocational education program.

The complexities of our scientific and technological industrial society requires, likewise, of a competent, up-dated body of vocational teachers and other professional personnel in this field to keep up with the demands of modern industry and commerce.

In a similar manner, as it is also felt stateside, private industry recruits constantly our best trained, and most competent vocational teachers, supervisors and specialists for their own plants and services. This requires continuous efforts on our part in preparing new personnel to fill the resulting vacancies.

Lack of salary scales that may allow us to compete with those of private industry leaves little hope with us in regard to solving this serious problem in a forseeable future.

The vigorous thrust that our Secretary of Education, Dr. Ramón Mellado, has given since his initiation in this position to vocational and technical education in the Puerto Rican public school system, has brought about much needed program expansions and improvement, and as a corollary to such efforts, the need to hire new hard-to-get teaching personnel. A clear example is the recently initiated project geared to provide all academic high schools with a varied number of vocational offerings, that may turn these schools into more comprehensive institutions. A total of 112 new shops will have been provided by June, 1971, in barely a 2 years' period. Such a fast expansion leads to a critical need for new vocational teachers. Lack of facilities and budget limitations in our teacher training institutions, such as the University of Puerto Rico and the private colleges and universities in the Island, add also to the problem of scarcity of qualified candidates to fill available teaching positions.

The most popular method for recruiting vocational teachers in Puerto Rico, particularly those in the vocational industrial field, has been that of bringing potential candidates direct from industry or from their particular trade. Once hired, these individuals must be provided with the necessary teacher training competencies. Sound, effective teacher education programs must be made available to this group to match the occupational experience they have already had in industry with educational.

The very nature of vocational education requires that every teacher, counselor, curriculum specialist, and others serving in this program, keep up with the new developments in their corresponding fields—new scientific and technological knowledge, new information, new skills, new processes and materials.

The Vocational Amendments of 1968 to the federal legislation known as Vocational Act of 1963, have also placed a challenging responsibility to each State and Territory which reimburses vocational education expenses from the available federal appropriations in terms of keeping up their teachers and other professionals in line with the new priorities set forth in the new legislation. Thus, training needs of *all* those serving in the vocational education programs include, among others: learning to work with disadvantaged youths and adults and with the academically, physically, mentally and/or emotionally handicapped; developing cooperative vocational programs; working with post-secondary enrollments and programs; dealing with consumer education problems, with revised guidance and counseling techniques; working in programs where community involvement is essential; research-directed vocational programs; the development of exemplary, experimental and pilot programs. These are the new emphasis in the recent federal legislation. It is, therefore, essential, that our teachers be knowledgeable on how to deal effectively with the various aspects of the law that needs to be stressed and turned out into sound programs. Here I would like to stress that this aspect should be taken well into account by the Colleges of Education of the different teacher training institutions on the Island in the revision of their teacher training plans—both for the pre-service as for in-service programs.

There is still another criteria to which we must abide in our efforts to serve the vocational education program in Puerto Rico in the best way possible to the eligible population of youths and adults interested in such services. It is the requirements set forth in the Commonwealth Plan for Vocational Education as these relate to academic requirements and teaching and occupational experience for the various professional positions in the Program. Such requirements makes it mandatory that plans be developed toward qualifying the various types of vocational employees in accordance to the approved Plan.

Where do we stand at present in terms of teacher training needs and where are we leading our efforts?

Even though emphasis has been given to staff development programs for vocational education through college courses, workshops, seminars, exchange of educational personnel with industry, among others, there is still a large percentage of noncertified vocational teachers serving in the system.

Out of 2320 teachers at the end of fiscal year 1968–69, a total of 654, or 28.18 percent, worked under provisional contracts. A total of 56 teaching positions could not be filled because of lack of qualified personnel. (Table)

In fiscal year 1969–70, some 2,016, out of 2527 teachers, participated in in-service training activities. Included were 57 provisional teachers who were granted leaves of absences to pursue studies toward their certification requirements. In all, 89 provisional teachers completed the requirements during that year. The proportion of provisional teachers in fiscal year 1970–71 is similar to figures for the past year, since 98 new positions were opened, thus requiring the recruitment of additional teachers. Most of these groups are serving under provisional contracts. The higher figures correspond to the vocational industrial program, industrial arts, vocational agriculture and distribution and marketing education.

The above situation tends to emphasize the need for intensifying both the pre-service and the in-service teacher training activities.

Preservice

Formal teacher training programs in the University of Puerto Rico for many years, for the preparation of new home economics, industrial education, business education and office occupations, vocational agriculture (Mayaguez Campus) and guidance. All but industrial arts are reimbursed for part of expenses, from vocational funds. (Lack of resources to provide adequate services in several of the above programs.)

Plans are underway for the establishment of a teacher training program for coordinators for the Distribution and Marketing Program (UPR, Rio Piedras).

Initiation in 1969–70, in Mayaguez Campus, of teacher training courses (2) for Industrial Arts teachers (in coordination with UPR, Rio Piedras Campus), (difficulty for Ponce and Mayaguez candidates to come to Rio Piedras Campus).

Courses in Vocational Industrial Education initiated 1970–71 at Mayaguez Campus (2 year curriculum—10 students—leaves with pay). Plans to organize a four year curriculum.

Teacher training program initiated 1970–71 in Mayaguez Campus for preparation of technical education personnel (candidates are students in Engineering courses—last three-years)—must take Education courses and special practice in industry (Summer) four students ($100 month sholarship—Office of Personnel).

Inservice

Leaves with pay—all programs, according to priorities set in terms of needs.

Summer courses (registration dues paid by Department of Education.

Special courses, workshops, clinics, seminars (in coordination with universities and other government agencies).

Studies, toward M.A. degree, Home Economics (N.Y. University—Puerto Rico campus).

Coordination with industry (industrial education) occupational up grading experience (requires, substitute teachers, additional incentives).

VOCATIONAL AND TECHNICAL EDUCATION PROGRAM—PROVISIONAL TEACHERS

Program	Total number of teachers	Number of provisional teachers	Percent of provisional teachers	Vacant positions
Trade and industrial education	224	76	33.0	1
Vocational agriculture	123	42	42.0	23
Office education	314	72	23.0	
Distributive and marketing education	41	22	54.0	
Home economics	702	110	15.7	1
Technical education	45	19	42.0	6
Industrial arts	609	261	44.7	24
Guidance	262	52	20.0	1
Total	2,320	654	28.19	56

TRAINING NEEDS OF THE REGULAR ACADEMIC PROGRAMS

Puerto Rico's public school system has been struggling for years with innumerable problems that handicap the teaching-learning situation and breed additional problems. Some of these are: overcrowded and uncomfortable classrooms with inadequate lighting and inadequate ventilation, lack of books and lack of equipment, and an ever increasing school population, to mention just a few. But the major problem that confronts us is the lack of teachers and the lack of teacher preparation.

To back my statement I will proceed to read a few statistics turned in by the department heads of our academic programs.

THE ENGLISH PROGRAM

Up to 1969, less than 1% of the total number of teachers teaching English in the primary level had the academic preparation required. The 3,710 teachers in the primary level had to teach all subjects in the curriculum—English included. In order to departmentalize the teaching of English in this level, about 2,000 teachers were needed.

Through the Bilingual Program, 534 teachers have received a pre-service training and have been appointed to teach English. One thousand four hundred and sixty-six (1,466) additional teachers will be needed to complete the departmentalization of the teaching of English in grades 1–3. All 2,000 bilingual teachers must continue to receive their academic training to acquire certification.

One thousand three hundred and eighty-six (1,386) teachers who teach English in the upper elementary level, the junior high school level, and the senior high school level have not completed their requirements for certification. These teachers need in-service training to complete their academic preparation.

THE SPANISH PROGRAM

Out of 1,187 teachers teaching Spanish in the elementary level, 88 have provisional appointments. Out of 795 teachers in the junior high school level, 99 have provisional appointment. The majority of the teachers at the secondary school level need preparation on how to teach the language arts. Those at the elementary school level need cultural background. Most of the teachers in the Spanish program need orientation on techniques of grouping, development of skills, evaluation, and the teaching of grammar and composition.

THE SCIENCE PROGRAM

In the San Juan Region, out of 363 teachers teaching science at the secondary level, 86 teachers do not have a single credit in the subject they teach.

The most critical situation is that of the 8th and 9th grade teachers of Introductory Chemistry and Physics. A fifty percent (50%) of these teachers do not have a single credit in their subject. This situation is doubly felt now that chemists are in such great demand by our developing economy.

THE SOCIAL STUDIES PROGRAM

Most of the 10,747 teachers teaching Social Studies in the elementary, junior, and senior high school levels need additional training to teach this subject. They rely almost exclusively on lectures and memorization of facts, thus conditioning the minds of our students to uncritical acceptance. A revision of the elementary Social Studies Program and in-service training of teachers are being planned.

THE MATHEMATICS PROGRAM

Out of 1,119 teachers of mathematics in the junior and senior high school levels, 407 have provisional appointments. In addition, most of the math teachers and school directors are unfamiliar with the new mathematics program. They depend solely on the mathematics supervisor who is in charge of half the school districts in an educational region.

THE KINDERGARTEN PROGRAM

Out of 397 kindergarten teachers, 238 have a normal diploma or less. Most of these teachers have very limited academic preparation in Early Childhood Education.

Every year, approximately 80,000 children enter the first grade. Only 19,900 have had kindergarten. One thousand two hundred six (1,206) additional teachers would be needed to provide kindergarten for all, at a rate of 50 children per teacher.

THE ARTS PROGRAM

The Arts Program includes Arts, Music, and Theater. Out of 507 arts teachers in the three levels, 245 have provisional appointments. The Arts Program needs 1,100 new teachers to function adequately.

SPECIAL EDUCATION PROGRAM FOR HANDICAPPED CHILDREN

There are 375 teachers in the Special Education Program. One Hundred and twenty-five (125) of them have 15 credits or more in Special Education. One hundred and seventy-five have less than 15 credits. Seventy-five (75) have no training. To handle the needs of our handicapped children, 2,000 trained teachers are needed. There is an urgent need of training in the following areas: emotionally disturbed, learning disabilities, speech problems, hard of hearing, deafness, and visual impairment.

THE PHYSICAL EDUCATION PROGRAM

We have 241 teachers of physical education in the three levels—41 of those have no preparation. One thousand five hundred and seventy-five (1,575) new teachers are needed.

The enrollment in our elementary level schools is 430,745 children. The 67 teachers of physical education in this level can handle only 26.800 children.

THE SOCIAL WORK PROGRAM

A minimum of 30 graduate credits is required to hold a school social worker position. To be fully trained, 2 years of graduate work are required.

We have 345 school social workers in our program; 194 have 1 year training, 58 have no training.

THE SCHOOL LIBRARY PROGRAM

We have 1,571 elementary schools. There are 96 libraries, and 96 librarians for this level.

We have 325 junior high schools. We have 163 libraries—one hundred and sixty-three (163) librarians for this level.

The library situation in the elementary level is critical because it is at this level that good library services are most essential.

THE AUDIOVISUAL PROGRAM

This program needs to train its personnel in the designing, production, and evaluation of instructional materials. It needs to prepare paraprofessionals to work with the logistics of educational technology.

THE HEALTH PROGRAM

There are 325 junior high schools on the island. A health course is taught in only 30 schools (9%). There are 114 senior high schools; 73 schools offer health education (64%). At least 336 new health teachers are needed to offer health education in the junior and senior high school levels.

The 102 zone supervisors in the health program need additional training in human growth and development, group dynamics, evaluation, mental health, nutrition, safety, drug addiction, and communication techniques to reach the community.

The 103 health teachers need additional training in group dynamics, and human growth and development.

———

The following letters to the Honorable Walter F. Mondale, and to President Richard M. Nixon, were received after "Part 5: De Facto Segregation and Housing Discrimination" had gone to press. They are included here for your information.

CIVIL RIGHTS COMMISSION,
Detroit, Mich., January 27, 1971.

Hon. WALTER F. MONDALE,
U.S. Senate,
Washington, D.C.

DEAR SENATOR MONDALE: Because of your interest and concern over the relationship between equal educational opportunity and equal housing opportunities as evidenced in the recent hearings of the Senate Select Committee on Education Opportunity which you chaired, we are enclosing a letter to President Nixon by our Commission, expressing our concern over his recent statements on the subject of "forced integration" of the suburbs.

Since its inception, the Commission has carried out its Constitutional mandate to safeguard the civil rights of all Michigan citizens. During the past several months, we have become increasingly concerned by the apparent reluctance of the Federal Government to exercise a leadership role in upholding federal fair housing housing guarantees. Our concern has been heightened by recent events in the Michigan city of Warren, which recently voted by referendum to discontinue the city's urban renewal program out of racial fear, in our judgment. Earlier, our Commission had taken sharp exception to Mr. Romney's statement about "forced integration" of the suburbs.

When President Nixon reiterated Mr. Romney's position in opposition to "forced integration" of the suburbs, our Commission felt impelled to write to the President and to take exception with his statements on the subject.

Our Commission is deeply concerned that its ability and effectiveness in achieving equal housing opportunities for Michigan citizens may be impeded by what appears to be a relaxation on the part of the Federal Government in efforts to carry out its own responsibilities in this vital area. We therefore urge you and your other colleagues in the Senate and the House to take appropriate action to prevent this possible turnabout in national policy.

Sincerely yours.

JULIAN ABELE COOK, JR., *President.*

Attachment.

JANUARY 11, 1971.

President RICHARD M. NIXON,
The White House,
Washington, D.C.

MR. PRESIDENT: The Michigan Civil Rights Commission was deeply troubled by your statement made during a press conference on December 10, 1970, and reiterated in your press conference of January 4, 1971, that forced integration of the suburbs is not in the national interest and that it was not the policy of the Federal Government to use federal funds in ways not required by law for the forced integration of the suburbs.

The use of the term "forced integration" has tended to legitimize the often-held views of white citizens that equal housing opportunities for all citizens is somehow an infringement on the rights of white citizens. It implies that certain black citizens are being sought out, even against their choice, in order to move into suburban communities. It carries the same meaning as the phrase "forced housing", which was used by the opponents of the Michigan and Federal Fair Housing Laws.

Mr. Romney, along with other leading citizens of the country, has repeatedly said that racial segregation and polarization is the most serious domestic problem facing our country and that the very survival of our Nation depends upon its resolution. It has also been acknowledged that the Federal Government from the early thirties until the early fifties played a marked role in creating this housing crisis through such FHA practices as encouraging and accepting the use of racially-restrictive covenants in federally-guaranteed mortgages, through the withholding of FHA insurance from central city areas, and by insisting that neighborhoods and new subdivisions reeciving FHA insurance be of homogeneous composition.

Other public officials and prominent private citizens of the country, including U.S. Senators Javits, Brooke, Mondale, and Ribicoff, Rev. Theodore M. Hosburgh, C.S.C.; and U.S. Representative William M. McCulloch, all maintain that the Nation's racial crisis will not be resolved unless the rigid patterns of racial segregation that exist in every metropolitan area of this country are eliminated, thereby enabling minority group families to acquire housing and employment opportunities in metropolitan areas where opportunities are developing.

There are numerous instances of communities that have prevented, often through rezoning, the construction of federally-assisted low- and moderate-income housing projects for fear that black citizens might be able to live in them. Many of these same communities are receiving federal assistance for their schools, police departments, recreational purposes, sewer facilities, and for urban renewal.

The Michigan Civil Rights Commission has the responsibility for guaranteeing equal housing opportunities of all the citizens of the State of Michigan. The Department of Housing and Urban Development has a similar responsibility. The aim of our agency is to insure that every citizen of our state can purchase or rent the housing of his *choice* without discrimination from any individual, organization or community. It is likewise the responsibility of our agency and it is our strong belief that the Federal Government has an even greater responsibility in this area, to undertake or require affirmative actions to achieve equality in housing.

Because federal housing programs and funds contributed in great measure to our existing patterns of residential segregation and exclusion, the Federal Government must use its powers and resources to compensate for past injustices perpetuated against some of its citizens. We believe this to be very much in the national interest. We therefore recommend the following:

(1) That the Federal Government take the necessary legal action to eliminate patterns of housing discrimination and exclusion that characterize suburban communities;

(2) That builders who participate in federal housing programs be required to take affirmative action to insure that the occupancy patterns of their projects are representative of the racial population in the community or metropolitan area;

(3) That builders who participate in federal housing programs be required to build some low- and moderate-income housing;

(4) That requirements which will insure equal housing opportunities be made a prerequisite to the receipt of any and all federal funds by a community;

(5) That federal funds be denied communities which refuse, through zoning ordinances and other actions, to allow for the construction of low- and moderate-income housing;

(6) That federal installations not be built or kept in communities which do not take steps to insure equal housing opportunities for minority group citizens.

Mr. President, it is our firm conviction that the Federal Government cannot remain neutral in the face of what many believe to be our most serious domestic problem. To remain neutral is to allow the racial crisis to threaten the very existence of our nation.

We urge you to firmly enunciate the Federal Government's policy of guaranteeing the right to equal housing opportunities for all American citizens. In addition, we urge you to use the full powers of your office to take affirmative action to unite our divided nation in the crucial area of housing.

Sincerely yours,

JULIAN A. COOK. Jr., *President.*

EXCERPTS FROM "THE WAY WE GO TO SCHOOL," A REPORT BY THE TASK FORCE ON CHILDREN OUT OF SCHOOL, BOSTON, MASS.

Foreword

This report marks the end of the first phase of a journey which began in December, 1968, when a conference was held to explore the problem of children excluded from the Boston Public Schools. Social service workers, mental health personnel, and community leaders, representing thirty-five agencies from across the city of Boston, agreed that the problem of exclusion from, and within, the school system constitutes an emergency situation. They resolved to act with dispatch and vigor to correct a shameful condition.

A follow up conference in January, 1969, joined by representatives of the Boston School Department, the State Department of Education, and the State Department of Mental Health, concluded with an agreement to set up a Task Force on Children Out of School. The Task Force was to focus on the full dimensions of the exclusion problem: its numerical magnitude, geographic scope, and relationship to the social service and mental health systems. The findings were to serve as a basis for immediate and long-range actions.

After a period of initial planning by agency and school representatives, and the acquiring of a staff, the Task Force began its investigation by holding its first meeting on October 1, 1969. It was launched as a collaborative action-effort of community agency representatives, educators, social service and mental health professionals, parents, lawyers, and persons from the political community. The Task Force focused on the phenomenon of exclusion as a community problem, although it was clearly understood that the Boston School Department and the State Department of Education hold major responsibility for its existence and eventual elimination. It was recognized also that the problem of exclusion is endemic to most urban school systems in the nation. Therefore, we were not exploring an isolated phenomenon characteristic only of the Boston Public Schools.

The Task Force staff sought out and interviewed a cross-section of people including Boston School Department administrators and personnel, social service and mental health professionals, parents, and community leaders. In the process of investigation the Task Force gained impressions, facts, attitudinal statements, and perceptions from these various groups. In addition, we collected data from researchers who have done, or are currently doing, similar studies in Boston and other parts of the country. The most valuable information, however, was obtained through testimony presented by school and mental health officials and community leaders at Task Force meetings.

We do not claim that our study is exhaustive. Indeed, it indicates where future research needs to be done. We do believe, however, that we have collected and analyzed a sufficient amount of data to understand clearly the various aspects of the exclusion phenomenon in the Boston Public Schools. The situation is too serious to permit delay for further study now. We have the basis upon which to chart a course of action.

While our findings are an indictment of the system of public education, above all else they are an indictment of the total community whose indifference and inaction promotes this shameful condition. The chief intention of the Task Force is to move beyond the comfort of indictment to the achievement of corrective action. History has shown that task force reports, after releasing ringing indictments, usually are consigned to the bookshelves for a quiet death, while the problem called into question lives on.

Our quest will not have ended until the tragic and indefensible situation we have found is corrected — whether it takes one year, five years, or more. To this end we are developing a program to carry forward sustained action in pursuit of our goals. We seek the public's support for our continued efforts. I believe that there is no more urgent task before the Boston community. So we continue a journey which must not end with failure, but must meet with success in the interest of the precious youth of our community.

Hubert E. Jones, Chairman

I. Introduction

This report probably will make you very angry. It describes the almost unbelievable experiences that happen every day to thousands of school-age children in Boston. If you are the parent of a child in the Boston schools, the facts we have uncovered about children excluded from the regular educational process may cause you great despair. If your child is among those treated in the manner we describe, then make no mistake in understanding that your child's life is being scarred. If you are an interested citizen, then you too must realize that this situation affects you as well as the children and their parents.

Children in our city are being denied the only opportunity permitted in a lifetime to prepare for the greater challenges of life. They are failing to receive the educational opportunity that we believe is the right of every child in our country. And their beauty — the inner beauty of children — is being scarred, perhaps unalterably.

At a time when the public schools must take giant strides to prepare children for today's world, some children are being excluded from school, others discouraged from attending, and still others placed in special classes designed for the "inferior." The following chapters describe the way these practices take place, and how they affect the lives of the children:

It must be recognized first, however, that this grave situation exists throughout the city. It is not the problem of one particular neighborhood, or race, or social group. Rather, it transcends cultural, social, and economic boundaries. Parents and citizens in the North End, South Boston, Roxbury, and all other parts of Boston, share the same grim problem.

The information contained in this report is the result of many months of work. It represents an intensive investigation into the needs of school children in Boston. To the best of our knowledge, we have collected all the studies and data compiled by others who are concerned about the same problems. We have supplemented this information with our own research and studies. In addition, we heard testimony from school officials, teachers, parents, community workers, nuns, psychiatrists, lawyers, doctors, social workers, and other professionals.

The mere compilation of a massive amount of information was not our intention however. Our major concern is what is happening to our children in Boston and why. At best, we can make an educated estimate as to the magnitude of the problem. We know of several thousand children that are affected directly. However, we believe this number to be the tip of an iceberg: there are many more children that no one knows about. But our chief concern does not rest with engaging in a numbers game.

Rather, we are reporting to our fellow citizens — and fellow parents — the situation that we have found, inviting you to join with us in taking action to alter that which is so intolerable. For though we were shocked, as you will be shocked, perhaps the most surprising aspect of this problem is that it need not exist. It is within our power to alter it. While new legislation and additional funds are urgently needed for certain changes, we can alter now the policies and practices of the school system and other city institutions which treat children in this manner. We cannot over-stress our most basic conclusion that the situation we have uncovered presents us with an extreme emergency.

II. Exclusion: What It Means To The Children

(Note: While the information about each of these children is true, their names, the location of their schools, and all other identifying information have been changed to protect their confidentiality and that of school officials).

We have found that children with many different types of needs are being excluded from the schools. In the course of our investigation, we made an intensive effort to locate many of these children. With the assistance of community organizations, social agencies, parents, nurses, psychiatrists, and others, we located hundreds of individual children from every part of Boston. We went into their homes to talk with them and their parents. We listened to them describe what it means for a child to go without an education while other children go to school. And we spoke with professional people from agencies about their efforts in behalf of these children.

After a while, the stories began to merge into a characterization of a pervasive problem. We began to get an overall picture of children out of school or children labelled and shoved aside within the system. Yet we were reminded that while we sought to understand the general problem, we must not lose sight of what happens to individual children. For to understand their needs, their hopes, and their fears, is, in a sense, the key to understanding what we all must do to change a situation that is so shocking.

THE STORY OF RICHARD
(As told by a child psychologist)[1]

I recall another situation: the case of a "quiet child" who holds his fear and anger and any other strong feeling deep inside himself, in hopes that the world will not recognize him for the vulnerable target that he is. I first met him when a counselor asked me to try to expedite placement in a special class of a "retarded boy" who had been tested two years before. Although recommended for placement at that time, he simply had been "held over" in the fifth grade for two years.

It was explained to me that since there were several children in the school awaiting special class placement, as well as a handful of aggressive children who misbehaved in classes, the principal decided to take pressure off the teachers by rounding up all these kids and putting them in one "class," to be presided over by a substitute teacher. I recall warning this principal previously of the dangers involved in combining assaultive kids with retarded and withdrawn ones, without the usual mass of relatively normal children as a buffer between them.

I went to the classroom where I met the teacher, who confided that there was "something wrong with that boy, he's backward". I took Richard to my office and decided to switch to a nonverbal medium – a series of abstract designs which I asked him to copy. These generally prove to be very difficult for retarded children. Richard produced the most perfect set of reproductions I have seen in hundreds of tests. Furthermore, he could recall eight of nine objects, a feat generally accomplished by highly intelligent children. When I showed him a simple book, he read words commensurate with his grade level, though he denied understanding their meaning.

Following the testing, I talked to several of his former teachers. They all considered him totally illiterate. He was considered a "good boy" but "very retarded". The fact that his elaborate drawings revealed great concentration and creative imagination didn't impress them. Their sole criterion of mental normality was verbal fluency. Back at the central office I checked Richard's file. Two years ago he had been tested and marked "severely retarded; he is to be placed in a special class for his own good as he will never learn to read or write".

Hence, our Richard, who reads and writes and draws fanciful pictures, is considered too limited even to be placed with educable retardates. I completed the testing, which revealed Richard was psychotic; his superior intellectual capacity allows him to function well in some areas, but his estrangement from reality and sense of fear prevent him from responding to much of the world around him.

His father came to see me, and explained that Richard, while always quiet and withdrawn, was quick to pick up complicated mechanical skills such as fixing radios and clocks; could it be that no school personnel had spoken to this man in six years?

We are attempting to place Richard in a private school for emotionally disturbed children if we can find a vacancy. Placement is required for those children who cannot be accommodated in the public schools. That is, if anyone notices them.

ORLANDO and MARIA MARTINEZ
ages 15 and 9

The Martinez family moved to Boston from Puerto Rico several years ago. They lived with some relatives in North Dorchester until Mr. Martinez was able to get a job. Now they live in Brighton, closer to his work. The parents speak Spanish, and though the children know some English words and phrases, they speak Spanish in their home.

When Orlando first went to school, he could understand no English at all. He sat in class for several weeks, but could not participate. A friend of his parents who could speak English talked to the teacher about this. Soon Orlando was told to go to the Day School for Immigrants. Most of the students at the school were older persons, and there was still no instruction in Spanish. He did learn to say a few English phrases though.

Orlando attended the school for almost two years and received a diploma. But he still can't speak English, nor can he read or write. He is out of school now. He talks about getting a job, but a friend told him he probably can't get one because he has no education.

Maria, his younger sister, has never been to school though she is nine years old. Mr. Martinez says he would like for her to go to school, but that Orlando never learned anything in school and he is afraid Maria would be treated the same way.

During the past summer, however, a summer school program was held in a school in the South End. It was for Spanish-speaking children, and Mrs. Martinez took Maria to the school every day. Bilingual teachers taught the children, and Maria enjoyed this immensely. She even learned to speak a little English. But when summer was over, the program ended and Maria had to stop going to school.

She begs her mother to take her to school, but Mrs. Martinez knows that there are no programs for a girl like Maria. She tells her that maybe she can go to school again next summer. By then, Maria will be ten years old.

MARY JANE and JOHN TURNER, IMMIGRANTS,
ages 17 and 15
(As reported by a counselor in a community agency)

My first contact with John and Mary Jane was last winter. They has just come to Boston from the South. As in the case of many poor, black families migrating North, one parent and the older children came first to establish themselves; then the other parent brought the younger children.

When I first met the Turners, they were all sick with the flu and colds. Mr. Turner had a job, but had not been paid recently because he was out sick. At age sixty, he earned only $62 a week. The children had no winter clothing but Mr. Turner borrowed a jacket that he said John could wear to school when he started. Both the parents wanted the children to go to school very much. This was one reason that they had decided to move North, where they heard the schools were better.

A school counselor reported to me that Mary Jane, at age seventeen, had the equivalent of a second grade education. There are no classes in the school system for children over sixteen who are so far behind — even when such a youngster wants to go to school. Another problem was that Mary Jane was so hard to understand because of her heavy dialect that I had to get a friend to interpret for me what she said.

John, at fifteen, also had the equivalent of a second grade education. He had been sent by the school counselor to the School for Immigrants, which he had attended for three weeks when I first met him. I remember that fact so well because I was startled to see his school work. He wrote at the top of all his papers: "John Turner, Immigrant." I couldn't help but question how good it was for him to go to a school where most of the students are adults who don't speak English, when he needs so much help with his own speech.

At mid-year, I told John to register at the school in his neighborhood, instead of the School for Immigrants. But when he went there they found out that he was almost sixteen with so little education, and they sent him home. After several phone calls to School Department officials, I got John's name put on a waiting list for the Barrett School, the only school in the city for children who have gone through school and still can't read or write. The school admits only 100 pupils, who have had good attendance and conduct records. To this day, I have heard nothing from the School.

I really don't know what to do next for John and Mary Jane. I've got to try something, but I know another school year will probably roll around and they still won't be in school. I haven't mentioned yet the other children: Lee Ann, 14, and James, 11. Lee Ann is in the fifth grade, but is so embarrassed to be in class with ten and eleven year olds. James seems bright, but I'm not sure what will happen to him.

It's really heartbreaking, you know. These good, illiterate parents are trying to give their children something they never had themselves. But I doubt if they'll make it. I really doubt it.

KATHY FITZGERALD
age 9

Kathy, her parents, and her thirteen year old brother live in Charlestown in the same house in which she was born. When she was almost four, her mother noticed one day that Kathy's body began to twitch or shake as she lay on the floor watching television. Though this lasted only a few seconds, Mrs. Fitzgerald became concerned and, on her husband's advice, called their doctor.

By the time she took Kathy to the doctor, the child had had two more shaking spells. After an examination and a series of tests, the doctor told the Fitzgeralds that Kathy had petit mal seizures – a type of epilepsy. He reassured them, however, that while they would naturally be concerned about this condition, most people who

have it live normal, healthy lives. By taking regular medication, the tendency can be kept well under control.

After several months of taking the medication, Kathy no longer had seizures. The doctor said that on her present level of medication, she could expect to participate in normal activities and look forward to a healthy life. The Fitzgeralds were quite relieved to hear this good news, for they had been very concerned about Kathy's future. The family began to function normally again, and Kathy showed the normal signs of vitality and good health.

When she turned six years old Kathy, like most children, was excited about starting to school. Her parents were very excited too because their lingering fears were put to rest when the doctor told them there was absolutely no reason Kathy shouldn't go to school. He gave her a clean bill of health.

When Mrs. Fitzgerald took Kathy to school for registration, she took along the medical certificate from the doctor. The principal, upon finding that Kathy had had seizures two years ago, told Mrs. Fitzgerald that her daughter could not come to school. He explained that the class would be overcrowded, and that he could not take the responsibility for her. Neither, he said, could the teacher watch her. He suggested to Mrs. Fitzgerald that she keep Kathy home for that year and arrange for a home tutor to come to the house.

Not knowing what to do, Mrs. Fitzgerald took Kathy home where she remained several months. After contacting the principal again by telephone, Mrs. Fitzgerald finally was able to get a tutor to come to the home an hour a day three days a week. But Kathy seemed quite withdrawn and upset, something very unusual for her.

Concerned about this, and because she felt Kathy was not receiving a good education, Mrs. Fitzgerald contacted a counselor at a family service agency. After talking with Kathy and both her parents, the counselor told Mrs. Fitzgerald that Kathy's mood seemed to develop because she was not allowed to go to school, something that had been a big disappointment for her. She suggested that together they try to get Kathy into public school.

The counselor called the school to talk with the principal about Kathy. He said, however, that because it was almost mid-year, Kathy should wait until next year. He could not be responsible for her now. Finally, the counselor was able to get Kathy into a private school for crippled children. Though she wasn't crippled, they

accepted her on a temporary basis until she went to
public school in the fall.

The next fall, Mrs. Fitzgerald took Kathy to register
or school. But this time, the principal said that because
Kathy had attended the special school, it would be best
or her to continue there. In distress, Mrs. Fitzgerald
called the family service counselor, but found she was no
longer at the agency. Not wanting to cause Kathy more
distress, Mrs. Fitzgerald took her back to the school for
crippled children and the director agreed to let her
continue there because of the unusual circumstances.
She is now nine years old and has never been in a public
school.

DAVID JACKSON
age 11

The first two years of school were normal and un-
eventful for David. He made average grades and enjoyed
going to school each day – a three block walk from his
home in Roxbury. His mother said he looked forward to
the time his baby brother reached school-age so they
could go to school together.

The summer before David's third year in school, his
father was killed in an accident at work. His mother
seemed to suffer deeply over the tragedy, and David
shared her grief. After several months, however, the
family began to adjust and accommodate to the new
situation.

During the school year, however, David began to miss
school periodically. He would tell his mother he didn't
feel like going to school, so she would allow him to stay
home on those days to rest. Eventually David wanted to
stay home nearly every day. His mother finally told him
he had to go to school, though over the next few months
she did allow him to remain at home occasionally.

One day a truant officer came to the house while
David was at home. He told Mrs. Jackson that David had
been truant from school on several occasions, days he
had left home to go to school. David seemed to be
frightened by the man, and wouldn't talk to him, except
to answer questions. The officer told his mother, in
David's presence, that if he didn't go to school, Mrs.
Jackson would be taken to court.

Mrs. Jackson told David he must go to school every
day or she would have to punish him. After about six
weeks, she found out that David had been punished at
school for misbehavior. He had been talking in class.
During the next year, David's behavior changed notice-

ably. His conduct in class was very aggressive, and he was
changed to a different class twice.

Finally, Mrs. Jackson got a note saying David had
been suspended from school. She went to talk with the
teacher who told her she would not let David back in the
class. Distressed, Mrs. Jackson kept him at home for
several weeks; then a social worker suggested she take
him to Children's Hospital for an evaluation. The psychiatrist told Mrs. Jackson that David was emotionally
disturbed and needed special help. He recommended
that he attend a day school for disturbed children.
Officials in the School Department told Mrs. Jackson
that there were no vacancies for David at the time. She
asked if her son could attend public school classes for
disturbed children during the meantime, but was told
there was no room there either.

David remained out of school for nearly eighteen
months. For a short time, he went to a learning center in
the neighborhood, but this was not permanent. Most of
the time he just stayed at home with nothing to do.
Finally, Mrs. Jackson told a social worker that David was
getting no help and no education. The worker called the
school, and, after several months, arranged for David to

enter a day school. He had been out of school nearly two years.

PATRICIA REILLY
age 16

Pat is the middle child in a family of five children in South Boston. Her two older sisters have graduated from high school, the same one Pat attended until the 12th grade. Her father and mother are separated now, but she and her brothers and sisters visit their father on weekends.

Her mother recalls that Patricia had some difficulty in her early years in school. She fainted once, and had crying spells in school. On these occasions, Mrs. Reilly was asked to keep Pat home from school. She was a very sensitive child and once, when the principal yelled at a group of children, she became very upset.

As she grew older, however, these problems seemed to go away and Pat did quite well in school. Her marks were a bit above average and seemed to improve each year. She talked with her mother about going to nursing school.

In February of her senior year, Pat found out that she was pregnant. At first she was afraid to tell her mother, but finally decided to do so. Mrs. Reilly naturally was upset but recalls that her first feeling was that she loved Patricia and wanted to help her. Together, they went to talk with the priest on three different occasions. He said they must make the best of this mistake, and encouraged Pat to continue her education and even go on to become a nurse.

Both Pat and her mother were encouraged and decided that they would work together. There were only twelve weeks of school left and Pat planned to go on to graduate. But when her teacher found out that she was pregnant, she was sent to the principal's office. After some discussion between the principal and the teacher, Pat was told that she must drop out of school. The principal said that it was neither good for her nor the other children for her to continue in school.

When Pat's mother found out about this, she called the school. The principal said that there was nothing he could do, but that Pat could come back to finish school some other year. Pat stayed at home, losing the semester, and therefore failing to graduate. Mrs. Reilly expressed concern over the possibility that Pat might not complete her education even though she is so close.

HARRIS WILLIAMS
age 10

Harris is an only child who lives with his mother and aunt in the South End. He is somewhat small for his age but has always been very active, playing with friends in his neighborhood.

During the spring of last year, Mrs. Williams got a note summoning her to school. The pupil adjustment counselor told her that Harris and another boy, who had once been his friend, had been fighting. Harris was not to return to school for a week. Mrs. Williams remarked that the teacher seemed to be taking the side of the other boy, but did keep Harris at home for several days.

When he returned to school he was immediately sent home again for no specific length of time, but until he "learns to behave". Mrs. Williams again went to school to see the teacher. It was at this time that she found out Harris had been placed in a class for retarded children since last year. She became very upset because she had not been informed of this. She recalled a note from someone last year saying that Harris was receiving some special help with his studies, but it said nothing about a class for retarded children.

Mrs. Williams visited the school several times regarding this matter. She asked to see her son's records and test scores, but was told that she couldn't because the information was "confidential". The teacher did admit that Harris' work had been better than the others, that he could be smart when he wanted to, and that she didn't really understand him. In particular, it seemed as though he had been placed in the class because of his behavior.

Mrs. Williams was not satisfied, and arranged for Harris to be tested at a private clinic. The psychologist gave him a thorough evaluation, and told Mrs. Williams that Harris had an I.O. of 96, a normal score. He said that he definitely should not be in a class for mentally retarded children. He felt that this would only cause him to act up more, rather than helping him.

A lawyer at a community agency told Mrs. Williams that he would help her get Harris into the regular class he should be in. He called the principal and the Director of the Department of Special Classes (for mentally retarded), and arranged to get Harris into his regular class.

Mrs. Williams is happy about this and Harris is doing better now. But she found out from a neighbor that several other parents whose children go to that school are upset because their children have been put in these classes too.

TONY MANGANO
age 14

Tony, his parents, and two sisters, live in the North End. His sisters, one older and one younger than he, do quite well in school but Tony has had difficulty from the very beginning.

When he entered kindergarten, he was excluded after a few months. The teacher said that he was very bright but that he was just too playfull and aggressive. The next year he entered the first grade with the same results — he was sent home. His mother was told that because he was not quite seven, there was nothing the school could do for him. Mrs. Mangano still doesn't understand exactly why this happened; she feels that he is a good boy and the schools should have a place for him.

The pupil adjustment counselor made an appointment for Tony at a clinic. The doctor couldn't see Tony for ten days and the principal said he couldn't come to school during that time. Mrs. Mangano was never told the results of the evaluation, so she called the clinic. She found out that three weeks earlier the doctor had recommended that Tony be returned to the first grade. His academic work was satisfactory and he had no emotional problems. The school hadn't told this to Mrs. Mangano, but she finally arranged for him to return at mid-year.

The following year, Tony was suspended from school. A note sent to his mother said he and another boy "were pushing at the water fountain and cutting up too much". Mrs. Mangano went to the school and the principal suggested she take Tony to another clinic so he could get an evaluation for disturbed children. A doctor at the mental health clinic said this was ridiculous because Tony, while mischievous and active, was not emotionally disturbed.

After that, the school refused to allow him back, but did send a home tutor. Mrs. Mangano said that several times the tutor failed to come to the home, and when she did, it was for less than an hour. She felt Tony wasn't learning anything this way because the tutor just gave him some things to read or write, but didn't really teach anything. She feels Tony lost a lot that year and fell behind his academic level.

The next year Tony again went to school. While he had no behavior problems, he seemed to have little interest in his lessons. The teacher told Mrs. Mangano that he seemed to be a "slow learner". This kept up for the next two years or more, as Tony's mother recalls, and he did progressively worse in school. Eventually, Tony began to be truant from school several times each month. His father whipped him at first, but Tony seemed to withdraw even more. His truancy continued, and finally he was formally suspended from school on two occasions.

After the second suspension, Tony didn't return to school. A worker noticed Tony coming to the Neighborhood Center daily. He called the school to find out why they had not contacted Tony or his mother; he had been out of school three months.

Footnotes

1. The psychologist's account of this child is reproduced here because it represents what happens to a number of children in the Boston schools.

III. Exclusion: An Overview

On the basis of our information, we have identified three broad categories or types of exclusion operating within the Boston School System, each one affecting different groups of children:

1. Children who are out of school or who have never been to school. The children in this category come primarily from cultural minorities; many of them are Spanish-speaking. Most of these children cannot go to school because the School Department has failed to establish educational programs for them;

2. Children who are not allowed to attend school, or who are made to leave school. This group is composed of children with physical handicaps such as those who are crippled; it also includes girls who are pregnant.[1] Generally, these children are not allowed to attend school even though, in the opinion of many experts, they are capable of participating in normal school activities;

3. Children who have unique needs which are inadequately or inappropriately met within the school system. Children in this category include those who are mentally retarded, emotionally disturbed, and perceptually handicapped. The School Department often confuses them by labelling a retarded child as disturbed, or vice versa. One result is that "special classes" become a catch-all for children with vastly different needs.

These three groups then are composed of children who are "culturally different," "physically different," and "mentally or behaviorally different," corresponding respectively to the listing above. While no one actually assigns these labels to the children, School Department operations serve to categorize them as decisively as though labeling were a formal policy. The irony is that these children get labelled arbitrarily according to their alleged "differentness," when in fact almost any child in school could be judged different from his peers in some way. Considering their educational needs, some children are "different" enough to warrant special recognition; many are not. But the one common experience that this arbitrarily mixed grouping of children shares is exclusion from school.

While exclusion in its narrow sense refers specifically to a decision by the school committee to prevent a child from attending school,[2] we found that it has a much broader meaning in actual practice. Seldom is such formal action taken against a child. Rather, according to the examples above which we shall discuss in the next three chapters, children are excluded from school altogether, or are excluded from a proper education within the regular classroom, in a variety of informal ways. In some cases, this exclusion is not done intentionally; sometimes, however, it is.

But intentional or not, exclusion from school severely affects the lives of many children. In the following three chapters we shall examine the characteristics and needs of these groups of children.

Footnotes

1. The inclusion of pregnant girls in this category is not meant to imply any relationship between physical handicaps and pregnancy. Rather, the typology outlined in this chapter is based on practices found operating in the Boston School Department.

2. General Laws, Chapter 76, Sections 16 and 17.

IV. Children Who Are Culturally Different

By far, the largest group of children out of school that we have been able to identify are those who are members of cultural minorities. Presently, Italian, Chinese, Cuban, and Puerto Rican children comprise most of this number, though it also includes a significant proportion of black children from the South.

The majority of these children came to Boston relatively recently. Immigration rates have fluctuated in the past, but there is now a steady flow of new residents. The figures on immigrants entering the Boston port show this trend:[1]

Year	No. Immigrants
1965	5,026
1966	9,903
1967	12,707
1968	13,663
1969	15,477

While many immigrant families take up residence elsewhere in the state, a large proportion of those entering the port make their permanent residence in Boston. In 1968, the Immigration and Naturalization Service listed 4,187 new immigrants residing in the city. Of this number, there were 520 Italians, 257 Chinese, and 326 Cubans. The Immigration Service does not record Puerto Ricans, who are citizens, but independent sources estimate the annual rate to approach 1,500 and probably more.[2]

Thus, immigrants continue to come to Boston in noticeable numbers. While Italians have been coming for many years, the immigration of the other groups is more recent. Chinese families from Hong Kong and Taiwan steadily take up residence, and the number of Portuguese families is increasing. Black families continue to migrate from the South, while Puerto Rican families make up the largest cultural group presently moving to Boston.

A large proportion of children from these ethnic groups are not being educated by our public school system. The regular school curriculum does not meet their needs and there is little recognition that programs should be provided for them. Consequently, they have no alternative but to remain out of school.

Spanish-Speaking Children — An Example

In addition to the large number of Puerto Ricans, Spanish-speaking families from other countries now live in Boston. This includes a significant number of Cubans as well as other Latin and South Americans. The number is growing each year. For example, the 1960 Census records 1,200 Puerto Ricans in Boston. Today, even modest estimates are in the range of 20,000.[3]

Public recognition of the presence and needs of these newcomers has been slight. Little has been known of them. Being citizens, the Puerto Ricans are not listed in official immigration records. And the annual police census fails to specify the number and origin of other Spanish-speaking families. In short, these people have moved to Boston relatively unnoticed. No agency — public or private — has accurate and complete information on their numbers.

A number of individuals and agencies have made an effort, however, to document the size of this population. Surveys have been made door-to-door in some areas of the city; interviews and studies have been conducted by laymen and academicians; and several agencies have begun to establish a partial picture, one that is incomplete at best. Because documentation has been difficult, it is important to consider the evidence at some length.

The data provided by these various sources enables us to compile a statistical picture with a high and low range. The following picture was compiled by the Mayor's Office of Public Service:[4]

Brighton-Allston: 2,500 to 4,000 Cubans
(Source: Cuban Refugee Center; APAC; Catholic Church)

Jamaica Plain: 3,000 to 5,000 Cubans and Puerto Ricans
(Source: Cuban Refugee Center; Jamaica Plain APAC)

South End: 4,800 to 8,000 Puerto Ricans
(Source: APCROSS: BRA: Cardinal Cushing Center)

Roxbury — North Dorchester: 5,000 to 10,000 Puerto Ricans, Santo Dominicans, and others
(Source: Denison House, Catholic Church; survey by Sister Francis Georgia)

South Boston: 700 Puerto Ricans
(Source: St. Augustine:s Church)

Columbia Point: 500 Spanish speaking people
(Source: Boston Housing Authority)

The information provided by these sources ranges from a low of 16,500 to a high of 28,200 Spanish-speaking people in Boston. The Office of Human Rights has estimated that the actual figure may be as high as 32,000, with the following composition: 22,000 Puerto Ricans, 5,000-6,000 Cubans, and 4,000-5,000 other Spanish-speaking.[5]

The Boston School Department itself accepts the figure of 20,000 Puerto Ricans alone (that is, aside from numbers of other Spanish-speaking people). In a report to the federal government, this figure was used by the School Department.[6]

As difficult as it is to determine the exact number of Spanish-speaking residents in the city, it is even harder to establish the annual rate of growth for this population group.

Statistics compiled by the Cuban Refugee Center in Boston show that an average of 550 Cubans have registered at that office each year since 1961. But it is known that not all Cubans enter Boston through that agency which is sponsored by Catholic Family Services. Other agencies sponsor Cubans too, and some Cubans arrive without agency assistance. It is known too that some who register go on to settle in other cities in the state. On the whole, the Mayor's Office estimates the Cuban population to be growing at the rate of 400-500 persons each year.[7]

Determination of the growth rate of the Puerto Rican population is more difficult since Puerto Ricans are not required to register. The rate must be estimated on the basis of several studies. Action for Boston Community Development (ABCD) conducted a Summer Migrant Study in 1968. Almost half of the families interviewed had arrived from Puerto Rico within the last three years. Similarly, the Boston Redevelopment Authority (BRA) study, 1966-67, showed an equal percentage of Puerto Rican families who had lived in the city less than three years. Finally, a study of new patients in the Out-Patient Department of Boston City Hospital, between January and March, 1969, showed that of almost two hundred patients born in Puerto Rico, the average length of residence in Boston was eighteen months.

Analyzing these data, a statistical consultant set the minimum annual growth of the Puerto Rican community at 1,000 persons.[8] If anything, this estimate appears to be low. The Puerto Rican population increased by over 15,000 persons in ten years (1960: 1,200; 1970: 16,500 minimally).[9] This is an annual average of 1,500.

Using the conservative figures then, the number of Cubans and Puerto Ricans coming to Boston each year is at least 1,500 (Cubans: 500; Puerto Ricans: 1,000), and quite likely even more.

Besides immigration, the birth rate contributes to the population growth of the Spanish-speaking population as well. A good deal of information is available on the household composition of these families: family size, ages of children, and ages of parents. Six studies have been made:[10]

Boston Redevelopment Authority, 1966
(89 Puerto Rican households)
Manuel Teurel, Harvard Honors Thesis, 1966
(49 Puerto Rican households)
Harvard-MIT Joint Center for Urban Studies, 1968
(1157 children)
Boston Housing Authority, 1968
(225 Puerto Rican households)
Massachusetts Department of Education, and APCROSS, 1968
(261 Puerto Rican households)
Sister Francis Georgia, 1969
(50 Puerto Rican households)

Several points are made clear by these studies:

1. Puerto Rican parents in Boston are young, in the child-bearing age. Most of them are between the ages of 20-30.
2. Puerto Rican families are large. The average household has four children.
3. The children in the families are very young. Three-fourths of them are under 12 years, and one-third of them are under age 5.

On the basis of the information discussed so far, we can draw a statistical picture of Spanish-speaking children in the city, based on the low estimate of the total Spanish-speaking population of 16,500 and the high estimate of 32,000:

Number and Ages of Spanish-Speaking Children in Boston

Population Estimate	Total[a] Children	School[b] Age	Below[c] School-Age
16,500	11,000	5,500	3,650
32,000	21,330	10,665	7,110

a. Four children per household of six persons.
b. One-half of total number of children.
c. One-third of all children.

In showing the number and age-range of the children, the studies implicitly brought out another issue of con-

cern. If half of the Spanish-speaking children are of school age, how many are in school?

The researchers and interviewers then began to try to document the number of children who attended school. Sister Francis Georgia, Consultant in Puerto Rican Affairs for the Mayor's Office of Human Rights, surveyed a ten block area along Dudley Street from Magnolia Street to Blue Hill Avenue. This door-to-door survey revealed 350 Spanish-speaking children of school age. Sixty-five percent of them had never registered in school; many others rarely attended or had dropped out altogether.[11]

A Puerto Rican community worker canvassed his own block in the South End. He found fifteen Spanish-speaking children on that one street who did not go to school.[12]

Nuns teaching at an elementary school reported that from their classroom windows, they saw Puerto Rican children each day playing in the streets during school hours.[13]

A grocery store manager told of the large number of children he sees regularly in the homes where he delivers food each day. In a short time, he pointed out over eighteen of these homes to the surveyor. Some of these families had six or more children in them.

During the summer of 1969, Spanish-speaking workers conducted a summer program for Puerto Rican and other Spanish-speaking children. Of 400 children who attended, one in eight had never been to school before. Many others had once attended but no longer did so.

On the basis of these individual studies and observations, Sister Francis Georgia declared:

"... by any standards, the fact is incontestable that hundreds and hundreds of Puerto Rican children are not in school at all. They are visibly roaming the streets or just allowed to stay at home. Any community resident who has taken even a minimal interest in this problem will attest to this condition ... "

But the question still remained: exactly how many Spanish-speaking children are actually out of school? To determine this, we turned to school records:

• In October, 1968, the Boston School Department reported to the Office of Education in Washington, D.C. that 2,516 children with Spanish surnames attended school in Boston.[14]

- On December 1, 1968, Assistant Superintendent William L. Cannon circulated a memorandum, and reported 1,127 Puerto Rican children in the Boston Public Schools.[15]
- On April 10, 1969, each school was surveyed again, this time for the number of all Spanish-speaking children in each school. The total reported was 2,107.[16]
- In April, 1969, principals of Boston's parochial schools reported 265 Spanish-speaking children in elementary grades and 44 in high school.
- The maximum number of Spanish-speaking children in school reported for the school year 1968-69 was 2,825.

On the basis of these official school records, it became possible to determine the number of Spanish-speaking children out of school. The graph below is based on the most conservative figures, e.g. comparing the *lowest* population estimate with the *highest* figure given for children in school:

Attendance Status of Spanish-Speaking Children in Boston Schools (1969)

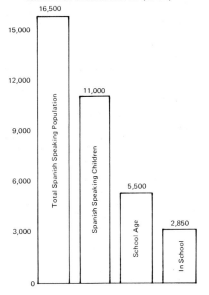

The evidence presented by these figures is clear: a minimum of 2,650 Spanish-speaking children are not being educated. The implications of this problem are magnified when we consider that these are the most *conservative* estimates. If we use the highest estimate given for the total Spanish-speaking population, by the Mayor's Office of Human Rights, (32,000), the total number of children out of school ranges as high as 7,800!

Thus, we can state with a marked degree of confidence – and alarm – that between 2,650 and 7,800 Spanish-speaking children of school age in Boston are not in school. There may be several reasons for this shockingly high number of Spanish-speaking children out of school. Two stand out.

First is the "cultural" reason. Most of the people in the Spanish-speaking community, especially the Puerto Rican community, formerly lived in rural areas. Being poor, their lives were devoted to economic sustenance. As among people of many lands, their cultural bond was strong. When they came here, they faced a completely

different life. Now they are city dwellers, expected to know how to utilize urban institutions and services. And above all, they suffer the handicap of not being able to communicate; they cannot speak the language.

The people, facing these bewildering barriers, remain within their community, drawing strength from their friends. Incidents of hostility and physical harm, directed mainly against their children, have had serious effects. There are some schools, for example, where Spanish-speaking children have been beaten up by other students. This problem, plus the problem of a new and bewildering life style, and the barrier of language, all work together to enforce a tendency to remain withdrawn.

At most, however, this "cultural" explanation is minor in comparison to the second reason: these thousands of children are out of school because there are no educational programs for them. The school system does not recognize that their needs must be reflected in the school curriculum.

"The school curriculum and language program is, in most cases, grossly inadequate to meet the needs of these children. The schools have very little. . .'holding power' for the children. .and the school system's methods for handling the language problem tend to reinforce a traditional pattern of leaving school at an early age." [17]

This problem is seen not only by community leaders, but is recognized by certain school officials as well. Reporting to the federal government, the Boston School Department stated: [18]

"The Spanish-speaking child finds himself in a classroom where the total curricula, methods, and medium of language are geared toward the native English speaker . . . It is unrealistic for us to suppose that if we then place a number of non-English speakers in this urban classroom, the teachers can meet the special needs of these children.

At present the children within these areas are unable to cope with the subject content being taught because of their lack of proficiency in English, and almost immediately encounter failure in the classroom. For many this failure pattern continues for a number of years until the child has gained the needed proficiency in English. By this time the initiative and positive self-image (so necessary for success in any educational endeavor)

of many of these children has been thoroughly thwarted."

Thus, the major reason most of these children are out of school becomes clear. The educational programs, by the School Department's own admission, are failing to educate the numbers of Spanish-speaking children who are in school. The people in the Spanish-speaking community — leaders and parents — know that the school system is failing to educate their children. Because there are no adequate programs for them, there is little alternative but to allow their children to remain out of school.

That this is in fact the case was shown during the summer of 1969. Spanish-speaking teachers and community leaders conducted a summer school program in the Mackey School for Puerto Rican children. Expecting 250 children, over 400 came to school each day. Many had never before been to school, despite being of school-age. The program demonstrated an important point: the children remain out of school involuntarily. When there is an educational program for them, they will attend. The positive response to this program was beyond the most hopeful expectations of the teachers and planners. The Spanish-speaking community does value education for its children — when the education is available.

In a larger sense, it is beside the point to discuss statistics, cultural variables, and programs. The most important aspect of this entire problem is how it affects the children themselves: what does it mean to a child when he can't go to school? What effect does it have upon his life?

The Spanish-speaking child does not have to know English to realize that other children go to school. He sees them pass his house each day. But he can't go; there is nothing at school for him. By implication, the child is told two things: first, that his language is of little or no value, and second, that his parents — the way they speak and their way of life — are of little value.

The child, in a huge, new country, is told to change his language, habits, and customs — his very being. He is forced to deny what he is, finding that his own self is not "proper" or not of value. And it is this message that the child has reinforced in his mind each day the school doors open for other children, but not for him.

One need not be a psychiatrist to understand the impact this has upon the mind of a child. Language is an extension of one's culture. If you destroy the language,

you destroy the culture. If a child is told his language is of no value, he is told his culture is worthless too. Soon, he will understand that he too is of little worth. This process, this message, lays the groundwork for self-hatred.

In testifying recently in support of a bilingual education bill, Father Ernest Serino, Director of the Cardinal Cushing Center, recalled how this message affected his own parents who came as children from Italy. In a short time, they understood that what they had, what they were, was of little value. They remained illiterate, suffering shame for the next fifty years.

If our schools have progressed at all in those years, certainly they must have developed more responsibility and more compassion for all children. One way to show children that they are important and of worth is to reinforce their self-esteem by building upon what they have. This can be done, as a start, simply by providing Spanish-speaking teachers to help the children learn both Spanish and English, while they retain their own cultural values. The School Department could indicate its sincerity also by hiring some Spanish-speaking school officials whom the parents could consult regarding their children's education. Above all, the schools could recognize the responsibility to provide educational programs for all of these school-age children.

The Boston School Department does offer programs for some Spanish-speaking children. It first began to recognize the need to educate these children in 1967. During that year, the first English as a Second Language program was established.

Today, the school system has three programs operating for Spanish-speaking children: English as a Second Language (ESL), Bilingual Classes, and Bilingual Transitional Clusters.

The ESL program during the 1969-70 school year included about 750 Spanish-speaking children who were taught by 20 teachers. In order for a school to be eligible for an ESL teacher, it must have thirty or more non-English speaking children in it. The teachers remove the children from their regular classrooms in a group for about forty-five minutes of instruction each day. The ESL instruction, however, is rarely co-ordinated with regular classroom instruction.

ESL instruction is very elementary, focusing primarily on beginning conversational English, rather than upon academic instruction. The program, which is the principle one in the school system, provides less than an hour of instruction daily for children who can neither speak English nor understand the regular classroom instruction.

Not surprisingly, the ESL program has not been adequate for most children to learn sufficient English to function productively in the regular classroom. The program has been discontinued altogether in a number of other cities because of its ineffectiveness.

The adequacy of this method of instruction is best summed up by a Puerto Rican leader who asked: "If most of our children are forced to vegetate at home, should we be happy that a few are allowed to vegetate in school?"

Another program, Bilingual Classes, began in 1968-69. Last year, 120 children were in the program. The program stresses the pedagogical soundness of teaching young children basic subjects in their own language.[19] This approach considers cultural as well as language factors in the curriculum.

The rationale for the Bilingual Classes is supported by several studies that show that bilingual children achieve better in school than their monolingual peers.[20] Though the program in Boston is relatively new, it appears to be having success. Its greates limitation though is that it includes only 120 children.

During the 1969-70 school year, a third program began. Approximately 150 children attended bilingual transitional classes, a full-time academic program taught in Spanish. The purpose of this program is to enable children to learn sufficient English quickly in a relatively isolated environment, so they can move rapidly into the regular school system. By having a higher turnover rate, the program is designed to accommodate more children than the other bilingual program.

The three school programs, then, contain a total of approximately 1,020 Spanish-speaking children. Of this total, 270 children receive a bilingual education, while the majority, 750, receive only forty-five minutes of ESL instruction each day.

The adequacy of these programs may be judged in two ways: one, according to the academic success of the children in them and two, by comparing the number of children they reach to the number of children who need them.

Judging by the first criterion, ESL, the major program, does not come off well — by the admission of the School Department. In its report to the federal government, cited earlier, the Department stressed this failure: that it is "unrealistic" to place non-English speaking children in a regular classroom and expect them to be educated.[21]

Yet, the School Department continues to keep the majority of these children (750 of 1,020) in the regular classroom, under the ESL program. And as predicted, the program is failing to educate the children. A survey of 400 non-English speaking children, mostly Spanish-speaking, was carried out by the Massachusetts Department of Education and APCROSS. The data, reported on by the School Department, showed that over 75% of the children were held back academically in school:[22]

26% held back 1 grade (132)
25% held back 2 grades (128)
12% held back 3 grades (62)
5% held back 4 grades (24)
8% held back 5 grades (39)
or dropped out
11% unknown (54)

Only 13% of the children surveyed were in their proper grade. Clearly, from the standpoint of academic success, the program is failing.

The success of the other two programs — bilingual programs — is more difficult to judge because they are relatively new. One began in 1968-69 and the other began in 1969-70. While first impressions are that the children in them are more successful academically, these programs must be judged according to the other

criterion as well: how many children they reach compared to how many children need them.

A total of about 270 children are in the two programs. In 1968-69, 120 children were enrolled in the bilingual classes. In 1969-70, about 150 more began in the bilingual transitional clusters. This means only 26% of the children in school who need bilingual education receive it. The others are in the ESL program.

But there is another group of children who need bilingual classes: the 2,650 or more children who are now out of school. As discussed earlier, they are out of school because the School Department provides no classes for them.

To understand fully the magnitude of the need, however, we must consider two additional facts: (1) each year, over 600 more Spanish-speaking children living in Boston reach school-age,[23] and (2) another 500 Spanish-speaking children who are of school-age move to the city.[24] Thus, in addition to the 2,650 school age children now out of school, there are 1,100 more each year who need an educational program. Leaving aside, for the moment, the 750 children in the ESL program who need bilingual instruction, the minimum rate of increase looks like this:

1969-70: 2,650 children need bilingual classes
1970-71: 3,750 children need bilingual classes
1971-72: 4,850 children need bilingual classes
1972-73: 5,950 children need bilingual classes

The Boston School Department has announced no plans to meet this rising need. Its only response has been to provide classes for approximately 150 additional Spanish-speaking children each year for the last two years, (120 in 1968-69, and 150 in 1969-70).

Assuming that this approach will continue, we have the following pattern annually:

1,100 children needing bilingual education
  150 children provided bilingual education
  950 more children each year for whom
       no education is available

Beginning with the 2,650 children now out of school, and adding these additional 950 children each year, we get the following picture:

Projected Number of Spanish-Speaking Children Out of School

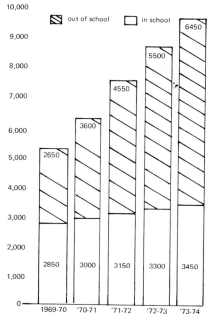

The bar graph takes on an even more sobering meaning when we realize that it is computed on the most conservative estimate of the total Spanish-speaking population. The data are based on a total population of 16,500, while all other estimates are higher. The highest estimate, from the Mayor's Office, is 32,000, indicating that the number of children who will be out of school may in fact be several times as high as the graph shows.

The problem then is increasing rather than decreasing. The programs for the children are inadequate at best. Last year, for example, only seven Spanish-speaking children graduated from high school in the entire city. Every year, larger and larger numbers of children remain out of school because the school system has failed to provide for their education.

Certainly, however, the responsibility for the situation does not rest solely with the School Department. It is a community problem when such large numbers of children are forced to go without an education. It is the responsibility of us all — citizens, professionals, and public and private institutions — to see that the children in our city receive an education. In a real sense then, we all bear responsibility for what is our collective failure in this instance.

Even so, one institution in our city — the school system — exists solely for the purpose of educating children. Its legal and moral mandate is to provide an education for school-age children. Thus, it is reasonable to expect that if the educational needs of children presently out of school are to be met, the Boston School Department must lead the way.

To date, such leadership has not been forthcoming. In fact, the Department continues with business-as-usual, ignoring serious warnings from other quarters. For example, the Massachusetts Commission Against Discrimination, in a recent hearing, found "probable cause" that the Boston School Department is discriminating against children who speak Spanish.[25] This preliminary ruling coincides with a policy memorandum distributed to school districts by the United States Department of Health, Education, and Welfare. It underscores the legal responsibility of the schools for providing educational programs for Spanish-speaking children; it prohibits the use of federal funds to school systems that discriminate as to race, color, or national origin.

Specifically, the memorandum states that where inability to speak and understand the English language excludes children from effectively participating in a school district's educational programs, steps must be taken to correct the deficiency, in order to open the school program to these children. Former HEW Secretary, Robert Finch, discussed how language barriers discriminate against Spanish-speaking students: "If students cannot understand the language their teachers are using, its hopeless to expect them to learn."[26]

In light of this federal policy, the preliminary findings by the Massachusetts Commission Against Discrimination indicate that the Boston School Department is not in compliance with the law. If the School Department alone is unable to fulfill the law, it certainly has the responsibility to inform the public of the problem and arouse public interest toward its fulfillment. Either way, alone or in conjunction with the public, the School Department must stand as protector

of the educational rights and needs of these children.

But this is not the case. Indeed, by most standards the Department is not very concerned with this situation. For the last four years, since February, 1967, community leaders have called upon school officials to take action in behalf of this growing number of children. Yet, the Department has announced no plans to meet this need. It continues each year to allow more and more children to remain out of school. And it has failed to call upon the people of Boston to take action in behalf of the children. In short, almost no effort is being made by the school system.

The only action taken within the last two years to provide an education for these children was development of the bilingual transitional classes. As noted earlier, this program presently provides for only 150 Spanish-speaking children, while several thousand currently are out of school. Yet, even this effort was not made by the School Department. It was conceived of and developed by a handful of community leaders.

In 1966, Miss. Virginia Dunn, a teacher in South Boston, began to notice numbers of Spanish-speaking children in the community who did not go to school. Finding that no educational program existed for them,

she made an effort to begin a small class. In the summer of 1968, she was joined by Sister Francis Georgia.

The Sister began to knock on doors not only in South Boston but in neighborhoods throughout the city. Working with other Spanish-speaking leaders, she surveyed the areas to document the large numbers of children out of school. She recalls going personally into the homes of more than one thousand children who were not in school. The Sister talked with them and with their parents. She learned from the parents that they desperately wanted an education for their children. But being new residents without the ability to speak English, they were bewildered. They knew that the school system offered no education for their children.

In April, 1969, Sister Francis Georgia went to school officials with the information that had been collected. She spoke with school committeemen, the Superintendent, and the Deputy Superintendent. She was received politely by most officials, but recalls that she and other community leaders had the problem dumped back in their laps: "We had to prove to the school officials that the need exists; we had to produce the 'warm bodies'."

Persisting in her efforts on behalf of the children, the

Sister was sent from school administrators to school committeemen to the Mayor's Office, and back to school officials. It did not take her long to discover that not only was there little or no communication among these officials, but that no one would accept the responsibility for taking action to provide an education for the children.

During these months of inaction on the part of school officials, the Sister began to meet with representatives of the Educational Development Center (EDC), a non-profit consulting firm. Together they developed the idea for bilingual transitional clusters, and drew up a proposal for implementation. The proposal provided for 280 Spanish-speaking children, with a budget of about $260,000. EDC officials offered to put up $60,000 for teacher salaries and training, if the Boston School Committee would provide the remainder. EDC stipulated that it had to give its contribution prior to the end of its fiscal year, and requested the School Committee to act on the proposal by October 1, 1969.

Sister Francis Georgia took the final draft of the proposal to School Superintendent Ohrenberger and Deputy Superintendent Tobin in August, and received their initial approval. That month she brought the proposal before the School Committee, and at the same time provided the committeemen with other information revealing several thousand Spanish-speaking children out of school. She requested the Committee, as the body legally responsible for the education of children in Boston, to take action to provide for their education.

The response of the School Committee brought mixed feelings: the members unanimously voted to agree that several thousand children out of school is a grave problem, about which something should be done. But it took no action on the matter.

Meanwhile, EDC officials were concerned that the School Committee would delay so long on the proposal that the $60,000 EDC had set aside would be lost. Their fears were not unfounded: as the school year began, the Committee still had taken no action on the proposal. Finally, on October 15, it approved the proposal – exactly two weeks too late. In so doing, the School Department lost $36,000 of the total which EDC had hoped to spend on the program.

Even this belated "action" on the part of the School Committee was not enough to get the program started. In fact, it was not until several months later that classes began.

The months' interlude was filled with such poor communication and inaction on the part of school officials that private citizens, most notably Sister Francis Georgia, had to assume the major responsibility for administrative tasks such as teacher recruitment, classroom space, and the purchasing of furniture.

After waiting several weeks for the school system to recruit bilingual teachers, the Sister went to the Supervisor of Personnel for the Boston School Department. Having not been informed that he was to hire bilingual teachers, he asked the Sister why she had come to him. He was upset that the Assistant Superintendent had not informed him of this matter, but promised to do what he could.

After another wait, community leaders were told by the School Department that it was having difficulty recruiting bilingual teachers. The next day, Sister Francis Georgia placed an advertisement in the paper, and got responses from ten bilingual teacher applicants.

It was left to her to locate classroom spaces as well. The Catholic Church had provided a building which the School Department refused because of structural design. The Sister then went to Denison House and St. Paul's Parish, arranging for a total of eight classrooms in the two locations.

After classroom space was provided, the School Committee sanctioned the purchasing of furniture. But the official in charge told the Sister that the furniture couldn't be provided for several months. In order for the classes not to be delayed further, she proceeded to locate the furniture herself.

Classes began for a small number of children on January 12, 1970. In all, it took five months from the time the proposal was written until the children started class.[27]

About 150 of the 280 available seats were filled. Community workers carried the responsibility of recruitment. One Puerto Rican explained the problem:[28]

"The (Spanish-speaking) people are very sensitive and proud. For years, the School Department has failed to provide an education for their children. In a sense, the Department was telling the parents: 'Your children aren't important enough to educate.' Now when some classes are available, you can't expect the parents to believe all of a sudden that school officials really do care. It will take a little time and an all-out effort by the School Department. It must provide classes for every one of these children, and in every part of the city."

By all indications, however, the School Department does not plan to provide an educational program for these children. In the fall of 1969, the School Committee adopted a resolution recognizing, that "between 5,000-7,000 Spanish speaking children are out of school," and pledging to provide "education programs to all Spanish-speaking children in Boston by September, 1970".[29] But this promise has not been honored. Nothing has been done to locate the children, recruit teachers, or provide classroom space. And the budget for 1970-71 remains substantially the same as last year's.

Meanwhile, the number of children out of school is increasing. And it will continue to increase until the School Committee recognizes the need and acts accordingly. So far, however, recognition of the need has in fact resulted in regression. There are more children out of school today than when the first program started several years ago. At best, the response of the Boston School Committee has been a feeble catch-up attempt, resulting in more and more children out of school.

Spanish-speaking children out of school are but the most obvious example of the large numbers of children who, in effect, are barred from an education. It indicates what must be happening to children of other cultural groups as well — Italian, Portuguese, Chinese, and Southern blacks. We have information on Chinese children who are out of school, but we have not been able to get conclusive information on the needs of Italian and Portuguese-speaking children or of black children from the South. However, given the lack of response to the needs of Spanish-speaking children, we fear the same situation holds for these other children.

The likelihood that this need is more widespread is indicated in a School Department report to the government: " . . . it is apparent that there is a similar need, albeit on a much smaller scale, for . . . programs for non-English speaking children of Portuguese, Italian, and Chinese extraction".[30]

The children's language or nationality, per se, is not of such importance. The crucial issue is what happens to large groups of children whom we fail to educate. What

are we to expect of them in the future? The Whiting Report, issued by the Mayor's Office of Public Service, addressed this question in regard to Spanish-speaking children. We feel it holds true for all groups of children:[31]

" . . . the present structure of the school programs, not being geared to the special needs of the Spanish-speaking, may produce a large number of teenage drop-outs within the next three or four years. This can be expected to contribute to Spanish juvenile delinquency and unemployment problems which have now barely emerged."

While all these children will not turn to delinquency, we can be fairly certain that the majority of them will earn poverty-level wages or be forced on welfare. By our collective failure to act, it is clear that we shall pay a social and economic penalty in the future. And more importantly, the children themselves will suffer from our failure to provide them an education. In this day, such a failure must be attributed in large measure to the institution in our city most responsible for educating children — the Boston School Department.

Footnotes

1. Immigration and Naturalization records, United States Department of Justice, Immigration and Naturalization Service, Annual Reports, 1965-1969. (1969: Table 5, page 39).

2. Whiting, Rosemary, "An Overview of the Spanish

Speaking Population in Boston," Mayor's Office of Public Service, 1969, page 3. This report cites data from several independently conducted studies.

3. Ibid, page 2.

4. Ibid.

5. Hemingway, Herman W., Administrator, Mayor's Office of Human Rights, reported that as many as 32,000 Spanish speaking citizens reside in Boston. Letter to the *Boston Globe,* January 29, 1969.

6. The Boston School Department reported this figure to the federal government in a proposal for funding: "Title VII E.S.E.A. Bilingual Education Program," Boston Public Schools, 1968.

7. Whiting, op. cit., page 3.

8. Walter, Rosly, "Proposal for Bilingual Transitional Clusters Within Boston Public School Districts," Educational Development Center, Newton, Massachusetts, 1969, page 7.

9. The 1960 United States Census recorded 1200 Puerto Ricans in Boston. Today, the most conservative official figures available indicate the number to be at least 16,500. The Boston School Department reports that the Puerto Rican population increased 19,045 in eight years, 1960-1968 (see footnote 6 above).

10. Walter, op.'cit, page 4.

11. Date made available to the Task Force staff by Sister Francis Georgia, Consultant in Puerto Rican Affairs, Mayor's Office of Human Rights.

12. Walter, op. cit., page 8.

13. Ibid, page 9.

14. These figures, reported to the Department of Health, Education, and Welfare by the Boston School Department, were made available to the Task Force on a school-by-school breakdown.

15. Office of Assistant Superintendent William Cannon, Boston School Department, memorandum, December, 1968.

16. Telephone survey of all principals in the city.

17. Teruel, Manual, "Puerto Ricans in Transition," unpublished honors thesis, Harvard University, 1969.

18. Boston School Department, "Title VII E.S.E.A. Bilingual Education Program" proposal, Boston Public Schools, 1968.

19. Center for Urban Education, *The Center Forum,* Vol. 4, No. 1, September, 1969, page 3.

20. Ibid.

21. Boston School Department, op. cit.

22. Vorhauer, Delia, "A Profile of Boston's Spanish Speaking Community: Characteristics and Attitudes," Association for the Promotion of the Constitutional Rights of Spanish Speaking (APCROSS) and Massachusetts State Department of Education, Migrant Division; compiled by Action for Boston Community Development (ABCD), April, 1969.

23. Table: Number and Ages of Spanish Speaking Children in Boston, this chapter, shows a minimum of 3,650 Spanish speaking children below school age e.g. ages 1-6. This is over 600 children in each age category.

24. Based on 1500 Spanish speaking immigrants to Boston each year, one-third of whom are school age children.

25. Hearing before the Massachusetts Commission Against Discrimination, June 8, 1970.

26. *HEW News,* U.S. Department of Health, Education, and Welfare, Office of the Secretary, May 25, 1970.

27. Refer to "Notes on the Chronological Development of Transitional Bilingual Clusters in Boston Public Schools," Educational Development Center, Newton, Massachusetts, for a 94 page summary of community efforts to motivate the School Department to take action.

28. Alex Rodriguez, former Director, Cooper Community Center.

29. Resolution, "Transitional Bilingual Classes for Spanish Speaking Children in Boston," submitted by School Committeeman Paul Tierney, and passed unanimously by the School Committee, November, 1969.

30. Boston School Department, op. cit., Part II, XIX-2.

31. Whiting, op. cit., page 8.

VII. Services to Children: The School Department

The preceding chapters identify problems and practices in the Boston School Department that adversely affect the lives of thousands of children. To consider one problem after another, and the impact that each has upon the lives of children, creates grave concern on the part of interested citizens. In fact the problems seem so immense that they may cause concerned people to become dismayed. Or perhaps they have an anesthetizing effect whereby concern and empathy is worn down by an apparently overwhelming situation.

If, in this day, the children of our city are to receive the educational programs and services they need and deserve, concerned citizens cannot be worn down. Instead, concern must lead to greater understanding and, ultimately, to action. Understanding of the problems requires more than awareness of what is happening however. It requires awareness of the organizational structures, procedures, and processes that cause and perpetuate problems. We realize that such a full understanding of the failure toward our children must consider national priorities and resources. But to be practical we must focus on the institutions of our own city that bear primary responsibility for the development of our children.

The information, testimony, and statistical data provided in previous chapters focus on the operation of the School Department in an effort to analyze the causes and consequences of excluding children from school. In our investigation we found a wide range of competency on the part of school administrators. Some are extremely perceptive and concerned, working in an inert bureaucracy, while others fail to understand the needs of children or the effects of certain school policies upon them. But we are not dealing with administrators who are inherently "good" or "bad", for all such persons will say that they want what is best for the children. Rather, we find that it is more useful to examine the concept of education held by school administrators, and the administrative structure as it operates under that concept and in regard to the needs of the children.

The concept of, and attitude toward, education varies with time. During the lifetime of Horace Mann, the Boston School System was a pioneer in the new belief that the concept of equal educational opportunity meant that all children, not just the rich, had a right to an education. Today, with an even greater commitment to a full educational opportunity for each child, the concept has a more advanced meaning. Equal educational opportunity refers not only to the "inputs" — the mere exposure of children to a classroom. It refers to the "effects" as well — how well children learn. In essence this means that schools are responsible for how well they do their jobs, for the results.

This advanced concept is widely held by educators, academicians, and laymen as well.[1] That the schools accept this responsibility, at least in principle, is indicated by the existence of programs offering "special services" within the school system. It recognizes that children come into the schools with different abilities and needs, but that the schools are responsible for how well they educate each child.

"It is archaic to continue the argument about whether or not the school should be responsible for the behavioral tendencies and emotional adjustments of the pupil. The hard fact is this: school events bear a functional relationship to the child's characterological outcome. Thus, the schools are responsible whether or not (some) educators accept and meet this responsibility. This is clearly true for the difficult child as well as for the one who is productive and content."[2]

Clearly, while other factors act upon children too, a major responsibility for their development is borne by the schools. In fact, there is considerable evidence to indicate that when children do not learn, it is the fault of the school and not the child.[3] This view is supported by evidence that all children have an in-born curiosity which drives them to want to learn; the failure of some children to learn stems from the failure to stimulate that natural desire.

One widely-reported study shows that the educational success of children depends upon the teacher: if a teacher expects a child to succeed, he actually will demonstrate greater intellectual achievement. This research concludes that "the difference between the special children and the ordinary children was only in the mind of the teacher".[4] This information has given rise to the term "self-fulfilling prophecy" – that if a child is treated as though he is smart or dumb, he actually will be, due to the malleability of the young mind. Children are very sensitive and learn what is expected of them. They judge their own worth according to the expectations of teachers or other adults.

> "When teachers, supervisors, and administrators receive students with these categorical labels (or assign the labels themselves), their expectancies then appear to become prophecies which are frequently fulfilled, to the surprise of no one."[5]

Two other sources hold similar views. Evidence in the nationally-known Coleman Report indicates that the sources of educational failure lie in processes which occur during the time children are in school, rather than prior to their entry. Schools then are a direct or indirect contributor to the educational failure of children. The U.S. Office of Education reports that many students fail because of the behavior of adults in the school.[6] The difficulty centers around administrators and teachers who cannot accept normal student-age behavior, or who are not able to help children with special needs. In other instances, failure is due to traditional instruction procedures generally directed toward forcing children to conform to the school's pattern, rather than encouraging them to develop their own potential.

Regardless of variation in the theme, the overall point is clear: the way children are treated in school largely determines their educational success or failure. School administrators bear responsibility for how well children in school succeed, much in the same way that doctors are responsible for the well-being of their patients and lawyers for their clients. The only difference is that the school system carries an even greater responsibility inasmuch as children are required to go to school. Within the last several decades, the responsibility of the schools has expanded rapidly due both to public and legal mandate. Today, the schools bear the major public responsibility for the socialization and development of our children.

Understanding this role and responsibility, we harbor grave concern because of ideas and attitudes held by some top administrators and politicians in the Boston School Department:[7]

● "There isn't much we can do with some of these children. Many of them are just slow learners."

● "We don't have inferior schools; what we have are inferior students."

● "The problems are not our responsibility. It's the fault of the families."

● "The crime no longer fits the punishment. The courts are too easy on school offenders."

● "[If they were allowed in school] you'd almost be giving your approval of what they'd done."

In the course of our investigation, we found that these attitudes, while not held by all administrators and teachers, are widely-held enough to be shocking. Some attitudes that were even more extreme, we had to dismiss as the opinion of a very small minority. From a moral and ethical point of view these opinions are distasteful, negating the assigned role of the school in each child's development. But even from a purely selfish viewpoint such attitudes are shortsighted, for we all shall bear the consequences of our failure to thousands of children. The toll shall be paid in human terms as well as financial ones: inadequate education or outright exclusion often leads to delinquency, lack of skills, unemployment, marital problems, crime, and other unhappy outcomes. From either viewpoint, a moral one or a selfish one, the attitudes expressed are startling.

Another part of the prevailing concept of education – one which is related to the attitudes just discussed – is an orientation toward children which is frequently punitive and inhibiting. Reflecting a narrow concept of education from times past, it stresses "sitting still, keeping quiet, and staying in line".[8] Based on the rationale that this climate will promote learning, it instead discourages inquisitiveness, independence, and creativity. The message operates to quiet minds as well as bodies; in many cases, the price paid for a calm child is a dull mind as well. Such a view seems to rest on the idea that form in education is somehow more important than content; that unnecessary order is more virtuous than stimulation of the young mind.

The significance of this concept is that it is in almost total contradiction to all that educators and psychologists know about how children learn:

- The young mind, being naturally inquisitive, responds best to highly creative stimulation.

- Many behavior problems and classroom failures on the part of children are simply the expression of frustration — a cry for help, a communication that something is wrong.

The view we find so prevalent in the Boston schools is the antithesis of the above:

- Children must be kept in line; those who are over-active must be punished into learning.

- Consequent misbehavior is a sign of disrespect for authority and the result of a bad home.

These attitudes reflect a concept of education that is not only outdated, but out of keeping with the needs of young children as well. The attitudes are not merely those of individuals however, for they become incorporated into the very structure and operation of the School Department itself. Attitudes of administrators in the school bureaucracy are reflected in the policies and practices toward children in the schools. For this reason it is important to summarize, on the basis of evidence in other chapters, the structure and operation of services to children in the School Department.

Within the School Department there are twelve separate departments or programs which, together, are referred to as "special services". A considerable part of our investigation focused on the operation of certain ones of them: the Departments of Attendance, Pupil Adjustment Counseling, Investigation and Measurement (testing), Physically Handicapped, Special Classes (mentally retarded), and the programs for Emotionally Disturbed, Perceptually Handicapped, and non-English speaking children. We evaluated statistical data from the

departments, and heard testimony from the various directors. We questioned them about their responsibilities, and we questioned people from community agencies about their relationship with the departments. And we focused on what happens to children who come to the attention of "special services"

The rationale for providing "special services" to children in school is quite simple: the full educational development of each child depends upon more than academic instruction in a classroom. Education in its deepest sense involves the general nurturing and development of the child. Recognizing this, and realizing that each child has his own unique needs, "special services" are provided to insure the full educational development of each child.

The educational process then includes more than regular classroom instruction. Persons with special training in certain areas function to supplement the "regular" educational instruction process. "Special services" therefore exist for the large proportion of children who at one time or another need special help. For example, a child having difficulties with his studies may be referred to one of the services, depending upon whether the learning difficulty is due to poor eyesight, hearing, or emotional problems.

The operating relationship between the overall school system and "special services" is this: the on-going education of children is provided in the regular classroom environment; when children exhibit needs which impede this educational process, "special services" are available to help them so their education can continue.

But our inquiry into this relationship revealed that it operates to exclude several thousand children from school; their educational development is not supported, but halted. For these children, neither the regular classroom nor the "special services" are working. Because of this, it is apparent that the relationship itself between the overall system and "special services" as described above is not working. It exists in theory but not in practice.

The school machinery as it presently operates pushes children out of, rather than drawing them back into, the educational process.

"The existing machinery for responding to students (in need) serves mainly to push away, to alienate, to cut off opportunity. While counseling . . and psychological treatment are not to be discounted, they are far less significant in the schools' response . . . than the routine practice of isolation from the classroom, assignment to a special classroom . . . (and) suspension . . . all of which serve to block future opportunities for pupils . . ."9

There is a wide range of mechanisms that operate to push away, isolate, and exclude the children thereby diminishing their opportunity for involvement in the normal educational process: assignment to special classrooms, removal to an isolated environment, and placement of overactive children in classes which provide only custodial care. Other examples of this isolation-exclusion orientation are denial of opportunity to participate in special activities, not allowing children with low I.Q.'s to eat lunch with other children, and not permitting emotionally disturbed children to participate in routine activities such as fire drills. The extreme forms of exclusion are the prevention of children from entering the classroom in the first place, and suspension from school of those who do attend.

The school system seems to operate on the implicit principle that schools exist for the instruction of a relatively homogeneous group of children, and that the educational process cannot tolerate the normal range of human differences that exists in the larger society. This principle presumably rests upon the assumption that classroom instruction can proceed better if "different" or "difficult" children are removed.

This principle of operation is contrary to the needs and rights of children in a democracy, according to the United States Office of Education:10

"School organization which isolates and excludes according to ability, race, or economic class, denies to youth the opportunity to meaningfully interact with diverse segments of society . . . (Such a) school does not present itself as a model of a pluralistic society."

If the schools are to be a model of a pluralistic society, then there is no rational basis for separating children according to arbitrary groupings while they are in school. Children educated in such a manner cannot be expected to relate successfully with different kinds of people when they become adults. The grouping, isolation, and exclusion of children not only shortchanges those who get separated, but it is abnormal and unfair to the children they get separated from. The creative capacities of children are developed by their learning to live in a microcosm of society — the classroom where

differences exist and are welcomed.

On the basis of the processes operating in the School Department, we conclude that it is responding to children on the basis of their *differences*, rather than on the basis of their *needs*. On one hand it fails to recognize, in the case of Spanish-speaking children, that their language difference requires special educational programs to meet their needs. On the other, as in the case of crippled children, it responds solely on the basis of their difference and excludes them. For example, a child becomes labelled a crippled child rather than a normal child who also happens to be crippled. Or a disturbed child becomes labelled as "crazy" rather than as a normal child who has an emotional problem.

With this orientation toward the children, the system operates to exclude those who are different rather than responding to them on the basis of their need, while including them. Using the earlier example, a child who is crippled becomes excluded because he is different, rather than being included and given special help if that difference affects his educational development. Thus, the very machinery — "special services" — which is supposed to help children do well in the regular classroom often functions in their removal from the classroom. Special programs become the vehicle through which children who don't "fit in" are removed from the regular classroom and often from school altogether.

"Special services" in the Boston School Department, then, serve the system rather than the children. They are utilized to relieve the regular system of its responsibility toward certain groups of children. Administrators and teachers in the "special services" are not utilized as specialists to help meet the special needs of children so they can continue to function in the regular classroom. Instead, they are forced to become "babysitters" for the children that the regular system does not want.

Consequently, there are two separate systems operating in the Boston School Department — the regular one and the so-called special one. Instead of co-ordinating their efforts to meet the needs of children, they operate separately, serving different functions. In so doing, neither has the ability to meet the needs of the children.

2. Thorne, Tharp, Wetzel, "Education and Mental Health: the Development of New Resources," Southern Arizona Mental Health Center, 1966.

3. See Jackson, Lenore, and Rosenthal, Robert, *Pygmalion in the Classroom,* 1969; Clark, Kenneth, *Dark Ghetto,* Harper, 1965, especially pages 111-153; and Howard, James "Schools Don't Have to Make Delinquents," *Christian Science Monitor,* May 31—June 2, 1969, page 13.

4. Jackson and Rosenthal, op. cit.

5. Cruickshank, W., Paul, J., Junkala, J., *Misfits in the Public Schools,* Syracuse University Press, 1969, page 132.

6. Task Force on Juvenile Delinquency, President's Commission on Law Enforcement and Administration of Justice, *Juvenile Delinquency and Youth Crime,* U.S. Government Printing Office, 1967, pages 222-277; Kruger, W. Stanley, "They Don't Have to Drop Out," *American Education,* Vol. 5, No. 8, October, 1969, U.S. Office of Education, page 7.

7. These comments are quoted from statements made in interviews, meetings, and public responses by various School Department Officials, during the course of the Task Force investigation.

8. For elaboration on this concept of education in the Boston schools, see Schrag, Peter, *Village School Downtown,* Beacon Press, Boston, 1967, especially Chapter IV.

9. Task Force on Juvenile Delinquency, op. cit., page 256.

10. Ibid, page 278.

Footnotes

1. For example, see Coleman, James S., et al, *Equality of Educational Opportunity,* U.S. Government Printing Office, 1966, Coleman, James S. "The Concept of Equality of Educational Opportunity," *Harvard Educational Review,* Vol. 38, No. 4, Winter, 1968, pages 7-22; and Kirp, David L., "The Poor, the Schools, and Equal Protection," *Harvard Educational Review,* Vol. 38, No. 1, Fall, 1968, pages 635-688.

VIII. School Counselors and Attendance Officers: An Example of Misplaced Priorities

The information in the preceding chapters points out the inadequacy and inappropriateness of certain school programs as they relate to the specific needs of the children. The data also reveals serious problems in the structure and operation of the overall School Department itself, with the result that large numbers of children are excluded from school. The "machinery" operates often to the detriment of the children; not only are their educational needs unmet, but their problems are compounded by treatment in the school system.

In our investigation we found this failure to help the children continues, in part, because of misplaced priorities in the School Department. Resources that could be used directly to help children are used instead for other purposes. Political nepotism, lack of awareness, and, at times, unconcern perpetuate continued failure. A comparison of two departments – Pupil Adjustment Counseling and Attendance – provides an example of the present priorities which must be altered if the School Department is to move to meet the needs of the children.

The Department of Attendance

The Attendance Department is designed to serve two main functions in the school system: one, to locate and keep records on all school-age children in Boston, and two, to insure the school attendance of all school-age children who reside in the city. This latter function is to be carried out by protecting the right of all children to attend school, and by counseling children who express their problems through truancy.

Testifying before the Task Force, one of the Co-Heads of the Department explained that the attendance officers serve as a co-ordinating link between the school and the community. The officers, he said, must be unusually perceptive of others' values while providing services to the children. They are to give counseling services to children on the streets, in their homes, and in

the schools. By providing such services, he explained, the role of the Department is a helping one and not a punitive one. It is recognized that children who are truant are not bad children, but youngsters who are in need of help.

Between September, 1968, and May, 1969, over 700 children were taken to court primarily due to their being truant from school.[1] The attendance officer is instrumental in this court action: he acts as the prosecutor, gathering evidence against the child and presenting it in court. It is at the discretion of the officer whether to take a child to court.

When one member of the Task Force asked the Co-Head how he feels about taking children to court, he responded:[2]

> " . . . we are often dissatisfied with the disposition because if a child gets off, others learn that going to court is not such a big thing. They don't fit the crime with the punishment anymore. That's the whole problem . . . "

Asked what kind of crime he was referring to, the Co-Head replied: "The crime of truancy."

Because of their dissatisfaction with court proceedings, the officers often use other methods in providing their services: "You've got to cajole or threaten. It becomes a question of forcing those wards (sic) to school. We tell the parents we'll take them to court or we'll stop their (pay) checks. It's not legal of course, but we tell them that anyway."[3]

The predisposition of the attendance officers to rely on court action and threats of court action stems, in part, from their backgrounds and training. The position of attendance officer is a civil service one, with preference given to disabled veterans, veterans, and other people in that order. Aside from their military backgrounds, most of the officers have training in police work. Most of the thirty-nine attendance officers now in the Department are former policemen.

In the course of our investigation we were told by a number of people, some within the School Department, that the position of attendance officer is a "political plum" — a highly paid permanent position meted out on the basis of friendships and political connections. The salary for example is fixed at $13,400 per year, one of the highest paid positions within the School Department. (It is more than a teacher with a Ph.D degree can make at the highest salary increment.)[4] The annual Attendance Department budget for salary alone is over half a million dollars ($522,000).

Recruitment procedures for the position are as questionable as are the officers' qualifications. The examination for the position is given sporadically at different periods during the year. We were told that the time depends on whether there are any openings for the position or whether School Department officials request new candidates. One person, a professional who works in a community agency, reported to us that he has been attempting to take the examination since 1968. He has received no answer to his letters requesting the date of the next examination. When he goes in person to take the exam he is told that it was just given, or that there are no openings. Yet, he reports that new officers have been added to the Department several times during this period.

One School Department official told us that when there is a vacancy the position is filled immediately by the friend of an attendance officer or high ranking school official, before interested citizens can compete for the opening. In support of this, he points out that none of the officers are Black, Puerto Rican, or Chinese, and that only four are women.

One of the Co-Heads of the Attendance Department acknowledged that selection for the position of attendance officer tends to be "informal".[5] He stated that when he sees a person who he feels is qualified to be an officer, he tells him to take the examination if a position happens to be open. Thus, it is understandable that this "informal" process works to the advantage of friends of officers already in the Department.

We determined it beyond the scope of our investigation to establish exactly how the procedure operates. According to our view, such a determination is not necessary because mismanagement of the Department is apparent anyway. Whether it is due to "political" or other reasons, the actual operation of the Department is

a cause for serious concern.

Dr. Pierre Johannet, a child psychiatrist, met with the Task Force when we heard from the Co-Heads of Attendance. Responding to their statements regarding how they do their job, Dr. Johannet discussed the meaning of truancy and the response that is necessary to help the children:[6]

"In most instances when a child behaves in a certain way, he's trying to say something. It isn't simply that a child is breaking a law, but rather, he's trying to make a statement. Now if that statement is received and it is possible to help the child, and to find out why he's staying out of school, then perhaps he won't be a repeater . . . I think that one of the duties of an attendance officer would be to be able to respond to that first call . . . (but) the background, training and experience of the officer is not appropriate to the duties."

A pupil adjustment official spoke of the illogic of hiring ex-policemen to do counseling and social work. Such a practice is as illogical as it would be to hire social workers to be policemen.

"An attendance officer is in an excellent position to detect serious behavioral and emotional problems . . . But we find that most of those in the Department are veterans with police backgrounds. The adequacy of such a background for helping children with serious emotional problems is questionable."[7]

Both from the testimony of the Co-Heads and from the observations of interested professionals, it is clear that the stated philosophy of the Department and its actual operation are two different things. The Department is not geared to provision of counseling services to truant children. Instead, its orientation is punitive. Truancy is seen not as a symptom but as a breaking of the law. Consequently, the officers, lacking the understanding and training necessary for working with children, gear their efforts toward preventing the "crime of truancy".

This is not to say that most of the officers don't have concern for the children and their needs. Rather, it simply is recognition that they have been trained for one type of job in the past, and are expected to do something quite different now. Their lack of training for their present responsibilities affects not only the way they do their jobs, but their attitudes as well. One of the Co-

Heads, for example, characterized all truant children as being "less intelligent, less well-scrubbed, crude, careless, and with pungent speech". Upon rebuttal to his statement, he responded: "Let's face it, these people are not school prone; they're just not. Their morals are certainly indicative of this."[8]

Aside from the counseling of truant children, the other stated function of the Department of Attendance is keeping track of school-age children in the city. The rationale for this is that protecting the right of children to attend school can be accomplished only if it is known how many school-age children there are, where they reside, and where they go to school. It is important as well in determining demographic trends which affect the schools' plans for the future.

Last year, according to figures from the Department, officers made over 67,000 investigations pertaining to the attendance of children. The following exchange then took place with the Co-Heads:

Q. How many different children does that figure represent?

A. We don't know that.

Q. It seems terribly important to know whether it represents five thousand or fifty thousand different children in the school system.

A. Concerning children out of school, we are disturbed by the unverified claims that there are as many as 5,000 such children in Boston. We would estimate over the course of a year that about 200—500 children are out at any one time.

Q. Are you aware that the School Committee and Mayor's Office have been given data showing over 5,000 Spanish-speaking children, alone, out of school?

A. We haven't seen them. Somebody should tell us about them. Nobody gave the names to us.[9]

Because of the internal operation of the Department, there is no way of knowing whether 67,000 different children are truant, or whether it might be that 5,000 different children are truant an average of twelve times each during the year. No such records are kept.

One of the most important responsibilities that the law places upon the Attendance Department of each city is the conduction of an annual census of school-age children, (Chapter 72, Section 2). The census records are valuable in determining present and future educational needs in the city. In Boston however, the Department does not conduct the census. It merely keeps records on the number of children who appear in school. As a result, there is no firm idea of how many school-age children in the city are out of school. Consequently, the attendance officers have no idea how many children they are failing to reach.

In summary, the Department of Attendance does not fulfill its main objectives: keeping records on all school-age children in the city; insuring the right of children to go to school by protecting them from those who impede that right; and counseling them when they express needs through truancy.

It does not do this for several reasons. First, the Department takes no census of the school-age children in Boston. Hence, it is not known how many children should actually be in school. Second, the officers are not able to deal with the needs of the children. They are veterans and ex-policemen, lacking adequate training in counseling and social work. Their orientation is legalistic and punitive. Third, they aren't able to utilize community resources well. Aside from lack of professional skills, they are all of one race, precluding in large measure their ability to relate to other racial and ethnic groups throughout the city.

The Department of Pupil Adjustment Counseling

This Department is somewhat unique in comparison to other "special services" in the School Department. Its uniqueness stems from its orientation: instead of addressing itself to one specific area of need as do other departments, it focuses itself in general to children with special needs. This broad focus covers several areas: children with school adjustment problems, children in crisis situations, and children who need clinical evaluation and treatment by mental health professionals. Covering this spectrum, the Department is generally the first "special service" to come in contact with children who need different kinds of special help.

The procedure by which children are referred to the Department of Pupil Adjustment Counseling varies, but generally it is as follows: a teacher recognizes in the classroom that a child is experiencing some difficulty or has some special problem; the principal is consulted on the matter, and at his discretion the pupil adjustment counselor is asked to see the child. The counselor may decide to try to counsel the child, refer him to the Director of the Department for evaluation, or refer him to a clinic for an evaluation.

While these decisions are made by the counselor, the success of the overall procedure — whether a child receives help or not — depends largely upon the teacher and principal. Some teachers are reluctant to refer too many children. Their main goal is to have a calm class. Children who are apathetic or troubled may not be referred unless they become disruptive.

Some teachers, on the other hand, point out that they often cannot refer children to the counselor because they must get prior approval from the principal. If the teacher requests supportive help for the child, the final decision whether the child actually sees the counselor depends on the discretion of the principal.

A large factor in the occasional reluctance to refer children is the overload on the counselors. There are only 29 counselors for the entire school system. This amounts to a counselor-student ratio of 1:3400. While this does not mean that each counselor must help 3400 children each year, it does mean that each counselor is responsible for special help which any one of that number needs during the year.

The actual burden on the counselors is great. For example, sources cited in Chapter VI indicated that a minimum of 4% of the total school population has serious emotional needs at any given time. This means that each counselor has about 135 children who need special help. Any counselor, social worker, or psychologist will attest to the fact that this is an impossible load.

The problem, however, is not even that simple. The figure of 4% is simply the minimum estimate. Other authorities place the figure at 35–40%.[10] This does not mean that this many children are seriously disturbed. It does mean that this many are likely, at any given time, to be in need. While many of them may be experiencing normal crises of growing up, they nevertheless need the attention of an adult trained to help them. This means that instead of 135 children needing the help of one counselor, eight to ten times that number may be in need of such help. It is clear that thousands of children who could benefit from counseling services are not receiving them. The counselors are being asked to carry out an impossible task.

The task is made more difficult by the hiring practices pertaining to new counselors. Selection is made not by the Director, but by the Board of Superintendents. The procedure is carried out on a rating basis. Teachers within the school system get so many points according to certain criteria, and are eligible for the position of counselor when they accumulate enough points.

We found that most of the present counselors are dedicated in their efforts to help the children. Being former teachers, they have had some training in regard to the developmental patterns of children. And they have had experience in working with children in their classes. But it must be recognized that some of them have little or no training in counseling itself. While their past experience is likely to make up for this deficit somewhat, formal training in counseling is usually an essential asset in working with the children. Because the counselors largely determine whether individual children receive clinical evaluations, such training is imperative.

Because of the present hiring practices, persons who have strong backgrounds in counseling, social work, or psychology cannot be considered for the position. The only prerequisite for the position is that the person must have been a teacher. Thus, for the position of pupil adjustment counselor, teachers with absolutely no training in counseling may apply, but persons with a university degree in counseling are not even considered.

Even if all the counselors were adequately trained however, utilization of their abilities within the School Department is poor. The counselors, who receive one of the highest salaries of all school personnel ($13,400), work only until 2:30 each day. Because of this high pay, and because their services are in great demand, there is no reason that they should not remain at school each day until 5:00, to counsel with children and their parents.

In summary, the Department seeks to provide an essential service to a very large number of school children. But its efforts to fulfill this mission are impeded in three ways. First, the ratio of one counselor for every three thousand four hundred children means that large numbers of children who need help must go without it. For many of them, their problems will intensify, until problems that were relatively normal will become very serious. Being responsible for so many children at a number of different schools, the counselor is forced to be crisis-oriented instead of prevention-oriented.

Second, the Director has no authority in the hiring procedure. She is unable to hire persons with special skills in counseling, unless they happen to have been a teacher in the Boston School System. Third, counselors are not used judiciously and resources available to help them in this work are extremely limited. In the event that children need services from more highly trained persons, such as a psychiatrist, it frequently is weeks or months before an "opening" is available. There is no formal working relationship between the school system and the mental health facilities.

Summary

In the Boston School Department children who have special needs are referred to the Department of Pupil Adjustment Counseling. Children with a wide variety of symptoms are referred: quiet, withdrawn children and loud, aggressive ones; slow learners and fast ones; children whose behavior is violent and those whose behavior is mild; children with organic problems and those with psychological ones. The symptoms vary but the Department seeks to determine the source of the behavior and the help needed.

Children who express one particular symptom however — truancy — are dealt with not by counselors but by attendance officers. The result is that a child having difficulties in school may receive the services of counselors who seek to provide help for his problems. But when those same problems cause him to be truant from school, he is no longer in the care of teachers who serve as counselors. Rather, the child is dealt with by former policemen who are attendance officers.

The child is the same; his problems remain the same. Yet at one point he is considered to need supportive services from experienced counselors. At another point he no longer receives that help. The School Department's orientation toward him changes from support and guidance by trained persons to more forceful measures by untrained persons.

The discrepancy in these orientations toward this child is an anachronism. Considering the help the child needs, there is no logical rationale for this different treatment. A child in trouble needs the same kind of help whether he is in school or not. Since the School Department already seeks to help him both in school and out, it seems logical to provide him with the same service (counseling) in school or out. A number of cities supplying information to us, for example, provide such services.[11] Having discarded the use of attendance officers, they have expanded the counseling program

providing it in the school and the community. "School-home counselors" or "visiting teachers" contact children who are absent. They have the same skills and training as the counselors who work within the school.

The failure of the Boston School Department to take this step means more than the continuation of an antiquated attendance program. The Department's priority continues to be upon dealing with problems after they get out of hand rather than meeting them early. It fails to apply its resources to prevent truancy in the first place through counseling and other services.

Yet, the School Department's priorities remain unchanged. It spends over half a million dollars each year to hire attendance officers who deal with truancy ineffectively after it happens. It employs fewer pupil adjustment counselors, at much less cost, to work with children before they become truant.[12] The priority is upon suppressing problems after they occur rather than upon meeting symptoms before they develop into problems.

Footnotes

1. John Fitzpatrick and Charles Parlon, Co-Heads of Attendance Department, Boston School Department, reported that 475 "habitual truants" and 254 "school offenders" were taken to court. Meeting at Dorchester House, June 18, 1969.
2. Charles Parlon, ibid.
3. Ibid.
4. Salary scale for school year 1969-70, is $11,900 for teacher with Ph.D degree at highest increment.
5. Charles Parlon, ibid.
6. Dr. Pierre Johannet, Child Psychiatrist, Boston University School of Medicine, Division of Psychiatry, testifying before the Task Force, November 12, 1969.
7. Katherine McLeod, Director, Department of Pupil Adjustment Counseling, Boston School Department, in Task Force meeting, December 10, 1969.
8. Charles Parlon, op. cit., testifying before Task Force, November 12, 1969.
9. Ibid.
10. See footnote 33, Chapter VI.
11. Indianapolis, Indiana; Philadelphia, Pennsylvania; Buffalo, New York; and Arlington, Massachusetts, to name a few.
12. The Boston School Department spends more money each year on salary for custodians than it does for adjustment counselors.

X. Administrative Responses to Children's Needs

We have described and summarized programs in the school system and mental health system which are failing, individually and collectively, to meet the needs of children. The inadequate structure of the programs is compounded by administrative procedures which are working to the detriment of the children. The functioning of these programs which serve to isolate and exclude children who need help is the natural consequence of certain patterns:

a) programs have no adequate central co-ordination, and no built-in monitoring mechanism to determine whether they are operating to help the children;

b) parents and professionals from the communities are not permitted to participate in determining policies and services, hence there is little responsiveness to the people; and

c) administrators and officials answer only to themselves, therefore there is no accountability to the public.

In this report, we have described in some detail the failure of the Boston School Department and auxiliary social services in meeting the needs of our children. Attention has been called to this failure by others.[1] Each time it has, the official response has been to shift the burden of responsibility from the school officials back to those who state the problems.

Provided below is an illustrative list of official responses:

1. **Denial.** I deny that children are being excluded from school, or that such things are happening to them. Prove it.

2. **Exception.** The examples you have given are exceptions. Prove that they are widespread.

3. **Demurrer.** I admit the facts, but feel that you have not presented a problem which is that important.

4. **Confession and avoidance.** I admit the facts and feel very concerned. But there are over-riding considerations which free me from responsibility for acting to solve the problems.

5. **Improper jurisdiction.** I understand the problem, but feel it is not the school's responsibility. It is the task of the family and other institutions.

6. **Prematurity of request.** We knew all along that these things were happening, and have made plans to correct the situation. Our efforts must be given a chance.

7. **Generalized guilt.** What you say is true, but other school systems have similar problems. We are no worse than they are.

8. **Improper forum.** The problem is really in the hands of the State and Federal government. There is little we can do.

9. **Recrimination.** I admit that children are out of school, but claim that it is their own fault. It wouldn't happen if they and their parents really cared.

10. **Further study.** The problem has been referred to the proper officials for further study. We hope to develop a plan sometime in the future.

We do not believe that any of these responses is appropriate in regard to the needs of the children. We hope they will not be used again to cover over the problems.

Footnotes

1. Kozol, Jonathan, *Death At An Early Age*, Bantam Books, 1968; Schrag, Peter, *Village School Downtown*, Beacon Press, 1967; in addition to numerous evaluations and reports done by local universities and community groups, which largely go unheeded or are attacked by school officials.

XI. Conclusion; Basis for Action

Conclusion

In this city, thousands of young children do not go to school. A minimum of 4000 school-age children are excluded from the Boston Public Schools; the likely number ranges as high as 10,700.[1] The majority of these children remain out of school because the School Department provides no educational programs for them. Children of Puerto Rican, Italian, Chinese, and other ethnic groups comprise the larger proportion of excluded youngsters. Other children – those who are crippled and girls who are pregnant, for example – are excluded from school in large numbers too.

Another group of children – between 2,800 and 4,800 – go to school but are excluded from the regular educational process.[2] Many of these children are misclassified and isolated. They are assigned labels denoting inability to participate in normal school activities. Mentally normal children who are labelled as "mentally retarded" comprise a large proportion of this group. Other children actually are retarded or emotionally disturbed and in need of special educational services, but they fail to receive them.

When public institutions, particularly one so basic as the public school system, fail to provide adequate services, it is an indictment of the total community. Failure in this instance indicates that private citizens, professional groups, and public officials either have not informed themselves about the exclusion of children from school, or they do not recognize it as an emergency situation requiring immediate action. In either case, it is clear that responsibility for this basic failure of the school system rests with the entire community.

Certain institutions and departments however exist to represent the public interest in regard to the educational development of children. Chief among these are the State Department of Education, the Department of Mental Health, the School Committee, the State Legis-

lature, and public and private social service agencies. These guardians of the public interest, each bearing a unique responsibility for children, are implicated individually and collectively in the failure of the public schools and the consequent exclusion of children from an education.

Two types of failure are apparent. First is the failure to provide services on the part of the child care network: social service, welfare, and mental health agencies. This service network neglects to provide adequate help for large numbers of children – emotionally disturbed, mentally retarded, perceptually handicapped, pregnant, disruptive, physically handicapped, and others.

The second type of failure is that of the regulatory bodies – those responsible for maintaining standards and developing educational programs for children: the Departments of Education and Mental Health, the Legislature and the School Committee. These bodies not only share responsibility for the exclusion of children by abdicating their designated legal authority, but they fail to alert the public to such a grave and monumental problem.

That the collective policies and practices of these institutions, departments, and agencies operate to exclude children from school is apparent. Yet, the situation of excluded children points directly to the institution bearing the major responsibility for their education: the public school system.

The failure to provide an adequate educational program for several thousand children points up some fundamental weaknesses in the Boston School Department. Basic among these defects is the school system's orientation toward children who are "different". Implicit in the operation of the School Department is the premise that it does not bear responsibility for the education of certain groups of children. Contrary to its legal mandate under the compulsory education law, the Department operates to isolate and exclude from the educational process large numbers of children who do not readily "fit" into the homogeneous school structure.

Two processes within the school system operate to the detriment of the children. First, large numbers of children in school are isolated from their peers; in many cases they actually are cordoned off from normal school activities. This isolation happens not only to children whose mental or physical needs require special attention (though even they should not be isolated); it happens to "normal" children as well — to children whom school officials merely *think* are unusual. This categorizing process has resulted in the erroneous labelling of several thousand children as "mentally retarded" or "emotionally disturbed." Meanwhile, children who actually are retarded or disturbed fail to receive adequate educational programs for their special needs.

Second, the School Department fails to provide any educational programs at all for other children. Most notable is the Department's apparent disregard for the educational needs of thousands of non-English speaking children in the city, most of them Spanish-speaking. Despite warnings that it is discriminating against children on the basis of national origin (something prohibited by the United States Constitution), and despite repeated pleas by community leaders that it recognize the existence of these children, the School Department continues to exclude them from school. Other children are excluded from school not because there are no programs for them, but as a convenience to school officials. Despite state laws and regulations to the contrary, crippled children generally are not allowed to attend school, and pregnant girls are excluded as well.

The operation of the school system is predicated on a pupil-excluding definition of normality which affects larger and larger numbers of children.[3] This narrow definition grows from a disease-oriented use of categorical labels which is inappropriate for the education of children. The schools focus almost exclusively on the "differentness" of certain groups of children, as if being different were indicative of shortcomings in the children.

Instead of mobilizing to meet the educational needs of various groups of children, the School Department places the onus upon the children to fit into the existing school structure. Hence, the School Department excludes so many children because it demands that they conform to its image, while ignoring its moral and legal

mandate to provide an education for them all.

Basis for Action

If, for our children, the concept of democracy is to be realized at all, the right to an education must be one of its basic tenets. The realization that every child has a moral and legal right to an education must form the central commitment of the public school system and other institutions. What is meant by a "commitment"? We mean more than a verbal recognition: we mean that the policies and practices of the institutions themselves must be geared to insure that right. We mean that the Boston School Committee and the School Department must act immediately to provide an adequate educational program for all children in the city. And we mean that other institutions, clinics, and agencies must act in conjunction with the schools to meet the needs of the children.

Such a commitment must incorporate four basic principles pertaining to the education of children. While these principles relate directly to the public school system, they place important responsibilities upon other institutions and agencies as well.

1. All children, regardless of differences and abilities, should be encouraged to participate fully in regular school curricula and activities. In the educational process, children should neither be excluded from a full educational opportunity nor isolated according to ability grouping. The only rationale for grouping is the provision of *temporary* help to accelerate the development of children with specific needs. As a rule, children with different abilities and needs should be integrated into the regular school environment. When certain children reach the limit of their abilities to function in that environment, then their specific needs must be identified and met — but not at the cost of excluding them from activities in which they are capable of participating. The exclusion of disturbed children from fire drill practice and the exclusion of retarded children from the lunch room are obvious examples of segregation. Yet, exclusion from certain academic activities is unnecessary as well.

In short, if the schools are to fulfill the public responsibility for the educational development of our children, they must be organized to do everything in their power to draw children into the educational process. Special services and programs must be utilized to help children remain a part of, or return to, the regular school process, instead of being used to remove them from participation.

2. The educational abilities and needs of children must be determined on an *individual* basis. Presently, children with special needs either are excluded from school altogether, or are inappropriately evaluated and labelled according to what they supposedly are — according to a static group stereotype. The labelling of a child as "mentally retarded" for example, while a convenient stereotype for school officials, does little to enhance the child's educational opportunity. One "re-tarded" child may be able to function productively in the regular classroom, while another may require special educational methods. Yet, the present labelling process places them both in the same class as part of a stereotyped group. Instead of categorical labelling, the schools and agencies must evaluate children according to their individual educational needs: what they have mastered compared to what they need to master.

3. The evaluation of children must include more than simple testing methods. Evaluation includes psycho-logical testing, pediatric physical examinations, neuro-logical examinations, psycho-motor functioning, psy-chiatric evaluations, and more.

Contrary to present practice, testing should not be used to label children according to intellectual ability. Because testing in no way measures fixed abilities, it is useful merely to indicate areas in which children need special attention. At best, testing is only a guide for introducing measures to strengthen the ability and intellect of children.

4. The education of all children requires the joint co-operation and planning of a number of systems and institutions in the city and state. The provision of adequate educational programs designed to meet specific needs is beyond the expertise of the school system alone. The State Department of Education, the Depart-ment of Mental Health, the Department of Public Welfare, public and private social service agencies, the universities, and the State Legislature all bear respon-sibility for the exclusion of children from the Boston schools.

Yet, a survey of these bodies finds them, if concerned about the children at all, doing the minimum required of them. But even if they were to assume their maximum responsibilities, more is required to educate the children. New models and innovative service patterns for children must be developed. Nothing less than a joint massive effort by these components will accomplish this task.

The incorporation of these principles into concrete programs and practices requires a major re-orientation on the part of the Boston School Department and other institutions. We do not claim to have all the answers to solve the situation we have found. To the contrary, we realize that the failure to educate thousands of children is such a serious problem that all citizens must work together to meet this emergency. Because the school system, alone, has been unable to meet the responsibility it holds, the burden falls upon us all to mobilize to meet the needs of our children.

That the public must share the burden of helping the schools function properly and adequately is a concept that is at the basis of American education:[4]

> "Professional educators are the chosen instru-ments for implementing policies determined by laymen . . . When the educational enterprise is going smoothly, the public does not often exercise its right to evaluate. It is after the system begins to break down and the public finds itself inadequate-ly served that the issue comes to the fore. (This is) the right of the laymen to an account for professional performance . . . Education is public business as well as professional business . . . (and) was never intended to be a professional monopoly . . . the scales must not tip toward a technocracy in which the public cannot exercise its right to scrutinize the professional process in education".

Realizing that our school system has faltered to the extent that the lives of thousands of children are in serious jeopardy, we accept our right and responsibility to act in their behalf. We call upon other parents, professionals, school officials, and citizens to join us. We face an extreme emergency, and the need for emergency action is apparent.

In recognition of the importance of the task, and in light of the investigation just completed by the Task Force, we intend to pursue the following action by the School Department and other institutions. We do so, however, not in the spirit of insisting upon the exactness of any specific change, but in the spirit of saying that no measures less comprehensive than these listed here will accomplish what must be done.

We recognize that some, though not all, of the changes require additional funds. As concerned citizens, parents, and taxpayers, we feel that these funds are a wise investment in the future. In fact, an investment now may be a savings in the future if we come to the aid of our children while there is yet time.

In the final analysis however, we look at the task before us not in economic terms, but in human terms. We carry the responsibility for the very development of the children in our city. And for that responsibility — that task, the only thing of real importance is that we not fail.

*   *   *

On the following pages are enumerated specific actions to be taken on behalf of children. They are organized according to the institution responsible for their implementation: Boston School Department, State Department of Education, Mental Health Facilities, Department of Public Welfare, Social Service Agencies, and the Youth Service Board. Action to be taken by the School Department is organized further according to substantive areas.

In most instances the changes can be initiated without legislative action. Changes that do require legislative action are indicated by an "L".

Boston School Department
(the School Committee and Superintendent)

General:

- Beginning in the 1970-71 schoolyear, issue a comprehensive annual report to the public, indicating the needs for, and plans to provide, educational services to children in Boston schools. This review and planning guide should include pupil services, consultation services needed, teacher recruitment, building construction, racial/ethnic trends, budget allocations, etc. The tone of the report is not to be "these are our accomplishments", but rather "this is what we as professional educators feel are the gaps in services, and these are our plans for the public to review".

- Conduct an an annual census of all children in Boston under the age of 18, for the purposes of: a) determining how many children are in/out of school, b) developing programs and resources to meet growing needs, and c) determining future educational trends and needs. (State laws and regulations provide for a general census as well as specific censuses of physically handicapped, mentally retarded, etc., none of which are conducted.)

- Contract with universities and professional groups for evaluation of all special school programs; the evaluation must be conducted independently of School Department personnel and officials.

- Computerize all school records pertaining to educational programs and services to children. Computerization will save money in the long run, inasmuch as departmental records now are inaccurate, unreliable, and unuseable for planning purposes.

- Develop jointly with public and private mental health facilities a plan for providing evaluation and treatment services to children according to areas of need: emotionally disturbed, perceptually handicapped, etc. Jointly work to develop new programs and services as needed.

- Whenever a child's regular educational program is interrupted or altered in any manner, school officials must notify the parents in writing. Notification must be made prior to action by school officials, and it must specify: the problem, action planned, nature of the child's educational program, and an invitation to the parents to participate fully in decisions regarding the child's education.

Non-English Speaking Children:

- Because the law requires the school committee of each city to provide for the education of all school age children, we call upon the Boston School Committee to:

  a) officially recognize that an emergency situation exists in the Boston Public Schools insofar as there are no educational programs for several thousand Spanish-speaking children,

b) institute emergency action and planning to provide bilingual transitional educational programs for these same children,

c) declare that it will meet this responsibility no later than the school semester beginning January, 1971, and,

d) report to the people of Boston by November, 1970, on the plans to resolve this emergency, and, at the same time, report on long-range plans to avoid such a situation in the future.

- For all children not fluent in English (Italian, Portuguese, Chinese, and others, as well as Spanish speaking), provide full-time bilingual transitional programs taught by instructors fluent in the children's native language as well as English.

- In order to recruit these teachers, waive the Boston Teachers Examination and other unnecessary obstacles which might impede the hiring of qualified teachers and administrators. It must be recognized that the need of the children for an education takes precedence over any barrier to the formation and operation of such educational programs.

- Employ bilingual parents and community leaders to serve as classroom assistants, as well as utilizing them in the development and evaluation of such programs.

- Start Kindergarten I and II classes for non-English speaking children, conducted in the language of the children.

- Provide counseling and tutoring programs for non-English speaking children to encourage them to stay in high school.

Physically Handicapped Children:

- Fulfill the legal responsibility for the education of the children by:

a) accepting handicapped/crippled children in regular classes unless a physician or psychiatrist of the parents' own choosing determines that the child is not able to attend regular classes,

b) conducting a search of all public and private institutions to locate children unnecessarily excluded from school.

- Arrange to accommodate handicapped children in school through such devices as building ramps for wheelchairs, re-arranging classroom locations, and developing "buddy teams" whereby other students share responsibility for helping handicapped fellow students during the day. (Any expenses incurred will be minimal compared to the financial and psychic cost of preventing children from attending school.)

- In recognition that the law holds the School Department responsible for provision of educational programs to handicapped children, provide special classes for handicapped children who cannot attend regular classes, but who are able to come each day to the school building.

- Develop a formal working relationship with other community resources for handicapped children, such as the Industrial School for Crippled Children, so that children too handicapped to attend public school will be educated. The formal responsibility for their education, however, remains that of the School Department.

Pregnant Girls:

- Issue a policy directive to School Department officials and teachers, made available to the public as well:

a) stating that because pregnancy is no basis on which to determine one's ability or right to attend school, the Department's policy is to encourage all pregnant girls to remain in their regular classes, unless instructed otherwise by their personal physicians,

b) instructing all personnel — teachers, counselors, and principals — that it is illegal to counsel girls to leave school, and that they are to support and encourage them to continue attending, and

c) providing counseling services through the Pupil Adjustment Department, to support the girls during their period of pregnancy.

- For girls unable to attend school, or who chose not to, develop and provide an alternative educational program at least equal to that offered in the regular classroom, for which the students receive full academic credit. Such programs must be part of the regular on-going school system, and be fully co-ordinated with it.

- For such alternative programs hire teachers from distinct ethnic/racial backgrounds who are able to work with girls from the same backgrounds.

- The present program, Centaum, must be discontinued altogether, or completely re-structured to meet the following standards:

  a) attendance in the program must be on a voluntary basis and not a forced one, (girls must be allowed and encouraged to remain in regular classes instead),

  b) the academic program must be equal to that offered in the regular school classes, including full academic credit,

  c) any pregnant school-age girl choosing to enter the program may do so, and may not be rejected by the Director,

  d) the racial imbalance must be corrected in the teaching staff, and

  e) a psychiatric consultant must help the Director and teachers develop attitudes to impart a positive self-image on the part of the students.

- Provide home instruction for girls who, under the direction of a licensed physician, cannot attend the school or a special program.

Children Retarded in Mental Development:

- Immediately discontinue the testing of children by School Department personnel. Contract with public and private mental health clinics in the city for the immediate re-evaluation of all children who have been identified as retarded, whether they have been placed in "special classes" or not.

- Continue this contractual arrangement for the evaluation of all children for determining their level of ability and needed educational program.

Re-evaluate annually children identified as retarded in mental development.

- The evaluation of children must include the following as determined by the psychologists or psychiatrists: psychiatric evaluation, pediatric physical examination with auxiliary studies, psychological evaluation, perceptual-motor functioning, school achievement tests, and clinical conferences.

- Discontinue the classification of children as "retarded" and the categorical placement of children in "special classes" for the retarded. Instead, identify children according to individual abilities and needs (by clinical evaluation), and structure their educational programs accordingly. (L)

- Test scores and evaluative records held by School Department personnel must be available to the parents of the child.

- Provide remedial reading help to all children having the ability to improve reading skills. This requires ending the cut-off point of 90 I.Q. or above for those receiving such help.

- Terminate the isolation of mongoloid children from other "retarded" children which is done now not on the basis of I.Q. or educational needs, but because their physical appearance is different.[5]

- Provide pre-school classes for children retarded in mental development, as ruled upon three times by the State Attorney General's Office.[5]

Emotionally Disturbed Children:

- Discontinue the exclusion of children from school prior to or pending a clinical evaluation. Abide by the intent of the "750" law: removal from class is a last resort, not the first.

- Provide school classes for disturbed children in each school district or geographical area of the city, so children may remain in their own neighborhoods.

- School administrators abide by the decision of the psychiatrist in regard to the child's educational needs.

- Work with the State Departments of Education

and Mental Health to develop community-based educational services to counterbalance the usage of residential facilities. (Refer to listing under State Department of Education and Department of Mental Health, below.)

Perceptually Handicapped Children:[5]

- Provide for an annual psychiatric evaluation of children who have learning disabilities.

- Provide special educational services for the children when their disability is diagnosed rather than waiting until a child is at least two years behind academically, as is done now.

- Continue the practice of part-time tutoring for children in addition to, but not instead of, their regular class work.

Counseling Services to Children:

- Increase the number of pupil adjustment counselors by September, 1976, to establish a counselor-student ratio of 1:400, increasing the number between now and 1976, each year, to reach this level.

- End the unnecessary pre-requisite of being a teacher for the position of pupil adjustment counselor. Hire social workers (M.S.W.), trained counselors, and other persons with expertise in working with children.

- Hiring of counselors must be under the supervision of the director of the department. Selection must be made from lists of qualified applicants submitted by agencies, clinics, and schools in each area of the city.

- Adjustment counselors in each school district must be designated to work in the community, counseling children out of school and acting as liaison between the school and the parents and community resources.

- Regular, on-going in-service education must be provided for the counselors.

- A pupil adjustment counselor or guidance counselor is paid a much higher salary ($13,400) than a teacher having comparable qualifications. Each works the same amount of hours each day

(8:10-2:45, usually). This inequity must be rectified:

- a) persons having the same qualifications and training should receive the same salary, regardless of whether they are teachers or counselors,

- b) if counselors are to continue receiving a higher salary regardless of training, their workday must be extended until 5:00 p.m.; the number of children in need of counseling services certainly supports the extension.

- In each school, one classroom should be established with a full-time teacher/counselor team for children who simply have a "bad day" and temporarily need special help.

Services to Children Who Are Truant:

- End the designation of "truancy" (attendance) as a special category of behavior, recognizing that it is a symptom not to be dealt with in isolation.

- Expand the concept of attendance to provide for the protection of children against illegal exclusion from school.

- Discontinue the punitive orientation toward children who are truant by:

- a) making services to the children a function of trained counselors who work in the community as well as the school,

- b) hiring counselors from lists submitted by community agencies, to reflect an ethnic spread in correlation with sections of the city, and including more women, and

- c) co-ordinating counseling services with community agencies that provide similar services.

- Discontinue the position of attendance officer, thus ending it as a Civil Service position with veterans' preference. (L)

- Terminate the services of the present attendance officers, and apply the $522,000 salary savings to the hiring of qualified counselors. If any of the present officers are trained in social work or counseling, hire them as counselors.

State Department of Education

- We call upon the Department, as the body legally responsible for the supervision of education in the Commonwealth, to use its authority to set and enforce educational standards in the Boston School Department. (The failure to conduct an annual census; the isolation of normal children in classes for the retarded; and the failure even to provide educational programs for several thousand Spanish-speaking children; are examples of areas in which the Department has failed to enforce standards in the Boston Public Schools.)

- For repeated and persistent violation of laws and regulations, we call upon the Department to withhold funds from the Boston School Department until it is in compliance. In situations where violations persist without remedial efforts, the Department must utilize its power to seek resolution in the courts.

- Above all else, the Department must provide leadership in sponsoring legislation, and developing innovative educational programs, in conjunction with the Boston School Department and the Department of Mental Health.

- One such program critically needed is the establishment of community-based day care programs for emotionally disturbed children. Funds under "750" must be diverted for establishment of these centers, which can serve more children at less expense. Innovative models for such programs are operating successfully in other states.[6]

Mental Health Facilities

Public (Department of Mental Health):

- The Commissioner of Mental Health and the Regional Administrators for Boston must act immediately to correct the present imbalance in services to children by:

a) applying over half of the Department's total annual budget increase to children's services on an on-going basis, until

b) the budget for children's services is at least in proportion to the percentage of children in the regional populations.

- We call upon Area Boards to exercise their legal authority in vetoing Department budgets which do not reflect equal priorities to children.

- Persons with administrative authority for delivery of services to children must be appointed in the administrative structure of the Department at regional and local levels.

- The Department of Mental Health, the body legally responsible for provision of mental health services in the Commonwealth, must devise a plan for providing consultation to the schools and comprehensive services to school children. This formal working plan with the School Department should be completed by January, 1971, and made available to the public.

- One model for provision of services is the establishment in each catchment area of a central service to evaluate children for a specific need: emotional disturbance, retardation, etc.

- Pre-school and after-school nurseries and centers for children with special needs, such as behavioral disturbances or retardation, must be structured and operated under the joint auspices of the Departments of Mental Health and Special Education. (One plan for day care centers for disturbed children has been developed by Children's Services, but must be enacted by local Area Boards.)

Private:

- Private agencies, clinics, and hospitals must adopt the policy that any child out of school or in need of special services represents an emergency situation. This requires walk-in service followed by evaluation, counseling, and treatment services provided as needed, without waiting periods.

- Private agencies, clinics, and hospitals receiving federal or state funds for services to children must set-up a formal working relationship with the School Department, either in conjunction with or independent of the Department of Mental Health's formal relationship.

• Psychiatrists and other professionals working with children must spend some time in the public schools each year, to understand the educational needs and problems of the children they treat.

Department of Public Welfare[7]

• The Department must establish a formal, on-going policy of surveying the educational status of all school-age children known to it, acting as their advocate whenever any child is excluded from school. Working with the parents to resolve educational problems or needs of the child must be one of the fundamental tasks of the Department.

• A directive must be issued to workers stating that whenever any child is out of school due to lack of clothing or transportation or lunch money, the Department authorizes immediate appropriations needed to return the child to school.

Social Service Agencies[7]

• Each agency in the city, public and private, must recognize its responsibility in seeing that all children known to it are involved in adequate educational programs. This requires each agency to develop its own "plan of action" to be followed whenever any child is excluded from school.

• Each agency must set aside a percentage of its time for services to the schools, including direct services to children and consultation for teachers and administrators.

Youth Service Board[7]

• The Board must assume responsibility for children released from its custody by following-up to insure

that they are accepted in a public school. The Board needs to follow a policy of notifying the School Department routinely when a child is released. (Currently, there is no communication, and children refused admission to a public school have no one to act in their behalf.)

• The Board must set aside a proportion of its budget to begin innovative community-based services for children.

Footnotes

1. Recognizing the futility of debating the exact number of children out of school, the figures are listed here merely to provide some idea of the magnitude of the problem of exclusion. For each group of children there are two figures: the absolute minimum and the likely maximum. There are other groups of children out of school but not listed here because no data is available on them.

Spanish-speaking	2,600-7,800
Pregnant girls	500-1,500
Disturbed/severe	
behavioral needs	500- 600
Crippled	400- 800

2. The figures listed here follow the same format as those listed in the footnote above.

Mentally retarded	2,000-2,500
Disturbed	300- 900
Perceptually handicapped	200- 600
Non-English speaking	300- 800

3. For a more thorough discussion of this concept, refer to Cruickshank, William M., et al, *Misfits in the Public Schools,* Syracuse University Press, 1969, Chapter IV.

4. *Reconnection for Learning,* also known as the "Bundy Report" on the New York City Schools, McGeorge Bundy, et al, 1967.

5. Space limitations prevented consideration of this subject in the text. For further information or written materials, write to the Task Force office, listed at the front of the book.

6. Refer to *Take A Giant Step,* Hoffman, Herbert J., Massachusetts Advisory Council on Education, 1970, for a discussion of the "re-education" model.

7. Space limitations prevented consideration of these institutions in the text.

Appendix C

Percent of High School Graduates Who Attend Degree-Granting Colleges
(Rank Order Comparison of Boston and Cities of Comparable Size)

Rank	City	% Attend College	Public School Population	City Population	Latest Year
1	San Diego	75%	130,217	680,000	1966
2	Denver	56%	96,634	480,000	1969
3	Kansas City, Mo.	52%	72,702	555,000	1964
4	Seattle	50%	89,502	550,000	1969
5	Minneapolis	50%	68,200	440,000	1969
6	Pittsburgh	49%	72,011	530,000	1969
7	Milwaukee	48%	132,500	750,000	1969
8	Indianapolis	45%	107,747	510,000	1969
9	St. Louis	39%	124,841	665,000	1968
10	Memphis	37%	133,000	545,000	1969
11	Boston	29%	96,534	570,000	1969

One measure of how well a school system is meeting the needs of its children is to determine how many children it equips and motivates to continue on in the field of higher education. A total of ten cities was selected on the basis of population and geographical location to compare to Boston. They represent a wide cross-section geographically, while having similar size public school populations, (e.g. medium size, ranging from 72,000 to 133,000 children).

Appendix D

Children Out Of School, By Age and Sex*

Ages	Male	Female	Total	Percent	Cumulative Percent
5-7	77	58	135	(17)	(17)
8-10	104	59	163	(23)	(40)
11-13	98	69	167	(23)	(63)
14-16	104	103	207	(27)	(90)
17-19	48	32	80	(10)	(100)
unknown	28	26	54	-	-
TOTALS	459	347	806	(100)	(100)

* The table above summarizes information on 806 children out of school, as reported to the Task Force during August and September, 1969. These individual cases were reported by public and private agencies that co-operated with the Task Force by supplying the information.

Although the information was useful in developing a profile of children who are excluded from school, the sample is not representative of all excluded children. For one thing, agency co-operation was voluntary; some did not report to the Task Force. Secondly, these cases represent only those children who had come to the attention of social service agencies. We believe that most excluded children never come to the attention of any agency. This appears to be true particularly for adolescents, since 63% of the cases reported involve children under the age of thirteen. If resources were available to locate other excluded children, the proportions shown here might change.

Sources of Information

Boston Children's Service
Martha Eliot Clinic
BU-BCH Child Guidance Clinic
Children's Hospital
Neighborhood Youth Corps
Beth Israel Hospital
Laboure Clinic
Children's Mission
Department of Public Welfare
Children's Protective Service
Bridge
Spanish Population Survey

Douglas A. Thom Clinic
Family Service Association
Judge Baker Guidance Center
Dorchester House
Visiting Nurses' Association
Roxbury Multi-Service Center
Boston Educational Service & Testing
Boy's Club of Greater Boston
United South End Settlements
Roxbury Court Clinic
Boston School Teachers
Miscellaneous Sources

THE
PUERTO RICAN
EXPERIENCE

An Arno Press Collection

Berle, Beatrice Bishop. **Eighty Puerto Rican Families in New York City:** Health and Disease Studied in Context. New Foreword by the author. 1958

Blanco, Tomas. **El Prejuicio Racial en Puerto Rico.** (Racial Prejudice in Puerto Rico). 1948

Carroll, Henry K. **Report on the Island of Porto Rico;** Its Population, Civil Government, Commerce, Industries, Productions, Roads, Tariff, and Currency, With Recommendations. 1899

Cebollero, Pedro A. **A School Language Policy for Puerto Rico.** 1945

Chiles, Paul Nelson. **The Puerto Rican Press Reaction to the United States, 1888-1898.** 1944

Clark, Victor S., et al. **Porto Rico and Its Problems.** 1930

Col! Cuchí, José. **Un Problema en América.** (The American Problem). 1944

Colon, Jesus. **A Puerto Rican in New York and Other Sketches.** 1961

Enamorado Cuesta, J[ose]. **Porto Rico, Past and Present:** The Island After Thirty Years of American Rule. A Book of Information, Written for the American Reading Public, in the Interest and for the Benefit of the People of Porto Rico. [1929]

Fernández Vanga, Epifanio. **El Idioma de Puerto Rico y El Idioma Escolar de Puerto Rico.** (Language and Language Policy in Puerto Rico). 1931

Fleagle, Fred K. **Social Problems in Porto Rico.** 1917

Friedrich, Carl J. **Puerto Rico: Middle Road to Freedom.** 1959

Gallardo, José M., editor. **Proceedings of [the] Conference on Education of Puerto Rican Children on the Mainland (October 18 to 21, 1970).** 1972

Geigel Polanco, Vicente. **Valores de Puerto Rico.** (Puerto Rican Leaders). 1943

Institute of Field Studies, Teachers College, Columbia University. **Public Education and the Future of Puerto Rico: A Curriculum Survey, 1948-1949.** 1950

Jaffe, A[bram] J., editor. **Puerto Rican Population of New York City.** 1954

New York [City]. Welfare Council. **Puerto Ricans in New York City:** The Report of the Committee on Puerto Ricans in New York City of the Welfare Council of New York City. 1948

Osuna, Juan José. **A History of Education in Puerto Rico.** 1949

Perloff, Harvey S. **Puerto Rico's Economic Future:** A Study in Planned Development. 1950

Puerto Rican Forum. **The Puerto Rican Community Development Project:** Un Proyecto Puertorriqueño de Ayuda Mutua Para El Desarrollo de la Comunidad. A Proposal For a Self-Help Project to Develop the Community by Strengthening the Family, Opening Opportunities for Youth and Making Full Use of Education. 1964

Puerto Ricans and Educational Opportunity. 1975

The Puerto Ricans: Migration and General Bibliography. 1975

Roberts, Lydia J. and Rosa Luisa Stefani. **Patterns of Living in Puerto Rican Families.** 1949

Rosario, José C[olombán]. **The Development of the Puerto Rican Jíbaro and His Present Attitude Towards Society.** 1935

Rowe, L[eo] S. **The United States and Porto Rico:** With Special Reference to the Problems Arising Out of Our Contact with the Spanish-American Civilization. 1904

Siegel, Arthur, Harold Orlans and Loyal Greer. **Puerto Ricans in Philadelphia:** A Study of Their Demographic Characteristics, Problems and Attitudes. 1954

[Tugwell, Rexford G.] **Puerto Rican Public Papers of R. G. Tugwell, Governor.** 1945

United States-Puerto Rico Commission on the Status of Puerto Rico. **Status of Puerto Rico:** Report of the United States-Puerto Rico Commission on the Status of Puerto Rico, August 1966. 1966

United States-Puerto Rico Commission on the Status of Puerto Rico. **Status of Puerto Rico:** Selected Background Studies Prepared for the United States-Puerto Rico Commission on the Status of Puerto Rico, 1966. 1966

United States Senate. Select Committee on Equal Educational Opportunity. **Equal Educational Opportunity for Puerto Rican Children (Part 8):** Hearings Before the Select Committee on Equal Educational Opportunity of the United States Senate. 91st Congress, 2nd Session, Washington, D. C., November 23, 24 and 25, 1970. 1970

Van Middeldyk, R. A. **The History of Puerto Rico:** From the Spanish Discovery to the American Occupation. 1903

Wakefield, Dan. **Island in the City:** The World of Spanish Harlem. 1959

White, Trumbull. **Puerto Rico and Its People.** 1938